More praise for *Inside Putin's Russia*

'This brilliant dissection of the anatomy of modern Russia and its leader deserves to be lauded' *Literary Review*

'A reasoned analysis . . . Jack's post has given him excellent access, including to "Vova" himself' *Times*

'Andrew Jack fills his book with chilling examples of the authoritarian nature of the country's president' *Spectator*

'An enthralling exposé of modern Russian politics' *Good Book Guide*

Andrew Jack was until recently the chief Moscow correspondent for the *Financial Times*. While based in the UK he was part of the award-winning investigative team reporting on the BCCI and Robert Maxwell scandals. He is the author of the critically acclaimed book *The French Exception*.

INSIDE PUTIN'S RUSSIA

Revised Edition

ANDREW JACK

Granta Books

London

Granta Publications, 2/3 Hanover Yard, Noel Road, London N1 8BE

First published in Great Britain by Granta Books 2004
This revised edition published by Granta Books 2005

Copyright © 2004, 2005 by Andrew Jack
Maps copyright © Katharine Reeve

Andrew Jack has asserted his moral right under the Copyright, Designs
and Patents Act, 1988, to be identified as the author of this work.

All rights reserved. No reproduction, copy or transmission of this publication may be made without written permission. No paragraph of this
publication may be reproduced, copied or transmitted save with written permission in accordance with the provisions of the Copyright Act
1956 (as amended). Any person who does any unauthorized act in relation to this publication may be liable to criminal prosecution and civil
claims for damages.

A CIP catalogue record for this book
is available from the British Library.

1 3 5 7 9 10 8 6 4 2

Typeset by M Rules
Printed and bound in Great Britain by
Mackays of Chatham plc

CONTENTS

DRAMATIS PERSONAE

ABRAMOVICH, ROMAN

(b. 1966). An intensely secretive orphan who became a successful oil trader during the 1990s. Through friendship with Boris Yeltsin's 'Family' and a series of business deals in association with Boris Berezovsky, he emerged as the multi-billionaire owner of an oil, aluminium and food empire before selling off many of his assets and acquiring Chelsea Football Club.

AUSHEV, RUSLAN

(b. 1954). Former Soviet army officer who became president of Russia's North Caucasus republic of Ingushetia in 1993, steering a more peaceful course than was pursued in neighbouring Chechnya. His policies clashed with those of Putin's Kremlin, and he stepped down in 2002, clearing the way for the election of an FSB (the Russian successor of the KGB) officer.

BEREZOVSKY, BORIS

(b. 1946). Fast-talking academic turned tycoon with wide business interests, including media outlets which he used for political objectives. The éminence grise of Boris Yeltsin's second term in 1996–9, he was secretary of the Security Council and the Commonwealth of Independent States. He helped promote Vladimir Putin to president but then became a strong critic and fled into exile abroad.

DRAMATIS PERSONAE

CHERNOMYRDIN, VIKTOR

(b. 1938). Energy ministry executive with tight contacts to the state-backed monopoly Gazprom, he was named a compromise prime minister by Yeltsin in 1992 after the turmoil of early market reforms. He remained in power until his sacking in 1998, and was appointed Putin's ambassador to Ukraine in 2001.

CHUBAIS, ANATOLY

(b. 1955). Economist turned ruthless 'Bolshevik'-style architect of 1990s market reforms, including privatizations which created a class of oligarchs. He helped mastermind Yeltsin's re-election in 1996, and was named head of UES, the state electricity monopoly, in 1998. He continued to pursue political ambitions as a key figure behind SPS, the liberal democratic Union of Right Forces.

DZERZHINSKY, FELIX

(1877–1926). Founder of the ruthless Cheka, the All-Russian Extraordinary Commission for Combating Counter-Revolution and Sabotage, the forerunner of the KGB, the Soviet-era secret police, and its Russian successor, the FSB. Dzerzhinsky's name is synonymous with the Red Terror he launched on behalf of Lenin, but his reputation has enjoyed a revival along with that of the KGB.

DUDAYEV, JOKHAR

(1944–96). Soviet air-force commander who became the first Chechen general in the Soviet forces. He returned to his native Chechnya in 1990, and led the republic into a chaotic self-declared independence. His erratic style and clashes with Yeltsin triggered the first conflict in 1994, and he was killed by a Russian missile after his satellite telephone call was intercepted.

GAIDAR, YEGOR

(b. 1956). Brilliant economist who was the intellectual father of Russia's liberal reforms under Yeltsin during the 1990s. Briefly acting head of government as deputy prime minister in 1991–2, he subsequently adopted a lower public profile, but continued to wield considerable influence over Putin's reform programme through his strong contacts in the government and Union of Right Forces.

DRAMATIS PERSONAE

GREF, GERMAN
(b. 1964). A graduate of Leningrad's law school, he worked with Putin in the city administration in the 1990s and joined the federal property fund in Moscow in 1998. He coordinated the drafting of Putin's economic policies from 1999, and became minister of economic development and trade in the new government, pushing through liberal reforms.

GUSINSKY, VLADIMIR
(b. 1952). Charismatic theatre director turned politically influential businessman, he built a banking group in the 1990s but increasingly focused on creating the professional NTV television network and other media assets. His falling-out with Putin made him the first oligarch to be driven into exile abroad in 2000, and led to the systematic stripping of his assets.

KADYROV, AKHMED
(1951–2004). Gruff former Muslim leader of Chechnya and anti-Russian warlord during the first conflict in 1994–6, he became critical of the leadership of Aslan Maskhadov. In 2000, Putin named him head of a pro-Kremlin puppet administration, and he was made president after highly contested elections in 2003. Killed in blast in Grozny in May 2004.

KASYANOV, MIKHAIL
(b. 1957). Slick finance ministry official with a reputation for charming foreign investors and maintaining tight associations with Yeltsin's 'Family'. Putin named him prime minister, and Kasyanov survived for almost the entire first presidential term despite persistent rumours of his immanent dismissal.

KHODORKOVSKY, MIKHAIL
(b. 1963). Soft-spoken oligarch with powerful political contacts who alienated shareholders as he struggled to win full control over the oil company Yukos in the late 1990s. Transformed into enlightened businessman, he helped pioneer a more transparent style of corporate governance and launched extensive philanthropic programmes before his confrontation with Putin put him in prison in 2003.

DRAMATIS PERSONAE

KIRIENKO, SERGEI

(b. 1962). Boy wonder who rose from his commercial and political power base in Nizhny Novgorod to become Yeltsin's youngest-ever prime minister in 1998. Fired after the financial crisis in August 1998, he was a key member of the Union of Right Forces, helping it win strong support in the 1999 Duma through Putin's help. Putin made him presidential plenipotentiary for the Volga region in 2000.

LUZHKOV, YURI

(b. 1936). Flat-capped mayor of Moscow since 1991, he worked his way up through the Soviet bureaucracy with a reputation as a tough boss, while his second, businesswoman wife benefited from many city contracts. A potential presidential rival who created the Fatherland-All Russia party that ran against Putin's Unity in 1999, he helped make peace and merge the two into United Russia in 2001.

MASKHADOV, ASLAN

(b. 1951). Chechen brought up in the Soviet army, he took charge of the military defence against Russian forces during the 1994–6 conflict. He negotiated a peace agreement, and his moderate line won him victory in internationally recognized elections in 1997. After the descent into anarchy that followed and the launch of the second war in 1999, he went into hiding as the formal chief rebel leader.

NEMTSOV, BORIS

(b. 1959). Energetic former governor of Nizhny Novgorod appointed Russia's deputy prime minister under Yeltsin's government of 'young reformers' in 1997, and pushed out with Kirienko after the August 1998 financial crisis. A key figure in the Union of Right Forces, he was its parliamentary leader in 1999–2003, before the party failed to win re-election.

POTANIN, VLADIMIR

(b. 1961). A child of the Soviet elite who controlled Uneximbank and became a deputy minister in 1996, he helped devise the controversial 'loans for shares' scheme which created Russia's oligarchs. That handed him control of the oil group Sidanco and the metals giant Norilsk Nickel. His Interros holding company remains one of Russia's most powerful business groups.

PRIMAKOV, YEVGENY

(b. 1929). Middle East intelligence expert who worked undercover for the newspaper *Pravda*, befriended Saddam Hussein from the late 1960s and pursued an academic career. Named head of the Foreign Intelligence Service by Yeltsin in 1991, he was foreign minister from 1996. He was prime minister in 1998–9, before being fired as his presidential ambitions and political influence rose.

SHAIMIEV, MINTIMER

(b. 1937). Communist *apparatchik* who held senior positions for the party in the ethnic republic of Tatarstan before taking formal control in 1990. Remained in charge ever since, despite the collapse of the USSR and his support for Kremlin opponents. A founder of the Fatherland-All Russia party of regional bosses that merged with Putin's Unity to form United Russia in 2001.

SOBCHAK, ANATOLY

(1937–2000). Putin's law school professor and political mentor. One of the pioneers of the democratic movement in the 1980s, he took charge of the administration of Leningrad and supported Yeltsin against the *putsch* in 1993. Lost re-election in 1996 to his deputy, Vladimir Yakovlev, and was subject to corruption investigations that drove him into exile in France. Returned as Putin rose to power, but died of a heart attack a few months later.

STEPASHIN, SERGEI

(b. 1952). Career interior ministry official who held a series of senior jobs in the security forces before becoming Yeltsin's most short-lived prime minister after Primakov's sacking in 1999 until the nomination of Putin. Named head of the parliamentary Audit Chamber in 2000.

VOLOSHIN, ALEXANDER

(b. 1956). Engineer who turned to business as a partner of Berezovsky in the early 1990s, before joining the presidential administration in 1997. Named Yeltsin's chief of staff in 1999, he is seen as the mastermind behind Putin's election and many subsequent political decisions. He resigned in October 2003, apparently in connection with the imprisonment of Khodorkovsky.

DRAMATIS PERSONAE

YAVLINSKY, GRIGORY

(b. 1952). Liberal economist and author of the '500 day plan' rejected by Yeltsin, he led the democratic Yabloko party from 1993, and was an outspoken critic of the privatizations of the 1990s that created the oligarchs. Sometimes attacking the authoritarianism of Putin's regime, at others he advised the president on issues including foreign policy. His party lost out in the 2003 elections.

ZAKAYEV, AKHMED

(b. 1959). A former drama student drawn into Chechnya's independence struggle, he was briefly Dudayev's culture minister before taking up arms against Russian forces in 1994. He became a deputy head of Maskhadov's administration, and his foreign emissary, even holding peace talks with a Kremlin representative after the second war began, before being pursued for extradition from Denmark and the UK since 2002.

ZYUGANOV, GENNADY

(b. 1944). An *apparatchik* who worked in the Communist propaganda department during the 1980s and maintained a conservative line as the USSR collapsed. Head of the Communist Party of the Russian Federation since 1992, he ran unsuccessfully against Yeltsin and Putin for president, and only just maintained the party's position as the largest opposition group in parliament in December 2003.

PREFACE TO THE
REVISED EDITION

WHEN I EXPLAINED THE PURPOSE of our meeting, the expression on the man's face quickly changed. I had just sat down to begin an interview in the Moscow office of an experienced western ambassador, and I told him that I was trying to probe the background of Vladimir Putin. The former secret policeman and enigmatic Russian president had risen quickly and discreetly to the pinnacle of power, and was now starting a second term in the Kremlin with more power than ever in his hands. It was essential to gather every piece of information that I could about his background.

'In that case, let's go up to my apartment,' said the diplomat immediately, rising to his feet. He unlocked the adjacent heavy door, climbed the stairs, and before uttering another word, he selected a compact disk of 'Boris Godunov' from his shelf, and put it into the player. Only then, with the sounds of one of Russia's most tragic operas drowning out our whispered voices like in some bad Soviet-era spy novel, did we sit down and start to talk.

The incident was a strange reminder of my arrival in Russia more than five years earlier. I had previously travelled to the country, but arrived full-time to work in the ruins of the August 1998 financial crisis. That had wiped out the livelihoods and spirit of many people, leaving the hopes and incomes of the fledgling middle class shattered. At first, I had been cautious about eavesdropping and even entrapment as I adjusted to the sombre Moscow atmosphere, full of the stories of the KGB past. There was little doubt that 'they' could still be listening.

But I soon let my caution go. It seemed then that the FSB, the post-Soviet internal security agency, was unlikely to have the resources to listen to, let alone translate, my conversations. With budgets reduced and staff demoralized, many employees seemed more interested in offering themselves for hire to the highest commercial bidder. In any case, I had nothing to hide. The essence of most of my conversations would be published soon enough in my newspaper for everyone to read, and my interlocutors rarely seemed reluctant to talk. Fear had disappeared. I preferred to give out my credit card number on an almost certainly tapped but neglected phone than by internet, where freelance hackers and corporate fraudsters were a far more potent threat.

Today, there are chill breezes returning from the Soviet past. The FSB has become more powerful, better funded and more centralized. Its officials, like those in the prosecutors' office and other uniformed agencies, are ever more frequently used in campaigns across the country against Russian journalists, or business people caught in political and commercial feuds. A new nationalistic feeling, stoked by economic recovery, disillusion with the ineffective westernization of the 1990s, and an absence of reflection on the horrors of the past, has become more dominant. The owners of big businesses are more cautious about their public statements, and more scrupulous in how they use their fortunes. For ordinary people, there is a clear disengagement from the political process, a mixture of cynicism, disillusionment and disinterest. Living standards have risen, but if fear has not returned, uncertainty about the future has.

Russia under Putin remains far from the police state that operated under Brezhnev, let alone Stalin. His 'liberal authoritarian' regime is mixing Soviet with distinctly post-Soviet themes to create something new. Since the turn of the millennium, the economy has been booming. In May 2004, the luxury Italian Mazeratti sports cars opened a showroom in Moscow; and *Forbes* launched a Russian-language edition, believing it could tap into a fast-growing market of the super rich. Moscow may concentrate such extravagance, but there are smaller-scale versions of new-found wealth and investment across much of the country. Market reforms are operating, and a distinctly post-Communist society is being created. Mobile telephone subscriptions are rising fast; ever-growing numbers of Russians are travelling and studying abroad. Many who left are now coming back, as the salaries in the US, or the security situation in Israel, make their adoptive countries less attractive at a time of rapid evolution at home.

But modern Russia does bear some resemblances to the vision of Yuri Andropov, Putin's last Soviet hero as head of the KGB and briefly leader of the country, whose name began to appear ever more frequently in the media. Like his former employer, Putin appears to believe that reforming the economy to modernize the country is a far more urgent priority than building a democracy that bears more than a superficial resemblance to the variants recognizable in the west. The extent to which he is right, and how far the reality of his first term belies a more complex series of processes at work in modern Russia, is one of the central themes of this book.

My meeting with the ambassador in 2004 was not the only incident to suggest a new caution within the country. A colleague was told when he visited a large state-controlled company that the authorities would have to be informed of the nature of their meeting. Even in writing this book, a few curious incidents took place. When my publisher used a courier service to send me a copy of the page proofs from London, the package that should have arrived within two days instead took two weeks to make it through Russian customs. A Moscow bookshop was reluctant to stock copies, pointing out that since 1999 it had been required to seek ministerial authorization for all the titles it sold, and had already had problems with critical political books. A pattern was beginning to emerge.

As I prepared to leave Moscow at the end of 2004, I went to the ministry of foreign affairs to receive my annual press accreditation card. 'Andrew, why do you keep writing about Yukos? Why not something more positive?' said my *kurator*, a young shaven-headed man who had recently replaced his end-of-career predecessor as 'handler' of the English-speaking media. 'That way when I show my boss your articles next year, he will be able to say you are a serious correspondent and offer no objection to renewing your card.'

This revised and updated edition of *Inside Putin's Russia*, including a new foreword and epilogue, is more timely than ever. Now well-established into his second term in office, Putin will remain in place as president at least until 2008, barring unforeseen circumstances. After that, he will continue to influence Russia's evolution, if not by modifying the constitution and staying in the Kremlin, then less publicly as a top official or adviser. By his own admission, he intends to cultivate and propose a successor, just as his predecessor Boris Yeltsin did with him. He is a constant with whom world leaders must learn to deal.

The spread of terrorism and the instability in Iraq have highlighted the need for intensified international cooperation. High oil prices have provided a new imperative to find alternative supplies outside the Middle East. Russia's increasing integration into the global community – such as its lobbying to enter the World Trade Organization – is raising its profile and giving it potential new leverage. The enlargements of both the European Union and NATO into the former Soviet bloc in 2004 have brought the boundaries of the west far closer.

Since Putin's spring 2004 re-election there have been important new developments which give fresh information about his leadership style, the challenges he faces, and the future evolution of Russia. There has been his government reshuffle; his oversight of the 'Yukos affair'; his foreign policy involvement in neighbouring Georgia and Ukraine; his handling of Chechnya after the assassination of its leader Akhmed Kadyrov; and above all, the mismanagement of the Beslan school hostage tragedy and its political aftermath. All will have an impact for a long time to come, with repercussions which extend well beyond national boundaries.

Russia may not currently be the top global priority. But whether it rebounds in the next few years, or goes into decline, it will likely have a growing impact that policymakers, business people, academics and others with interests beyond their own borders would do well to heed. Putin's role in that process will prove essential.

CHECHNYA

1. Lipetsk
2. Mordovia
3. Chuvashia
4. Mari El.
5. Ul'yanovsk
6. Karachayevo-Cherkessia
7. Kabardino-Balkaria
8. N. Ossetia
9. Vladimir
10. Ivanovo

RUSSIA'S ADMINISTRATIVE REGIONS

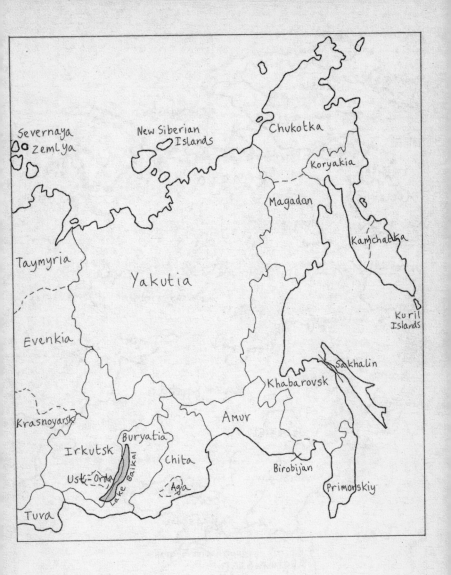

Severnaya
Zemlya

New Siberian
Islands

Chukotka

Koryakia

Magadan

Kamchatka

Taymyria

Yakutia

Evenkia

Kuril
Islands

Sakhalin

Krasnoyarsk

Khabarovsk

Amur

Buryatia

Irkutsk

Chita

Ust-Orda

Lake Baikal

Aga

Birobijan

Primorskiy

Tuva

RUSSIA AND ITS NEIGHBOURS

INTRODUCTION: IN THE
KREMLIN LIBRARY

A WALK ACROSS RED SQUARE on a dark winter's evening, a security check at the giant gates, the scrutiny of a metal detector, and we reached the heart of Russian power. Along with my two colleagues, I surrendered my mobile phone, waited in a reception room, and was ushered down sterile gilded corridors to the inner sanctum of the Kremlin. It felt as though we were alone in the entire building. Then Vladimir Putin slipped into the library to join us almost unnoticed, shook hands, and sat down to offer us his undivided attention.

It was 13 December 2001, and Putin had every reason to be irritated. Just a few weeks before, the Russian president had defied domestic public opinion and western expectations alike by pledging his wholehearted support to the US-led international anti-terrorist coalition created after 9/11. In another signal that the Cold War was over, he had closed Soviet-era bases in Cuba and Vietnam. But on the day of our meeting, George W. Bush had responded by announcing to Congress that he was unilaterally withdrawing from the 1972 Anti-Ballistic Missile (ABM) treaty, a cornerstone of international strategic stability and one of the few remaining agreements that gave Russia some leverage and status abroad.

Putin had been warned in advance, of course, in a private conversation between the two heads of state. But it was fortuitous timing for a meeting with foreign journalists, giving him a chance to express his

1

misgivings at length, on home ground, to an international audience. It was still relatively early in his exposure to the western media, little more than eighteen months since he had become president, and the bodyguard hovering in the corner of the room added a slightly sinister tone to the atmosphere. Putin came across far better than the stereotypes which had dogged him because of his past in the KGB, the Soviet secret police. He was not someone to talk in slick sound bites, but his lengthy replies were measured and thoughtful, nuanced and conciliatory. He used a little flattery and an occasional turn of humour, demonstrated considerable technical knowledge and a good turn of Russian phrase as he explained the likely ineffectiveness of the USA's proposed missile defence plan as trying 'to hit a bullet with a bullet'.

Bush's decision, he said bluntly, was 'a mistake' that ignored proposed Russian treaty modifications and risked triggering a new arms race. He graciously conceded that the USA had the right to make its decision, and that he had no plan to stoke any 'anti-American hysteria'. Most important, he was pragmatic, recognizing that from a position of weakness it was best to turn the situation to his advantage. Russia could no longer afford to maintain the large Soviet stockpile of 7,000 nuclear weapons, and he was keen to see it cut to a more realistic maximum of 2,000, matched by a similar reduction by the USA. But he also laid out his demand for a new legal treaty to fix those numbers. Six months later, the two leaders signed the Treaty of Moscow as Putin had wanted, overcoming insistence from American advisers that a verbal agreement would suffice.

We talked for more than ninety minutes, and had the impression that – were it not for the prompting of his press secretary – he would have been willing to go on all night. At one point, a telephone on his desk rang but he let it go unanswered: perhaps the only man in Russia who could afford such indulgence. There was none of the nervousness of many of his fellow officials and business people, and no demand to inspect and censor the quotes ahead of publication. He seemed at the height of his confidence and power.

In a wide-ranging interview, he stressed his determination to paying back international debt and actively pursuing reform. 'Of particular importance is the positive development of the economy. We believe this is the most important thing,' he said. Throughout his first presidential term, he kept his word, overseeing a period of unprecedented growth and stability. He proved a tough negotiator, expressing his desire to join the World Trade Organization – but only on standard terms rather than accepting additional conditions he considered unfair to Russia.

More open to debate has been his effectiveness in meeting the hopes he expressed to us then of developing democratic institutions, a free media and civil society within Russia. There were doubts about his commitment to such values when he first came to office, reinforced by some of his initial actions. But there were also reasons to give him the benefit of the doubt initially, as he attempted to rebuild on the Communist legacy and the post-Soviet mess he had inherited. However during his second term beginning in 2004, growing restrictions on freedom gathered pace, and the risks of a more authoritarian system became far more real.

What came across in our discussions was the importance he attached to military-style loyalty and honour. He expressed no disappointment with Bush personally as a result of the ABM decision, stressing: 'On no occasion did he deceive me or mislead me. He always does what he says, and in that respect he is a reliable partner.' Amid the well-rehearsed answers, there was just one moment – in response to my final question – when he appeared unsettled. I asked about the growing numbers of people from his native St Petersburg that he had brought into his administration. 'If you look into the percentages . . . you will not find many,' he began defensively. But then he added: 'I try to hire people for jobs based on their moral and professional qualities. I have to know [them] well. The point is that I know they are fit for making decisions in this sphere.'

The question of his collaborators was perhaps Putin's greatest challenge. After spending fifteen years in the KGB, until the USSR collapsed in 1991, he had experienced a meteoric rise through local administration in his native St Petersburg and the federal government in Moscow. He changed jobs every year, becoming prime minister in 1999, and then – defying all initial predictions – was elected president in spring 2000. That gave him little time to broaden his circle of acquaintants, forcing him to rely on his own close colleagues or those imposed on him by his predecessors. His natural caution meant that his own people – and style – would only gradually emerge. And not all of them had evolved as far as he had, or were willing or able to compensate for his own limitations.

The direction of Russia, a vast country with a long tradition of centralized rule, has always been set by the leader – whether tsar, Politburo head or president. Boris Yeltsin, the man who dissolved the Soviet Union and made himself head of a nominally democratic state, engineered a constitution that in fact put most powers in his hands. It was no honorific role. He had created a supra-presidential system. And, though severely weakened by ill-health and palace intrigues in his second term in 1996–9, he was able to all but name his successor. Putin, a far younger, more energetic man, took the post and strengthened it still further, rebuilding the institutions of state. His role in defining the course of the country from 2000 to 2004 was extremely important. And the likelihood that he will remain in office at least until 2008 makes understanding his character and values vital.

This book attempts to describe and analyse both Putin and the country he inherited, which merits greater understanding by the rest of the world. Historically, Russia's official state Communist ideology helped define the central struggle of the twentieth century. At the start of the twenty-first, its economy is modest and its military might diminished. But its vast reserves of natural resources, its gigantic land mass – one-eighth of the world's total – and its strategic position on the axis of Europe and Asia will ensure that this country of 145 million well-educated people remains fundamentally important in international affairs over the coming decades.

The first chapter, 'Coming to Terms', addresses the Russia that Putin inherited. It was a country severely weakened and demoralized, riddled with corruption and sharply divided between rich and poor, old and young. The bloody repressions and miserable living conditions of totalitarianism had been replaced by a limited democracy and a painful economic transition to wild capitalism in the 1990s that left some freer and richer than they had ever been, but others abandoned, embittered and nostalgic for the past.

'The Man from Nowhere' charts Putin's own rise to power, as someone whose character was fundamentally shaped by those evolutions. Born when Joseph Stalin was still in office, he was inspired by Yuri Andropov, the former KGB leader and briefly Brezhnev's successor as leader. He worked for the KGB during a period of stagnation until the system fell apart, and was then thrust into politics and administration at the heart of the fledgling democratic movement. His rapid promotions reflected both his own skills and the strong support of a tight group of individuals around Yeltsin.

'Prisoner of the Caucasus' explores a theme that was central to Putin's rise to power, the conflict in Russia's tiny North Caucasus republic of Chechnya. It proved an important factor throughout his period in office, and has dominated western perceptions of his rule. While an extreme case, it had been the ultimate symbol of the excesses of Yeltsin's policies and personality. His successor's approach has proved at best palliative and at worst incendiary.

'Shooting the Messenger' highlights the sorry story of the evolutions of the Russian media after the end of Communist state censorship. What could have been an important counterbalance to the authorities and the basis for establishing democracy and civil society was instead too often corrupted by mercantilism and pride, and a tool in the hands of competing business clans. Putin's clampdowns cowed it and restored television in particular to its traditional role as a mouthpiece for the authorities.

'Autumn of the Oligarchs' describes Putin's uneasy relations with the handful of politically influential businessmen, created by Yeltsin, who wielded tremendous power and helped select the country's new leader, but then found themselves struggling to maintain influence and redefine their role under the new regime. They symbolized a very curious, Russian-style form of capitalism. They were forces for growth and progress, but also meddled in politics and tried to impose a highly monopolized form of development.

'The Price of Reform' studies the changes to the political institutions that Putin engineered during his first term, establishing a form of 'managed democracy' designed to tame the regions and the parliament to his will. It explains the limitations of the previous very imperfect system he inherited from Yeltsin, and studies its changing role in pushing through the new president's economic and other policy initiatives.

'A Bridge Too Far' analyses the new twists in Russian foreign policy under Putin: first towards its traditional Soviet allies, then to an explicit embrace of the USA and Europe, and then back again as the international environment itself changed. Putin has done much to boost his country's credibility abroad, proving a more consistent, reliable partner than Yeltsin. He has been aided by the changing external threat of terrorism and a growing demand for Russia's abundant energy supplies away from the unstable Middle East. But there was also a more nationalistic neo-imperial underside that warned he was not simply turning Russia into a western nation.

'Towards Liberal Authoritarianism' takes stock of Putin's first four years in office by examining the concluding events of the period. Many of his actions that were criticized abroad were popular and more comprehensible at home in the context of the Russia that he had inherited. But as his first presidential term came to an end, his achievements were mixed. The economy was in much better shape, but there was also a shift away from western-style democracy that suggested he had created a very specific form of 'liberal authoritarianism'.*

Russia remains a secretive country where theories and conspiracies often dominate over facts, and the truth is hard to extract. That is never more the case than with Putin, who spent most of his life in closed Soviet institutions – the KGB and the Kremlin – where information has always been tightly controlled. This book cannot claim to come up with definitive explanations, but it is intended at least to provide readers with some greater understanding of the complexities of a fascinating country, based on the author's own observations as a witness of many of the events that have characterized Putin's Russia over the past few years.

I would like to thank my agent, Andrew Nurnberg, for his friendship and support; George Miller and his team at Granta for their professionalism and understanding under extreme deadline pressure; Bruce Bean, John Hamilton, Anton Ivanov, Andrew Kuchins, Alan Rousso and Steve Solnick for thoughts on particular chapters; my *Financial Times* colleagues John Thornhill, Robert Cottrell, Charles Clover, Rafael Behr, Arkady Ostrovsky, and Katya and Lena, for their constant ideas and collegiality; my parents for everything including scrutiny of the text; and Victor and above all Sandra for great tolerance and wisdom.

---

*It is a sign of the economic stability of Putin's Russia that the exchange rate has remained relatively constant for most of his period in office at about Rbs 30 to $1.

COMING TO TERMS

ON 21 DECEMBER EVERY YEAR, Yevgeniya Ivanova respectfully raises a glass of vodka to her persecutor on his birthday. She toasts the Soviet dictator Joseph Stalin, whose portrait still hangs on her wall even though his bloody regime condemned her to more than a decade in the country's horrific Gulag labour camp system. In 1943, at the age of fourteen, Ivanova was arrested by the secret police in her native Leningrad, her only 'crime' that her uncle supposedly collaborated with the Germans. She passed through a series of prisons and work camps before arriving in the Kolyma river basin in Russia's extreme north-east district of Magadan in 1949. Though freed in 1956, she long remained under police observation, and was only formally rehabilitated in 1993. For the past forty years, she has lived near Susuman, a township of crumbling concrete buildings constructed on pillars above the ground to withstand the extreme conditions. 'I don't consider myself an enemy of the people, but my conscience is not clean,' she said, puffing on a *papirosa*, a Soviet-era cigarette made with coarse tobacco. 'We studied Stalin's words in school, sang "Thank you, Comrade Stalin" – and rightly so. I was raised in that tradition. I have nothing against the Soviet system.'

Some argue that her views are the result of continued fear, others of delusion. 'They found you a relic,' said Miron Etlis, himself a former political prisoner and the Magadan representative of

Memorial, a human rights organization, when he heard her comments. But Ivanova's nostalgic sentiments – or a milder echo of them – remain too common in modern-day Russia to be dismissed so easily. They reflect a continued ambivalence of Russians in coming to terms with their painful history. Few physical markers record the history of the Gulag today, and those victims who survived the system are fast dying out. An older Russian generation often prefers to emphasize the positive aspects of the past and forget the bad except in their own private grief. The young simply see it as irrelevant and uninteresting. Mikhail Gorbachev removed the fear from the old Soviet system and laid the groundwork for its destruction. Boris Yeltsin carried out the demolition work, and established some aspects of a more democratic society in its place. In the process, he made substantial compromises, and failed to purge the old or win over many Russians with his approach to the new. Vladimir Putin, in his turn, provided consolidation and stability, capitalizing on the continuing ambivalence and nostalgia among many Russians for the past after a disruptive first post-Communist decade of mitigated success. In so doing, he has done little to lay to rest the spectre of the past.

Nowhere is the tension over Russia's twentieth-century history more striking than in the hilly republic of Magadan, a focal point for Stalin's repressions. Under Lenin, in 1918, a decree on Red Terror already permitted executions without trial and the creation of the Gulag. The move marked some continuity with an often authoritarian tsarist past. But it was extended to unprecedented lengths under the Bolsheviks. Across the Soviet Union between 1930 and 1956 alone, even the most conservative estimates suggest that nearly nineteen million people were imprisoned and four million killed, crushing the genetic backbone of Russia's intellectuals, artists and political opponents. Millions more were deported, had their lives destroyed or perished in famines. Eight time zones east of Moscow, with winters that can drop to below minus fifty degrees Celsius, and sweltering, mosquito-ridden summer temperatures above forty degrees, Magadan became a centre for prisoner-slaves. 'Kolyma was the greatest and most famous island, the pole of ferocity of that amazing country of Gulag,' wrote Alexander Solzhenitsyn.

Stanislaw Kowalski remembers initially being struck by the beauty of the region. He was rounded up in his native Poland in 1940, and like many – Russians and foreigners – who fell into the hands of the secret police, he spent months in successive prison camps moving ever further east. His first view of Magadan offered a brief respite after an agonizing insanitary eight-day journey by ship, squeezed into five-tiered bunks in an unventilated hold. The impression would not last long. Held in Camp Number Four near the capital Magadan, he recalls a hard-labour regime which began at 5 a.m. and continued until 11 p.m. every day. 'We had 350 grams of bread and a soup of seaweed in the morning, then nothing till a little soup and salted herring in the evening,' he remembered. Later, he would be taken by truck for thirty-six hours along the 'road of bones', built by and on the bodies of prisoners for hundreds of miles from Magadan to Susuman and beyond. He marched for another day through the woods to Pioneer Camp, where he spent months digging for gold and felling timber. He was trapped by the cold-blooded logic of the system: his low output would be penalized by a reduction in already meagre rations, making the impossibly large work quotas yet more unattainable, and survival still less likely. A small number of common criminals kept order on behalf of the authorities, living in better conditions while terrorizing and stealing from others. The death toll was staggering. 'People just disappeared. They stayed in the barracks and the corpses were removed,' he said. 'The prisoners had a saying: "Kolyma means death." It was just sheer accident that we got out.' He was lucky, one of 100 Poles released as a result of the treaty with the Soviet government at the end of the war. Another 400 died before the agreement was fully implemented.

Intrigued by the region's gruesome but little-researched legacy, the historian Robert Conquest wrote a book on Kolyma in 1978 in which he estimated that three million perished. 'You can't get the full statistics because many prisoners were released severely weakened just before they died,' he said. Today, adjusted for a lower number of prisoners shipped in than he had previously thought, he believes the true figure of deaths is between 700,000 and one million. 'That sounds about right,' said Etlis. 'But I don't like to count the numbers, it degrades what happened.' The figures remain chilling nonetheless. So does the fading of history. Far from centres of population, deliberately hidden and always built to be temporary, Kolyma's camps – like hundreds of others across the former Soviet empire – are rotting fast in the harsh environment. Soon, nothing will be left of either the physical remnants or the living memories of those who laboured inside them.

9

The Soviet system was happy to reinterpret others' history. Many of Hitler's concentration camps fell into Communist hands after the war and were deliberately preserved by the USSR as symbols of the evils of defeated Nazism. Visiting the concentration camp of Buchenwald in east Germany shortly after reunification in 1991, I was struck by the displays. They still reflected the distorted interpretation of the former leadership of the German Democratic Republic: there was plenty of space devoted to the cowardly killing of Communist Party leaders by the Nazis, but little mention of the tragedy that befell other groups, notably the Jews. In 1960s and 1970s Germany, rebellious baby-boomers brought up in a new era of freedom questioned and criticized their own parents as they came of age, and launched a fresh and profound reflection on de-Nazification. In the Soviet Union, with tight state control over the media and intimidation of individuals, such debate was suppressed and internalized. It was limited to the whispered conversations around the kitchen tables of those – a very large number – who were touched more or less directly. After a period of openness in the late 1980s and early 1990s, today talk of those years has all but ceased. Memoirs have been published, archives have been at least partially opened, documentaries and plays are shown, and discussion is no longer forbidden. But indifference has all too rapidly replaced intolerance, at a time when most Russians spend more time struggling to survive the present than thinking about the past. The economic boom since the turn of the millennium has if anything given rise to a resurgent nationalism and pride that further glosses over the Soviet regime's colossal crimes.

In autumn 2002, I paid a visit to the former Nazi camps at Auschwitz in Poland. Local trains make frequent connections to Krakow, from where free buses regularly shuttle visitors to the different sites. The environment is harsh, the memories painful, but coachloads of people – including dozens of schoolchildren – wander around, often spending several hours between the internment huts with their painful exhibits and videos on the Holocaust. The following spring, I visited Perm 36, a former camp two hours' drive from the Russian city of the same name. First opened in 1943, it became a centre for arrested dissidents, including many nationalists from Belarus and Ukraine. It was a reminder that the repressions were not specifically Stalinist: while the techniques applied may have become less brutal, the practice of depriving people of their liberty as a punishment for being too free-thinking continued until much more recently. Perm 36 was closed to its last inmate in only 1988. A few months later, after a Ukrainian film pictured the site, the authorities tried to destroy it with bulldozers. 'I'm an archaeologist, and there are fewer remains from the Gulag than from the temporary settlements of the Stone Age,' said Lev Timofeyev, a local historian who has helped convert the site into Russia's only purpose-built political prison camp to be conserved and turned into a museum. 'The prisoners only had the possessions that they could carry with them: a fork, a towel.' With some assistance from the local government and US foundations, but little Russian federal help, he began to take over the site, research its history and restore it in the early 1990s. A decade later, the chilly, spartan and semi-ruined barracks are a more potent reminder than any sophisticated visual aids of the conditions in which political prisoners lived. But without any easy public transport, I had to hire a car to reach Perm 36. And without any widespread interest or resources today, few even of the more enlightened residents of the city of Perm had come to look. I met no other visitors during my trip. At best, a few thousand come each year – a figure that Auschwitz surpasses in just a few days.

Elsewhere across Russia, tucked away in former camps and cemeteries, there are dozens of privately funded small monuments to victims of the repressions, but few of any scale or prominence. By contrast, in a building behind Lubyanka, the KGB's own long-feared headquarters in central Moscow, there is a small 'Historical demonstration hall'. Previously called the Chekist hall of the KGB, it contains extensive displays on tsarist-era counter-espionage, and on contemporary activities in the fight against terrorism. But there is little on the Stalin era, other than mentions of the KGB's subsequent 'scrupulous work in the rehabilitation of victims of groundless repressions'. Near to Russia's western borders, there is one impressive museum which covers the period, complete with a reconstructed wooden prison barrack, documents and artefacts. But this is the Museum of the Occupation in Riga, the capital of the independent Baltic republic of Latvia. It focuses on the successive 'occupying totalitarian regimes' of Nazism and Communism, while glossing over the role of Latvians themselves in the crimes committed in their country. In any case, for such former Soviet satellite states, which can portray themselves as victims of 'colonization', it has proved psychologically easier to reflect on their history than for the colonizer itself.

Museums are not the only way of remembering and reflecting on the past. But there are plenty of other indications that people prefer to forget or romanticize. An opinion poll in 2003 suggested that 29 per cent of Russians considered that Stalin did more good than bad, citing above all the victory over Hitler and a return from chaos to order. Many still argue that the Soviet dictator was unaware of the evils being perpetrated in his name; others that Russia needed tough leaders then and now. While Germany has paid out money to Russian victims of Nazi forced labour camps, and returned confiscated trophy art, there have been no reciprocal gestures. Many school history textbooks still gloss over the repressions, and the time spent by teachers on the subject is minimal. Igor Obrosov, a Moscow artist whose father and brother were arrested and sent to the Gulag, invited me to his dusty studio one day. In a corner, he showed me the powerful series of canvases that he had painted in secret in Soviet times, depicting the arrest and interrogation of his family. He is now drawing up plans for a monument he would like to see built. But even he is reluctant to focus on the Red Terror, proposing instead a memorial to 'victims of political repressions' in general, rather than one specifically to the crimes of Stalin or even the Soviet regime.

Perhaps because of its especially brutal legacy, Magadan has done more than most places to remember. A tortuous ten-hour drive along the 'road of bones' from the regional centre is the settlement of Yagodnye. Here, Ivan Panikarov, a journalist who came to the region from Rostov in 1987, has spent his own money assembling a modest display in a three-room flat in a crumbling 1960s apartment block. The handful of visitors each month can see a wheelbarrow from the gold mines, bullets gathered from camp pits, and gruesome photographs of some of the skeletons that are still being unearthed by modern gold prospectors. In the city of Magadan itself, a large room in the municipal museum offers one of Russia's few state-supported permanent Gulag exhibits. There are just a few copies remaining of an exhibition booklet produced a decade ago and never reprinted, but documents, photographs and crude winter clothes still pay testament to the executions, disease and grave injustices of the period.

Most striking, a towering concrete monument to the repressed sits on the hill overlooking the city, itself somewhat totalitarian in style. The *Mask of Mourning*, a grieving head with the faces of victims pouring down its face like tears, is one of the few such memorials of any scale in the country. Its sculptor, Ernst Neizvestny, who emigrated to the USA in the 1970s, said he first drew up a design when discussions began under Nikita Khrushchev's 'thaw' in the 1950s. A change in the political mood in the Politburo cut efforts short, but he continued to dream. 'It was my duty. People who don't think about the past don't think about the future,' he told me. When he raised the idea again during a visit to Moscow in the late 1980s, Gorbachev himself was not responsive. But there was interest from the regional authorities in Magadan, as well as in Sverdlovsk and Vorkhuta, sites of other labour camps.

By the time the sculptor's project finally began to advance in the early 1990s, Boris Yeltsin was in power. 'A lot of politicians around him were against,' Neizvestny said. 'They were worried about provoking the Communists.' Ultimately, Yeltsin used the monument for his own political ends, inaugurating it in 1996 just ahead of the second round of presidential elections that he was fighting on a strongly anti-Communist platform. Since then, Neizvestny's plans for the other two monuments have withered. His only other significant work relating to the period was commissioned for Elista, the capital of the ethnic republic of Kalmykia. Russia's only Buddhist region, it was eliminated and its entire population deported under Stalin. Eased by an up-front payment made directly by the local businessman-president, Neizvestny cast and inaugurated *Exile and Return* in memory of the Kalmyks a few months later.

As we walked down Magadan's streets, Etlis pointed proudly to numerous 'Leningrad-style' façades on offices and houses built by prisoners. After his own release from a labour camp in Kazakhstan, he came voluntarily to the city that he now calls home. But he prefers not to linger in front of the statue standing in front of the city hall: that of Edward Berzin, the first head of Dalstroi, the Far Eastern Construction Company which organized Kolyma's slave labour. Berzin himself was eventually arrested and executed, in the bloody spiral of paranoia and recrimination under Stalin. As in many other Russian cities, there has been little effort to change other Communist-era relics in Magadan. There are still Lenin, Proletarian and Soviet Streets too; there is even one in honour of Felix Dzerzhinsky, the

13

ruthless creator of the Cheka secret police, which coordinated Stalin's repressions. Yet Etlis seemed reluctant to stir the shadows of the past. 'They already turned Stalin Street into Karl Marx Street. Why should we change the names again?' he said.

Valentina Soboleva, in charge of external relations for the Magadan regional administration, replied in the same vein when I asked why the old street names remained. 'That is our history too.' A copy of *Magadanskaya Pravda*, the local newspaper established in 1935, sat on her desk, a Soviet-era hammer and sickle logo on its masthead. She showed me a short article for a book on the region that she had drafted for the governor which referred elliptically to 'not a few dramatic pages in our history'. Then she added: 'People got married in these streets, and they have memories here. I don't like it when people just talk about the Gulags. It's our history, unfortunately, and you can't rewrite it. But those who live here also love the area, and are working to make it a dignified place.'

Stanislaw Kowalski, perhaps with the greater distance that his Polish origins and his new life in the USA have given him, is less sanguine. 'So many people died, you could call it genocide. The world should know about Kolyma. But there is no interest. There is a belief that it would be better if it was forgotten.'

Reviving the past

On 21 December 1999, Vladimir Putin gathered the heads of the parties of Russia's newly elected parliament. He could have offered to toast democracy, or even their success fresh from campaigning. Instead, he raised his glass to Comrade Stalin, and all but one of the politicians joined him in fêting the Soviet leader's birthday. It was one of many gestures that showed Putin's continued links with the past. He made no secret of his respect for Yuri Andropov, the KGB's former chief who, like him, would go on to lead the country. He laid a bouquet at his grave in Red Square in July 1999, and in January 2000 restored a memorial plaque at Lubyanka, the KGB headquarters. At a gathering of FSB (the security service) officers on 20 December 1999 after the parliamentary elections, he joked that 'the group charged with taking the government under control has achieved the first step of its assignment'. He stressed that it was important not to paint all

Soviet history black. By the end of the following year, Putin had approved a new Russian national anthem. The tune was the old version first adopted under Stalin, and the lyrics were updated by its original author, the ageing poet Sergei Mikhailkov.

On 9 May 2000, just two days after his inauguration, Putin presided over a parade in Red Square commemorating the fifty-fifth anniversary of the end of the Second World War. He was standing next to Lenin's tomb – though not on it, like his Soviet predecessors – and behind him was the backdrop of the Kremlin's multiple towers, displaying variously the tsarist double-headed eagle, the tricolour flag and the Communist red star. Three years later, Putin was still playing with images, endorsing a red flag for the Russian army anointed with both stars and eagles. The result was a thoroughly postmodern mixture of Russia's different eras. If opinion polls suggested that ordinary people endorsed the choices, they pointed above all to a populace living in total confusion with its own past. The majority were in favour of both the restoration of the Soviet army flag and the re-adoption of the pre-revolutionary tricolour. Most did not even know from which era the symbols dated. It was symptomatic of a society known abroad both for its distinctly contemporary commercial teenage lesbian pop duo Tatu and for the national airline Aeroflot, still sporting its hammer and sickle logo and the old Soviet Union identification label 'SU'. But amid the uncertainty, Putin's clear imprimatur was the restoration and clear reaffirmation of pride in the Soviet Union, stripped of its former ideology.

Many younger people were indifferent to such symbols, but for an older generation of Russians, they struck a clear chord. I headed to Red Square on 5 March 2003 for the fiftieth anniversary of Stalin's death. Shortly before the appointed hour, just a few dozen nostalgics had gathered. But as the Kremlin clock struck 11 a.m., a line that ran to hundreds of people began to file respectfully across the cobbles, laid flowers and passed through Lenin's mausoleum before paying their respects at Stalin's tomb behind. Gennady Zyuganov, the leader of the Communist Party – the largest single party in parliament with just over a quarter of the total seats – held an impromptu press conference. His only criticism of Stalin was to suggest an excessive 'personality cult'. The repressions, he suggested, were nothing compared with the 'genocide' of ordinary Russians caused by the economic reforms of the 1990s. Millions of families of victims of the purges might have disagreed, but there was nobody nearby, in front of Lubyanka, to protest against the KGB's bloody history.

If Putin personified the past, he soon benefited from a Brezhnev-style cult of personality of his own, not seen under Yeltsin and with more than a nod towards the regimes of Central Asia. On his fiftieth birthday, on 7 October 2002, he was showered with extravagant tributes, from a crystal crocodile to a slow-growing Siberian pine, from carpets to a Turkmen horse. Bronze busts, carpets and other artefacts bearing Putin's image went on sale. Tomatoes, roses and even a street in the republic of Ingushetia in the North Caucasus were named in his honour. A female teen pop group composed and sang a sycophantic song, the lyrics pleading that they sought 'a man like Putin'. Small museums sprang up in villages and factories he had visited. A children's textbook distributed in St Petersburg uncritically described young Volodya's rise to power. Just as under Yeltsin tennis had become the sport of choice for Russia's elite, so Putin's interest in skiing meant it suddenly became popular with other leading Russian figures (his first love, judo, was presumably too difficult to find favour). Businessmen flocked to develop the Krasnaya Polyarna winter sports resort near Sochi.

Others eager to show their loyalty sponsored biographies of Putin. Several novels and hagiographies of him soon went on sale. Roy Medvedev, a historian once persecuted for his dissident views but who rejoined the Communist Party just as the Soviet Union was collapsing, wrote a book called *The Unknown Andropov*, which brought him to the new president's attention. He followed up with the *The Time of Putin*, which was soon on sale in the bookshop of the Kremlin itself. In the kiosks inside the Duma and the Federation Council, and even in ordinary stores in Moscow and beyond, dozens of different portraits and photographs of Putin were available. They proved popular wall decorations for those government officials not lucky enough to have a photograph of themselves in the presence of the head of state. Putin himself coyly stressed his embarrassment. 'Everything is all right in moderation,' he said. He did little to stop them, with Kremlin officials only stepping in very occasionally when his brand might be damaged, such as when a young entrepreneur opened a Putin Bar in Chelyabinsk, offering the Vladimir cocktail and the Putin pretzel. It seemed there was a generation ready and eager to revive their old instincts.

Putin's genuflections to the Soviet era horrified many dissidents and intellectuals, stirring painful memories of their persecution and imprisonment. It seemed as though the old hardliners were constantly pushing to test the limits of tolerance of modern Russia. Putin periodically played the 'good tsar', reining them in only if public reaction became too negative. Just ahead of the sixtieth anniversary of the battle of Stalingrad in 2002, a group of local deputies began discussing the idea of changing the city's name back from the latter-day Volgograd. Debate went quiet after Putin magnanimously said he 'personally' was against. In 2002, Yuri Luzhkov, the mayor of Moscow, proposed re-erecting the giant statue of Dzerzhinsky that had stood outside Lubyanka until 1991. He earned a scornful anonymous rebuke from a 'Kremlin source' quoted by official state press agencies. Shortly before Putin paid a visit to Magadan, the regional parliament even voted through a resolution proposing that his presidential term should be extended from four to seven years. He hinted shortly afterwards that four years was perhaps too short, but that the destabilization that could be triggered by changing the constitution was too great to risk.

Playing with Soviet symbols sent a more sinister signal to many in a society long attuned to reading between the lines to interpret the thoughts of the leadership. The taste of the past became more real when the prestigious Academy of Sciences attempted to return to the Soviet-era practice of requiring its members to report on any contacts with foreigners. United Russia, Putin's party, increasingly began to resemble the Communist Party, a 'party of leaders' compromising the old *nomenklatura* (elite). His background gave new confidence to the security services. On 27 October 1999, with Putin already installed as prime minister, officers of the FSB came to the home of Igor Sutiagin to arrest him. An arms researcher, he was charged with espionage on the grounds of preparing a report on Russia for a UK consultancy firm. He claimed his information all came from open sources. But he was detained, branded as guilty in public, charged in vague terms based on the secret Ministry of Defence Decree 005, which he was not allowed to see, denied access to independent experts, and tried in private. His case was characterized by a series of procedural violations according to Russian law, not to mention that the very fact of the FSB conducting criminal investigations and operating detention centres was in breach of the principles of the Council of Europe, to which Russia belongs.

Sutiagin's case followed the pattern of a number of others already under way before Putin's rise to power. Two naval officers and journalists, Alexander Nikitin and Grigory Pasko, were first arrested in the mid-1990s on suspicion of espionage after denouncing pollution by the Russian navy into Russia's Baltic and Japanese Seas respectively. Their cases began under Yeltsin, and they were released from prison – though not technically acquitted – under Putin. But their pursuit was symptomatic of a growing 'spy mania' in the country. Vladimir Shchurov was arrested shortly after Sutiagin. Valery Kovalchuk was charged in August 2000. Oleg Kalugin, a former KGB senior officer who fled to the USA and become an outspoken critic of Putin, was tried in his absence for treason in the summer of 2002. Such judgements served as warnings, discouraging others from conducting sensitive research or speaking out.

Gorbachev never destroyed the KGB, and was in many ways in its debt: the Soviet leader was the protégé of Yuri Andropov, its head from 1967–82. Yeltsin split the organization into different units but continued to draw on it – not least in his choice of prime ministers. He always resisted 'lustration' – opening the secret files revealing the identities of informants that made up the backbone of totalitarian control – for fear it would spark a civil war. Many victims of the repressions were rehabilitated under a 1991 law, but the compensation they received was often less than the pensions of their former persecutors and guards. While researchers continued to delve into the history of the repressions, the FSB became increasingly resistant to their requests. Alexander Yakovlev, one of the architects of glasnost, who was appointed by Yeltsin to research the most sensitive political archives, said: 'I still have good access. But when I am gone, and someone else does the asking, I fear it will be different.'

On a chilly spring day in 2000, I paid a visit to a small wood enclosed by a high fence in Kommunarka, just beyond Moscow's ring-road to the south of the city. The old green-painted *dacha* (cottage) and meadows and trees behind looked at first sight innocuous. But the absence of indications of its bloody history was itself chilling. It was here that the NKVD (Soviet secret police) shot hundreds of victims in the 1920s and 1930s, dispatching them with a single bullet to the back of the head and dumping them in pits. Some were dead on arrival, gassed in trucks on the way. All had been rounded up, swiftly 'judged' and condemned to death. The site held the country residence of Genrik Yagoda, the brutal head of the NKVD, who was himself 'repressed' in 1937. The FSB website today lists his biography, but makes no mention of how he died. And the FSB continued to control the site until 1999, when it finally relinquished ownership to the Orthodox Church. Only then could Memorial, the human rights group, gain access, put up a small plaque and, after several years of effort, complete a painstakingly compiled list of victims.

Many Russians welcomed Putin's embrace of the Soviet period. People may have forgotten – or preferred to revise their views on – the Gulag, but the memories of the later Communist period remain both vivid and, in much of Russia, rosy. To see why, a good starting point is the winding road that stretches northwards from Magadan to Susuman. The route is as far as it is possible to get from Lenin's tomb anywhere in the country, yet still firmly in his shadow. I spent ten hours travelling its length with Volodya, a local man who drove an ageing black Volga saloon car. We passed a succession of towns that had been abandoned, factories that had closed, machinery left rusting, schools half-constructed, and pipelines that had broken. Over the past decade, the 'road of bones' had become a dusty track of socialist ruins. The region – like so many in the extremities of Siberia – was developed under the warped economics of slave labour and distorted transport tariffs, and the military-industrial imperative of development at any price. In post-Stalin times, its citizens were looked after paternalistically. Despite its harshness, Magadan was far from belonging to the Third World. Everyone had jobs, housing and sustenance. There were roads, signs, petrol stations, social services, electricity and heating for all those who lived even in the most remote towns. And living conditions, heavily subsidized, even made it attractive. Yet with the collapse of Communism and the accompanying state infrastructure, and the advent of the market in the most harsh conditions, the entire system started to crumble. There was money in Magadan. When Valentin Tsvetkov, the governor, was gunned down in central Moscow in October 2002, suspicion immediately fell on those struggling for the lucrative gold, fish and timber concessions which he controlled. But the post-Soviet distribution of wealth was hugely skewed, with just a few benefiting. Some professional gold-miners were able to make a living even in places like Susuman. They went elsewhere when the long winters began, leaving the long-term residents with little except memories of better times.

'For me, life under Communism was better,' said Volodya. 'People worked and lived well. Democracy? Freedom of speech? So what? The Communists planned everything from 1937; the "democrats" only look as far as their own pockets.' He arrived in Magadan in the 1980s from Donbass, a coal-mining region in Ukraine, in search of a better life. 'Under *perestroika* [Gorbachev's economic restructuring that laid the foundations for a free market], the shifts in the mines fell from three, to two, to one a day, and then everything shut down. Here, the salary, the apartment and the pension were better. I'm really sad about all these closed factories. We used to have a convoy of 140 lorries driving down this road every day. Gorbachev killed us morally. He said he would open us up to the world, but we just saw how poor we were. We believed that the Volga was the best car in the world. Now we understand what shit it is.' For many residents of Magadan, and those across the rest of Russia, political freedoms were abstract and irrelevant, and free markets an all too painful reality that had replaced queues and rations with a wide variety of goods at prices they could not afford. Many of the Soviet *nomenklatura* were able to trade their old privileges and contacts for money; many others struggled even more to survive than they had before. 'They say we are a democratic society and have joined the market economy,' said Vladimir Chekhovskikh, a local photographer. 'But it's not true. Perhaps in Moscow or St Petersburg, but not in the periphery. Everything has been destroyed here. We have freedom, but not financial freedom.'

A number of former prisoners and their families stayed in Magadan after de-Stalinization: initially because they were not allowed to leave by the KGB; later because they became used to the conditions and the local networks of friends, or they simply had nowhere else to go. Many residents had come far more recently. A period in the extreme conditions of the regions of the far north in the Soviet Union meant promotion, a much higher salary and pension, long holidays in the 'mainland' to the south, access to an apartment and other social facilities. When Communism collapsed, the situation was turned on its head, and these migrants suffered disproportionately. They had all the disadvantages of others living across Russia, as their savings were wiped out and their state-funded wages failed to keep up with market prices. But their extra benefits were inverted, with the subsidies on food disappearing, leaving the cost of goods in the local shops – most brought in by plane or boat – far higher than elsewhere. Bread – the yardstick of subsistence across Russia – cost Rbs 12 in Susuman, twice as much as in Moscow, hardly the cheapest of cities. The reasons had shifted from political to economic, but many of the residents remained prisoners nonetheless. Many did not even have the money to leave a region that has no roads or rail links to the rest of the country. 'I came from Ukraine in 1990, partly for the health of my children,' said Pyotr, a mechanic at the airport, who earned extra money driving a gypsy cab and fishing for crabs, but for whom the airfare was now equivalent to five months' salary. 'In the past, I could fly away any day I wanted. Now we are trapped here like hostages. The last time I went home was four years ago.'

Such stories of regret over the changes of the past decade were typical in many of the more remote parts of Russia. In 2002, I travelled to Mirny in Yakutia, in the far north, which had lived since the 1950s on the extraction of diamonds from a gigantic 1,800-foot-deep opencast mine in the town's outskirts. Unlike many of the country's other remote regions, Mirny had survived as a 'company town' under the protection of Alrosa, the diamond monopoly controlled jointly by the federal and local authorities. The high value of its production, and continued state support, meant it could still assist the local population, unlike many other single-company towns from the Soviet era. Alrosa ran the hotels, the restaurants, the airline and even an old collective farm. It began completion of a hydroelectric dam abandoned in the late 1980s for lack of funds. When freak floods in 2001 washed away part of the town of Lensk, a river port and entrepôt several hours' drive south, the company spent millions of dollars flying in new houses in pre-fabricated kits, and constructed a high ditch to act as a future flood barrier. Alrosa was paternalistic, inefficient and untransparent, but at least it helped the local residents survive the turmoil of the 1990s. Yet even here, company employees lamented the past, and called for the reinstatement of Mirny's Soviet status as a 'closed town', to which outsiders could not travel – let alone come to live – without authorization from the security police, under the blanket cover of protecting state secrets.

It was a refrain I heard in many much poorer places too, like Sarov, the former secret scientific research centre in the Urals that was home to the Russian atomic bomb programme. In much of Russia, the collapse of the state since the late 1980s had destroyed any social contract between the government and the people. Public sector wages and pensions were delayed and reduced to miserable levels; public transport deteriorated; and much of the semblance of law and order collapsed. Privatized companies tried to shed what they called their 'social assets' – the costly services that they had previously been required to finance although they were not directly part of their business. They pushed hospitals, schools and tramways into the hands of local authorities which had little competence or money to take up the slack. By controlling new arrivals, closed towns managed to maintain a greater degree of comfort in their isolation. They felt increasingly threatened by 'welfare scroungers' arriving from elsewhere to take advantage of even marginally higher social benefits, and by what they perceived as criminal elements among immigrants, notably from Central Asia and the Caucasus. In the absence of tighter social controls, and the presence of growing income disparities, problems of drugs, alcoholism and violence were emerging. The return of controls on travel in and out did not smack to them of sinister repressions; many saw it instead as a sign at last of the restoration of justice, a sense that someone was again helping them plan for the future.

I travelled in January 2003 to a town near Petrozavodsk in Karelia, in Russia's north-west. The image as I arrived in the main square could have come from India were it not for the snow. Dozens of people were lined up with buckets, waiting to receive drinking water from a big tanker that had been driven to the site. There was a series of portable outdoor toilets for the residents. The surrounding 1960s concrete apartments looked normal from the outside, but the heating and water had failed. Natalya showed me the problems she faced. There were sheets of ice on the inside walls, and the toilet and bath had cracked after the water froze. So had the radiators. At least the gas still worked for a few hours a day, so she kept warm by keeping the gas stove turned on permanently, with its door left open. The local engineers blamed the reforms of the past few years, as they discussed underfunding of the infrastructure, and how all the best staff had left to seek better-paid jobs elsewhere.

The danger was that the problems of the present led to an over-romanticization of the past – and not only of the era of stagnation under Brezhnev, but even the outright repression under Stalin. 'If we didn't have a tough leader, we would not have the country we have today, or have won the war,' said Tatiana Dzhagoeva, a librarian in Susuman. 'Stalin brought order to Russia in place of corruption.' Tears poured down the face of Vera Rytel, who was living on a pension of Rbs 2,500 a month, as she recalled how her father had been arrested and brought to Magadan as a Baptist minister. But she was pleased about the return of the old national anthem. 'I was very happy when the hymn was restored,' she said. 'I stood up at home when I heard it. It was the right decision by Putin. It gave me a feeling of pride. We worked from plan to plan, not just to show off. We worked for the people's fate then, not the interests of people.'

Putin's warm attitude towards Soviet history no doubt partly reflected a genuine pride in the system which he had once sworn dutifully to uphold; and partly a recognition that objectively conditions had been better for many Russians then. More cynically, it was a cheap way to console the country's lost generations. While state support for serious discussion about the repressions was absent, substantial resources were pumped into the annual commemorations of the 'Great Patriotic War' of 1941–5. The fact of Stalin's collaboration with Hitler in 1939–41 was glossed over, let alone his ruthless purges of the officers' corps which crippled the Red Army before the war and contributed to the large death tolls of his own people during the fighting.

Within Russia, at least, it should not be surprising that Communism is not viewed in the same way as Nazism, despite the resemblance of the two totalitarian systems. Robert Conquest argues that the philosophy of the camps was entirely different. 'The NKVD said to some that they had come to die, but the Nazis operated on a different scale,' he told me. 'Death was not premeditated in the Gulag as it was in the concentration camps.' Stalin was not militarily defeated like Hitler; on the contrary Russia, which had suffered huge casualties during the war as it helped defeat Germany, saw itself as the victor. It was treated as such by the Allies, and Communism was fêted in intellectual circles in the west long after the truth of its dark underside was known. Since the death of Stalin, furthermore, the Soviet system did evolve significantly of its own volition, becoming far less bloody even if it continued to use repressive methods to maintain control.

Whatever the pressures from abroad, it was ultimately Russians themselves who 'de-Stalinized' their system; and they too who created the conditions for its collapse and forged the new post-Communist system. The country was not overtaken by a foreign power which imposed a new constitution, leadership and ideology. There was no clear, imposed rupture as happened when the Allies changed the systems in Germany and Japan after the Second World War. The old Soviet apparatchiks are still influential today – both those who have remained in their jobs and those who have become new Russians in business. Unlike in other Soviet-bloc countries, there has been no *nomenklatura* 'purge'. Many of the country's current governors are former Communist Party regional first secretaries. Few have been removed, or asked to face up to their past. Khrushchev dabbled with a 'thaw' in the 1950s after the death of Stalin, but he did so for his own political advantage by targeting his opponents rather than as the start of a systematic process of de-Stalinization. He had been complicit, as a senior official during the persecutions that sent so many to their deaths. Gorbachev, who could never bring himself to criticize Lenin, was a pure product of the Soviet system, and a protégé of Yuri Andropov, who actively persecuted dissidents in the 1970s while head of the KGB. It was Gorbachev, for example, who personally signed the order authorizing the internment of Andrei Mironov, a dissident who in 1985 became one of the last to be imprisoned. Yeltsin dismantled the Communist Party, but never disbanded the KGB or opened its archives.

It is not only leading politicians and members of the security services who have smoothly made the transition from Communism to capitalism. There are many more still in place at every level, who shaped the minds and determined the fate of current and future generations: school teachers, government officials, doctors. If many of the brighter and younger ones have left, an older and less reformed generation has remained behind and is perpetuating itself. Tucked behind a high wall and video cameras in central Moscow stands the Serbsky Institute. It was notorious among dissidents in the 1970s for its role in diagnosing 'creeping schizophrenia' – a mental illness not recognized internationally, but which allowed for long-term internment of critics of the regime, and 'treatment' with drugs that induced sometimes permanent physical disabilities. While science had long been annexed by the Soviet authorities for political purposes, it was under Andropov at the end of the 1960s that the use of psychiatry escalated most sharply.

Dr Fyodor Kondratiev, one of those responsible for the controversial diagnoses during the period, and now in his seventies, is still practising as head of the department of endogenous psychoses. He has since been involved in other high-profile cases, part of the team that concluded that Colonel Yuri Budanov, on trial for murdering a young Chechen girl in 2000, was 'temporarily insane' and therefore subject to diminished responsibility. He also ruled sane Salman Raduyev, a Chechen rebel, allowing him to stand trial ahead of a curious 'illness' which left him dead in his prison cell aged thirty-five. When I met Kondratiev, he played down the total number of dissidents that had been diagnosed. He stressed that many had in any case been genuinely mentally disturbed; and suggested that they were better off in hospitals than in prison camps. In an article he wrote in the mid-1990s he went further, accusing critics of Serbsky of indulging in 'anti-Soviet propaganda'. No surprise, then, that a younger generation of psychiatrists at Serbsky held similar views. Yevgeny, a young psychiatrist brought up under his tutelage, drew a curious parallel with the treatment given to Soviet-era dissidents whom Khrushchev had argued must be insane by definition to even question Communism. 'Any state has laws against, for example, attacking the president,' he said. 'The man who attacked the British Queen is still in a psychiatric hospital, for instance.'

Education is also caught in the middle, trapped between a Soviet and a post-Soviet world. Since the start of the 1990s, a series of new history textbooks has been issued, written from a variety of ideological approaches. Some cover former taboos from the Soviet era, including the repressions and the secret Molotov–Ribbentrop pact; while others remain fixed in a near-Communist ideology. Few spend much time on the repressions. David Mendeloff, an academic who has studied a dozen officially sanctioned school textbooks produced over the past decade, argues that even if franker books represent a great improvement on Soviet-era texts, their interpretations remain restricted: in their rosy portrayal of relations with ethnic minority groups such as the Tatars; or in their argument that the Molotov–Ribbentrop pact was defensive rather than part of Stalin's plans for territorial expansion.

The limited funding available means that few schools can afford to use a range of different texts, or chose the more critical ones. And however good the history books, many of the teachers remain from the Soviet era, and often feel uncomfortable with open class discussion of more sensitive subjects. In November 2003, the ministry of education decided to remove from the curriculum the historian Igor Dolutsky's twentieth-century textbook, which had cited as a topic for student discussion commentators' critical comments on Putin's regime as an 'authoritarian dictatorship' and 'a police state'. On the same day, Putin himself gave a speech warning that 'textbooks should not become a ground for new political and ideological fighting . . . they must cultivate a sense of pride among youth in their history and country'. That is not to say critical analysis does not – or did not – take place. At the Institute of History in Moscow, I met professors who had taught courses in the 1980s such as 'The Problems of Bourgeois History of the USSR' – a pretext to read precious, closely guarded and officially banned western texts on Russia. But access was restricted to a few. The absence of any profound or sustained public debate today has severely stunted reflection on the Communist past, and left a new generation largely ignorant and indifferent.

'Victors write their own history,' said Catherine Merridale, an academic who has interviewed dozens of victims of repression for her book *Night of Stone*, and laments how little time is spent in classroom discussion on the repressions. She says that the families of victims often seem to assume their own guilt or suppress all memories of the period. 'Some people believe discussion rips society apart. There are many old people who feel depressed and cheated; lots more are stoical. But there are horrible psychological results. The consequences are less for individuals than for the state of society as a whole. If you don't discuss the illegal use of state power, you repeat it, such as in Chechnya.'

Sergei Kovalev, a dissident scientist turned human rights activist, agrees. He remembers in the 1970s reading an illegal *samizdat* (self-published) copy of *Into the Whirlwind*, the memoirs of Yevgeniya Ginzberg, who was an inmate of Kolyma, a victim of Stalin's 1930s purges. Its mere possession formed one of the charges brought against him by the Soviet authorities, which dispatched him in her steps to Kolyma. It was a reminder of how the legacy lived on long after Stalin's death. Kovalev was sent there into internal exile as recently as 1981, and spent three years as a political inmate in a prison 250 miles from Magadan city. He was only released in 1984, shortly before Ginzberg's book could at last be published and turned into a play once Mikhail Gorbachev was president. 'We have never shed our Soviet bones,' he says. 'The authorities only talk about human rights with the media or foreign colleagues. Citizens are seen as instruments of the state.'

Surviving the present

At Moscow's Smolenskaya-Sennaya Square, in the shadow of the Stalinist 'wedding cake' tower that houses the Ministry of Foreign Affairs, today's two Russias come jarringly together. Dozens of expensive foreign cars – the latest models of Japanese and German jeeps, gleaming black Mercedes, and an occasional Ferrari or Bentley – hover as they wait for the traffic lights to change. Street children beg at their windows, or begin – unsolicited – to wash their headlamps. Middle-aged Russians walk alongside peddling goods in a society where everything can be bought for money, such as the illegally obtained subscriber lists of mobile telecom companies or car vehicle registrations. In the pedestrian subway nearby, well-dressed middle-class Russians walk to and fro while pensioners beg for near-valueless kopeck coins. Vendors of all ages display cheap pirated videotapes, or books at whatever price they choose, including a mark-up to cover periodic shakedowns from their criminal 'protectors' and police alike. Nearby, a luxury guarded apartment block houses some of the city's richest businessmen and celebrities, their needs serviced by the ritzy department store Stockmann, with prices well above those charged in its parent store in Helsinki. Not far away, there are still old *kommunalka* (communal) apartments housing three or more families, each in a single cramped room, sharing an ageing bathroom and kitchen and struggling to afford the goods in the shops.

In a single decade, Moscow, once the self-proclaimed capital of the idealistic socialist world, has become a place of very real extremes in inequality and injustice, law and disorder. The city is a paradoxical place, where the poor are often richer than they seem, and the rich poorer. It is also exceptional, a symbol of the excesses of the new Russia taken to the utmost limits. In a few years, a drab city has been transformed into a western-style metropolis, with new office and apartment complexes, advertising banners and boutiques. You can buy anything in Moscow – at a price. Just over the river lies Kutuzovsky Prospekt, the main west-bound thoroughfare that leads to some of the capital's most exclusive suburban homes, a prize location for billboards, and where it is now almost impossible to buy an ordinary loaf of bread but there are rows of luxury shops. Near my office stands a gleaming Porsche show-room. When I went to visit just after it opened in 2001, I was surprised to see only tiny model cars on display. 'We didn't expect such interest. They've already all sold out,' Oleg Pashin, the manager, explained.

In the late 1980s, the city's wide roads, including the inner 'garden' ring-road – its grass long since dug up to allow for as many as six lanes of traffic in either direction – were almost empty except for official cars. Now, in a sign of growing wealth, they are heavily congested with traffic. And today's typical vehicles are not the rusting Soviet cars – the Moskviches, Zhigulis and Volgas of old – that once required years on a waiting list for an ordinary Russian to obtain. Nor are they even the former luxurious Zils for the Soviet elite, now being sold off cheap. Instead, the traffic jams are dominated by foreign cars. Many are second-hand, bought and imported or stolen and smuggled for resale in Russia. But others are brand new, with the luxury car of choice the latest model of customized Mercedes or the military combat-style Hummer jeep. S600s and the box-like G Wagon jeep, at $100,000 a piece, are more in evidence in Moscow than in any western city. As much of the rest of the world was struggling with a sharp economic downturn at the start of the millennium, Moscow became the salvation of many manufacturers of cars and other luxury goods, the market they sought to crack.

The Soviet elite always had special access and privileges. But both the volume of cash and the disparities in its ownership have exploded since the collapse of Communism, as income from all manner of legal, borderline and illegal activities has emerged from the shadows. Those with connections now not only have money, but also spend it without shame. And those that have money usually have influence – or the ability to bribe their way out of trouble. Government ministers in Italian designer suits drive around in the latest chauffeur-driven cars, travelling to and from their expensively furnished country houses each day, edging other cars aside with their blue flashing lights and disregard for normal traffic laws. Yet they declare official incomes of just a few hundred dollars a month, and the tax inspector never comes to visit. One contractor told me how he had built an Olympic-size swimming pool for a recently fired government minister, a lifelong civil servant, that alone had cost more than $1m. Given the Soviet past, the money had certainly not come from a rich relative's legacy. 'Parliamentarians have an allowance for a Volga, but 300 of them drive Mercedes with chaser vehicles,' said Pavel Borodin, the former head of the Kremlin's property department, responsible for overseeing state assets.

In some ways, Russia's rich are poorer than they seem. Many sacrificed whatever vestiges of high personal values they had in the often violent tussle to take control of assets, at a time of little law and a widening moral vacuum. Most have shown only marginal compassion in sharing their wealth with others. Financially, a second tier of Russians is also not as rich as their wild spending habits suggest. After years of living with miserable Soviet goods, many are keen to finally spend with little regard for the long term. Suspicious of banks and inspired by a culture of extravagant gestures and years of pent-up frustrations, they spend without thinking. Psychologically, they are also in poor shape, with the need for personal security to help them maintain their business interests. Wherever there is a sleek Mercedes saloon in Moscow, there is usually a dark-tinted jeep behind carrying bodyguards. A handful of sometimes spectacular contract killings can give an exaggerated impression of crime in Russia; nevertheless, for those in some way linked to the criminal world, the settlement of accounts can be ruthless. Bold, eye-catching contract killings do take place, often involving sophisticated surveillance and powerful weapons, including, in St Petersburg, shoulder-launched missiles to destroy reinforced jeeps. These days, the guards are sometimes for show, or because their employers became 'hostages' to their own security services, which knew everything about them. In one Moscow restaurant at lunchtime, I spotted a ten-year-old boy, presumably the child of a tycoon, eating with a bodyguard complete with dark suit and earpiece.

Conversely, many of the poor are richer than they seem. While official incomes are undoubtedly extremely low, the figures can be deceptive. The methods used by Goskomstat, the state statistics agency, both in assessing income and in defining poverty are open to debate. In reality, many Russians have both hidden sources of earnings and very low real costs. In their official employment, many earn a significant part of their salary in an undeclared 'envelope' of cash, on which they pay no tax. Often, they have a second or third job on the side. In urban areas, they may have access to a *dacha*, a country house which – however humble – gives them a small plot of land for cultivation, and the possibility of renting out one of their two properties. Most also received the apartments in which they live for free, when they had the chance to 'privatize' their homes at the start of the 1990s. That has left them with a valuable asset that is rising in value, with no mortgage or rental payments. Add to that subsidized heating, water, gas, electricity and telephone bills, and their outgoings are modest, leaving a high proportion of their income for food, clothing and leisure. At the federal level alone, there are more than 150 categories of people eligible to receive further privileges such as free travel on public transport, from war veterans to labour heroes, invalids to civil servants. In total, such concessions benefit two-thirds of the population, regardless of their level of need.

Duma deputies only officially receive $600 a month. But, as one party leader confided to me, corporate contributions allow him to pay his politicians a further $1,000 in cash – untaxed – and additional allowances covering a car and chauffeur, and mobile telephone bills. Thanks to the property department of the presidential administration, they also have subsidized holiday vouchers, and apartments in Moscow – which are not always returned even if they fail to be re-elected. The result, he estimated, was a monthly income of nearer to $5,000 – even before any outside work or bribes they might receive. Such undeclared top-up systems are widespread. I once saw the editor of a small-circulation but Kremlin-backed Russian newspaper driving a brand-new Toyota jeep, valued at many times his official annual salary. Another magazine editor had a luxury *dacha* in one of the most exclusive suburbs of Moscow, way beyond his apparent means.

Russia has a huge shadow economy, estimated by different experts at between a quarter and half of GDP. Most of it is hidden in the statistics but clearly visible on the ground. There are signs of growth and conspicuous consumption, of new boutiques, luxury cars and expensive restaurants, far outside Moscow. In the North Caucasus, in Ingushetia, North Ossetia and Chechnya, which are among Russia's poorest republics, there are surprising signs of wealth. Driving through villages with shops that are little more than lean-tos selling a basic array of goods, I would come across large newly built brick mansions with high walls and guards. In Vladivostok in the far east, whole tree-lined districts in the suburbs with luxurious houses had been built for members of the local elite. The money was there, albeit spread very unevenly.

Those on lower incomes have often proved resourceful in making ends meet, demonstrating a remarkable versatility and entrepreneurship. Even the elderly women who staff Moscow's theatres, galleries and concert halls do their best to supplement their meagre official earnings with such 'survival mechanisms'. The cult of the cloakroom in Russia means that no one in any sort of coat or hat dares enter a public building and keep it with them; rather they hand it in for safekeeping. Given the bulky wrappings required during the long winters, there is a logic to the system, although it creates long queues before and after performances. Except in snobbish restaurants, no one would think of tipping. But the attendants in theatre 'garderobes' do their best to add on fee-paying services: renting opera glasses, charging to look after bags, selling newspapers or books. In the Bolshoi theatre's new annexe, the staff have reintroduced an old 'service': pay for opera glasses and you can jump straight to the front of the queue. The main Bolshoi itself was riddled with scams until reformed under its new director. It had a system of distributing free tickets to trade unions, government ministries and its own employees. Many would end up being sold on at large mark-ups by well-dressed touts standing openly on the steps of the theatre, in clear collusion with the management inside. The official ticket office, hidden away in a side street, often claimed that all seats were sold out.

The same money-making offers apply to many government institutes and universities attempting to make ends meet. To find my way to interviews with distinguished professors or the heads of obscure think tanks, I often had to pick my way past endless offices in dusty corridors informally sub-let to travel agents, import-export companies and all kinds of other commercial organizations that were taking up most of the space. I interviewed Yuri Levada, one of Russia's most respected pollsters, who then ran the All Russia Public Opinion Research Centre (VTsIOM), in his office in an annexe of the Russia Radio Institute, an academic engineering research centre now full of commercial radio stations. His own organization was nominally part of the ministry of labour, but it had received almost no official funding in a decade. Its computers, office equipment, rent and salaries were instead paid largely thanks to his ability to attract outside funding from companies and – often foreign – research agencies.

I stayed with Igor and Tamara for a month in St Petersburg. Both had done well under Communism, he as a university teacher, she as a museum curator. They had little time for any of the post-Soviet political parties, and viewed Putin sceptically. They had survived, but their quality of life had substantially dropped, and the future was unclear.

Their income was modest, but their outgoings low, with an apartment, a car and occasional use of a friend's *dacha*, and support from a wide circle of acquaintances. 'At least fear no longer exists,' I suggested over vodka in their kitchen. 'One type of fear has been replaced by another: lack of money,' replied Tamara. She was worried above all about retirement, when her modest pension would barely cover medicines or the maintenance costs on her flat.

The end of Communism brought a collapse in any formal system of rules, regulations or even nominal attachment to equity. In its place came brute force, money and opportunism. Near my office, people living in the adjacent apartment blocks simply grabbed parcels of land to build metal garages for their cars. A restaurant on the first floor of one building took over the entire public courtyard in front for its own use, turning a car park into a raised area, filling it with earth and then planting trees. A developer near the US embassy seized an entire street, closing it for months during construction of an office building, and leaving it sealed afterwards. Guards linger on public pavements outside shops and offices, reserving 'their' places outside. Tenants stake their claims by putting up lockable metal barriers at night. There is no uniform system of tariffs for parking. Surprisingly, I could often easily park unhindered and for free just around the corner from Old Square, the former Communist Party Central Committee headquarters which still contains top Kremlin offices. However, half a mile further north, near the TsUM shopping centre, a green uniformed attendant who had bought the rights off the Moscow city authorities would usually appear from nowhere and demand Rbs 20 an hour. Another half a mile north, away from the centre but in front of two upmarket restaurants, the price demanded was twice as high again – regardless of whether you had been eating inside.

Despite hidden income from such money-making initiatives, post-Soviet Russia has created a new category of the very poor. The average wage is less than $200 a month, and the difference in income between the bottom and top 10 per cent of the population has more than trebled since the late 1980s from 1 to 4 to 1 to 14. The proportion of the country living below the official but disputed 'poverty level' is one fifth of the population. Most worryingly, many of the poorest are not the unemployed, but those on low wages, forced to work very long hours and take on several jobs to make ends meet. A detailed analysis carried out by the Interactive Research Group, a consumer agency, in

2003, classified 3 per cent of Russians as rich, 30 per cent as middle-class, and 67 per cent of the population as disadvantaged or 'little moneyed'. While it remains difficult to compare the manipulated statistics of Soviet times – and to account for the poor quality of life – the standard of living today for many remains arguably lower than it was before 1991. The overall size of the economy is also smaller than it was fifteen years ago. Since then, $150bn has left the country, and perhaps just $30bn been reinvested.

In rural areas, people can eke out a subsistence living on their own smallholdings. In cities, there are often petty jobs they can take to supplement their incomes. But those in smaller towns without such opportunities, and especially single-parent families or pensioners living without assistance, suffer far more. Visible signs of economic prosperity are not in any case proof of material well-being. Much misery remains hidden inside shelters and apartments, with the harsh environment keeping people off the streets in winter – or making them pay the price. Each spring, workers find 'snow drops', the homeless or alcoholics who have collapsed, died and been frozen under the snow, their bodies only recovered months later with the thaw. In a homeless shelter in St Petersburg, I met Stanislav. He found himself without a roof after he and his mother were conned out of their privatized apartment in the mid-1990s by a developer who promised money. Once they left, the payment never came. As the authorities attempted to 'clean the streets' of the city ahead of the 300th anniversary celebrations in 2003, to be attended by more than fifty foreign dignitaries, police asked for his papers. Without the official – but constitutionally illegal – documents showing that he was registered in St Petersburg, they bundled him into a waiting bus and took him, along with dozens of others, to old disused barracks nearly sixty miles from the city centre. He was told to stay there until the festivities were over.

Yeltsin's achievements during the 1990s should not be under-estimated. He swept away the residual foundations of the planned totalitarian state, neutered the Communist Party, and launched the market economy when he abolished prices and launched mass privatizations. He at times berated media owners, and toyed with banning the Communists and postponing the 1996 elections, but his more democratic instincts prevailed. He opened Russia to foreign investment and western institutions, from the International Monetary Fund (IMF) to the G8. He joined the Council of Europe, and re-committed to the

Organization for Security and Cooperation in Europe. He oversaw the unwinding of the Soviet empire, which shrank overnight by a quarter of its land mass and half its population. Russia survived the transition with very little bloodshed. Just three people died during the failed coup in 1991, and its 'decolonization' of the former Soviet states was relatively peaceful by international comparisons. But in the process, Yeltsin made a series of grand bargains: undermining the institutions of state, leaving civil servants and pensioners impecunious; privatizing state assets on the cheap in a way that created a small but very powerful business class; and failing to implement sufficient economic reform to touch a broader segment of the population, the consequences of which are still being felt. Natalya Rimashevskaya, one of the country's leading poverty researchers, called the 'shock therapy' or overnight price liberalization adopted in January 1992 by Yegor Gaidar, the economist Yeltsin appointed as his deputy prime minister, 'an operation without anaesthesia for millions of Russian citizens'.

The pain of Yeltsin's revolution was primarily felt not in blood and bullets but in the 'shock without therapy' that resulted. His choices may have been necessary, even inevitable, and simply accelerated the inevitable collapse of a hugely inefficient system. But they triggered agonies for the population that went well beyond the purely economic. These are most strikingly demonstrated in health statistics. Russia has the highest per capita rate of suicides in the world after tiny Lithuania, and far greater in absolute terms, at 60,000 in 2002. Mental illness and stress have risen sharply. Life expectancy dropped throughout the 1990s, notably as alcohol abuse led to a growing number of accidents and fatal diseases. The average age at death in Russia today is fifty-nine years for men and seventy-two for women – the highest gap in the world. The birth rate remains very low, partly reflecting pessimism about the future. Tuberculosis has re-emerged as a serious infectious illness, and the rate of HIV infection is rising fast. 10 per cent of conscripts to the army are malnourished, and 40 per cent of pregnant women are anaemic. Such figures bear heavily on the present, but will bear more on the future.

The uncertain future

Moscow may be becoming a credit card-friendly city, but I never dared leave home without at least a Rbs 50 note in my pocket. The reason lies in three letters that have replaced KGB as an institution striking exasperation if not fear into Russian hearts: GAI, the long-standing acronym for the state traffic inspectorate, which was recently renamed DPS in a failed attempt to improve its image. In Europe or the USA, police are on the whole fair, and their presence perceived as neutral-to-positive. In Russia, the police are almost universally perceived as a menace. Although the *GAIshniki* are armed with guns, their most important weapon is a little black and white stick which, with a flick of the wrist, they use to stop cars at random. In a hangover from the Soviet period, every town and city has GAI checkpoints on its exit roads, carefully scrutinizing the passing vehicles. And on just about any other street, often hidden behind a lamppost or just round a corner, GAI are constantly appearing at the most inconvenient moment, waving down cars with little justification.

The GAI are a metaphor for post-Soviet existence: necessary but corrupt and arbitrary. They are necessary, because Russian driving is reckless and needs some control. Many Russians never had a car until the 1990s, and have since bribed their way to receiving driving licenses. As I drove around Moscow each day, I saw speeding, tail-gating, cutting up, drunken driving, illegal turns, jumping of red lights. At night, I would have to be constantly wary of people over-taking on the inside lanes, and driving without headlights – let alone steering through mud-caked windscreens with minimal visibility. Whenever I walked, I weaved between cars parked across my path, and occasionally leapt out of the way as one drove past on the pavement to bypass the traffic jams. The GAI are corrupt, because the endless forms and time-wasting procedures they are supposed to follow only serve to push drivers to slip a Rbs 50 note to their tormentor to bypass the rules. They are arbitrary, because it is a courageous GAI who stops a sleek Mercedes with accompanying bodyguard-filled chaser vehicle, knowing that he risks threats or worse in response. And because of this they often spend less time dealing with the important matters that could improve road safety than in maintaining a system of privileges. They have proved powerless, for example, to stop the Moscow authorities erecting huge distracting televisions carrying advertise-ments at intersections, the likely cause of numerous accidents. But they spend plenty of time stopping the traffic to allow preferential access to the roads for some 4,000 people in Moscow who have been authorized or have bribed their way into receiving blue flashing lights and special number plates. These anointed ones can drive with impunity, even using specially reserved central traffic lanes on some of the city's main thoroughfares.

The GAI are also an example of the arbitrary state because, as in other aspects of Russian life, it is always possible to find a violation as the basis for persecution. That has long been the principle at the very heart of Russian life. Everyone is guilty, or can be treated as so. As Dzerzhinsky said: 'Find me the man, I'll find the crime.' Everyone is potentially 'on the hook', compromised whenever necessary. The speed limits are too low, left turns are almost impossible, filter arrows are conceived to trap all but the most experienced, dotted lines to demarcate where you can drive across the road are faded by age or hidden by snow. I was once stopped and fined over the contents of my *doverenost*, the authorization that bureaucratic Russia requires when you drive a car registered in someone else's name. My 'crime' was that the date was written out in words, not in numbers. Officials can threaten to confiscate the car, or driver's documents, for trivial offences. And ultimately, as a GAI once said to me with a wink when he claimed that the traffic light I had passed through was already flashing green on its way to orange, 'It's your word against mine.'

That arbitrary exercise of authority remains one of the hallmarks of modern Russia. In Moscow and many other cities, the authorities have proved able to ignore the constitution and even direct legal challenges in maintaining the Soviet *propiska* system requiring all local residents to be registered. That allows them to decide who can live and work in Moscow, and provides a further tool in the 'everyone is guilty' armoury: anyone can be stopped by the police, and ordered out of the city if they are not registered there. At worst, the police are frequently accused of violence and torture of those taken into detention. Those who suffer disproportionately are people with so-called 'Caucasian faces'. While Caucasian means 'white' in the west, in Russia it refers to the dark-skinned residents of the North Caucasus and Central Asia, who are widely despised.

Sergei Mishketkul, whose case is now before the European Court of Human Rights, was one such victim. Having experienced a previous conviction, he turned and fled when he saw two policemen coming towards him one night in Moscow in April 2001. They were hunting the burglars of a nearby apartment, described as 'Caucasians' by the victims. They gave chase, caught him, and beat him so badly that officials in a pre-trial detention centre refused to accept him for the night for fear they would be accused of brutality. The police took him to the apartment, and planted a passport and watch in his pockets as proof of his 'guilt', although the owners later said neither item had been stolen. When his friend – with a solid alibi – came to the police station the following morning to help, he too was arrested and charged as his accomplice. The courts sentenced them both to four years imprisonment. 'In Soviet times, the law was much more respected than now,' said Yuri Vasichkin, a former state prosecutor who is their lawyer. 'The professionals have quit for better-paid jobs, the standards and morals have gone down and the level of corruption increased.'

Sergei Pashin is well placed to understand how far the Russian law enforcement system works against the accused – and its accusers. He was a Moscow city judge, who began to receive calls from the public prosecutor, the police organized crime squad and the FSB when he took on a case involving a gang suspected of kidnapping a businessman. 'They said I should pay serious attention to the case, and that it should be decided "in the proper manner,"' he told me. The evidence was weak, but there were clear signs of torture. The suspects had been handcuffed for long periods, electrocuted and had their heads dunked in water to extract confessions. After he refused to convict and began to criticize the judicial system in public, he received no more 'important' cases, and was subject to two attempts at dismissal before eventually resigning.

Corruption and pressure have always been part of Russian life. According to the sociologist Igor Kliamkine, until the mid-eighteenth century civil servants were not paid at all but had the right to 'receive presents'. Afterwards, budget constraints meant they were poorly paid, offering little prospect of breaking the previous system. In tsarist and Soviet times alike, turning a blind eye to corruption ensured that bureaucrats remained loyal, because they were always under the threat that they could be prosecuted. Many aspects of the Soviet system were already hugely distorted, with the diversion of goods onto the black market, and a widely developed system of bribes and mutual favours in operation. But such techniques were given full rein over the following years, once the former counterbalancing powers of variously the Communist Party, the KGB and the state planners were removed.

In the words of Jacques Sapir, a French analyst: 'The advocates of privatization thought they were attacking the base of the former society. In reality, without really wanting to, they eroded the very basis of the *idea* of society. "Everything is possible" became "everything is permissible".' Everyone who had a chance to make additional money took advantage. Some 2,000 activities required licences from the state, providing a huge potential for bureaucrats to extract bribes on businesses. In Rostov, I met one children's book publisher who complained that he even had to get approval from the ministry of health on 'sanitation' grounds for each new title he produced.

The same logic applied to government officials, who sometimes charged cash simply for meetings, let alone for reaching decisions that accelerated, circumvented or contradicted official procedures. One modern Russian joke tells of a group of striking miners who managed to force their way into the reception room of the prime minister's office. 'They don't have any money and they want to see you,' explains his assistant. 'Let them in anyway,' the prime minister replies. Commercial 'expediters' with extremely close links to officials opened doors that were often otherwise firmly closed. Judges had long been accustomed to a system of 'telephone justice', with political authorities making decisions that they rubber-stamped. Now they sometimes switched their allegiance to whoever bid the most, adding commercial to political pressures. Bailiffs charged with implementing court decisions would enthusiastically enforce them, or entirely reverse and ignore them, in exchange for an appropriate fee.

The police force was 'privatized', with uniformed officers with standard-issue machine guns and cars with flashing blue lights unashamedly hiring out their services to guard buildings or accompany important businessmen on the roads. Their neglect of their principal activity of keeping the peace meant an explosion in private security companies – again often with connections to the police. Even the FSB, the security service, went up for sale, giving access for a fee to their phone taps and surveillance information, or specifically gathering new material by command on commercial rivals. 'Every year I read my own FSB file to see what's in it,' one Russian businessman confided to me. Telephone transcripts of the results would regularly fall into the hands of the media, sometimes doctored and often inaccurate, but usually designed to embarrass companies or officials, and deliberately placed by their rivals.

The positive aspect of all this activity was to indicate how much latent Russian entrepreneurship existed, despite eighty years of theoretical anti-capitalism. More pragmatically, it allowed many government officials to survive at a time of pitiful salaries. One example was the visa-issuing system in Russian consulates around the world, a cynical mix of Soviet-style bureaucracy and unfriendly staff combined with very western-style fees. The revenues – on a sliding scale, with premium rates for same-day delivery – were all kept by the embassies, to top up diplomats' salaries. The negative side was to still further increase injustices and inequalities, making access to public services fee-paying and the outcomes unrelated to merits; to introduce huge inefficiencies; and – as time went on – to create significant additional financial barriers and vested interests opposed to reform of the old ways of operating.

Sheremetyevo airport was a typical case of a public asset managed for private gain. Moscow's main international gateway, it was more of a national disgrace. There was no train or direct bus connection to the city. A taxi mafia with tough rules to minimize competition did their best to fleece those arriving. Luggage carts were rarely available and, when so, only at a price. The facilities were tatty and poorly equipped, although the airport was charging substantial tariffs to the airlines that used its services. The passport-control desks were systematically understaffed, creating a free-for-all as tired arriving passengers fought in a mêlée – sometimes for hours – for the pleasure of being barked at by officials who took an inordinately long time to scrutinize their travel documents. The slow pace of reform partly reflected a fierce struggle for control, given the substantial financial stakes. But there was also little pressure for change, since those who might have had lobbying power went unaffected. Visiting politicians and Russian government officials would be whisked through the VIP lounge without suffering any of the normal inconveniences. Others willing to pay $100 a throw could also bypass the entire process, skipping the queues and leaving the proles behind them.

Georgy Satarov from the INDEM think tank carried out detailed surveys across Russia's regions, and estimated that corruption had become an industry worth $30bn a year. The most significant 'additional payments' were in those areas of life with which ordinary citizens came into daily contact, notably health and education. The daughter of an acquaintance, a brilliant student, should have got into medical college on her own merits, but was told that the price of entry to an institution that was nominally free would be $5,000. What message did that send out about the future quality of the nation's doctors? Special individual 'tuition' was a standard way to 'earn' access to higher education. In the health sector, a typical visit to a doctor would involve a 'present' of some sort. Basic care might be provided for free, but a fee would be solicited for everything beyond the most rudimentary service, for food, cleaning and better-quality medicines. Doctors with ten years of training found themselves treating teenagers clutching mobile phones and wearing expensive leather jackets that they could not afford on their own modest salaries. The approach was understandable but invidious. One result was that ordinary Russians could end up paying more in side payments than they would have done had they simply gone to a private clinic. Another was the maintenance of a hugely inefficient network which was poorly adapted to improving the health of the nation. In place of modern multi-drug treatment, an older generation of doctors which dominates thinking still practises the removal of lungs to treat TB, supporting in the process a network of operating rooms and sanatoriums. The health system is technocratic, geared to specialists, hospitals and showpiece equipment that politicians could point to with pride (and which provided ample opportunity for kickbacks). It is ill adapted to the less glamorous but more effective use of primary health care and the work of general practitioners.

If the gap between rich and poor has grown sharply, so have the divisions between the classes and the generations. In the last ten years, the group which by values, education and jobs would be considered middle class in other countries has been filleted. Tens of thousands of doctors, engineers, scientists, social workers and others on the pittance the state pays have often abandoned their professions, turning instead to market trading, taxi driving or other activities where they can make far more money. A generation of specialists has been demoralised and destroyed, creating a huge gap in professions which hold scant attraction to younger people. That creates a major challenge for the future.

When I arrived with my family in Moscow in 1998, the choice of potential nannies for our young son was embarrassingly rich. Among those willing to abandon their careers for the prospect of earning just a few dollars an hour – considerably more than in their existing jobs – were a paediatrician, the head of the gastroenterology department of a Moscow hospital and an accountant. In Akademgorodok, a huge university campus near Novosibirsk in Siberia with thousands of students, and once the pride of Russia's education system, I met professors even in the economics faculty – potentially one of the more marketable departments – who could only continue to teach because they were supported by spouses working in the private sector. Faith Fisher, the daughter of an American preacher, came to the town in the early 1990s, and launched an aid programme of food parcels to help many malnourished families of scientists.

A younger generation with a far more modest education and less experience but engaged in more or less reputable business activities pushed aside their elders financially, psychologically and even physically. More than in most cities in the west, people in their early twenties are highly visible, spending extravagantly in restaurants, driving in expensive cars, and dressing in pricey foreign clothes. The older generation has been abandoned or bypassed by many employers, creating an inversion of Russia's former social structure. Age discrimination is widespread, with many companies preferring to hire only recent, more malleable, graduates. And the rapacious post-Soviet decade has permitted many businesses to be taken over on the cheap, sometimes imposing new, young, aggressive owners from the outside. The result in many companies is that people in their twenties or thirties are managing staff twice their own age. Some of the older staff may justifiably be considered too imbued with Soviet culture to adapt effectively to new times. Others have selfishly held on to what power and privileges they have, failing to think about a transition to the next generation. But, even aside from the normal personal tensions of such a management approach, it is far from clear that the younger group – brought up during the amoral period of the late 1980s and early 1990s – represents an improvement in human values.

I remember standing in an Aeroflot check-in at Paris, waiting for a flight back to Moscow. Around me were several dozen ordinary Russians, some of whom had obviously spent months or even years saving up to buy an economy-class ticket for the holiday of their life. Next to us, a group of young Russians in their early twenties, with thick necks and shaved heads, dressed in expensive suits, bearing all the marks of rapidly and dubiously acquired wealth, whisked through the first-class desk. The inequalities and injustices fit to trigger a new revolution were being put in place.

THE MAN FROM NOWHERE

THE MAN ON THE TELEVISION SCREEN cut an awkward figure. For most Russians, a short broadcast in August 1999 was the first time they had seen Vladimir Putin, and there was little to impress in the bland, diminutive official now on show. A bureaucrat who had lived most of his life in the shadows, he had suddenly been thrust into the public eye by Boris Yeltsin's latest bombshell. The ailing Russian president, himself out of public view for weeks on end while supposedly 'working with documents', had stirred from his slumbers to kick off a renewed round of political upheaval. On Monday 9 August, fresh from week-end consultations, he announced to the nation his new prime minister, and the man he described as his choice to be the country's future president. It was Yeltsin's last chance, a gamble that was the best he could manage after months of agonizing over his choice of a successor as he felt his political power slipping away. Few believed then that Putin would be installed in the Kremlin within a few months, and heading towards a period of Russian leadership which may stretch at least as long as Yeltsin's.

Russians had become accustomed to 'August angst'. Almost exactly a year before, on 17 August 1998, the government announced a simultaneous debt default and rouble devaluation, triggering economic turmoil and drawing unwelcome attention from around the world. In August 1968, Soviet tanks had rolled into Prague, crushing the fledgling democratic movement. A group of Soviet hardliners took advantage of Mikhail Gorbachev's August holidays on the Black Sea coast in 1991 to put him under house arrest and announce their brief, ill-fated coup. Its failure triggered the collapse of the Soviet Union, and the rise of Yeltsin to power. And in August 1993, Yeltsin attempted to impose a new constitution that sparked a confrontation with the Congress of People's Deputies. He resolved the conflict by force, imposing a new system dominated by the president, while the parliament was sidelined. Perhaps it was the short, hot summer holidays that provided the conditions for events extraordinary even by Russia's extreme standards, when many decision-makers as well as ordinary citizens were themselves resting. That thinned Moscow's already shaky lines of command and control, and created an opportunity when the public's usually high level of indifference or powerlessness was at its peak. This time, however, the initial Putin aftershock was more subdued.

In most countries, the nomination of a new prime minister would create a political storm. But in the Russia of the late 1990s, it had become commonplace. It seemed trivial compared with the economic turmoil and social upheaval facing the country. From 1992 till 1998, Yeltsin had frequently reshuffled his ministers, while retaining Viktor Chernomyrdin as the head of the government. Then he fired the prime minister in spring 1998, replacing him with the youthful Sergei Kirienko. The new incumbent did not last long. He was dismissed just months later in the wake of the August financial crisis. After the president's attempts to appoint other candidates were rejected by the parliament, the former foreign minister Yevgeny Primakov was named in the following weeks. Then in May 1999, Yeltsin sacked him in favour of Sergei Stepashin, in an accelerating round of musical chairs. So when Vladimir Putin was named less than three months later, it was with no great irony that Boris Nemtsov, a liberal politician himself once tipped as a future successor to Yeltsin, joked that there would be another five heads of government before the presidential elections scheduled for summer 2000.

Mikhail Gorbachev, the last Soviet leader and a long-standing enemy of Yeltsin, was among the public figures who criticized the latest reshuffle. Media commentators dwelt on Putin's background in the KGB, the country's Soviet-era secret police. Yeltsin's backing of his own anointed successor seemed more like a kiss of death than a useful endorsement at the time. His own popularity rating languished in the low single digits, and powerful rival political clans were gaining momentum in their efforts to overthrow him and his ruling clique. Yeltsin had barely escaped an impeachment vote inspired by the Communists in the parliament in May, his health was shaky, and his key supporters were on the defensive, ensnared in corruption allegations. His reputation had been sullied not least by the continuing poverty of many Russians, in stark contrast to the vast wealth of a handful of politically influential oligarchs he had helped create. He was also seen as directly responsible for the hugely unpopular first war in Chechnya, followed by an even more unpopular and poorly implemented peace agreement that had tipped the tiny breakaway republic towards anarchy. Insurgencies by Chechen bands across the border into the neighbouring Russian republic of Dagestan had taken place, and there was widespread talk in the country of introducing a state of emergency and postponing the parliamentary elections scheduled for December 1999.

Most Russians seemed largely indifferent to Putin's nomination, however. It was hard to believe that he would last long in his new job, let alone take over the presidency. 'Military men carry out the orders of the president without questioning them,' he told reporters after his nomination, the unquestioning salute of the former KGB lieutenant-colonel to his political masters all but visible. He went further in his first significant interview, on that same August evening's *Hero of the Day* programme on NTV. When asked whether he was ready to be president, he replied: 'It would be ridiculous to say that I am not ready when the president has already said [that I am].' It hardly spoke of the ambition or autonomy of a future leader of the country. But it did set the tone for what was to come. He defined his top priority with the words: 'The main problem we have is the absence of political stability.' He pledged continuity, with no government reshuffles, and the assurance that there would be no federal state of emergency. Parliamentary elections would go ahead as planned, in December.

Putin had been propelled remarkably quickly through a succession of top government jobs over the previous decade, but most had had little public profile. If his long-standing career in the KGB had been purposefully lived in the shadows, his subsequent moves also remained out of the limelight. In less than a decade, he had been promoted from an adviser to the St Petersburg mayor to a deputy governor; from a Kremlin official advising on administrative and regional affairs to head of the FSB, the KGB's successor body; and then secretary of the president's Security Council. It was the sort of meteoric rise that could only have happened in the socially fractured post-Soviet landscape, and with considerable help from powerful sponsors. But this last move to prime minister and dauphin was far more surprising than the rest. Putin was an official who served the state, not a politician accustomed to public life. He was someone more used to low-key management and the implementation of orders than to taking high-level political decisions himself. By his own admission, he was a good bureaucrat, not a politician.

Within weeks of his appointment, the greyness would disappear. Like George W. Bush after the 11 September terrorist attacks two years later, Putin would become a symbol around which widespread Russian support crystallized. He was helped above all by an intensive military campaign in Chechnya, which proved unexpectedly popular in the wake of a series of murderous apartment bombings. Aided by ample positive media coverage, Putin's image was rapidly transformed into that of a tough, decisive, dynamic leader. Within three months, he seemed to have acquired a golden touch. His own popularity ratings were sufficiently high that his mere mention of support for Unity, a party created from scratch after his nomination, was enough to push it to an extraordinarily strong result in the parliamentary elections in mid-December. Serious rivals for the presidency began to withdraw. On New Year's Eve, Yeltsin pressed home his advantage: he unexpectedly announced his premature resignation, making Putin the acting president. By now, the new prime minister had a clear incumbent's advantage. Yeltsin's gamble had paid off.

Putin's paradox was that he was the antithesis of the man who had chosen him, Boris Yeltsin. The outgoing president was impulsive, confrontational, irrational, instinctive and often inactive through ill-health or drunkenness. Putin, by contrast, was abstemious, healthy, energetic, evasive, secretive and cautious. He was modest, low-profile and non-conflictual, a technocrat who preferred to shirk responsibility and defer decisions, an anti-politician. Born in 1952, he was from a different generation than Yeltsin, but also markedly younger than Yuri Luzhkov, the mayor of Moscow, and Yevgeny Primakov, the former prime minister, his closest rivals just a few months before. Putin was in many ways a product of Yeltsin and his 'Family', the entourage of relatives and powerful figures around the outgoing president. But he also developed and evolved in the new job. And he brought with him certain values of his own, while promoting or recruiting colleagues and friends drawn from his past jobs and his home city of St Petersburg. Their varied and sometimes conflicting approaches would help define the direction of his period in office.

It is not easy to understand Putin. He spent fifteen years of his professional life in the KGB, known for its tight loyalty and intense secrecy. Even his own wife, Ludmilla, says that, in accordance with the usual rules of the agency, her husband rarely discussed his work. In politics he kept a low profile, dealing mostly with politicians, businessmen and officials, rather than the general public or journalists. Throughout the 1990s, he refrained from moving into business like so many of his peers, sticking instead to government. He worked first in the discreet corridors of the presidential administration in the former Communist Party Central Committee building; and then in the Kremlin itself, which he made still more closed than it had been under Yeltsin. His own version of his life – most notably as he describes it in *First Person*, an extended pre-election interview with three Russian journalists – seems often too good to be true, a romantic attempt to build up an image as a decisive, patriotic and macho man of the people. It is the sort of mixture of plausible fact and unverifiable myth that a professional KGB agent would weave, supplemented by advice from slick post-Soviet political spin-masters. At other times, however, given the spontaneous nature of the original conversation, it is surprisingly frank, hinting at his style and character if not always the substance of his past or his own real opinions.

Putin's Russian biographies – official and unofficial – veer to the sycophantic. Several key people around him who knew him best can no longer talk. His father, Vladimir, died just before his nomination as prime minister in August 1999, and his mother, Maria, at the end of 1998. Anatoly Sobchak, who championed democratic reforms and was Putin's political mentor, died from a heart attack in February 2000, and Artem Borovik, one journalist investigating his past, perished in a plane crash in March 2000. A political opponent of Putin's and Sobchak's from St Petersburg, Yuri Shutov, has been held for more than four years in detention without trial. Others have disappeared from view, like Marina Salye, a politician from Leningrad who accused him of corruption at the start of the 1990s. So have documents – if they ever existed – of many of the transactions to which he was party. Even School 193, where he studied for several formative years, has since been demolished.

During one of my repeated trips to St Petersburg to trace his past, I decided to see how he treated the memory of his own parents. As I walked through the sprawling Serafimovskoye cemetery past a series of monuments to the victims of the brutal siege of Leningrad in 1941–3, I wondered if the grave at least would offer some unusual clue to Putin's personality: extravagant and granted a prestigious corner position, perhaps, or callously neglected. Instead, what I found was characteristically modest but respectful, understated but dutiful. It stood in a plot of little more than average size, with no special location other than a view towards an overgrown creek. Two flowers had been placed recently at the base, with tasteful shrubs growing around. There was a large black stone cross, higher than those around it but not excessively so, without the pictures or ornaments that often adorn Russian graves. There was just a simple, tasteful engraving of their names and dates in gold, below the inscription 'God, thy will be done'.

Many who do know Putin and are still alive are reluctant to talk; others who are willing to share their thoughts seem almost universally to have vague and positive memories, citing the sort of personal 'he was so strong that he didn't know his own limits' qualities that would make all but the most naïve employer squirm in a job interview. This speaks either of Putin's objectively extraordinary qualities, or of his ability to cover his tracks, win loyalty, and co-opt or generate fear. Perhaps it should be no surprise that some of his most vocal critics are today in exile abroad – and often with an axe to grind. In the circumstances, painting a definitive portrait of his life is all but impossible. But by studying Putin's background and career, and triangulating the different views of him, it is possible to give some indications of his views and his style. They help explain how he would subsequently behave in office, and what impact he would have on Russia.

The four faces of Vladimir Putin: student, sportsman, civil servant, spy

With the Mercedes parked outside, the historic pink façade recently repainted, and a satellite dish attached to the wall of the inner courtyard, 12 Baskov Pereulok in St Petersburg looks like a comfortable enough place to live today. The front part of the building is now occupied by the offices of Telekombank. Next door has been taken over as if in tribute by Baltnefteprovod, a subsidiary of the state-controlled monopoly oil pipeline operator Transneft. The address where Putin passed his childhood reveals much about the man and his entourage. He grew up in Russia's former imperial capital, the second city by size and importance after Moscow. That made him the first Soviet or post-Soviet leader in nearly a century who did not come from a provincial town. The city was built by Peter the Great, who had a modernizing vision, but whose chosen location was hopelessly impractical. Construction of his European-style city in the cold north on swampland demanded ruthless methods which left many thousands dead. The city's residents had been hardened over three centuries by tsarist oppression, Soviet repression and German aggression alike. St Petersburg was a centre of culture, intellectuals and wealth, a 'window on Europe', physically close to and intellectually mimicking the west. But it was also a centre of rebellion, the heart of the Bolshevik Revolution, and later – partly in response – a focal point for the military and the security police determined to keep its population in line. The city also had its fair share of ordinary Russians such as Putin, drawn in no particular ideological direction, and concerned above all with surviving the austere post-war years and the stagnation that would follow.

On the same road where Putin grew up stood his school, where he first picked up a taste for the German language which would help shape his subsequent career and outlook. Opposite lived Anatoly Rakhlin, who would become his long-time judo trainer and friend. A few minutes' walk north stands the *Bolshoi Dom*, the 'Big House' at 4 Liteiny Prospekt which was home to the feared KGB internal security police. It was so named because its agents joked that from its top floor they could see not only the entire city but even Soloviki, the island monastery in Russia's far north that became part of the Gulag prison system. A little further to the east of his home is Smolny, then headquarters of the Leningrad regional Communist Party. The gloomy building has changed tenants, but still bears the Soviet address of Dictatorship of the Proletariat Square. Its long corridors would later be very familiar to Putin in his job as the city's deputy governor after the building was taken over by the local administration in 1991. By 2003, when St Petersburg under Putin's tutelage came to celebrate its 300th anniversary, Baskov Pereulok would be a short distance from the bustling activity of Nevsky Prospekt, the city's main thoroughfare, rapidly awaking to consumerism, with new restaurants and boutiques opening on every corner, and Internet cafés providing uncensored information from the outside world.

But in 1952 the future in Leningrad – the former name of the city in very different times – seemed far less clear or bright, the horizons much more limited. Vladimir Vladimirovich Putin grew up in cramped conditions. The sole surviving child after two older brothers died young, he lived with his mother and father in one of the typical communal apartments that then existed throughout the city, many of which remain today. There was one room for all three of them on the fifth floor. They shared a windowless hallway with a sink and gas stove also used by two other families. There was a vile toilet, no hot water or bathtub, and, according to Putin, large rats on the rickety stairs outside, where he often fought with other boys. The conditions made him, as he has said several times, close to the problems of ordinary Russians without the *blat* or contacts of the ruling Soviet class and its privileges.

In fact, his roots were not entirely disconnected from power. His grandfather Spiridon, also from St Petersburg, was a chef who moved to Moscow, cooking at the suburban residence where Lenin lived, at one of Stalin's *dacha*s, and then at a guest-home for the Moscow City Communist Party. His father, Vladimir, worked during the Second World War for the NKVD secret police, and, in an incredible story related by Putin, was supposedly involved in sabotage behind German lines, even surviving an ambush by hiding in a swamp and breathing through a straw. After the war, he worked in a factory, where he was secretary of the Communist Party organization. Such connections, if not instrumental in forging the young Putin's career, at least helped shape his views. And his tough living conditions no doubt motivated him to do the best he could to get ahead.

Sergei Rodulgin had already met Vladimir Putin several times, but did not yet know his big secret. There was no obvious common link between the two men, but they were becoming good friends. Rodulgin, brought up in a military family, was born in Sakhalin in Russia's remote far east and raised in Riga in Latvia. He had come to Leningrad in 1970 to study the cello at the prestigious Leningrad Conservatory, and was devoting his life to music. He had met Putin shortly afterwards through his brother, a fellow student in the university law faculty. It was only when the two young men were walking past the Intourist hotel in the centre of Leningrad one day that Rodulgin understood his friend's secret employment. He recalls: 'Putin proposed that we went inside for a drink in the café. I said, "We can't", but he said, "It's OK. I'm special militia."' An everyday event in the west, access to such hotels in the USSR – with their 'subversive' foreign guests and tempting special goods for sale – was far more difficult. The fact that Putin could enter without problems showed that he was no ordinary citizen. Rodulgin says Putin never talked about his work, but explained that he worked for the KGB, later describing himself as 'a specialist in human relations'.

Rodulgin is one of a number of long-standing Putin friends who have done well in his subsequent career, and is witness to the fact that the future president did not only draw professional KGB colleagues into his inner circle. He first taught Putin how to appreciate classical music, and inspired his two daughters to learn instruments. He is even godfather to one of the girls, and the friendship between the two men continues with regular meetings to this day. Seated in his dark wood study, with Rubinstein's grand piano in one corner and his cello in another, Rodulgin, softly spoken and grey-haired, gave the impression of a deeply cultured man who had risen in his profession on his own merits, and approved of Putin's own ascension to power in the same way. 'Putin is a very good guy, down to earth, very nice, who can find a suitable language for simple people and VIPs alike,' he said. 'He is good company, but not very happy with others, and loves being alone. He likes horses and dogs.'

Rodulgin's acquaintance with Putin probably did him no harm when, not long after he moved from his job in the orchestra of the Mariinsky theatre to the Conservatory to teach and perform, he was elected rector by the faculty in December 2002. Putin certainly helped him and his peers when, at the start of the following year, the Kremlin authorized special additional financial aid to ten cultural institutions including the Conservatory, allowing a sharp increase in salaries to the staff. Rodulgin helped cultivate Putin, explaining classical music to him and helping give him a pride in the culture of his home town that is reflected in the programme of frequent visits he makes with foreign dignitaries to St Petersburg.

Putin, by his own account, had long dreamed of joining the KGB. After initially toying with becoming a sailor or an aircraft pilot, he settled on intelligence work. He says that, aged just sixteen, he went to its headquarters in the Big House and asked how he could be recruited. He claims to have been lured by the romanticism of such popular films of the period as *The Sword and the Shield*, portraying the adventures of a Soviet secret agent in Germany. 'What amazed me most of all was how one man's effort could achieve what whole armies could not. One spy could decide the fate of thousands of people,' he said. In that year, 1968, Soviet tanks had rolled into Prague to crush Alexander Dubček's fledgling democratic reforms. Memories were still fresh in many families' minds of the Stalinist repressions of the 1930s, implemented by the KGB. Yuri Andropov had taken over control of the organization in the late 1960s, cracking down after the 'thaw' that followed Nikita Khrushchev's initial rise to power with new arrests and the use of psychiatric internment for dissidents. But Putin claims he knew little about the purges, only of Stalin's personality cult. 'I was a pure and utterly successful product of Soviet patriotic education,' he said.

Vladimir Gelman, a sociologist from the European University in St Petersburg, argues that the explanation is plausible. 'The KGB, especially under Andropov, invested considerable efforts in laundering its image, creating the impression of honest, intellectual spies fighting against enemies. It was rather an effective PR campaign, and many people were affected by Soviet propaganda. The Brezhnev era was a time of stability and predictability. For intellectuals, to join the KGB voluntarily would be absolutely atypical. But the impact of intellectuals should not be overestimated. What Putin did was just promote himself. He was born in a typical blue-collar environment, in poor conditions. People there were interested in their own survival, it was very different for them than for intellectuals concerned about the fate of their country. Collaboration with the secret services was not considered as a moral choice, it was a rather typical career. It was a good opportunity for promotion. It was a very effective choice for a self-made man who had no relatives to promote him.'

A number of Putin's friends and teachers lend support to his own description as someone from a humble background with few advantages, who advanced through a mixture of his own qualities and the strengths of the Soviet system that made the most of his talents, giving him access to a good education. Neither money, contacts nor ideology seemed to play a significant role in his early progress. His schooling and university education were free, and he paid nothing for his judo lessons, the sport that he embraced young and has stuck with ever since. At School 193, his German teacher, Vera Gurevich, recalls in her memoirs, he was one of just two or three students who was not taken into the Young Pioneers, partly because he was cheeky and not studious. He did not appear especially political in his teens either. He attended the summer camps and other events organized by the Komsomol, the Communist youth league, like his classmates, but did not become one of its leaders.

Despite the experience of the 'great patriotic war', including Leningrad's particularly bitter siege by the Nazis, in which his own family suffered, Putin like many other Russians appeared to have no special animosity to Germany. That may have reflected the long-standing imperial German links to Russia, and the 'good' Germans from the east absorbed into the Communist bloc as the German Democratic Republic, compared with those in the vilified west. Gurevich relates how difficult it was for her to find work in the late 1950s, at a time when English had become the first foreign language of choice. Putin came to study German almost by accident, when he was allocated to Gurevich's class. Her encouragement – visiting his parents and continuing to tutor him even after he switched schools – played a role. His abstemiousness and discipline – albeit spurred as much by sport as by study – perhaps created a certain empathy in him for the Teutonic over the Slavic culture.

Putin moved for his final two years before university to School 281, which specialized in chemistry. Tamara Stelmakhova, one of his teachers, recalls a hard-working but unexceptional pupil. He was a political *informator*, someone who would speak about current affairs to the other pupils during weekly presentations. 'Just like now, I remember back then how he would hold on to the lectern as he spoke,' she says. She also recalls that he had a picture of Felix Dzerzhinsky, the founder of the Cheka, the precursor of the KGB, on his wall at home. 'Volodya believed in his country and his city. He was one of the rare students who had a very clear idea about his future. He was focused, determined, with a strong character, very serious, responsible and just. He was small, not a boy you usually noticed. It's a good thing that he is president, but it is unexpected. It was such a big leap. He was ordinary, there were so many like him.' Now in her seventies, Stelmakhova continues to work, partly to make ends meet. Neither she nor School 281 appears to have benefited from the connection with the future president, reflecting his transitory passage. His photo does stand at the centre of a small display just inside the main door of the building, but it was put up by the staff themselves. He did not visit during the fiftieth anniversary in 1998, and has not come back since. 'We never asked anything of him. It's not comfortable,' she says.

One activity that did have an important influence on Putin's life – then and since – was sport. He did not choose a team game such as football, but instead opted for individual, competitive and combative alternatives. Aged about ten, first he tried boxing, before switching to the martial arts of sambo and then judo. They may have helped initially to enhance his street-fighting skills, compensating for his small size with powerful technique. But judo in particular also imposed a discipline on him, and a different outlook on the world. 'It was sports that dragged me off the streets,' as he put it. 'Judo . . . is a philosophy. It's respect for your elders and for your opponent.' Because of his father's work, he passed into the network run by the Trud club, linked to the trade unions. He first practised at the second-floor sports hall on Decembrist Street – that has long since moved – under Anatoly Rakhlin, his long-standing trainer at the Pipeline construction sports club.

Today, Rakhlin, who also remains a confidant of Putin, sits in the well-renovated office of Yvara Neva, a St Petersburg judo club of which Putin is honorary president, on Kameny Ostrov, one of the many islands around which the Neva river winds. 'Football is popular because it is easy: you can play with any ball in any street, in the open air, and people who have been working can come along, bring beer, shout and smoke. In judo, that is not possible. You are in a sports hall, and it is very disciplined,' he explains. 'You cannot use just a single technique. Putin would very quickly change. He was never afraid. He was always sober. He also made mistakes: he had a big desire to win, and didn't take his strength into account. That's a weakness in sport.'

Commenting on Putin today, Rakhlin adds: 'He doesn't forget his friends. Of course he helps us. Every country should have its sportsmen. Putin has his work and I have mine. But he doesn't forget people.' Judo provided an important early test of one of Putin's enduring characteristics: loyalty. On entering university, he came under strong pressure to switch sports club from Trud to Burevestnik. But he refused. Once in the KGB, as Rakhlin relates, he was subject to renewed efforts, this time to switch to his employer's usual sports club, Dynamo. Again Putin refused, maintaining his connections with Trud instead.

There are not many world leaders who are also talented athletes, but Putin became an accomplished one. He earned the title 'master of sport' in sambo in 1973, and in judo two years later. In 1976, he rose to become Leningrad city judo champion. Had he chosen to continue, some of his peers believe he would have reached international standard. He still practises regularly today, using a small gym at his residence and sometimes inviting Rakhlin or his students to compete with him. The legacy of a tough sporting regime has kept him fit, giving him the stamina for a life of hard travelling and long days. Its rigorous training schedule also discouraged him from an early age from smoking or drinking, contributing to the almost anti-Slavic austere, ascetic image he has since developed.

Whether teaching him or simply reflecting his own nature, judo's imprint can still be seen in Putin's psychological comportment: a mixture of humility and cunning, someone who prefers ruses and indirect approaches. When visiting Japan in 2000, he took part in a judo demonstration, but also showed a certain respect and humility in allowing himself to be thrown by a small girl. 'People on the Russian side thought that he should not have done it, but I said his authority remained intact,' said Rakhlin. 'The Japanese reaction was very positive. I was just afraid that she would hurt her head when she threw him.' Some of Putin's interlocutors suggest that he behaves like a judo player as well as a KGB operative in discussions, digging to find background information about those with whom he will talk to win them over, or throwing them off guard by revealing information to destabilize them at the last minute. When an English colleague of mine came to interview him in 1999 despite the illness of his mother, Putin surprised him by expressing his concern. Strobe Talbott, the US deputy secretary of state and a Russian scholar who had translated Nikita Khrushchev's memoirs, recounts how Putin made clear that he was aware of Talbott's own academic dissertation subject at an early meeting between them.

Sport may have played a role in gaining Putin access to higher education, with his attendance at the law faculty of St Petersburg state university. His teachers say his marks were good, easing his way in. He says that competition for entry was intense, with forty school-leavers for each of a small number of places, most of which were in any case reserved for those coming out of the army. However, Rakhlin writes in his memoirs that getting into the law faculty at the time was not that difficult. He encouraged Putin to apply for partly selfish reasons, since university training meant that he would be exempt from otherwise obligatory military service. That way, his pupil could continue to train and compete in Leningrad rather than being sent away somewhere in the army.

By his own admission, Putin's choice of law was determined by others, rather than reflecting any special personal interest. According to his version of events, when he went to the KGB's local headquarters as a teenager, he was advised to get some training and work experience first. When he asked what degree to obtain, he was told to opt for law – one of a number of specialisms from which the KGB recruited. Whatever the truth, his studies did give him a foundation in the subject, which has remained with him ever since. 'Dictatorship of the law' became one of his slogans, and efforts to push through long-proposed changes to the civil, criminal and administrative codes were a priority after his election as president. He also appointed fellow lawyers in key positions as Kremlin advisers, including Dmitry Kozak and Dmitry Medvedev, both graduates of his old faculty.

'Never in Russia's history has there been such a storm of reform of the law as with our president-lawyer,' says Vadim Prokhorov, the former dean who was one of Putin's seminar advisers and who still teaches at the university. 'Volodya [Vladimir] Putin has deep respect for principles. He was thoughtful. He was a good, normal, ordinary student, not distinguished from the others, which shows that the later development of his career was the result of his personal qualities. He succeeded well, did his work, took part in discussions.' Some argue that the Soviet system followed the legal form while often letting respect for its underlying principles bow to political expedience. Even at the height of Stalinist repression, the KGB was always scrupulous to demonstrate violations of a law – regardless of its injustice, the ruthlessness of the techniques used in extracting a confession, and the pressure on the judges and prosecutors to come up with the 'right' result. Prokhorov does not want to be drawn into a wider debate, but says: 'The idea of respect of the law in the legal faculty always existed. The practice of violating the law was an exception, like the excesses of Christianity during the Inquisition.'

Valery Musin, one of Putin's professors who has acted as an occasional legal adviser to him ever since, says he was 'very cautious, very well balanced . . . very industrious and clever'. He dismisses suggestions that politically inspired 'telephone justice' was widespread in Soviet times. When I asked him about a high-level legal scandal in 2003, when federal prosecutors raided the offices of the personal lawyer of the tycoon Mikhail Khodorkovsky as part of a spiralling investigation widely seen as political, he replied: 'Frankly speaking, my father was a surgeon, and he used to say that he could not make a diagnosis without looking at the patient. This case indicates very clearly that our state and our leaders would like to show that everyone in this country should be law-abiding regardless of their financial position.'

Nikolai Kropachev, the current dean, also plays down the extent of interference in the judicial system. His own dissertation was on the rights of the individual versus the state, and he stresses the faculty's long tradition of independence from the authorities. He cites its resistance to the Soviet attacks on intellectuals couched as 'cosmopolitanism'. He says the faculty resisted considerable pressure to remove from its library books written by Olimpiad Ioffe, a distinguished lawyer on the staff who was stripped of his professorship and Communist Party membership and fled the USSR after a scandal in the 1970s when his daughter married a foreigner and emigrated. Kropachev says: 'Putin is first of all a lawyer. He is trying to realize his vision and training from law school today. If it had not been Putin, but a non-lawyer after the [1998] Russian crash, the country would not have been ruled by law but by force.'

But there are alternative ways to use that legal training. Power as much as principles, men as much as laws, play a dominant role in contemporary Russia, however much arbitrary acts are wrapped up in legal justification. Putin's professors must take some responsibility for him and his fellow students over the years. In Kropachev's office, a photograph of him with Putin – a near-ubiquitous decoration for those of Russia's contemporary officials who have met the president – sits on his bookshelf. He boasts that 'in the last hundred years, we have taught twelve leaders', citing Alexander Kirensky (head of the last pre-revolutionary government) and Lenin, as well as Putin. The faculty's recruitment brochures proudly set out the names of esteemed graduates. For an institution dedicated to training members of the supposedly independent judicial system, it seems strange that there are no judges, academics or well-known lawyers among the list. Instead, the focus is on alumni such as Putin and those in his inner circle – led by Dmitry Medvedev and Dmitry Kozak – who have joined him in the Kremlin.

Today, the law school has certainly done well for itself. The neo-classical main building on the Vasilevsky Island in central St Petersburg has been freshly painted. In contrast to the tatty surroundings in most Russian higher-education institutes, there is a state-of-the-art confer-ence hall. Dozens of expensive flat-screen computers sit in the well-stocked library for use by students. Half of its 700,000 volumes have been electronically scanned. But asked whether the Kremlin has helped the law school, Kropachev replies: 'We help them, not the other way round.' He cites advice and research on legal issues. He has played a direct role, too. He helped draft and was co-signatory of a letter in spring 2000 that called for sanctions against NTV for its satirical *Kukly* puppets programme, which had mocked Putin. 'I'm in favour of free speech, but not insults,' he says. 'The president should be treated absolutely like everyone else. It's wrong to insult people.' And in late 2002, when Vladimir Yakovlev, Putin's political rival in St Petersburg, tried to push for a third term as governor despite a local constitution limiting the head of the city to two terms in office, Kropachev was among the judges who ruled against. 'It was purely a legal decision,' he stresses.

If law – with whatever interpretation – was a formative influence on Putin, economics and foreign affairs also played their role. He spe-cialized in international law, according to Prokhorov, and chose as his undergraduate thesis in 1976 'The Principle of the Most Favoured Nation in International Law'. That may have played a role in his sub-sequent interest in liberal economic reform, in his work abroad, and in Russia's accession to the World Trade Organization in particular. The conclusions of his research are unknown. The university today says it no longer has a copy of the document, since student papers were destroyed as a matter of routine after five years. However, one academic at the faculty says that a fellow classmate, who is now an important legal figure in the region, copiously plagiarized Putin's thesis. Where Putin had received the top mark of 5, six years later his friend was able to earn a 4 largely on the basis of the future presi-dent's work.

It was at university that Putin was finally recruited into the KGB, where he would pass fifteen formative years of his professional life. He says that after his premature teenage application, he was not approached again until he was coming to the end of his final year, when he was singled out at the employment commission that decided students' careers. Tellingly, in Putin's version, unquestioning loyalty and obedience by the new recruits were valued far above any personal preferences or points of principle, and he was clearly willing to demonstrate his enthusiastic compliance. 'You can't pick your nose and say, "I want this and I don't want that."' They can't use people like that,' he told his interviewers.

Others say Putin's entry into the KGB may have come a little earlier. Konstantin Preobrazhensky, an undercover KGB agent in Japan until he was unmasked, has became a strong critic of the agency, and now lives in the USA after intimidation and threats to him and his family. He suggests that Putin was recruited in his third year at university, as a *seksot* or secret collaborator, an informant charged with unearthing anti-Communist staff and students. His success in the role may explain why he was hired as a lieutenant in the agency immediately on graduation, rather than after the two-year probation period that normally applied to those of his age. Preobrazhensky also casts doubt on whether the agency would have accepted Putin at all if he had knocked on its door at age sixteen as he claims. 'They were very much afraid of such people, and considered them crazy,' he says. Putin himself says that the man who met him at the *Bolshoi Dom* warned him that the agency did not take *initiativny* (those who came forward of their own volition).

Yuri Shvets, another former KGB agent who worked undercover as a journalist in Washington, DC, and who now lives in the USA, believes that Putin may indeed have volunteered as a teenager. But he too suggests that, if so, he probably spied on his fellow university students afterwards. 'The chances are very high,' he says. 'If you applied to the KGB, they would recruit you as an informant.' That would also fit with Shvets's personal experience of Putin, with whom he studied at the Red Banner Institute in Moscow, now the Academy of Foreign Intelligence, in 1984. 'We had "uncles" who wrote our references on graduation. They needed to know as much as possible, and used "elders" or the leaders of the groups, who reported to them. Vova [Vladimir] was a leader – a snitch. Everybody hated the leader.'

Intriguingly, while Putin himself denies being an informer at the law faculty, he does in *First Person* justify *seksots* as agents 'who decide to work for the interests of the state'. He also hints at their importance, claiming that 90 per cent of intelligence information came from ordinary Soviet citizens. His editors were perhaps sensitive to the angry reaction such remarks could trigger so soon after so many in Russia had lived in fear and under surveillance. Although printed in the original newspaper interviews, this passage was excised from the Russian-language book-length version that was distributed free of charge in large numbers during his 2000 election campaign.

When he joined the KGB in 1975, Putin says, he began working for the secretariat of the directorate and was then assigned to counter-intelligence work for five months. He received six months' training in a secret Leningrad institute, during which time he was recruited by foreign intelligence, which sent him for a year's training in Moscow. He returned to work in Leningrad's First Department for intelligence for four and a half years, and then attended the elite Andropov Red Banner Institute for intelligence training before his posting to the German Democratic Republic in 1985. The picture is attractive: fast promotions, and above all a rapid switch away from the stigmatized domestic function of the KGB, snooping on Russians, towards the more glamorous role of foreign agent, carrying out his patriotic duty abroad. Even today, employees of the SVR, the foreign intelligence service, draw a clear distinction between their elite work and that of the FSB's internal policing activities. By portraying himself as a secret agent abroad, Putin could approvingly cite Henry Kissinger, who once told him during a meeting in St Petersburg: 'All decent people got their start in intelligence. I did too.'

But Oleg Kalugin, the head of the Leningrad KGB during the 1980s, paints a more sinister picture of Putin's years in the security police. 'He was a typical uncritical Soviet person,' he says. 'He was very opportunistic, envious of people's success, devious. He was a faceless, colourless figure.' He believes it is perfectly possible that Putin knocked voluntarily at the KGB door as a teenager, motivated by a mixture of romanticism and a desire to overcome his weaknesses. 'I think he joined because he is physically short. He was often beaten by bigger boys at school; he recovered his dignity at judo school by learning how to repulse their attacks, but then realized that physical fitness was not sufficient.' He says Putin was employed as an informant at university, before beginning work in the feared Fifth Directorate, which specialized in undermining and prosecuting dissidents and the intelligentsia. After attending School 401 in counter-intelligence, he was switched to the First Directorate, in charge of intelligence gathering, where he spied on foreign visitors, tourists and scientists in the city. Kalugin says Putin remained in Leningrad for the following nine years, receiving only local language training. He says he was never formally transferred into foreign intelligence, but merely seconded from the Leningrad field office's First Directorate – initially to the Red Banner Institute, and then to East Germany. That is corroborated by public statements from both Vladimir Kryuchkov, the head of foreign intelligence at the start of the 1990s, and Yuri Kobaladze, its spokesman in the mid-1990s, that Putin was never one of their agents.

Preobrazhensky also has some indirect supporting evidence for this less glamorous and more sinister version of Putin's career path. Himself the son of a KGB general, he was recruited and sent to the agency's counter-intelligence school in Minsk in Belarus in 1977. He says that there were two sections: he was in one, dealing with supervision of secret military plants; and Sergei Ivanov, under cover as a lieutenant of the radio communications troops of the ministry of defence, was in the other, which prepared employees for the Fifth. He says Ivanov went back to Leningrad to work in the Fifth together with his close friend, Vladimir Putin. 'They must have worked together, because KGB procedures forbade friendship between staff in different departments.' Putin also forged a friendship with Viktor Cherkesov, his fellow graduate from the Leningrad university law faculty, who was hired to the investigations department of the KGB and went on to take charge of the interrogation of 'undesirables' on behalf of its Fifth Directorate.

Even Kalugin, who says he joined the KGB as a romantic during the time of Stalin, before Khrushchev's secret speech to a special closed session at the conclusion of the Communist Party Congress in 1956 that helped raise awareness of the evils of the repressions, tries to paint a relatively mild picture of the activities of the Fifth Directorate. 'We never attacked dissidents directly, we manipulated them: we created rival dissident organizations – such as poetry, music, rock groups to keep them under control, and to weed out the dissidents,' he says.

But Slava Dalinin, a dissident from Leningrad who is now a human rights activist, has a different recollection. He vividly remembers

Cherkesov's interrogations. His experiences are a sobering reminder of the more sinister side of the KGB, as recently as the late 1980s. He was arrested in June 1982 and duly charged by Cherkesov – as always strictly in accordance with a law, however unjust. He was accused of a classic dissident transgression: violation of Article 70 of the criminal code, for 'anti-Soviet propaganda'. His 'crimes' included possession of illegal home-produced *samizdat* copies of Alexander Solzhenitsyn's novels which described the horrors of the Gulag prison camp system, as well as union publications including some from Solidarity, which was putting severe strains on the Communist regime in Warsaw. 'I spent nine months in a KGB prison,' says Dalinin. 'Cherkesov was a man without a face, with no personal feelings and a primitive outlook on the world, focused on his career. His conversation was uneducated and formal.' Cherkesov threatened Dalinin with a technique refined to cynical perfection under Yuri Andropov when he took charge of the KGB at the end of the 1960s. He proposed debilitating psychiatric treatment, after a diagnosis of that politically inspired illness, unrecognized outside the Soviet Union, 'creeping schizophrenia'. In the event, Dalinin was sent to a political prison camp in Perm, and then to the remote Komi republic. He was only freed in 1987, two years after Mikhail Gorbachev came to power.

The relationship of Putin with Cherkesov and Ivanov remained close over the years. When Putin rose to power in Moscow, Ivanov was appointed first as head of the State Security Council and then as minister of defence. Cherkesov became Putin's presidential representative for Russia's north-western region, and played a central role in the battle to oust Putin's rival Vladimir Yakovlev from power as governor of St Petersburg. And another key friend, Nikolai Patrushev, who also joined the Leningrad KGB in 1975, and followed Putin to Moscow, succeeded him as head of the entire FSB. Putin repeatedly proved his loyalty to his friends and colleagues.

Putin himself has revealed nothing of the precise nature of his work in Leningrad. But when asked directly by journalists whether he had helped in the harassment of dissidents, he replied elliptically: 'My group was not particularly involved in these activities.' There seems no doubt that he was transferred away from such work, attending the Red Banner Institute in Moscow in 1984. In line with the practice of the time, he was assigned a codename which kept the first letter of his real surname: Comrade Putin became Comrade Platov. Shvets recalls that as a student Putin was noticeable 'for his obsession with martial arts. Ninety per cent of our guys believed that they came to train their brain, and went to the library to read. A much smaller group came to train their muscles, and they went to the gym.' The Institute gave him the chance to perfect the people skills that he would be able to use so often later in life: a Teflon personality designed to draw out his interlocutors without revealing much about himself, saying what they wanted to hear and promising what they sought, while not necessarily believing it or planning to implement it.

Putin's adherence to the KGB in the 1970s means Yuri Andropov was his role model, albeit a distant one. It explains his subsequent signs of deference to the man who took charge of the KGB in 1967, and was the only leader of the organization until Putin who went on to head the country. Andropov restored the pride and efficiency of the agency, shifting emphasis from repression to 'preventive' measures, while continuing to clamp down on dissidents. He created new networks of informants, launched trials against human rights activists, and sent the most high-profile ones – such as Solzhenitsyn – into exile. When he became General Secretary of the Communist Party for a mere fifteen months in 1983, while Putin was in the middle of his KGB career, Andropov was the embodiment – and last hope – of those who still believed in reform of the Soviet system. He brought fresh energy after the stagnation that built up under the geriatric Leonid Brezhnev. Drawing on his experience as a diplomat, he was active in foreign policy. He developed a reputation as a 'liberal Chekist', keen to bring about gradualist, technocratic economic restructuring while convinced that political reform was unnecessary. 'First we'll make enough sausages and then we won't have any dissidents,' he once reportedly said.

There are some other tempting personal parallels with Putin. Andropov had a reputation as a German and English speaker; a modest and reserved man who shunned social events, but had an occasionally earthy turn of phrase; a workaholic and teetotaller who pioneered an anti-alcohol campaign. There were also some fundamental differences. Andropov was a hardline ideologue, a firmly convinced Marxist-Leninist and anti-American, where Putin was from a younger, more cynical and opportunistic generation. Andropov attempted to impose workplace discipline including punctuality, never a strong personal quality of Putin. He probably appointed more people to senior positions from non-traditional backgrounds than Putin. And also he was chronically sick and quickly incapacitated in his post, which he achieved at an age twenty years older than Putin. But that probably made even stronger Putin's frustration at Andropov's rapid demise. It was no accident that when defending himself against a hostile crowd of relatives following the botched rescue operation for the *Kursk* nuclear submarine in August 2000, Putin said that he could be blamed for the events during his term in office, but not for those over the past 'fifteen years'. His reference point, from when he traced Russia's decline, was the end of Andropov's era.

In 1985, Putin was finally able to capitalize on his linguistic skills when he received his foreign posting: to the East German city of Dresden. He says that he might have had the chance to work in West Germany, but that would have required up to three years' preparation in the relevant department in the KGB in Moscow first, and he was impatient to leave on mission. Others are more scathing. 'East Germany was relatively prestigious, if you compare it with Bulgaria or Mongolia,' says Kalugin acidly. 'Something went wrong. With his German, you would have expected him to go to West Germany or Austria.' Shvets adds: 'We had a saying: "A chicken is not a bird, East Germany is not abroad." East Germany was not a very important country, it was where they sent people usually approaching retirement age, or as a consolation for those who had had problems – who had been divorced, or had their covers blown. And Dresden was like a black hole, a trip to nowhere. It was like sending a four-star general to direct the traffic next to Red Square.' He says the posting was a punishment for a rare drinking incident involving Putin and some friends at the Institute, just when the authorities were in the middle of an anti-alcohol campaign.

Dresden may not have been the most luxurious or prestigious location, but it certainly offered Putin more money than at home, the prospects of more rapid promotion, and a move away from the cramped apartment that he and his wife still shared with his parents in Leningrad. While the living conditions and the job terms were better than in Russia, East Germany was more ideologically hardline and repressive than the USSR of the time. There was not even access to western television channels. As one journalist from East Germany posted to Moscow in the late 1980s recalls: 'It was very frustrating.

Mikhail Gorbachev's *glasnost* meant that the Russian media was becoming very critical, and we could at last get to interview officials. But my paper in East Germany was still under tight censorship, and I couldn't report any of it back home.' Putin did not have the exposure to western ideas and the free market as a result of his time in Dresden, unlike those of his colleagues who were sent to more prestigious postings outside the Communist bloc, or even to Berlin, a very important KGB station. Nor did he come back convinced of the need to swiftly destroy the system. Indeed, while conceding that a divided Germany was unnatural, he told journalists that he believed the Soviet Union should not have withdrawn so quickly from the country.

Despite the limited window that he had directly on the west, Putin did at least have the chance to observe the weaknesses of Communism in another country outside his own. He saw the writing on the wall in the frustrations of the local people – literally, when the Berlin Wall came down in 1989, while he was still in post. He was the first Russian leader since Lenin to speak a foreign language well, and the first to travel and live abroad. Through his studies, language skills and practical contacts, he also developed an enduring interest in and love for Germany – West as well as East. That would create an important foundation for the future, signalling an orientation towards European culture and ideas. His daughters, who spent their early years in Germany, remained in German school after his return to Russia and ascension to the Kremlin; and Putin is clearly influenced by German cultural and political ideas. He has a number of close personal and business friends from the country. His contacts and linguistic fluency would serve him well, helping him to tap German foreign investors for St Petersburg during the early 1990s. He was so intrigued by the German analyst Alexander Rahr's biography, *A German in the Kremlin*, that he even invited him for a private dinner in the Kremlin. At a press conference in summer 2003, he liberally sprinkled German ideas into his answers: 'They have a word for that in German: *ja-nein*,' he said in reply to one awkward question. To another, on a possible shift of the Russian capital to St Petersburg, he cited the example of Germany, with its federal functions split between different cities.

For the second half of the 1980s, Putin worked as part of a team of just nine people at 4 Angelikstrasse in Dresden, directly opposite the local headquarters of the Stasi, the secret police, supposedly as a manager of the German-Soviet Friendship Association. It was an ideal 'cover' for continuing what he had already been trained to do: keeping an eye on others at social gatherings where barriers were down and tongues might wag. Putin himself is modest about his achievements, denying media reports that he was involved in recruiting western scientists as Soviet informants or in the transfer of technology to the east. He was promoted twice during his five-year posting, and in February 1988 he was awarded a bronze service medal of the National People's Army. But of another thirty-seven agents decorated on the same day, most received more prestigious gold and silver medals. There was little to spy on in the city, the most sensitive plant being the cumbersome Robotron electronics factory. 'He was a junior operative, and moderately successful,' says Kalugin. 'He worked with the Stasi to monitor visitors. His main job was to maintain the stability of the local regime. Intelligence was secondary.'

Putin says he gathered information on political figures and parties, and on 'the main opponent' – NATO. Documents from the BSTU, the German repository of files from the Stasi, provide a few clues. He is rarely cited directly, but in a 1997 letter he was asked to recruit someone who lived near the German Communist Party guest-house in Dresden, who could spy on visitors. The task was not accomplished. On another occasion, he contacted the local head of the Stasi to ensure that a scarce telephone connection that had been cut off was re-established to a former police officer-turned-informant. Most traces suggest that Putin's work was mundane. Either he was a master-spy prematurely promoted and able to entirely cover his own tracks and destroy all incriminating documents about himself, or more likely he was a dull junior officer in a backwater with few chances to shine and limited influence.

Shvets recalls: 'There was a gap between what we learned at the Red Banner Institute and what we did in practice. It was like a cold shower. The system had degenerated under Brezhnev. Our teachers were real Cold War professionals who had dedicated their lives to espionage. But we discovered that what was important was not what we did but what we reported. It was mainly about paperwork.' One former colleague of Putin from Dresden gave an interview in the daily newspaper *Izvestiya* in 2003 that is typical of the genre. Even under conditions of anonymity, he talked at length while providing little information, and refused to acknowledge a single negative quality in Putin. The greatest revelation was that Putin's favourite book was Gogol's masterpiece *Dead Souls*, a witty satire on Russian corruption and officialdom, which must have helped prepare him for the future. But he did reveal that the work in Dresden was largely about gathering routine information, analysing it and sending it back to headquarters.

There were suggestions that Putin was involved in Operation 'Luch' (Lightbeam), designed to recruit a ring of Stasi agents who would continue to spy for Moscow after the GDR collapsed. Putin himself denies that he was involved, although one man did confess to the West German counter-intelligence agency and claimed to have been recruited by Putin as part of a local espionage network which collapsed as a result of his defection. But it seems probable that if Putin was involved, the German authorities would have known by the early 1990s, and refused him re-entry on his frequent travels to the country during the period when he was still a minor official in St Petersburg. Putin was no James Bond. He was probably – as with so many of his intelligence counterparts around the world – an unglamorous but probably quite effective paper-pusher.

Usually, after foreign postings KGB agents were sent to Moscow. But Putin instead returned to Leningrad at the start of 1990, where, after what Kalugin says was a three-month delay without employment, he was allocated to the 'active reserve' of the agency, as assistant rector in charge of foreign relations at his old university. It meant, in other words, surveillance of foreign students and of the foreign contacts and trips of the teachers. 'It was even less important than working for Intourist, or the foreign trade delegation,' says Kalugin. Putin says he chose to return home because he could see that the Soviet system was crumbling, and he had no desire to wait for its ultimate collapse. To another interviewer, he claimed that he wanted to move his family back together with his ageing parents, rather than changing city. He said the posting at Leningrad university provided him a way to prepare for the future, possibly for an academic career, and in the meantime to work on a doctoral dissertation. The academic Musin, who was set to be his thesis adviser, says the subject was German corporate law. He says he had no idea that Putin, who described himself as working in 'the diplomatic service', was a spy.

There may have been another more mundane explanation behind Putin's low-level assignment on his return to Russia. A KGB colleague told Oleg Blotsky, one of Putin's biographers, that he advised Putin to return to Leningrad: a job had been allocated to him in Moscow, but the system was at breaking point. The Soviet Union teetered on the verge of collapse, and agents were returning home from around the world – above all from the fast crumbling Eastern bloc – seeking fresh employment and accommodation back home. There was no guarantee that Putin would be allocated an apartment in the Russian capital. At least in Leningrad he had a home base, and contacts to help him begin a new life.

The break with the past

In 1990, Putin took what he describes as 'the hardest decision of my life'. After more than fifteen years in his chosen profession, he wrote a letter of resignation to the KGB. A few months earlier, he says, he had already begun mulling a change of career when – at the suggestion of a friend from the law faculty – he went to see one of his old professors. Anatoly Sobchak had emerged as a powerful orator and one of the leading advocates of democratic reform as the USSR was crumbling. He was elected leader of the Leningrad City Council, and Putin offered to work with him as an assistant. It began a new chapter in his life, earning liberal democratic credentials that would become an important part of his psychological make-up as the new post-Communist Russia emerged. Putin says he explained his KGB background to Sobchak, but the politician said 'what the hell' and agreed to hire him anyway. It was only a few months later that he decided to resign, after being subjected to periodic pressure from his KGB colleagues and threats from opposition political figures that they would blow his cover and create a scandal.

'I couldn't quite put my finger on it,' said Putin, trying to explain why he ultimately decided to write the letter abandoning his long-time employer. The ambiguity is telling. As Russians say, 'A KGB officer never resigns,' or 'You can join but you can never leave.' In any case, by Putin's own admission, his first resignation request was ignored, and only a second demand was acted upon several months later, in mid-1991. In the meantime, Putin remained in the 'active reserve', on the KGB's payroll and at least theoretically under its instructions. Subsequently, he maintained tight links with the security services and the police in his work in the city administration, helped by nominations such as that of his friend Viktor Cherkesov, who was appointed to run the St Petersburg division of the KGB in 1992.

During the ill-fated *putsch* in August 1991, Vladimir Kryuchkov, the then head of the KGB, played a central role. Mikhail Gorbachev was placed under house arrest in his holiday villa in the Crimea. At the national level, Yeltsin saw his chance, championing democracy and denouncing the putschists when he famously stood on a tank in Moscow and called for popular resistance to the coup. In provincial Leningrad, Sobchak did the same, pledging his support for Yeltsin and risking arrest. He flew back to the city, where Putin – who had himself returned swiftly from a holiday in Kaliningrad – met him at the airport with an armed guard and whisked him away to safety. His act was in clear defiance of Kryuchkov, the man who was still his ultimate boss, although not in opposition to the sentiments of many inside the KGB itself.

It is possible that people within the KGB nominated Putin to his job with Sobchak. After all, Putin had not stood out for taking his own initiative in the past or defying the 'party line'. He never resigned his membership of the Communist Party of the Soviet Union, simply putting his card in the back of his desk drawer. He would later admit that the putschists' goal of preserving the USSR was 'noble', even if their methods were counterproductive. And there was an element of opportunism when he told journalists, 'When I saw the faces of the coup plotters on TV, I knew right away it was all over.' Only after their failure, with his assessment of the future made, did he make his second attempt to resign from the KGB. Much has been made of the fact that Putin hung a portrait of Peter the Great on his wall in the mayor's office. In fact, he was following the lead taken by Sobchak in his own office. The filmmaker Igor Shadkin says that when he visited Putin in 1991 to make a documentary about him, there was also a bust of Lenin in his room. The chances are that he really had quit the KGB, while not turning his back on its training or values.

Just as curious as Putin's decision to work for Sobchak was Sobchak's to hire Putin. Given his reputation as an ardent anti-Communist, why should one of the country's leading critics of the Soviet system have hired an agent of the KGB, which embodied more than any other institution the sinister legacy of the past? Boris

Vishnevsky, a political analyst and activist for the reformist Yabloko party in St Petersburg, says: 'I always thought Putin knew something about Sobchak. They were very different people from different worlds. The KGB presented Putin to Sobchak. It probably had compromising material on Sobchak, perhaps that he denounced others.'

But there was a more practical reason. In the lawless period of the early 1990s, Sobchak needed someone with good links to the security services to provide order and protect him from the rapidly emerging criminal sector. Even Kalugin, who today is no fan of Putin or the KGB and its methods, argues that he did make a clear break with his past, resigning and putting his fate instead in the hands of his new employer. 'Putin was totally dissatisfied and frustrated,' he says. 'He quit the KGB because he felt he had no future. The university was the end of his career. Russia was in chaos, and Sobchak offered him a chance. I don't believe he was still working for the KGB. Sobchak came to me because he wanted to find someone he could rely on. He was surrounded by enemies, by people who wanted to get rid of him. He wanted someone inside the KGB, and he found his former student.'

There was also more in common between the two men than it first seems. Many observers of Leningrad politics of the time say that while Sobchak was an eloquent anti-Communist speaker, he was also authoritarian, and like many of that first generation of fledgling democrats, he was far less skilled at applying his ideas than in speaking about them. As a result he may have had few qualms about working with the KGB, as long as their agents were diverted to his own purposes. The local politician Alexander Belayev was among those to criticize Putin for using KGB-style sources and tactics to keep an eye on local companies. Marina Salye, a city councillor at the time and a critic of both men, says that Putin took a particular interest in officials' sexual proclivities – suggesting a KGB-style appetite for gathering compromising materials that helped keep Sobchak's rivals in check. Boris Pustintsev, a dissident who now runs Citizens Control, a human rights group in St Petersburg, recalls: 'Sobchak was no democrat. He showed a Soviet-style arrogance.' He cites Sobchak's decision to make job appointments and dismissals secret; and his failure to name and support an independent human rights commissioner for the city even at the peak of Russia's democratic revolution.

Dmitry Travin, a journalist and commentator who now works for the local newspaper *Delo*, says: 'Sobchak's relationship with every-one – perhaps with the exception of Putin – was that of a professor to his students.' Others cite constant clashes with the city legislature, which Sobchak attempted to marginalize and ignore. Vladimir Gelman, the academic who observed the period closely, says: 'Sobchak was a controversial figure. He portrayed himself as a democrat, but as chair of the city council he was like a dictator. He was a good public speaker, but never bothered about the routine processes of decision-making. He needed someone absolutely loyal to him for the daily work.' Leonid Romankov, another Yabloko deputy, says: 'Sobchak was a big figure, but I was disappointed. He was very pragmatic. But his rela-tions with others were negative. If you are a democrat, you respect the divisions of power: the court, the legislature, the executive. His idea was to rule by himself. He could speak for forty-five minutes, but it was like a lecture. He was not a man of dialogue but of monologue. People say his talent was to create enemies.'

Even Putin concedes that Sobchak was not an easy man, telling his biographer Blotsky: 'Sobchak was a wonderful orator, a dignified mayor, but a very difficult person.' Putin seemed to fit in well with his boss's authoritarian style, while his far calmer temperament helped smooth the stormy relations with the City Council. He developed the reputation as Sobchak's *éminence grise*, controlling things behind the scenes. He was quickly promoted from an assistant to Sobchak to his adviser. He chaired the city's foreign affairs committee from June 1991, becoming head of the committee on external relations in 1994, and then a deputy governor. His skills as an administrator served him well, and developed fast. 'You should not judge a person by his back-ground in the KGB, but on his work,' says Vatanyar Yagya, an academic and member of the Council's foreign relations committee. 'Putin never acted in KGB style. He always supported democratic principles, respected people, and talked calmly. He was a very good organizer, a good interlocutor, who always thought about the interests of Russia and St Petersburg.'

As a KGB agent, Putin had been used to preparing information to be passed on to others who would act on it – or, as the Soviet Union teetered, who increasingly did nothing. Suddenly, as he put it, he was among the people taking the decisions, and the new responsibilities pleased him. 'I was taking decisions IN-DE-PEN-DENT-LY . . . I had to make decisions myself,' he told Blotsky breathlessly. The very admission hints at someone who had previously been reluctant to be at the pinnacle of power, who preferred others to be in the front line, assuming responsibility. It was a classic KGB officer's mentality. Nevertheless, he appeared to adapt well to his new role. Alexander Rahr argues that Putin demonstrated 'excellent managerial work in the civic administration', dealing with the operation of the city's casinos, the renovation of Pulkova airport, customs collection, the Litovsky commercial centre, and the Goodwill Games. Another acquaintance says: 'He was always responsible. While Sobchak was off partying or attending glamorous conferences, Putin would deal with the essential things that no one wanted to touch, like repairing the sewers.' Ludmila Narusova, Sobchak's widow, says: 'We knew Putin as competent. He was chosen for his professional qualities. He was not just very professional. He was reliable.'

Putin had a good combination of skills for his new job as head of the committee on foreign relations. Germany was one of the most logical western commercial partners for Russia, given its long historical links, geographical proximity and powerful economy. Reunification gave him a chance to apply his knowledge of East Germany into the newly expanded, much richer country created as a result. He used his language skills extensively, acting as an interpreter when Sobchak travelled to meet Helmut Kohl and other prominent politicians. But he was also far more actively involved in city administration, dealing with the legal nitty-gritty of contracts and investments. He was instrumental in trying to implement the mayor's dream of turning St Petersburg into a financial capital for Russia. A currency exchange was opened, and Putin attracted a number of investors, including the first Russian branches since the Bolshevik Revolution of Crédit Lyonnais and BNP-Dresdner. He negotiated the switch in use of the former East German consulate in the city into the German House, a base for some 150 German business representation offices in the city. He supervised the restoration of major hotels, such as the Astoria. He also laid the foundations for subsequent investment in the region by companies such as Coca-Cola, Wrigley and Gillette. He travelled frequently to Germany, but also visited other countries, most notably neighbouring Finland, ostensibly for skiing holidays, to the point that the protocol associated with his displacements became a tiring embarrassment for Finnish diplomats.

Most people who recall Putin from that period have bland but positive things to say of a man they recall as discreet but efficient.

'People always said two things about him: he's KGB, and from City Hall,' recalls one foreign diplomat who worked in St Petersburg in the early 1990s. 'He was first to arrive at receptions, and the first to leave. He shook hands, and he never said anything.' Romankov says: 'Putin was a closed man, not very emotional. He was not the sort of person to cheerily slap you on the back. But his committee on international relations was efficient, especially in establishing links to German businessmen.' Mikhail Piotrovsky, the head of the Hermitage Museum, a compulsory stop on any itinerary for foreign statesman brought to St Petersburg by Putin today, says: 'Putin invented the idea of foreign relations. He brought in foreign banks and created an international image here. He knows the Hermitage from his childhood, and doesn't feel uncomfortable with imperial things.'

The experiences of Graham Humes, an American who ran the non-profit body Caresbac-St Petersburg, were typical. His organization was established in 1993 to sell donated US butter in Russia and lend the $9m proceeds in local small businesses, reinvesting any profits. He quickly ran into objections from the Federal Humanitarian Aid Commission, which was sceptical that such activity could be considered charitable. He got little help from the US Consulate, and it proved impossible to see Sobchak. But he eventually managed to meet Putin, triggering a lengthy negotiation that culminated in a pragmatic deal: $2.2m of the money was 'donated' to purchase cut-price German equipment for a local dental clinic, a Sobchak priority. The rest he was allowed to invest as planned. The Aid Commission was bypassed through a special prime-ministerial order that Putin slipped under the nose of Viktor Chernomyrdin to sign when the moment was ripe, overriding the regulations in force. He remembers during one meeting Putin taking a call from Sobchak and smiling as he held the phone at arm's length, so loud was the shouting. 'I think we can both hang up our phones. I can hear you fine without,' he said, showing his willingness to stand up to the mayor. Overall, Humes says Putin was 'direct and very businesslike, not lacking in humour but maintaining control of each meeting . . . professional and skilled in political tactics, enabling him to dance around the old *apparatchiks* in order to achieve a St Petersburg open for foreign capital to benefit fledgling Russian businesses.' He adds that Putin kept a low profile, did not seek to benefit personally, and that there was never any attempt by city officials to divert money.

In Russia, however, westerners are often handled with kid gloves, especially when it comes to bribes. In relation to domestic transactions, Putin's six-year period in St Petersburg was not free of criticism. In 1991–2, with 'shock therapy' under way, prices liberated and inflation skyrocketing, the city's usually harsh winter was made far worse by the newly turbulent economic climate. There were severe food shortages, and Sobchak's administration received permission to barter metals and oil in exchange for food from abroad. But the programme was a failure. The commodities were sold cheaply, and the food bought was over-priced despite offers of aid from Germany. Much of it was never even delivered. In May 1992, the City Council produced a scathing report, questioning agreements made with a series of intermediary firms, 'the majority of which are not known as serious commercial structures, having insufficient experience in export-import operations, but which at the same time either have tight links with officials in the mayor's office or were created shortly before the signature of the contracts'. While not suggesting any direct personal enrichment by Putin, it criticized him for hiding information behind the pretext of 'commercial secrecy' and accused him of 'incompetence' and being insufficiently conscientious. The twenty-page document, No. 88, dated 8 May 1992, still sits in computerized form on the Council's database. Recommendation 8.2 is categorical: 'Strip V. V. Putin and A. G. Anikin [his deputy] of their responsibilities.' But its calls for the city prosecutor to investigate led nowhere.

Over the years, other accusations would emerge. The most damning relates to SPAG, a German-Russian joint venture called the St Petersburg Real Estate Holding Company. Established in 1992, its founding shareholders included the German Rudolf Ritter and Vladimir Smirnov from St Petersburg. The city of St Petersburg itself took a 20 per cent stake, and both Putin and German Gref, his City Hall colleague whom he later appointed as his economic development minister, became members of the advisory board. In 1994, Putin signed an affidavit handing the city's voting rights to Smirnov. The company did little to fulfil its mandate, developing just one office building in St Petersburg and working on one other still not completed. But in May 2000, Liechtenstein prosecutors opened a case against Ritter for money-laundering, linking SPAG to the Cali cocaine cartel. German prosecutors believe the company was also associated with Russian organized crime. Vladimir Kumarin, who has since changed his name to

Barsukov, and whom some Russian media linked to St Petersburg's notorious Tambov crime gang, was a partner of Smirnov, and in Znamenskaya, one of SPAG's subsidiaries. In 1994, Putin granted Smirnov's PTK Petersburg Fuel Company a near monopoly on the city's petrol supplies. In 2000, Smirnov was appointed to the Kremlin's property department, and then became head of Techsnabexport, the foreign sales branch of the ministry of atomic energy.

Other allegations that surfaced in the Russian media suggested that Putin took money abroad illegally; bought a house in the south of France or Spain; obtained an apartment for himself and for his mother in central St Petersburg for almost nothing; and was involved in kickbacks from the city's criminalized port. Putin and his supporters have vigorously denied the charges, suggesting in most cases that they were invented by political opponents, notably during the bitter 1996 election campaign against Sobchak. Vatanyar Yagya, who worked with Putin in the early 1990s, dismisses Marina Salye's 1992 report, calling her a 'quasi-democrat' frustrated at her own lack of power. 'She wanted to be one of Sobchak's deputies, but she never got to power,' he says. Putin even took Alexander Belayev to court in 1996 for libel after allegations that he had bought houses abroad. Today, Belayev says he merely took the materials from published reports, and that he had no concrete information from any independent sources. With Putin's move to more powerful positions in Moscow, any serious inquiries were soon dropped.

In the chaotic post-Soviet St Petersburg of the early 1990s, laws were meaningless, poorly paid government officials were quitting or abusing their functions, social controls were crumbling under the harsh new economic realities, and the old counterbalances were collapsing. It seems almost inevitable that Putin would have had dealings – even unwillingly and unwittingly – with the fast-expanding criminal structures of the time. Whether significant personal enrichment was involved is another matter. 'At the start of the 1990s, you could not do anything without criminals,' says Lev Lurye, a long-time political observer of the city, arguing that there was nothing unusually untoward in Putin's experiences. 'The administration was very uncorrupted,' says Sergei Vasiliev, another member of the young team of economic reformers that emerged at the start of the 1990s in the city before heading to Moscow. 'Sobchak was unwilling to deal with criminal businesses.'

The higher Putin rose in Sobchak's increasingly embattled City

Hall, the more he was drawn into the mud-slinging. In the 1995 federal parliamentary elections, he was the local campaign manager for Our Home is Russia, prime minister Viktor Chernomyrdin's party. He was even more exposed as manager for Sobchak's own re-election race in St Petersburg in 1996 which he called three months early in an attempt to wrong-foot his opponents, mirroring Yeltsin's tactics in 1999. Sobchak symbolized the first wave of disillusion with democratic reform. His personal style antagonized many within the city, and he began to appear as a political threat to Boris Yeltsin, sparking an intense and dirty campaign against him launched from Moscow. Putin's own unsophisticated tactics as a political manager may not have helped. But Sobchak was already substantially weakened by his many enemies, and Vladimir Yakovlev, one of his own deputy governors, rose to the challenge. In standing against him, he dared challenge his former boss. That demonstration of disloyalty 'broke the code of *nomenklatura* ethics', in the words of the journalist Dmitry Travin. Putin would not forgive Yakovlev for his treachery.

If Putin's resignation from the KGB was the decision that he personally considered the most difficult, his resolve to stick with Sobchak after the electoral defeat of 1996 was the one most remarked upon by others. Putin dubbed Yakovlev a 'Judas' during the campaign, and was behind the statement issued by Sobchak's senior staffers that they would not serve under him if he won. 'I would rather be hanged for loyalty than rewarded for treason,' as he put it. After the defeat, Putin was true to his word, rejecting an offer from Yakovlev to remain in his job. He says he was sceptical when Sobchak promised him an ambassadorship, and others claimed that they would hire him. He was left unemployed for three months.

To make things worse, a fire burned down his country house, destroying many possessions. He says one of the few objects to survive was a crucifix given to him by his mother, a symbol of his faith which he wears to this day. It was a story he used to win over George W. Bush when the men first met. Putin says he was secretly baptized, and has maintained his faith ever since. He visited Jerusalem several times, and was blessed by Alexei II, the Russian Orthodox patriarch, immediately after his inauguration as president in 2000. He has also visited the Pope in the Vatican, and indicated that he would welcome an official trip to Russia – which still remains blocked by the Orthodox Church. He even maintains a small chapel next to his office in the Kremlin.

Whatever his true religious beliefs, Putin's loyalty to his friends and backers seems unshakeable. One of Sobchak's own books approvingly reproduces a letter from Putin as head of the Our Home is Russia Party, criticizing prosecutors for abusing their office and carrying out investigations for political ends. With corruption probes and the threat of indictment looming, Sobchak began to suffer heart trouble. Putin flew to St Petersburg to visit him in hospital. Shortly afterwards, Sobchak was bundled aboard a private charter plane brought from Finland. Ostensibly flown out for medical treatment, he was soon safely in exile in Paris. Although Putin himself remains coy about his involvement, even Boris Yeltsin in his memoirs suggests that Putin engineered Sobchak's flight to freedom. It seems just as clear that in 1999 Putin – by then in charge of the security services in Moscow – was instrumental in securing Sobchak's return to Russia, with all charges dropped. Sobchak's hopes of a fresh political career were soon dashed by his death in Kaliningrad. Putin, loyal to the end, shed a rare tear at his funeral in February 2000.

The legacy Putin left behind him in St Petersburg was mixed. His KGB contacts and training helped him in his work, just as did his German language and cultural skills. But his rapid promotions suggest that his calm temperament and fast-developing administrative and managerial skills also played a significant role. As a campaign manager, he clearly failed: Our Home is Russia came third in the 1995 elections in St Petersburg, and Sobchak was not re-elected as mayor in 1996. His role as the implementor of Sobchak's vision of creating St Petersburg as Russia's financial capital also did not succeed. Foreign investment petered out, shifting instead to Moscow – and even to the surrounding Leningrad region, outside the city limits. No major international hotel chain was lured into the city, and smaller, medium-priced hotels to capitalize on the city's enormous tourist potential were chronically slow in developing. Crime remained high throughout the period, with some eye-catching contract killings. There again, Moscow was also laggardly, and had a huge advantage as the capital of Russia and the entire former Soviet empire. It bled St Petersburg of money, population and influence. The former imperial city's failures were all the more obvious because of its historical role. But it fared no worse than many other Russia cities over the past decade, and much better than most. Blame for many of the criticisms that can be levelled at the city's management today must be shared with Yakovlev. It was Putin's principled opposition to the new governor, and above all his loyalty to Sobchak, that stuck out. His new masters in Moscow would deeply appreciate that quality, and put it to good effect at the highest levels of state.

The rise to the top

Anyone wanting to understand Putin's Russia should take a visit to the St Petersburg State Mining Institute. The prestigious Gorny Institute combines service to the state with slick corporate sponsorship, and western-style management training techniques with a distinctive post-Soviet twist. On the tip of Vasilevsky Island, a short walk from its traditional rival, the law faculty, where Putin first studied, it boasts a prestigious history dating back to 1773. There are long corridors with portraits of its successive rectors, with the usual Stalinist peak: there were eight successive heads of the institute during the 1930s, and two in 1937 alone, at the height of the repressions, compared with just eight more in all the seventy years since. The institute seems to have easily reassumed its imperial past. Where most higher education institutions are gradually crumbling today, it sports fresh yellow paint and neoclassical columns at the entrance to its main building, the result of an extensive reconstruction in 1995, during Putin's period in the city. Inside, the recently redecorated offices house New Russian furniture, flat-screen televisions and aquariums.

Different departments and lecture rooms full of the latest technical equipment and computers are sponsored by a range of Russian and foreign companies: Surgutneftegaz for oil research, Gazprom for gas, Alrosa and de Beers for diamonds. Staff and students alike wear blue cadet uniforms, and walk about with a proud military air. It was here that Putin prepared and received his 'Candidate of Economic Science' doctoral degree in the mid-1990s. His decision to pursue higher academic studies, and his choice of economics after law, says something about his priorities – or at least those that he wanted to display publicly. 'His strength is not only politics but economics,' says Vladimir Litvinenko, a large, white-haired man with a deep, booming voice and garrulous style who became rector in 1994. 'Putin was a hard-working, concrete, resolute person. He distinguished himself from other students – perhaps because of his special-services background – by being very careful, scrupulous, but quick to take decisions.'

Litvinenko pulls out a copy of Putin's thesis, long removed from the library for safe-keeping in the cupboard in his own office. The document, signed by Putin and defended on 27 June 1997, is entitled 'Strategic Planning of the Renewal of the Mineral-raw Materials Base of the Region in Conditions of the Formation of the Market Economy (St Petersburg and Leningrad Region)'. With more than a taste of a Soviet central plan reworked for the new era, the text is a rather turgid justification of the infrastructure projects that Putin mulled while working for Sobchak. At least it shows an interest in economic issues and natural resources, which would prove central to his future presidency. There is a little more to be gleaned from an article he published two years later in the institute's journal, called 'Mineral-raw Material Resources in the Growth Strategy of the Russian Economy' – although its 1999 date means it was even less likely than the first to have been penned by Putin himself, as he was already deeply occupied with federal affairs. The author stresses that raw materials are the basis for Russia becoming an economic superpower in the short term, and that there should be tougher state regulation alongside market mechanisms. He says there is a need to create competitive and effective companies, to reduce taxes while increasing the 'rent' levy on natural resources, and to support social stability. He also emphasizes the need to create the conditions for investment, including from foreign companies in appropriate circumstances. The elements are a blueprint for his subsequent economic policy.

The Mining Institute is a reminder not only of Putin's intellectual interests and desire for a certain social status, but also of his continued close connections with St Petersburg after moving to Moscow in 1996. Litvinenko, periodically tipped as a prospective governor or head of an important state company, became the regional chairman of Unity, the pro-Putin political party created in 1999. He ran the St Petersburg office for Putin's presidential election bid in 2000, and for that of Valentina Matvienko, Putin's choice as governor, in 2003. In conversation, Litvinenko, who drives around in a chauffeured black Mercedes, is a vigorous defender of Putin's actions, stressing the importance of the market economy balanced by firmer authority from a more effective, disciplined state. In the two pages of the institute's

1999 recruitment brochure devoted to sporting activities, three of the five photographs show judo matches, as if already paying homage to its most high-profile graduate. Putin has drawn people for his own circle from among the institute's alumni, including Sergei Mironov, who became speaker of the Federation Council, the upper chamber, in 2001.

But it was other members of Putin's tight St Petersburg network who facilitated his arrival in Moscow. Briefly in the wilderness in summer 1996, he received a call from Pavel Borodin, the head of the Kremlin property department, which managed $600bn in state assets. Borodin had no direct links with St Petersburg, but he had met Putin a number of times there over the years in the course of his work. He called Nikolai Yegorov, the head of the presidential administration, who proposed Putin for a job as his deputy. But then Anatoly Chubais, a St Petersburg economist and politician who masterminded Yeltsin's re-election, took over from Yegorov and blocked Putin's nomination, preferring that the new arrival should not have such a high-ranking post. Alexei Kudrin, one of Sobchak's other deputy governors and a long-time friend of Chubais, had also recently been appointed to the Kremlin. As Putin drove back with him to the airport, uncertain of his future, Kudrin called Alexei Bolshakov, a former Sobchak aide and head of the Belarus-Russia Union, who had been named first deputy prime minister. Bolshakov called Borodin who swiftly appointed Putin as his own deputy in charge of legal affairs and the foreign assets owned by the Russian state.

Within a year, Putin became head of the Kremlin's Control Department, responsible for scrutinizing state functions, which he said was so unexciting that he considered quitting public service and starting a private law practice instead. He even prepared a report on mismanagement in Borodin's department, but Yeltsin refused to act on it. It was in this function that Putin was introduced by Chubais to Valentin Yumashev, head of the presidential administration. Yumashev admired his strong character, and brought him to Yeltsin's attention for the first time in 1997. He soon promoted Putin again, making him his first deputy, a job he described while prime minister as the most interesting in his career. His role was to handle relations with Russia's eighty-nine regional governors – without public exposure. It showed him at first hand, in his words, 'how the vertical chain of command had been destroyed and that it had to be restored'. Coupled with his own experience in Sobchak's administration in St Petersburg, his new contacts and knowledge prepared him well for the future. Early in his presidential term, Putin would draw on his experience to tackle the governors head on, sharply diluting their powers and removing some from office. And he would also build bridges to them, working to win their support for the Unity Party in order to push through parliamentary votes.

In summer 1998, Yeltsin asked Putin to return to the FSB. In a pre-electoral interview, perhaps trying to stress his democratic credentials, Putin said that he had no desire to 'step in the same river twice', re-entering an agency full of pressure, tension and secrecy. He spurned Yeltsin's offer of promotion to General, instead becoming the first nominally civilian head of the organization. But his return was natural, given his past experience. Putin, Yeltsin writes, was 'intellectual, democratic, could think in a new way, and was firm in the military manner'. The post also gave him the chance to reassert his influence over the mechanisms of control in Russian society, and allowed him to gather material on his enemies. Just as important, Putin's nomination was an attempt to neutralize the FSB with Yeltsin loyalists against a coming challenge. A few weeks later Yevgeny Primakov was named prime minister. The former foreign minister, Primakov had been chosen as a compromise candidate to run the government, but his old-style views and new-found political ambitions soon began to be seen as a threat to those around Yeltsin. 'The reformers needed an ally in the FSB,' says one member of their group.

In contrast to Putin, then aged just forty-six, who had shown both his loyalty and his liberal credentials, Primakov, who was already sixty-eight, was part of a Cold War generation that was suspicious of business and of all things western. Brought up in the Caucasus, he had long been an agent for the KGB abroad, working under cover as a journalist and specializing in the Middle East, where he cultivated Saddam Hussein in the late 1960s. At the start of the 1990s, Primakov took charge of the Foreign Intelligence Service (SVR), and put his supporters into many key positions. He attempted to impose his SVR spokesman, Yuri Kobaladze, as head of RTR, the second largest state television network, and when that failed, he appointed him instead to run Tass, the state press agency. He consolidated government agencies under his control, promoting his protegé Igor Ivanov as foreign minister, and attempting to subjugate the FSB to his authority.

Yeltsin writes that 'Primakov had too much red in his political palette' and risked winning support as 'a figure who could provoke strong emotions'. Primakov would certainly prove very popular, bringing consensus to the fractious parliament, and acting as a consolidating figure in society.

In public, Primakov said he would offer amnesty to common criminals to make space for those guilty of economic crimes. In private, he hinted at taking 'hostage' a key shareholder in each of Russia's large business groups, in order to bring the others into line. He made little secret of his contempt for the 'Family' or tight circle around Yeltsin, citing the inordinate influence of Valentin Yumashev and Alexander Voloshin, heads of the presidential administration; Tatiana Dyachenko, Yeltsin's daughter; and the wealthy, politically influential business oligarchs led by Roman Abramovich and Boris Berezovsky. These men, beginning with Berezovsky, a fast-talking former academic who openly boasted of using his commercial interests for political purposes, began to come under heavy pressure. Primakov had initially agreed that he would be Yeltsin's prime minister until the presidential elections in 2000 and then step down. But, according to one Kremlin insider: 'He discovered it was not as difficult to manage the country as he had thought. Power pleased him.' Primakov's ambitions rose, and he began to be seen as a serious threat for the presidency itself. Some argue that the very idea of the 'Family' was an artificial construct devised to undermine Yeltsin. But there was little doubt about the existence of a tight influential group around Yeltsin. Their struggle with Primakov became the country's defining political battle at the end of the decade.

Putin received mixed reactions within the FSB to his own leadership. He launched a purge of the old guard, bringing in acquaintances from St Petersburg to take their place. He sharply cut the head-count in the agency, and resisted calls for significant wage increases. If there had been an expectation that their old colleague would restore the agency to its former influence, many were disappointed with the results. Putin did offer some concessions, ensuring that wages were at least paid on time, and rekindling – or at least tolerating – a resurgent 'spy mania'. It was during this period that a series of high-profile espionage cases was launched. Work even began on the prosecution of Oleg Kalugin, Putin's former KGB boss who had fled to the USA, and who was ultimately tried in his absence for violating state secrets.

But no struggle was more important to Putin – or to the Kremlin – than that against Yuri Skuratov. Russia's 'general prosecutor' or chief criminal investigator since 1995, Skuratov had not been known for his successful prosecutions of important crimes. He promised convictions yet delivered few results. But with Primakov installed as prime minister, he opened probes into some extremely sensitive cases. None was more delicate than that surrounding Mabetex. A Swiss-based construction company run by the Yugoslav-born businessmen Behgjet Pacolli, Mabetex had had its first break in Russia in the remote Siberian city of Yakutsk at the start of the 1990s. It worked for the mayor, Pavel Borodin. Pacolli was able to exploit his contacts, winning work in former Soviet republics, including the presidential palace in Astana, the new capital of Kazakhstan. Yeltsin met Borodin in Yakutsk, and invited him to Moscow in 1993, drawing him into his circle. Mabetex came with him. Over the next few years, the company was involved in managing the reconstruction of the Russian government's White House, the buildings of the Duma and the Federation Council, a series of regional presidential residences, and even the refurbishment of the presidential aeroplane. Most striking of all, it renovated the Kremlin itself. The results were a matter of taste: a 'New Russian' kitsch imitation of imperial style, cavernous and sterile. But they were all on a grand scale, lavish in gold leaf and other extravagant materials.

Mabetex even redid the State Audit Chamber, the parliament's financial watchdog. But it was Swiss investigators who unearthed a series of highly incriminating bank transfers and other documents pointing back to Russia. They calculated that of $492m in contracts Mabetex and its affiliate Mercata Trading handled by Borodin's office, it paid out $66m in 'commissions' to top Russian officials, including more than $22m directly to Borodin and his close relatives. There were credit cards in the name of Yeltsin's family, including his daughter Tatiana Dyachenko. By the start of 1999, Skuratov had launched his own investigations into Mabetex. At the same time, he began examining allegations of fraud against Boris Berezovsky at Aeroflot, the national airline. 'We had tons of material before, but the special services did not cooperate,' Skuratov says. He denies that Primakov ordered any such investigation directly. 'He is far too subtle. But he created the atmosphere in which it was possible. He gave his position on the need to fight economic crime and corruption, and on the first day after his confirmation as prime minister he met all the heads of the law enforcement agencies, including me, and promised technical and financial support.' A Primakov confidant says: 'He frightened Dyachenko into sincerely believing that she would go to jail. Primakov didn't start the Mabetex case, but he didn't stop it either. The 'Family' overread the situation. They thought he hadn't used his influence enough to end it.'

Whatever the reality, in the byzantine workings of Russian politics myths play a powerful role, and the perceived threat took hold. The cases began to rattle the 'Family'. Skuratov says that Borodin paid him several visits to try to persuade him to drop his probe. Nikolai Bordyuzha, the head of the presidential administration nominated in November 1998, summoned him to the Kremlin for talks. Others, too, tried to intervene. But none of the private discussions seemed to be working. In March, Borodin got wind of trouble ahead and, in a time-honoured Russian practice, checked into hospital to protect himself from arrest. Skuratov ordered his offices to be raided by investigators. The media was full of the scandal.

Then the counter-attacks began. Skuratov's house was searched. Cooperation from other law enforcement agencies ceased. In the evening of 16 March, ORT, the main Russian state television channel, broadcast a short video of 'a man resembling Yuri Skuratov' cavorting with two prostitutes. Cassettes depicting the scene were soon circulating around Moscow. Some reports suggested that the women had been paid for by criminal bosses that Skuratov was supposed to be investigating. But it was a classic KGB-style entrapment. As different Kremlin officials tried to persuade the Senators in the Federation Council to dismiss the prosecutor, Putin emerged from the shadows. He appeared on national television to claim he had conducted a scientific examination of the video, and there was no doubt that it showed Skuratov. He demanded that the prosecutor quit, arguing that the events had compromised his work. By Putin's own admission, he was deeply involved in the case, attending the decisive meeting in March with Yeltsin and Primakov at which Skuratov agreed to sign his own resignation letter after Yeltsin brandished a copy of the video and photographs printed from it.

Skuratov says he unearthed no evidence linking Putin to the Mabetex scandal. But Putin was aggressive in defending the political masters who had put him in office, as well as Borodin personally, his first employer in Moscow. He may also have had a more personal grudge that helped motivate him to act. Skuratov had systematically pursued Putin's mentor Sobchak after he fell out with Yeltsin and was defeated in St Petersburg in 1996, driving him to flee Russia. With Skuratov out of office, Putin could intervene to arrange Sobchak's return. Skuratov plays down any personal motive in Putin's actions. 'He has the psychology of a person from the special services,' he says. 'His role was my neutralization. While for us the law is God, for him the president is god. The interests of the state come first.'

The Skuratov affair was a key final test for Putin in his rise to power. It showed his determination and loyalty to the 'Family' which was crucial to their endorsement of him. With Skuratov gone, the Mabetex investigations soon lost their momentum. The new team of Russian investigators claimed that the former general prosecutor had not followed basic procedures, and they ceased cooperation with their Swiss counterparts. They rejected photocopies of bank statements showing the flow of funds, arguing that the signatures could not be verified without the originals. The case was formally closed on 8 December 1999, and 19,000 pages of documents locked away into classified archives. But, with foreign investigators also involved, the story did not finish quite so soon. Borodin fiercely rejects the charges against him, and argues today that he was simply caught in a political campaign, while refusing to be drawn on the names of those involved. 'Let God judge,' he says, smiling and raising his hands skywards. He still sits in part of the old Communist Party Central Committee building on Old Square behind the Kremlin, a short walk from his previous office in the same complex. The charges against him were serious enough that, in early 2001, the Swiss managed to have him arrested and brought over from the USA, where he had been attending the inauguration ceremony of George W. Bush. The Russian government launched an official diplomatic complaint, and put up $3m in bail. Borodin agreed to travel back and forth between Switzerland and Russia several times in the following months, but refused otherwise to cooperate. Nevertheless, in early 2002, a Swiss court fined him $175,000 for laundering $22m.

Yeltsin's other challengers did not quit the scene so easily. The parliament was an important conflict zone for the Kremlin. The Communists forged close links with Primakov – notably through his long friendship with Yuri Maslyukov, his deputy prime minister. They pushed ahead with their long-demanded impeachment vote of the president: seeking to lay the blame on Yeltsin for the collapse of the USSR, the subsequent 'economic genocide' of the Russian people and the 'crime' of the first Chechen war. Taming the Communists and creating a more consensual parliament would be an important priority for Putin. The Federation Council – the upper parliamentary chamber dominated by the regional governors – became another focal point in the struggle for power. Although Skuratov had written his own resignation, the Council rejected it five times as the senators asserted their independence from Yeltsin. It was only in April 2000, a month after Putin's election as president, that it finally relented. The upper chambers' tenacity was an object lesson to him. Dilution of its influence became one of his earliest reforms once he was inaugurated as president. Primakov himself was becoming too powerful a figure. In March 1999, Bordyuzha – whom Yeltsin judged overly sympathetic to Primakov – was ousted as head of the presidential administration in favour of Voloshin, an ally and former business partner of Berezovsky. Two months later, Yeltsin dismissed Primakov himself, nominating Sergei Stepashin – another former spymaster – in his place. But Primakov's popularity continued to strengthen. In alliance with Yuri Luzhkov, the mayor of Moscow, he lent support to a political movement among Russia's governors. His government by consensus had won him considerable backing. Even without any government post, he was emerging as a very serious threat to Yeltsin. 'Over the summer, everyone was raising their glasses to Primakov and toasting the future president of Russia,' says one of his friends.

As much of the Russian elite sensed the balance of power tilting away from Yeltsin, they rushed to support Primakov. Sergei Yastrzhembsky, the presidential spokesman, a man tipped as a future foreign minister, joined his team. Stepashin, who had always got on well with Primakov, was also inclining towards him. However much Yeltsin rationalized it afterwards in his memoirs, in mid-1999 it looked as though he was flailing around, increasingly desperately to find someone reliable to assure his succession. For the third time in a year, he would change prime minister.

In his memoirs, Yeltsin claims that he had long had an eye on Putin, ever since he first noticed him in the Kremlin's Control Department in 1997, noting his 'will and resolve'. One insider says Yeltsin had decided on Putin by spring 1999 in the wake of the Skuratov affair, but was loath to appoint him as prime minister immediately. 'With a year to go before the presidential elections, he thought that too many negative things could happen: wage claims, pension crises and so on.' He opted for Stepashin as a first step, but was already thinking beyond him. Putin showed military-style loyalty and honour, respecting those who served him but never tolerating those who crossed him. 'It's very difficult for a westerner to understand Putin's logic,' says Sergei Vasiliev, who first got to know him in St Petersburg. 'He's a military man, a man of honour. He gets very distressed when someone does not fulfil his promises.' Or as Vera Gurevich, his German teacher from School 193, who remains in touch with him to this day, writes: 'I think Volodya is a good person. But he never forgives people who betray him or are mean to him.'

Putin also had other distinguishing characteristics. One was a certain callousness, a Soviet-style domination of the State over the individual. For all the public relations slickness in *First Person*, he does admit in the extended interview to an incident when in his youth he ran over a man in his car. 'It wasn't my fault. He jumped out in front of me or something . . . He was an idiot.' In December 1997, his speeding government car killed a five-year-old boy on the Minsk highway outside Moscow. The driver was not arrested and in 1999 was granted an amnesty. Putin did shed a tear at the funeral of Sobchak in February 2000. But more generally it was his coolness that came to the fore, illustrated by the *Kursk* submarine tragedy six months later. 'What happened?' asked the US TV talk-show host Larry King during Putin's appearance soon afterwards. 'It sank,' came the flippant reply. After journalists met Putin in the wake of a raid by Russian special services on the Chechen hostage-takers in the Moscow theatre siege in late 2002, one participant told me: 'I got the impression he was more interested in killing terrorists than in saving hostages' lives.' It was one aspect of his chilly personality, a characteristic that helped explain why Anatoly Chubais, the former top government official, opposed his nomination as prime minister. While he liked Putin's liberal credentials, he was concerned about how the constant reshuffling of top jobs could be seen as a sign of weakness in the Kremlin. And he was worried about the new candidate's lack of political experience. As he confided to one foreign delegation: 'Putin doesn't know how to smile.'

By mid-1999, Yeltsin was struggling with ill-health, and increasingly nervous about the corruption scandals touching his family and the political threats to his legacy. He began discussing with friends the idea of resigning early. It would be a powerful gesture, the voluntary departure of a Russian leader for the first time in the country's history. It would also give his chosen successor a significant political advantage, catching potential rivals off guard and with little time to prepare a campaign. But to do this, Yeltsin needed someone who would be entirely loyal. He and his supporters sought a successor who could provide assurances that they would be safe under a new regime. They thought they had found their man in Putin. In many ways, Putin would not disappoint. His first gesture as acting president on New Year's Day 2000 was to issue a decree granting Yeltsin immunity from prosecution. Many of the advisers and officials he inherited remained in place well into the new century. But Putin would not simply be a puppet. He brought with him the legacy of his own background, and former colleagues who would ensure that he was not just a tool of the old regime. His circle included both those from his years in the KGB, and a more liberal group of advisers who had worked under Sobchak. Their counterbalancing influence would help define the evolution of Russia during the second post-Soviet decade. Yeltsin wrote in his memoirs that his dauphin had 'an enormous dedication to democracy and market reforms and an unwavering patriotism'. As the future would show, not all three beliefs had equal priority.

PRISONER OF THE CAUCASUS

AS ACTORS IN 1940S AVIATORS' UNIFORMS began the second act of the cult musical *Nord-Ost* with a tap dance, the real combatants moved into action. A minibus drew up at the Theatrical Centre on Dubrovka, close to the heart of Moscow, and within minutes, Chechen fighters in modern camouflage armed with kalashnikovs were on the stage. Women in black with explosives strapped to their bodies filled the aisles. The world's attention had been shifting to Iraq, but the audacious siege on the evening of 23 October 2002 was soon dominating international bulletins and headlines, bringing to Russia a rare and unwelcome spotlight not seen since the *Kursk* submarine tragedy more than two years before.

For the next two days, forty men and women held more than 900 members of the cast and audience hostage, culminating in a storming that left 130 dead. The saga was harrowing for Russians, drawing to national attention the continued tensions in the North Caucasus which most preferred to forget. It was also painful and unsettling for many foreign diplomats. Some of their own citizens were victims of the siege. And the handful of interviews granted by the hostage-takers in the hours following the start of the attack had revealed that their leader was a soft-spoken, inarticulate twenty-four-year-old called Movsar Barayev, whose ruthless uncle Arbi had been linked to a series of brutal kidnappings and murders.

Nord-Ost had just celebrated one year as Russia's first home-grown, western-style musical. It had been a huge commercial success, drawing large crowds from among the country's emerging middle class, keen to witness a symbol of new-found revival after the painful post-Communist period. It made the perfect symbolic target for Chechen rebels frustrated by the agonizing stalemate in their republic. They planned an audacious attack in the heart of the capital that was bound to bring widespread attention to their cause.

October 2002 also marked three years since Vladimir Putin, then prime minister, had authorized a fully fledged military campaign in Chechnya. Like his predecessors in 1994, he had anticipated a 'short, victorious war' over a few months in order to re-establish Russian control in the republic. It was a period that coincided with his electoral campaign for the presidency, and his tough leadership on the issue played a major role in putting him into the Kremlin in spring 2000. But Putin would discover that the Chechen conflict could not be resolved so swiftly and easily by military means. Dubrovka showed that the repercussions were set to overshadow his 2004 re-election campaign and beyond.

To some degree, Putin was a victim of circumstances. Chechnya and Russia have been at war of one sort or another ever since the two cultures first collided three centuries ago, when Peter the Great led an expedition to the region in 1721. As prime minister in 1999, Putin inherited the abnegation of responsibility, or deliberate manipulation, of his predecessors in Moscow; and a state of criminality, radicalism and quasi-anarchy within Chechnya that was beginning to poison the neighbouring republics of Dagestan, Karachayevo-Cherkessia and Ingushetia. He could not ignore the provocative Chechen challenge that he faced, and the potential destabilizing effect on the rest of Russia. More open to question was his own role and that of his backers in provoking the conflict, and the methods they employed to resolve it.

Chechnya is in many ways a unique and extreme case in Russia's recent history. But it is also symptomatic of the attitudes and approaches of the country's leaders, officials and citizens, highlighting the dangerous undercurrents of the society today. It will continue to be an important policy issue in the future, and it remains a significant factor in the international perception of Russia, influencing foreign affairs. It is inextricably linked to Putin's own rule, making it impossible to ignore in any assessment of his period in power. However much he might like to portray himself as the architect of the resolution of the problem of Chechnya, he risks becoming its prisoner.

A vicious legacy

Akhmed Zakayev bitterly recalls the way 23 February was celebrated each year when he was at school. Across the Soviet Union, the girls in the class gave the boys presents to commemorate Soviet Army day – the date in 1918 when the Bolsheviks called on workers to defend St Petersburg from the White Army. It was only when Zakayev went home in the evening that his father would tell him the other more tragic and personal events that had overshadowed the same date for his family – and those of all his classmates – just a few years before. In the space of a few weeks at the start of 1944, preparations had been made for the complete liquidation of the Chechen-Ingush republic in accordance with Stalin's orders. By the early morning of 23 February, when the operation began, some 100,000 troops and 12,000 train carriages had been assembled for the rapid, mass deportation of the entire republic. By the end of the month, all 500,000 residents had been transported away. Many would perish in transit. Most of the survivors ended up in Kazakhstan, where Zakayev and his peers were born.

The early Khrushchev years following Stalin's death in 1953 brought a temporary political thaw across the USSR, but it came with considerable limitations. The Chechens were allowed to return home after 1956, but they faced opposition from local party functionaries, as well as very practical barriers from ethnic Russians, Cossacks and the occupants of the surrounding regions who had taken over their homes. There was little sign of open revolt, but a dangerous absence of any attempts to resolve the tensions created. For the following thirty years, the Soviet system – with its tight control over individuals, organizations and the media – allowed almost no public discussion of the repressions. 'My generation didn't learn its own history in school,' says Zakayev, an actor who would be enrolled into the anti-Russian resistance in 1996 shortly after his nomination as the Chechen republic's minister of culture.

Under Boris Yeltsin, 23 February was renamed Defenders of the Fatherland Day. But it remains largely an excuse for a holiday. Most of those who reflect on its historical significance at all cling to the positive memories and nostalgia of Soviet Army Day. There is little discussion of the mass deportation of Chechens, just as the Stalinist repressions in general are a subject most Russians prefer to forget. Vladimir Putin himself first made reference to the events in a televised statement as late as March 2003, as the Kremlin poured resources into making a success of the referendum on a new firmly pro-Russian constitution. Keen to strike a conciliatory tone alongside promises of a bright future if Chechens voted in favour, he referred to 'the tragedy of the Stalinist deportations . . . [and] the hardships of the forced resettlement'.

Chechens and Russians have clashed viciously almost ever since their contacts began at the start of the eighteenth century. Muslims from the mystical Sufi tradition, the Chechens had a reputation as ruthless fighters and were demonized by Russian soldiers, who showed equal harshness in response. General Alexei Ermolov wrote in 1818 that he would 'find no peace as long as a single Chechen remained alive'. Today, their aggressive image remains, and it is no mere stereotype. They are often the ringleaders in the widespread 'hazing' or violent bullying and intimidation of military conscripts. The long involvement of some Chechens in organized crime in Russian cities has not helped their reputation. The result today is that disturbingly many Russians in ordinary conversation will mutter that 'a good Chechen is a dead Chechen', tacitly endorsing Putin's tough approach and even genocide.

The thirty years after the Chechen return from mass deportation represented one of the longest periods of peace and coexistence with Russia. But Chechens and their traditions continued to suffer in many ways even during the late Soviet period. 'Russians told us off in the street and said, "Speak a human language," if I talked in Chechen,' says Zakayev. Jabrail Gakayev, a Chechen historian, remembers how students were evicted from classrooms if they wore the traditional *platok* or headscarf. Islam was suppressed. Chechens were discriminated against in higher education, comprising a far smaller proportion of those passing through the local institutes and universities than even their counterparts in the neighbouring ethnic republics. Now a highly regarded specialist at the Russian Academy of Sciences, Gakayev was able to rise through the system only because he emerged as one of its brightest stars: the recipient of a Lenin stipend, the holder of a 'red' diploma, and the best among a group of doctoral students. Most important, he avoided courting political controversy, opting during Soviet times to specialize in less sensitive pre-revolutionary history – and certainly nothing related to Chechnya.

Chechens tended to be more rural and less integrated into Soviet society than Russians and other ethnic groups. They received little positive encouragement and plenty of discrimination to maintain the status quo. They describe waiting lists of twenty to thirty years to receive an apartment in the regional towns and cities, while Russians received priority. Jobs in industry were difficult to find – and those Chechens lucky enough to get them tended to be given the more menial tasks. Gakayev says that of the 40,000 people employed in the local oil refining sector just 1,500 were Chechen, for example. The same applied in politics. In many Soviet republics, there was a local ethnic representative as nominally the highest official in the region, while the real decisions were made by a 'Second Secretary' firmly under Moscow's control. But it was only in 1989 – well into Mikhail Gorbachev's term in office – that Doku Zavgayev became the republic's first Chechen First Party Secretary. His subsequent lobbying led to the selection of the Chechen Ruslan Khasbulatov as First Deputy and then Speaker of the Russian parliament; and Jokhar Dudayev as the first Chechen general in the army.

The late Soviet period may have represented a time relatively free of open conflict with Russia, but it gave the Chechens little scope to liberate themselves physically and psychologically from their long period of repression, let alone to develop a modern political culture. As the USSR crumbled, they found themselves dragged straight from totalitarianism into near-anarchy. They were torn between a dissolving federal system and an incoherent local one; between an unpredictable national president in the form of Boris Yeltsin and an equally erratic Dudayev, who came to power as a political neophyte. They were captives of a Soviet Union preoccupied with its own collapse and a Chechnya ill-prepared for its self-declared independence. Yeltsin may have become a national and international hero in 1991 as a defender of democracy against the putschists, but his shelling of the Russian parliament in 1993 would be a precursor to the bloody battle in Chechnya in the following year.

Yeltsin's policy of 'divide and rule' may have kept Russia together when many feared it would fall apart. He famously allowed regional leaders to 'take as much autonomy as you can swallow'. That gave them substantial freedom to determine economic and social policies and even develop contacts with foreign countries while still adhering to the Russian Federation. But Dudayev choked on the amount of liberty he grabbed. Long absent from the republic, he had served in Estonia in the late 1980s, absorbing the rising nationalist, anti-Russian sentiment that would prove explosive on his return to Chechnya. He brought to power his own people from the mountain regions in the south of the republic – poorer, more traditional and rural in outlook, less Russified or educated. He released an estimated 16,000 criminals from prison. More concerned with grand gestures than with the practicalities of day-to-day administration, he allowed the territory to deteriorate into a series of warring fiefdoms.

Chaos reigned during the first period of uneasy peace up till 1994. Chechnya was not recognized as an independent state abroad, but it was also largely ignored – or exploited – by a Russia struggling to re-establish its own coherence after the collapse of the Soviet empire. Goods arrived duty-free from other countries, then crossed into the rest of Russia without any border checks. The republic became a centre for drugs production and trafficking, oil theft and illegal refining, counterfeiting, diamond smuggling and contraband alcohol. It was the focal point for the 'false avisos' scam, by which the Central Bank paid out large sums in response to fraudulent transfer documents, allowing an estimated Rbs 270bn to be siphoned out of the system – to the benefit not only of Chechens but many Russian collaborators too. Dudayev's defiance of Russia's authority, and Yeltsin's inability to compromise, gradually escalated. Moscow first supplied arms to anti-Dudayev forces and was drawn ever deeper into the conflict until it was engaged in full-scale war by summer 1994.

Ethnic Russians living in Chechnya had already found themselves abandoned by the federal state, becoming scapegoats targeted by the local population and ignored by Dudayev's regime. Without institutional support or the traditional clan protection of the Chechens, they became significant – if not disproportionate – victims. They lost their jobs. Some were beaten, robbed or killed, while others were evicted from their apartments at gunpoint, or forced to sell them at knock-down prices. Many fled in the early 1990s. During the war, they also suffered heavily as the victims of intense, indiscriminate military action, if only because their higher status in Soviet times meant they often had apartments in the centre of the battle-torn capital Grozny – and nowhere else to seek shelter. Their numbers fell sharply over the decade. Just as important, much of Chechnya's intellectual class was killed, or fled elsewhere in Russia, abandoning the weak and powerless in the republic to the strengthening grip of militants, criminal groups and radicals.

The contrast with neighbouring Ingushetia is striking. The Ingush are ethnically extremely close to the Chechens. Merged into a single autonomous republic in 1936, they suffered the same persecutions and deportations. Yet the parallel nationalistic feelings which emerged in the late 1980s were channelled more constructively. More moderate leaders held the reins of power, and when Ruslan Aushev became president of Ingushetia in 1993, he inherited and developed a very different strategy. Like Dudayev, Aushev was a Soviet army officer and Afghan veteran. But he had already gained political experience in the regional assembly, and his ability to steer a more balanced course through the post-Soviet landscape was significantly greater. Aushev provided a valuable buffer to Chechnya, welcoming refugees who fled the conflict across the border and frequently acting as a political intermediary. He was not popular with the Kremlin, and his regime was marked by cronyism and extravagance, including the elaborate gold-domed palace he built for himself as the centrepiece of his plan to recreate the ancient Ingush city of Magas. But he had no desire for his people to follow the same course as the Chechens, and his skill in avoiding that outcome is his enduring legacy. 'Leadership made a difference,' says Akhmar Zavgayev, Doku's brother and a Duma member. By contrast, he argues that Dudayev's own circle was so criminalized that even if the Chechen leader had attempted to make peace with Moscow and bring order to the republic, those around him would have prevented or killed him.

If Yeltsin and Dudayev share the blame for their headstrong styles at the political level, ordinary Chechens and Russians alike would suffer the consequences. The disastrous first Chechen war during 1994–6 led, at a conservative estimate, to 50,000 deaths. The bloodshed would trigger repeated calls led by Russia's Communist Party for Yeltsin's impeachment. The military campaign – partly employing the intensive bombardment tactics that Dudayev himself had used in Afghanistan on behalf of Soviet forces a few years before – poisoned public opinion. The Russian media was still in a golden period of freedom: aggressive, indignant and independent. Its role in criticizing the war – and in raising the political pressure as Yeltsin's re-election drew close in summer 1996 – was fundamental in bringing hostilities to a halt. Keen to be rid of the burden of Chechnya, the Kremlin agreed to a ceasefire, leading to the Khasavyurt peace agreement in August 1996. It called for an end to armed conflict, a political solution and economic reconstruction. Dudayev's assassination by Russian forces paved the way to presidential elections won by Aslan Maskhadov, the Chechen military leader, in January 1997. The vote was endorsed by Russia as a member of the Organization for Security and Cooperation in Europe, which observed the ballot and declared it fair. But Khasavyurt deferred a final agreement on Chechnya's relations with Russia for a further five years, endorsing in the meantime the continuation of a quasi-independent state. Any belief that the agreement would lead to lasting peace or stability was short-lived.

Hostages to fortune

The assignment was risky, but very short. Peter Kennedy's temporary employer seemed well prepared, and the money was useful as he saved to buy an apartment for his daughter. A specialist in satellite technology and a long-time employee of British Telecom, he agreed in 1998 to a brief secondment in Chechnya with Granger Telecom. The UK company frequently worked in difficult environments, and it had signed a $300m contract to install communications equipment. It arranged with its local client, Chechen Telecom, to provide a twenty-four-strong bodyguard. Kennedy joined up with three Granger staff – the Britons Darren Hickey and Rudolf Petschi, and the New Zealand-born Stanley Shaw.

But on 3 October, a band of twenty armed men came to their compound in Grozny. Despite the proximity of the Chechen authorities' own anti-hostage task force, the men managed to overpower the four guards on duty at the time and seized the Granger team. Over the next two months, the British authorities applied pressure on the Chechen government, which launched a fruitless search. The men were held in captivity, regularly beaten and left half-starved. They were subject to ransom demands totalling millions of dollars, and forced to watch videos of other prisoners being beheaded. At first it looked as though a solution could be found. Robert Jarvis, a Granger director, said later that he was hopeful they could be released in time for Christmas that year. Instead, on 8 December, the severed heads of the four men were discovered in sacks by a road not far from Grozny.

The British Foreign Office, like its US and other counterparts, had long warned its citizens not to travel to Chechnya. Its officials had very concrete reasons to justify their concerns. Only the month before the Granger kidnapping, Camilla Carr and Jon James, two British aid workers, had been released after more than a year of barbaric captivity. James had been regularly beaten and humiliated; Carr was repeatedly raped over several weeks by one of her captors. British diplomats themselves were categorically banned from travelling to the republic and the surrounding region, and when the bodies of the Granger employees were found, they had to arrange for the remains to be shipped across the border to Azerbaijan before they could take personal charge and supervise the repatriation of the mutilated corpses. It was no surprise that they had been keen to debrief Granger's employees so that they could gather rare first-hand information on the situation in the republic. Now that avenue was definitively closed.

The saga was a chilling reminder of how lawless Chechnya had become in the late 1990s. It would be distorted to concentrate on foreign captives, who represented a very small proportion of the total number of victims. A few dozen aid workers, journalists, missionaries, scientists and businessmen from abroad were taken prisoner. But well over 1,000 hostages were held in Chechnya during 1997–9. Some were used as slaves; others ransomed. Some were killed, the murders periodically filmed on videotape to be distributed as a warning, or to raise funds from radical Islamic organizations. Others were beaten, or had fingers chopped off and sent to relatives to encourage them to pay up. During the two-month search for the Granger employees in late 1998, the authorities claimed to have discovered and freed another sixty people held captive. Most victims of kidnapping were Russian citizens. The biggest proportion came from Chechnya itself or the surrounding republics such as Dagestan. The ransom business began to seriously destabilize the region, imposing huge human and economic costs. The Granger saga indicated how even the taboo in Russia of touching westerners – few of whom had fallen victim to serious crime in post-Communist Russia – had been breached.

Kidnapping is nothing new in the Caucasus. Culturally, the region has long practised bride-snatching as part of the wedding ceremony, albeit in a custom usually prearranged with the respective families if not always the wife-to-be herself. Some aspects of supposed hostage-taking can also be misinterpreted. The academic Jabrail Gakayev argues that many Russians 'released' in recent years were in fact tramps created by the post-Soviet turmoil, and taken in to work by Chechens in exchange for board and lodging. He stresses that Russian forces in the nineteenth century took Chechens hostage as part of their own strategy of intimidation of the local population. In its modern guise, the practice established during the 1994–6 war by Russian federal forces of releasing a captured Chechen in exchange for every two of their own soldiers had the perverse effect of encouraging more kidnapping of Russian soldiers as a human commodity to swap.

The conditions in Chechnya were not simply criminal. As in similar conflicts elsewhere – from Northern Ireland to Corsica and Algeria – there were links between politicians, security forces and criminal groups. Shamil Basayev, one of the most ruthlessly effective rebel leaders during the 1994–6 war against Russia, had previously fought on Moscow's side during incursions in Abkhazia, the breakaway region in Georgia. There are some indications that the local representatives of the FSB security police had considerable influence over regional Chechen warlords including both Arbi Barayev, the man accused of masterminding the Granger kidnapping, and his frequent accomplices the Akhmadov brothers. Like so many potential witnesses, Barayev cannot confirm his version of the story: he was killed, apparently during a struggle with Russian troops in summer 2001. According to some reports, he was captured, interrogated and then executed by the GRU, Russian military intelligence, a traditional rival of the FSB which also had strong links in the region.

Zakayev argues that the Russian special services were determined to undermine Maskhadov's regime from its very beginning in 1997, and that kidnapping was one of their tools, alongside criminality and the encouragement of religious extremism. 'After the first war, the army left and another war began,' he says. 'The FSB had operated a system of fear for seventy years. All this machinery was left in place. Humanitarian organizations had to be pushed out first to starve the population and isolate us from the rest of the world. Then journalists would follow, so that no one would see.'

There is no doubt that many in Russia's 'security ministries' felt angry and frustrated at the peace negotiated with the Chechens in 1996, and believed that they should have been allowed to continue the war to its end. Whether such people would match their words with deeds – or whether there was any direct control from Moscow if so – is more open to debate. But as one official closely monitoring Chechnya on the ground at the time puts it: 'There was at least the potential for some elements in the FSB to be playing dirty tricks in destabilizing the society. It was not necessarily a coherent policy, but there is a great deal of informal, personal contact by individuals and groups. The Chechens could move around in Russian society, they were integrated in the old Soviet system. It would be surprising if there was not contact with the FSB, the army, the interior ministry. There were material financial interests in prolonging instability, or in provoking the return of Russian forces.'

Whatever the cause, the uncontrolled growth of kidnapping highlighted the weakness of Maskhadov as president. A respected military commander, he proved a cautious leader, ill-equipped to address Dudayev's chaotic legacy, and unwilling or unable to take on the republic's feuding warlords. Ransoms provided an important source of income, and if Maskhadov was immune from the temptation, he was impotent to bring the practice to an end. According to Russian official claims, members of his own government were directly involved. His vice-president in 1997, Vakha Arsanov, a former field commander, allegedly received money for the release of Zavgayev's education minister, though he denies it. Nurdi Bazhiyev, the deputy interior minister, reportedly took money for the release of Russian television journalists from the ORT and NTV channels. Magomed Koriyev, head of the organized crime department, supposedly killed hostages. Those of Maskhadov's ministers who stood out against criminality paid the price. General Shaid Bargishev, the head of the Chechen government's own anti-kidnapping unit, was killed in a car bomb in late October 1998.

'Maskhadov was not elected on his merits; it was a choice between peace and war,' says Abdul-Khakim Saltygov, Putin's former human rights representative for Chechnya. With the warlord Shamil Basayev the main alternative candidate in the 1997 presidential vote,

Maskhadov seemed a far more attractive option, he says. He won an overwhelming victory with 59 per cent, but he faced considerable resistance from his opponents. If the test of democracy is how far the losers are willing to accept the result, then new-found Chechen democracy was weak indeed. Maskhadov began by attempting to co-opt and work with his former rivals for the presidency, bringing Basayev and Movladi Udugov, an advocate of Islamic radicalism, into his cabinet. But the coalitions were doomed to failure. Local warlords ignored or threatened Maskhadov's authority, and criticized his attempts to make peace with Russia. 'Chechens understood that there would be a second war, and decided it was necessary to keep united and to try to avoid civil war,' says Zakayev. 'But I don't idealize Maskhadov. We are paying today for his actions.'

During his period in office, Maskhadov also proved unable to prevent the spread of Wahhabism, a radical form of Islamic fundamentalism supported by financial contributions from the Middle East, which served a multitude of purposes in Chechnya. It provided legitimacy to rebels such as Khattab (the *nom de guerre* of Habib Abd al-Rahman), a Saudi Arabian who had previously fought in Afghanistan. The theoretical teachings of the Koran as propagated by Wahhabism certainly did nothing to limit practices such as kidnapping by self-proclaimed protagonists like Barayev senior. Chechnya provided fertile ground for proselytism, offering the prospect of some degree of meaning – as well as arms and money – to the lives of its adherents at a time when the federal and local administrations alike did so little for them. Maskhadov not only failed to clamp down on its excesses but entered into an alliance with Wahhabite dogma, going as far as nominally declaring *Sharia* (Islamic religious law) in the republic.

But in many ways, Maskhadov's options were few. He inherited a territory in ruins. Billions of dollars of damage had been inflicted during the first war, above all in Grozny, which in large part still resembles little more than piles of rubble after constant bombardment and intense, repeated ground combat. 'No country could come together after such destruction,' says Aushev. 'There was no economy, no cooperation with other governments, no advisers around Maskhadov, the risk of extremism, and pensions to the police had not been paid in two years.' When I first visited in 2001, Grozny reminded me of the pictures of Stalingrad after the devastating battle with the Germans during the Second World War. Driving through the city today, it is hard to distinguish the effects of the different periods of destruction. Much of the devastation after the second Chechen war remains a legacy of the first. Little had been – or has been – rebuilt. Water, sewerage, electricity and gas infrastructures have collapsed. Few buildings are fully intact: most still standing have holes in the roof and walls caused by missiles and bullets. Flying out at night by helicopter (because the mined roads were too treacherous to use), the view of bright lights below at first gave the impression of normality. Only when I looked more closely did I realize that I was seeing naked flames burning, where residents without electricity had pierced gas pipes and set the leaks alight.

In theory, the terms of the peace treaty in 1996 provided the basis for post-war reconstruction. But neither side kept its pledges. The Chechens promised but failed to return hostages and prisoners of war, and to disarm their militias. As Anatoly Kulikov, then interior minister, complained to the Russian parliament in October 1996, just two months after the signature, 'the Khasavyurt agreements are not just violated, they are harshly crushed at every corner'. There was no serious discussion of the political status of Chechnya, a question which was deferred with a final decision due to be taken in 2001. In Russia's chaotic political life at the time, that was an eternity which provided an excuse to procrastinate and forget. 'No one wanted to speak about Chechnya in Moscow,' says a senior official from the Council of Europe, the intergovernmental human rights organization based in Strasbourg. 'We didn't see any serious interest. We had worked with Tatarstan and Bashkortostan –' referring to two other ethnic Muslim republics which negotiated additional autonomy from Moscow in the mid-1990s without any of the same bloodshed, – 'but never with Chechnya. The Russians intentionally left it alone. They said, "We have five years with Khasavyurt, so goodbye."'

Zakayev and Ivan Rybkin, head of Russia's Security Council at the time, met in accordance with the Khasavyurt agreement in 1997 to draw up plans for the reconstruction of Chechnya. They came up with the extraordinary figure of $275bn to replace the devastated infrastructure. But very little money was ever released. Much that was, ended up stolen – often even before it left the Russian capital. Pensions and salaries went unpaid, including those of the local police. That demoralized officials, debased law enforcement still further, and exposed the inhabitants of Chechnya to ever more desperate conditions. Moscow held talks over paying a regular transit fee for the oil transported from Azerbaijan by a pipeline through part of Chechnya. But the money never materialized. The Chechens, who promised safety for the pipeline, never managed to control oil theft. Moscow instead set to work building a new pipeline route that bypassed the republic entirely, isolating it still further.

By abdicating its responsibilities, Russia further undermined Maskhadov. With him went the best chance of finding a candidate who was acceptable to Chechens and – given his Soviet army upbringing and culture – with whom it might be possible to find a common purpose. By 1998 Russia was also going through an economic crisis, which undermined its ability to subsidise any republic, least of all stigmatised, anarchic Chechnya. Politically, much of the commitment at the time of the 1996 elections had already faded away. Key policymakers lost interest. 'Our biggest error was that we bowed to the propaganda that said the Chechens won the war. There was no victory,' says Zakayev. Psychologically, too, many Russians were traumatized by the humiliation of the ceasefire in Chechnya, disgusted by the loss of blood and content simply to wash their hands of responsibility for the republic. 'Both sides were to blame,' says Rybkin. 'But in any fight, the stronger and the wiser is the more guilty.'

Nor did Chechnya ever receive any meaningful international recognition which might have prevented its further deterioration. Maskhadov went on a number of foreign trips to drum up support and investment, including visits to the USA and the UK. But they were fruitless, as officials stressed that Chechnya was part of the Russian Federation, and warned that the security climate made the likelihood of investment scant. Most countries did little even to apply pressure on Russia to improve the situation. One of the few regimes which recognized 'Ichkeria' – the name the Chechens gave to their republic – was the Taliban in Afghanistan. They, too, might have been less likely to take an extreme direction and forge a pact with Osama bin Laden had the international community helped them more. Maskhadov was ultimately left as Hamid Karzai of Afghanistan was to be after the war in 2001 which installed him: nominally controlling the country, but with scarcely the money, military support or legitimacy to run his own capital city. And he did not have the backing of Russia, let alone the USA.

The Chechen connection?

On 7 August 1999, a band of several thousand armed men marked the warlord Khattab's birthday in a dramatic way. Led by Shamil Basayev, they crossed the mountainous border from Chechnya into the neighbouring republic of Dagestan to the east. They seized villages in the Tsumadin and Botlikh districts, and dug in. Three days later, they held an Islamic *shura* (council), where they declared Dagestan's secession from Russia. The rebels would not succeed in staying long, but their presence provided a trigger for the second war with Chechnya. Their removal marked the first decisive steps taken by Vladimir Putin as Russia's new prime minister, indelibly linking Chechnya to his political fortunes, the forthcoming parliamentary and presidential campaigns, and his entire period in power.

If anti-Chechen sentiments were strong in much of Russia, there was also a sense that many would prefer simply to forget the bitter experience of the first war three years before and turn their backs on the North Caucasus. But that would soon change. Early on the morning of 9 September, a powerful blast exploded in the cellar of an apartment block in the suburbs of Moscow. The building, put together haphazardly from prefabricated concrete slabs, collapsed one floor onto the next, crushing ninety-four people in their sleep. A week later, on 13 September, an identical blast cut through the middle of another residential block not far away, killing another 124 people. I rushed to the scene, where disbelieving relatives gaped at the ruins. The central section of the eight-storey block had disappeared into a messy pile of rubble, leaving an almost surgically sliced hole between the two wings of the complex. 'We had saved up money so my daughter could buy an apartment here. That's her,' said Sergei tearfully, pointing to rubble being pulled away as rescuers searched for bodies.

Yuri Luzhkov, the mayor of Moscow, was swift to cite a 'Chechen trail' behind the blasts. Putin himself was measured, stressing during a session of parliament on 14 September that there was a Chechen connection, but also the need to distinguish ordinary Chechens from terrorists, and to argue that there was no justification for annihilating the Chechen people. But the signal had been sent. The supposed collective culprits had been identified; and the mood across Russia became more frightened and aggressive. In a spirit of communal solidarity, neighbourhood committees swiftly formed. Volunteers in

Moscow and other cities patrolled the streets and passageways around their homes by day and night, in search of anything suspicious. Attacks on and intimidation of Chechens by the police intensified around the country. By the end of September, Russian shelling had driven Basayev's band out of Dagestan and troops had followed him back into Chechnya. How much further the army would go was still unclear, but the second Chechen war had begun.

In the volatile political climate of the period, conspiracy theories soon emerged suggesting that it was the Russian authorities rather than the Chechens who were behind the attacks. The aim was to create a populist wave of support for Putin that would sweep him into office. In retrospect, it is easy to construct a cynical, bloody trail connecting Dagestan and the Moscow blasts to Putin's meteoric ascendancy. His hardline approach to Chechnya undoubtedly raised his profile, turning what looked like another short-lived hapless Yeltsin nominee into an unchallengeable presidential successor within a few weeks. But does that mean Putin – or those who backed him – were responsible for manipulating the events for their own gain? There has been no shortage of material in the Russian and western media – and by critics of the current regime such as Boris Berezovsky – to suggest so. There is some circumstantial evidence. And the classic question 'Who benefits?' can certainly be asked. But the answer is not clear-cut.

The strongest suspicions come from events at Ryazan, a city east of Moscow. On the evening of 22 September, a local man spotted a car with its number plate disguised, whose occupants were unloading sacks. He called the police, who on arrival found the sacks along with detonators in the basement of an apartment building. Initial analysis by local experts suggested that they contained hexagon, a scarce and powerful explosive used in the Moscow blasts. There were reports afterwards of intercepted telephone calls to the FSB headquarters. When the news leaked out, public statements by officials – including Vladimir Rushailo, the interior minister, and Putin himself – suggested a thwarted terrorist attack. But two days later, with the sacks safely transferred to the FSB's headquarters in Moscow, and signs that suspects were shortly to be arrested, the FSB switched its version. It claimed instead that Ryazan was a 'training exercise' in public vigilance and that the 'explosives' were really sugar. The inconsistencies suggested that in fact the FSB had been caught red-handed preparing a new bombing, implying that it had been behind the previous ones. FSB connections to the Dubrovka siege three years later would again raise allegations of their shadowy involvement.

Defenders of the FSB–Kremlin conspiracy often contrast it with the alternative, official version of a Chechen plot. They argue that it would have been strange for the Chechen leadership to launch a provocative campaign of bombings against ordinary Russians so far from their republic, in a way that seemed only likely to provoke an aggressive response just as they were trying to argue instead for greater independence. It was curious that the blasts should stop as soon as war got under way, rather than accelerate in retaliation to the military action. It also seemed unusual that Basayev and Khattab, never shy of claiming responsibility for such acts in the past, should remain quiet and later deny all involvement. They can point to the swift removal of rubble from the blown-up apartments, leaving little time for detailed examination, as well as the fact that all subsequent trials of alleged culprits have taken place in secret, allowing for no public scrutiny of the evidence. Nor has there been any independent investigation of the Ryazan incident. The Russian parliament refused to launch an official inquiry, and the former dissident Sergei Kovalev, who began his own informal investigation, received scant cooperation from the authorities.

The Dagestan invasion leaves just as many questions unanswered. Members of the Maskhadov administration say they repeatedly warned Moscow of a likely attack. The radical calls by Basayev and others for the creation of a secessionist Chechen-Dagestan Islamic state were no secret. A number of Russian officials also say there was intelligence on the manoeuvre for several months before it took place. Sergei Stepashin, Putin's predecessor as prime minister, claimed that a military operation against Chechnya had been in preparation since spring 1999. Turpal-Ali Atgeriyev, Maskhadov's vice-premier at the time, claims to have personally telephoned Putin to warn of the imminent invasion, but the tip-offs and subsequent offers by Maskhadov to help with operations in Dagestan after the invasion went unanswered. When Maskhadov sent an emissary to Moscow to meet Putin, the Kremlin stonewalled, and he was instead briefly arrested. Instead of being reinforced, the thinly spread local border guards appear to have been withdrawn from key access points shortly ahead of the raid. And Basayev was able to slip back into Chechnya with few casualties when he decided to retreat, despite intense Russian federal troop ground and aerial presence by that time.

Some reports claim links with Boris Berezovsky, a key kingmaker for Putin, and Alexander Voloshin, his long-time business partner who had become head of the presidential administration. Allegedly intercepted phone calls between Basayev and Berezovsky published shortly afterwards suggested that the two men had jointly planned the incursion into Dagestan. Once he had fled into exile, Berezovsky was even directly accused by the Russian prosecutor's office of authorizing the transfer of funds to Chechens, including at least $2m directly to Basayev. *Le Monde* suggested that Basayev had met Voloshin in the south of France. Within the Russian political elite, talk of a Chechen 'provocation' had been discussed since the spring, and Berezovsky told people that he believed a crisis was the best way to establish a new political leadership in the country. It all seemed to suggest that the Kremlin had engineered the invasion as a pretext for launching a fresh war in retaliation, giving Putin the chance to shine as the victor ahead of elections.

But the conspiracy theories also have their limitations. If the Kremlin, or some hardliners, deliberately engineered Basayev's invasion of Dagestan, they were taking considerable risks. They could have destabilized the whole region, triggering a far more difficult challenge to which federal troops would then have had to respond – and creating precisely the conditions for the wide-ranging radical Muslim insurgency within Russia that many claimed to fear. If the special services were involved in the apartment blasts, there was a danger that information would leak out and be swiftly exploited by the competing clans then vying for power, notably around Primakov. It is possible – albeit difficult to believe – that Ryazan was a training exercise, accompanied by a subsequent cover-up. Or that the security services, as often happens in Russia, wanted to plant materials so that they could then claim a counter-terrorist 'success', boosting their own budget, reputation and power in the process.

If justifying a war against Chechnya was the primary tactical objective, the ultimate outcome was far from clear. In retrospect, the conflict boosted Putin's popularity and created a groundswell of support for his election victory. But in mid-September, Primakov was leading in the polls to be future president, with 19 per cent in one FOM (Public Opinion Foundation) survey compared with just 2 per

cent for Putin. The pro-Putin Unity party would only start to gain significant support just ahead of the December elections. With fighting
already three months under way and the risk of a high loss of life,
there could already have been a backlash against Putin by December,
let alone by the time of presidential elections some months later.

If the consequence of the conflict had been a state of emergency –
with the aim of postponing the elections in Russia as Yeltsin hardliners
had already unsuccessfully sought in 1996 – then Putin's ratings might
have dropped still further as the conflict ran its course. All of his
advantage as incumbent and the first to declare could have been
dissipated as a result. The Kremlin elite remembered the political
catastrophe of the previous war all too well, and how it had very nearly
cost Yeltsin the presidential elections in 1996. One very senior official
from the period says they were panicked by the lack of preparation by
troops on the Dagestan border. 'If the FSB did blow up apartments, it
was not to make Putin president. War was an enormous threat to the
elections.' He dismisses as bravado Stepashin's claims that military
operations were long planned. 'Two weeks before the invasion,
Stepashin went to Dagestan and said everything was calm. He was
ineffective. Nothing was prepared for the attack. We were not ready.
Putin could lose, people didn't want to fight, and the polls were
against war.' If there was a plot from the top, its instigators were dangerously confident of their own abilities to carry it through.

Most of the information on conspiracies has come from Russian
media reports and political declarations, which have to be viewed
with some scepticism. If confirming any fact in Russia is difficult
enough, with Chechnya – where first-hand information is rare and
manipulations are widespread – it is exponentially harder. Both
Berezovsky and Voloshin have vehemently denied that any meetings
to plot the Dagestan invasion took place in France. Berezovsky argues
that his transfer of funds to Basayev was an approved Russian government transaction at the time the latter was part of Maskhadov's
administration. The decision by Russia's prosecutors to open an
inquiry against him proves little apart from political expediency. Why
else was the case not opened long before – or expanded to include a
broader range of officials supposedly concerned? Regarding the
Moscow blasts, one friend of Berezovsky's describes how the tycoon
was recovering from hepatitis in hospital when he was informed, and
appeared genuinely shocked. Another Kremlin official from the period

relates how they spoke afterwards and Berezovsky expressed his worries that the war risked jeopardizing Putin's campaign chances.

The multiple allegations surfaced during a period of intense political activity and uncertainty in the build-up to Russia's parliamentary elections in December 1999. A fierce battle was taking place between the pro-Putin Unity party and the Fatherland-All Russia movement of Luzhkov and Primakov. The Berezovsky phone intercepts were published in *Moskovsky Komsomolets*, a newspaper closely linked to Luzhkov. They may well have been supplied – or doctored – by Alexander Korzhakov, Boris Yeltsin's former chief bodyguard who became extremely influential before being ousted after the 1996 elections. General Alexander Lebed, who had negotiated the Khasavyurt peace accords, hinted at Kremlin conspiracy in the apartment blasts in an interview in the French newspaper *Le Figaro* before later retracting his words. But he too had become a rival of Yeltsin and a possible candidate. 'If there was a plot, the information would have leaked out and been used by Yeltsin's enemies,' says Yegor Gaidar, Russia's former deputy prime minister and an economist with continued strong links to the administration. Instead, as for those who argue that the Chechens were behind the blasts, there was little support beyond speculation, circumstantial evidence and anonymous sources.

The fact that Berezovsky himself has raked up the idea of an FSB plot since late 2000 is also curious if he is implicated. After he left for exile abroad, he initially claimed to me that he had no information on any such links, and would start an investigation simply using the Internet. While desperate to destabilize Putin's regime, and with more knowledge of Kremlin intrigues than almost anyone else, Berezovksy has since failed to produce any significant proof. He has merely repackaged reports originally published in Russian media such as *Novaya Gazeta*, notably concerning the Ryazan 'training' exercise. He has claimed alternately that the FSB and its rival the GRU were responsible. There is no doubt that he had close contacts with Chechen leaders, including Basayev. But if he himself was involved in any plot, his denunciations are part of an extremely dangerous double game, drawing attention to himself and inviting others to investigate his role. And if he was not directly involved, but has access to others who were, it seems surprising that he has not drawn on their information. It is at least as plausible that he is seeking merely to maximize his visibility as a critic of Putin, in the process capitalizing on his attacks to the point that he was able to qualify for political asylum in the UK in autumn 2003.

If Maskhadov and the Chechen leadership were not behind the Dagestani invasion and the apartment blasts, it may well be that radical Wahhabis linked to Basayev and Khattab were. Many converts from the North Caucasus had been drawn to Dagestan in the mid-1990s, and forged links with the Chechen rebel leaders after meeting hostility from the less puritanical Dagestani Muslims. In 1997, Wahhabis even signed a 'military mutual assistance treaty' with Salman Raduyev, another Chechen leader. In April 1999, Basayev assembled troops for the creation of an independent Islamic state. Wahhabis – both ethnic Russians and some foreigners – took advantage of the anarchy within Chechnya to attend Khattab's training camps, where some may have learned terrorist skills, including the use of explosives. Such fighters probably only represented a very small proportion of the total Chechen force which would confront Russian troops in the months ahead. And they were too easily used as a scapegoat for the prolonged conflict. But their presence and financial support did illustrate an 'international terrorist' link of sorts.

The Moscow apartment blasts – whilst the most dramatic incidents of the period – cannot be taken in isolation. They were part of a broader pattern of explosions, whose timing dovetails with the intensifying clashes between Russian troops and the Wahhabis in Dagestan during August and September. On 4 September, five days before the first attack in the Russian capital, more than fifty-eight people died when a military servicemen's apartment block was blown up in Buinaksk in Dagestan. On 16 September, three days after the second Moscow blast, seventeen died in an identical attack in Volgodonsk. The modus operandi was the same, but after the Moscow blasts, was there the need for additional provocation if the motive was purely to whip up anti-Chechen sentiment? The nature and location of the attacks suggest a link with the Dagestan conflict. The absence of any claims of responsibility, and the nihilist approach of gratuitous attacks on civilians, hint more at Al Qaeda extremist-style tactics.

Robert Bruce Ware, an American academic specializing in Dagestan, argues that Wahhabis are the most likely culprits. He cites Basayev himself, rarely unwilling to take responsibility for terrorist attacks, who said in an interview with the Czech journalist Petra Prokhazkova on 9 September 1999: 'The latest blast in Moscow is not our work, but the work of the Dagestanis. Russia has been openly terrorizing Dagestan . . . And blasts and bombs – this will go on, of course, because those whose loved ones, whose women and children are being killed for nothing will also try to use force to eliminate their adversaries . . . Each action generates a reaction.' And a week later, Khattab, who was himself married to a woman from Karamakhi, one of the Dagestani villages under Russian bombardment, told Associated Press: 'From now on, we will not only fight against Russian fighter jets [and] tanks. From now on, they will get our bombs everywhere. Let Russia await our explosions blasting through their cities.' He would later deny any involvement in the Moscow blasts.

Ware also points to parallels with a blast in 2002 in the Dagestani town of Kaspisk, and an abortive attempt two years earlier in Victory Square in Makhachkala, the capital. If it had exploded, it would have killed hundreds of bystanders. It would have been so unpopular that it was unlikely to have been planned by local political rivals; and killing loyal pro-Moscow officials would have no interest to the Moscow establishment. That suggests instead that the Wahhabis, sowing more general chaos in the republic against their enemies, were the most likely culprits.

The official Russian investigation has equally focused on Wahhabis. Detectives point to the creation of a terrorist cell in the town of Uchkeken in Karachayevo-Cherkessia, an ethnic republic west of Chechnya. Young radicals recruited by Achemez Gochiyaev – who has never been caught – were allegedly trained in Khattab's camps in Avtury and Shatoye in Chechnya, and then sent to engineer all four explosions, as well as others planned in Moscow, St Petersburg and beyond. Four men were convicted in March 2001 for the blast in Buinaksk, and another five at the end of that same year for planned attacks during 2000.

Ironically, this version is embarrassing for the Kremlin, and contradicts both the initial official explanations and the very justification for a second war. All of the suspects were from Karachayevo-Cherkessia and none from Chechnya itself. Many of the Wahhabis who invaded Dagestan were also not Chechen. Chechnya, riven by anarchy, served principally as a convenient launching pad for military action, a training site for radicals, and a possible hiding place afterwards for some of the masterminds, such as Gochiyaev. Most ordinary Chechens hated the Wahhabis as outsiders who brought terror and a form of religious extremism far from their own traditional Sufism. That suggests there could have been ways for the Kremlin to cooperate with Maskhadov and other moderate Chechens to drive them out.

What this explanation does not rule out, however, is possible manipulation by – or at least a common interest with – Russian hard-liners. That could simply be at the level of local operatives of the FSB or GRU. But it is clear that a significant part of the leadership of the Russian military and security establishment was keen for revenge in Chechnya, a desire to 'finish the job' they had begun. With blatant insubordination to their political bosses, for example, both Konstantin Pulikovsky and Gennady Troshev, commanders of the combined federal forces in Chechnya during the first and second wars respectively, write scathingly in their memoirs about their former colleague and subsequent commander, Alexander Lebed, and his Khasavyurt peace agreement in 1996. Many senior officers believed that they were close to winning the war in 1996 and were irritated that a ceasefire had been called. They also had personal motives for returning to the field of battle for revenge. Generals Pulikovsky, Shpak and Sergeyev all lost sons in the first war. Many others saw close comrades injured or killed.

If Dagestan and the apartment blasts provided the pretext, prepara-tions for a new conflict had been under way since the moment of Russia's withdrawal in 1996. Michael Orr, a military analyst, argues that many of the lessons of the first war were directly behind the restruc-turing of the armed forces which took place from 1997: military districts were modified to make them more coordinated and opera-tional, for example. Anatoly Kvashnin, the chief of the general staff, ran exercises involving all the relevant ministries to simulate 'local war'. In July 1998, he conducted an exercise in the North Caucasus designed to respond to hypothetical 'bandit' attacks and terrorist actions. It was Kvashnin who helped coordinate a new military doctrine for Russia which stressed the growing importance of mobile units to fight con-ventional conflicts on the country's southern borders. He would ultimately win out in a struggle for resources and influence against Marshal Igor Sergeyev, the defence minister, a 'Cold Warrior' more focused on the continued threat of war against the west and a defender of the nuclear Strategic Rocket Forces. Sergeyev was ousted by Putin in 2001, while Kvashnin retained his position.

Stepashin later claimed that an invasion of Chechnya had been prepared from March 1999. Yet people who met him at the time said he was then opposed to military action. As a former head of the FSB, he had closely followed the first Chechen war, and seemed to have no appetite for a repetition. 'He was actually open-minded, and genuinely wanted to seek a solution,' says a diplomat who met him at the time. 'He had experience of the disastrous 1994–6 campaign, and my impression was he had learned something from it. Russia had to look for another approach. People were sick and tired of the whole thing. They didn't want to lose more lives.' His boast of preparations for military action while he was head of the government may have represented his attempts – shortly after he was fired by Yeltsin – to suggest that he too was a tough leader. But as Zakayev argues: 'Stepashin knew about war in Chechnya. He was ready to resolve the conflict, so he was fired.'

Stepashin was not alone in seeking alternatives to a new conflict. General Kulikov, the former head of the Russian armed forces and interior minister, had a reputation as a hawk. But in summer 1998, during a presentation in the USA, he argued strongly that 'a renewed attempt to solve the Chechen problem through military force is out of the question'. Instead, he stressed the more dove-ish line of the need for Moscow to participate in the reconstruction of Chechnya, while ensuring that the funds reached their intended beneficiaries. He called for the involvement of the Chechen diaspora, and spoke of the need to restore faith in Russian institutions.

How far Putin personally shared the desire for an assault on Chechnya is unclear. In early 2000, he claimed that he only decided to invade the republic after the apartment blasts. The foreign diplomat who met Putin in April 1999, when he was in charge of the Security Council, says: 'He was very preoccupied with the security situation, partly because of militant Islam, and the use of Chechnya by narcotics dealers, smugglers and producers. His main objective, if not launching a military offensive, was at least containment.' Half a year earlier, in August 1998, Rybkin from the Security Council says he held extensive talks with Putin on the subject. 'He talked about a peaceful resolution, and the need for economic reconstruction,' he says. Putin's subsequent wholehearted pursuit of conflict suggests either that he was disingenuous in previously arguing for a peaceful resolution, or that he was too weak to prevent the army and the hawks in the administration from imposing their will. Or, most likely, that he changed his views as he saw the situation evolving.

The idea of a cordon sanitaire around Chechnya had long been discussed by policy-makers. By securing the northern part of the republic above the Terek river – flatter, easier to patrol and traditionally more pro-Russian – they believed that they could create a 'demonstration zone', showing to the Chechens in the south the attraction of Moscow's rule. When, by late autumn 1999, Russian troops arrived at the Terek, many argued that they should stop there. Berezovsky says: 'Russians believed that they had won, and the Chechens that they had lost.' That would have been the ideal point to broker negotiations. There was certainly much hostility among Chechens to the Maskhadov regime at the time – including many who fled the fighting to seek shelter in Ingushetia. It might have been sufficient to bring about popular endorsement of a return to Russian rule.

But others who were involved question how realistic such an idea could be. Yevgeny Primakov, Stepashin's predecessor as prime minister, says that a 'liberated zone' was seriously discussed. But he believed that to work, it needed the perimeter of Chechnya to be sealed, in order to cut off rebel supplies. While Russia arranged to close its internal borders, he says the whole plan was finally rendered impossible when Eduard Shevardnadze, the president of Georgia on Chechnya's southern flank, reneged on plans for joint operations. The army would instead get its way, as it pushed south of the Terek to reach and then go beyond the boundary which had been set three years before.

A long and dirty war

Roza Akayeva earns a third of the salary of her colleagues in a Moscow chocolate factory, but she considers herself fortunate. She managed to flee Grozny in October 1999 before the fighting began, and she found shelter and employment far from the conflict. Her brother was less lucky. In mid-January 2000, with Russian troops already occupying the Staropromyslovsky district of the city, Adlan Akayev was brutally tortured and killed. When Akayeva heard the news, she travelled for the burial to the Chechen village of Voznesenkoye, where his corpse had been taken by friends. The left side of his face was bruised; his collar-bone was broken; and seven bullets had passed through his body. The large exit holes on his front showed that he had been repeatedly shot from behind. Akayev was forty-five, and his pockets contained all the signs of his professional status: his passport, a driving licence and an identity card showing his job as head of the physics department of the Grozny Teaching Institute.

She also found a letter that he had written to her in November 1999. 'He wrote how he had tried to leave Grozny four times but that all men younger than sixty were considered rebel fighters and were not allowed to leave,' she told me. 'He tried to give the letter to others attempting to get out, but without success.' Akayeva travelled on to Grozny, where she found her brother's hat in his courtyard, and cartridges lying around. She has no doubt that he was summarily executed by Russian troops. Opposite, in a neighbour's house, she found signs of another massacre: five bodies dumped in a pit in the garage. Later, in Ingushetia, she met a sixth person who had survived. 'She told me that soldiers came and when one woman cried out, "We are Russians," they fired, there were lots of ricochets, and the brains of one man were left splattered on the wall. One of the soldiers said, "What have you done? She's Russian," but the other said, "What's done is done."'

'This war was worse than the previous one for its cruelty, and the local people didn't expect that,' says Akayeva, whose house was destroyed during the first conflict. 'I can't say that life was good under Maskhadov. I didn't like his regime. I would like to go back to the Soviet period. No one in our family supported the rebels. They were like a sect, like zombies. I knew lots of people who had sons who went to the Wahhabis for support, and who then said, "We have invested hundreds of dollars in your children, you will have to pay to have them back." My brother was once hit with a rifle butt in the street after he refused pressure to give good marks to one pupil. Adlan was always a principled person.'

Akayeva is typical of generations of educated Chechens who had every desire to remain part of Russia – citizens on whom the federal authorities firmly turned their backs. 'Our friends were Russian. We grew up together. I am very grateful for Russian education. It deeply changed my way of thinking,' she says. But her persistent efforts to bring her brother's killers to justice went nowhere. Military prosecutors gave contradictory responses as to whether they had even opened a formal investigation. Despite her testimony, no one came to study her brother's letter, his bullet-ridden sweater, or other vital clues. No effort was made to find eyewitnesses to the massacres in Staropromyslovsky. After she filed a complaint to the European Court of Human Rights, the Russian authorities offered her compensation in exchange for dropping the case, but she refused. 'I'm someone who has lost everything. There are things I value more than money. I'm offended that my brother, an honourable man and a patriot of his country, was killed. It's important that this case – which is only one of thousands – is heard. I can survive hunger, cold and bombing, but not injustice.'

Her story was not isolated. In November 1999, Russian forces attempting to encircle Grozny found themselves locked in combat with Chechen rebels near the town of Alkhan-Yurt, seven miles to the south of the capital. A delegation of elders visited rebel commanders in an attempt to persuade them to leave. They were brushed away, on threat of being shot. They tried to persuade the Russian commanders to cease the intensive shelling, also to no avail. The civilian population was caught in vicious clashes between federal forces and rebels – their number supplemented by foreign fighters pledged to a jihad – who dug in among the locals, triggering a long struggle for control of the territory and attacks which killed at least eight civilians.

If innocent casualties in such circumstances were all but inevitable, the reign of terror described by eyewitnesses once Russian troops finally entered the town on 1 December certainly was not. Over two weeks, according to evidence gathered by Human Rights Watch, they threw hand grenades into the cellars where people were sheltering, insulted and humiliated people, sought women to rape, looted houses and set them on fire. Residents were told to go to the nearby village of Kulary, but were shelled and shot at as they went. When they returned, they discovered the bodies of friends and relatives who had been killed after torture: there were people with eyes missing, half the nails cut off their fingers and burns on their hands. Local commanders refused to allow rapid burial in accordance with Islamic tradition, and ignored calls to stop the pillaging. At least fourteen civilians were killed during the period. The corpse of one woman, Nabitst Kornukayeva, aged more than 100, lay riddled by machine-gun bullets in her backyard, along with that of her sixty-five-year-old son, Arbi. Ibrahim Hankurnanov, wounded by shrapnel, was run over twice by an armoured personnel carrier. Aindi Altimirov was found beheaded in a field.

Nikolai Koshman, then Russian deputy prime minister with responsibility for Chechnya, and Malik Saidulayev, an influential Chechen businessman from Alkhan-Yurt based in Moscow and with close links to the authorities, were shocked by what they saw during a visit to the town on 17 December. They gathered first-hand accounts of the events and pledged a swift inquiry. Locals had other materials – from photos and videotapes to details of car registration plates used by the military – all of which could have provided the basis for prosecutors' cases. But the promises of an investigation came to nothing. The Russian authorities denied any abuses, or suggested that they had been perpetrated by Chechen rebels. Major-General Vladimir Shamanov, the senior commander based in the region during the period, allegedly insulted Chechens who pleaded with him to curtail the atrocities at the time, and harshly criticized journalists who attempted to probe the incident. Like those under his command, he was never reprimanded. Instead, he was awarded the Hero of Russia medal at the end of the same month, and has since been elected governor of the Ulyanovsk region.

Alkhan-Yurt was only the first of a number of such incidents during the Chechen war. It was followed by reports of similar large-scale abuses in Staropromyslovsky, Aldi and other districts. While many of the reported human rights violations and war crimes were committed by Russian forces, Chechens also perpetrated crimes. Their partisan tactics did not help. The rebels mixed with the local population, which often supported them more or less enthusiastically. By taking up positions in houses, hospitals and schools, they turned civilian objects into military targets, increasing the prospect of the deaths of non-participants and the destruction of local infrastructure and property. On a visit to Grozny in 2001, I heard local human rights activists complaining about a recent incident in which an armoured personnel carrier had sprayed bullets into a residential courtyard just behind their own office. But they then admitted that it had been in response to sniper fire aimed at the Russian troops – themselves young, inexperienced and nervous – from inside.

In pure military terms, the first phase of the second Chechen war was considerably more effective from the Russian viewpoint than the first war had been. In a few months, the army had reasserted nominal physical control over most of the territory. Setbacks such as the repeated seizures of and withdrawals from Grozny in the previous conflict were far less frequent. There was tighter coordination and intensive, specialist training provided to troops in anticipation of a new war, greater delegation to local commanders, and more time allocated for rest by front-line troops. Mirroring NATO tactics in Yugoslavia, greater emphasis was placed on surveillance and the use of overwhelming firepower in order to minimize direct confrontation and Russian casualties. Bislan Gantemirov, a Chechen imprisoned after the first war for embezzlement, was released and allowed to form his own militia to fight in Grozny, pitting Chechen against Chechen.

Just as important, by late 1999 Russia had already won the propaganda war. In 1994–6, the media had played an enormous role in inflaming public opinion against Russian military intervention. Journalists travelled freely across the front lines, showing the devastation and deaths caused by a war which many had seen as unnecessary. In the second war, there were no such parallels. The Dagestan invasion and the apartment blasts had helped turn a mood of exhaustion with Chechnya into hostility. In just a few months between summer and winter 1999, the mood in the federal parliament switched from keenness to impeach Boris Yeltsin for the crime of the first Chechen war to near-unanimous calls for a second. Journalists themselves, witnesses to and sometimes victims of the crime and kidnapping of the interwar years, were less personally sympathetic to the Chechen cause. Most were attached to Russian military units, and adopted their jargon: they were fighting a 'counter-terrorist operation' rather than a war, and the army was involved in 'special operations', 'working' rather than bombing territory.

Journalists were also more concerned about the physical dangers that they ran in travelling about the republic. Communication with rebel leaders became more difficult, making access rare even for those who wanted to portray the other side of the story. The Russian authorities introduced tough restrictions on reporting, with a system of accreditation and tight control on access, even while insisting that there was no war nor any need for a state of emergency which might have legally justified such measures. When necessary, pressure was applied by the regulators – such as the press ministry, which threatened action against media that interviewed rebel leaders including Maskhadov. In a reflection of NATO's military briefings during Kosovo, the government in December 1999 created Rosinformcentre, the Russian information centre, which held regular press conferences, controlled the distribution of military data including casualties, and – selectively – circulated articles about the conflict. It was rapidly renamed Disinformcentre by its many critics.

Putin himself set the tone – and sent a warning to others – with his involvement in one of the most extraordinary cases of journalistic pressure in Russia in recent years. Andrei Babitsky was a reporter for Radio Liberty, the US-financed radio station, and among the few who witnessed the conflict from the Chechen as well as the Russian side, sending video material for broadcast in Moscow which contradicted the official version of events. Arrested within the republic in December 1999 by pro-Moscow Chechens, he was taken to the notorious Russian pre-trial detention centre of Chernokozovo, where he was beaten and humiliated alongside many Chechens suspected of being fighters. In a highly contrived deal, he was handed over to Chechen rebel leaders, supposedly at his own request, in early February 2000 in exchange for three Russian servicemen. Video material shot of the exchange showed a tired and clearly unenthusiastic Babitsky being led to his new captors.

Putin was extremely well informed about the case. Before Babitsky's own colleagues were aware of whether he was alive or not after the exchange, Putin told three Russian journalists who interviewed him about a video showing the correspondent. He made it clear that he had no time for Babitsky, arguing that he was a 'traitor' who had 'fought on the side of the enemy' by producing allegedly pro-rebel pieces. Putin said Babitsky should 'behave according to the laws of his own country if he wants those same laws to be applied to him'. In line with similar phrases from senior Russian military and political figures, he added that he would have been ready to exchange him for 'just one Russian soldier'. It later emerged that the whole handover was manufactured, that no soldiers had been released, and that the rebel leaders were in fact Chechens controlled by pro-Russian forces. Babitsky was probably saved by the widespread media attention that the case caused. The Russians spent much of the time during his captivity attempting to find charges to justify his detention. They came up with vagabondage and 'theft' of a fragment of burnt wood from an icon, evaluated at Rbs 10. He had taken it during his most recent trip as a souvenir from the rubble of the church in Grozny where he had got married, and which had since been destroyed by Russian shelling.

While the second war may have employed better military tactics, a serious long-term strategy was absent. In place of the young, inexperienced conscript soldiers of the first war whose bereaved mothers helped stir public opinion against the fighting, *kontraktniki* or paid contract fighters did much of the work after 1999. Hardened soldiers, they fought principally for money, and many had been psychologically damaged by the previous war. It was they who perpetrated many of the human rights violations which took place. The military used intensive firepower, and such controversial weapons as fuel-air explosives, which created a partial vacuum above the ground, causing horrendous deaths for those in the vicinity of the attacks. Such techniques helped reduce military casualties, while creating greater devastation and civilian deaths. They did much to damage any residual goodwill among Chechens for Russian forces, even though many had already been disillusioned by Dudayev's and Maskhadov's rule.

One of the most important lessons from the Soviet occupation of Afghanistan – Russia's 'Vietnam' – went unheeded: it is impossible to win a partisan war. There was scant sign of any attempt to win the 'hearts and minds' of the local population. Instead, the army poisoned relations with a future generation of Chechens. Frustrated by their inability to bring the conflict to an end, Russia's leaders were quick to suggest they were fighting 'international terrorism'. Implausibly, just after the 9/11 attacks, the security services went as far as to claim to have found in Chechnya a map with Arabic notes showing the Twin Towers of the World Trade Center encircled, and a CD of how to fly a commercial airline. But while foreign fighters and money were undoubtedly present in the republic, the logic of the Chechen conflict was essentially rooted in local grievances.

Such a partisan war was not purely the army's fault. The Russian leadership long resisted shifting the conflict in Chechnya away from military control. Even with repeated insistence from the authorities that the FSB had taken charge, the influence of the armed forces remained strongly in evidence. Some 80,000 troops were still based in the republic in late 2003, long after the 'military stage' was supposed to have ended. At the time of a referendum on a new constitution in March 2003, a controversial decision was made that soldiers 'permanently' stationed in the republic could vote. That figure alone amounted to around 30,000. Chechnya had become the military's *raison d'être.* The fighting justified its existence and continued funding. Chechnya was the testing ground for the military doctrine around which the military chief of staff, Kvashnin, had built his latter-day career: a belief in the need to redirect resources away from preparations for a Cold War-style battle in mainland Europe, and towards the threats posed by attacks along Russia's southern borders, requiring small, mobile units to fight conventional wars.

Just as important as any official ideology, Chechnya had become a huge generator of income and vested interests. It absorbed large amounts of federal funding, providing supplementary salaries and resources for the purchase of weapons and logistical supplies alike. It built careers, giving rapid promotions to those who had served there. But it also became a giant illegal source of revenue. Many of the Chechen oilfields or their revenues appeared to be controlled more or less directly by the military hierarchy. At lower levels, illicit sales of weapons and equipment were rampant. Checkpoints provided a source for racketeering from all who passed, and a place where people could be arrested and kidnapped for ransom. Locals were forced to pay in order to learn who was on lists of those to be detained, to remove them from the lists, and to find those who had 'disappeared' and liberate them – or to recover their corpses. From the Chechen side, too, war became an economic end in itself. Given the high rate of unemployment and physical destruction, involvement in criminal activities was one of the few ways of earning money. And there is some evidence that attacks against Russian soldiers, laying mines and other rebel actions were paid for.

Through fear, incompetence or complicity, the Russian establishment failed to investigate and hold the army to account for the violations that occurred. By the start of 2003, the authorities said just fifty-seven cases had been brought to court by military prosecutors. They did not provide the names or further details of those tried, raising questions about whether justice was done, let alone seen to be done. The Council of Europe was given little attention by Russian officials on its fact-finding missions, the Organization of Security and Cooperation in Europe was unable to re-establish the presence it had during and after the first war, and other international organizations such as Human Rights Watch and even the United Nations special rapporteurs on torture and extrajudicial executions were repeatedly refused access to the republic.

No example of the impunity of the army is more unsettling than the case of Colonel Yuri Budanov, almost the sole significant case to be brought to open trial. On 27 March 2000, he entered a house in the Chechen village of Tangi-Chu and seized a teenager, Kheda Kungaeva. He took her back to his tent, beat and strangled her. According to an initial military report, he also raped her. That charge was later dropped, after one of his staff claimed instead to have mutilated her afterwards. Budanov was put on trial three times, and subjected to five different psychiatric examinations. I travelled to Rostov to see one part of the hearings in 2002. Budanov, with his cropped hair, sat inside a cage in the courtroom, sometimes deliberately ignoring the pleadings by reading a magazine, at others openly insulting Kungaeva's family. Outside, there were demonstrations calling for his acquittal. Everyone seemed to detest Chechens and believe Budanov should be released. Sergei Ivanov, the defence minister, set the tone with comments in the *Izvestiya* newspaper, where he expressed 'sympathy' for the colonel, whom he called 'a victim of circumstances and inadequate legislation'. It was only after the case became a cause célèbre that Budanov was finally condemned in July 2003. It had long seemed that even one scapegoat would be judged unacceptable by the authorities.

If Budanov's crime was atrocious enough at the time of a fully fledged war, even more unsettling were the ruthless torture, killings and disappearances during the uneasy peace that followed. During spring 2003, the pro-Moscow Chechen administration itself confirmed that there were forty-seven graves containing one or more victims discovered across the republic; and 1,500 'disappearances' during the second war – compared with 1,000 during the first. A year later, it doubled these estimates. Many initially occurred during *zachistki* or 'mop-up' operations, when Chechens were arrested in security sweeps by soldiers. As pressure from human rights activists increased, leading to regulations demanding that village elders and local prosecutors be present during such raids, the tactics switched. Small, completely unregulated night-time operations began instead. There were even gruesome instances of destroying the traces of torture through blowing up corpses of those kidnapped and killed. By early 2003, disappearances were running at three a day, according to Human Rights Watch, higher than at any period during the war. The organization dubbed the conflict a 'dirty war', comparing it to the Latin American conflicts of the 1960s and 1970s.

Not all human rights crimes were perpetrated by Russian forces. With access to researchers restricted, and Chechens afraid to talk about violations committed by their own side, it is difficult to gather evidence. But it is clear that members of the pro-Moscow administration were frequent targets of threats and assassinations by rebel forces. Others fell victim to ordinary criminals. The Kremlin gradually pursued a policy of 'Chechenization', appointing the former rebel leader and mufti Akhmed Kadyrov as head of a pro-Moscow administration in 2000 and delegating increasing power to him and his team. The more influence he had, the more his officials became drawn into the front line as targets of attack – and the more they were accused of abuses against others.

Eyewitness reports typically describe raids by men in masks and uniforms with machine guns, speaking unaccented Russian and often with armoured personnel carriers or other clearly identifiable vehicles outside. That suggested the extensive involvement of Russian forces. In a striking example, a mass grave was found by the village of Dachny in early 2001. It contained fifty-one bodies, including a number of men last seen in the custody of Russian federal forces. Many had their hands tied and bore signs of torture, including scalping. Given its location a mere half-mile from the main military base in Chechnya of Khankala, heavily guarded with checkpoints all around, it seems hard to explain how it could have been other than the work of Russian troops. As one anonymous and unrepentant Russian officer quoted in *Izvestiya* claimed in spring 2003, 20 per cent of the 'disappearances' were the work of rebels, 30 per cent of criminals, and half perpetrated by Russian forces.

Russian attempts to track down Chechen criminals and rebel leaders for trial were of limited success, though their capture and long-term interrogation could have proved useful for investigators. The Russian military claimed responsibility for the death of one key field commander, Khattab, whom it said was killed in the field as the result of a 'special operation'. A video later released showed his body, and supported suggestions that he had been poisoned. By whom was unclear, since his body was never found. Despite frequent claims by the Russian military that it had killed rebel leaders, it only managed to capture one person of much significance and put him on trial: Salman Raduyev. Within months of his conviction, he was found dead in the cell of his high-security prison in central Russia in December 2002, supposedly from internal injuries, aged thirty-five.

Even on the rare occasions when justice was seen to be done, the result was unjust.

An inconclusive peace

He said it would take a bullet to stop him from running in Chechnya's presidential race. In the event, a simple call from the Kremlin was enough to persuade Aslambek Aslakhanov to withdraw his candidature. With Russia firmly claiming that Chechnya was again part of the Russian federation, Putin wanted to finalize his conception of a political resolution to the conflict. He put his weight behind regional elections on 5 October 2003, but he forgot one thing: the need to give the impression of democracy. A process that seemed constructed to win endorsement by the west ended up being run in a very eastern way.

Akhmed Kadyrov, the gruff, bearded head of the pro-Russian administration named by Putin, was determined to win. Ruslan Khasbulatov, the former speaker of the Russian parliament and an outspoken advocate of talks with Chechen rebels, first announced that he would run against him, but then pulled out before filing his registration papers. In the following weeks, a dozen people officially put their names forward. But the handful with any serious chance soon started to have second thoughts. Husein Dzhabrailov backed out without clear explanations. Then Aslakhanov, a former interior ministry official who had proved unexpectedly popular as Chechnya's representative to the federal parliament since 2000 and who had called for negotiations with Maskhadov, changed his mind after discussions with the Kremlin. That left one person who was scoring well in the polls, and represented a challenge to Putin's choice.

I met Malik Saidulayev in his office in central Moscow, the well-guarded headquarters of the lottery and industrial empire that he had built up over the previous decade. He was tough, successful and reputed to be supported by the FSB – the sort of businessman who you would rather have as a partner than as a rival. Photos on the wall showing him with leading Russian political figures left little doubts of his contacts, and of his interest in power. He had long given money to Chechnya through a charitable trust, and had tried to act as an intermediary to bring the conflict to an end. With local polls suggesting that he would easily beat Kadyrov – and some possible prompting by the Kremlin – he decided to run. A few campaign trips started to make him feel less easy, however. He told me how he and his bodyguards had been surrounded by machine-gun-toting supporters of Kadyrov. There had been intimidation of his supporters. And he related how a professional hitman had even come to his Moscow office with an order to kill him, but had instead decided to confess all, realizing that he himself would be likely to be eliminated afterwards. Saidulayev said that he received calls from Vladislav Surkov, one of Putin's key political advisers in the Kremlin, asking him to stand down. He refused to do so. It was then that the Chechen electoral commission stepped in, with the Kadyrov-sympathetic Grozny court striking him out on the alleged grounds that many of the signatures of local people supporting his candidature had been forged.

'From that moment on, the elections – which were a farce – turned into a veritable theatre of the absurd,' said Tatiana Lokshina, the director of the Moscow Helsinki Group, a human rights organization which called for the elections to be boycotted. Despite laws that theoretically prevented political leaders from favouring one candidate over others, Putin made no secret of his preferred choice. At a time when he ought to have been campaigning on the ground just one week ahead of the vote, Kadyrov accompanied Putin in his delegation to the general assembly of the United Nations in New York. State television prominently showed the two men talking at length on the flight home. It also broadcast images of Kadyrov holding statesman-like meetings with top administration officials. The 'people's choice' had already been decided, Soviet-style. During his three years as the appointed leader, Kadyrov had firmly made his mark, naming his own people to key posts. That started with his bodyguards, drawn from his own village, who even looked like him. But on successive trips to Grozny, I found *kadyrovtsi* everywhere, from top government officials to ordinary drivers. The 'administrative resources' of his position allowed him to use public employees to his advantage, with police, officials and local election commission staff clearly in his favour. Just to make sure of his success, he put in an ally to head the press ministry. The Grozny court was used to rule on another aspect of Russia's curious electoral laws, which prevented the media from providing 'biased' coverage of campaigns. The result was to fine two local newspapers which took an anti-Kadyrov line.

With his last serious rivals, as well as any pretence of freedom of speech, removed, Kadyrov won more than 80 per cent of the vote – as far as the figures could be believed. While the date had been fixed months in advance, Russia only invited western election observers a few weeks ahead of voting, far too little notice for them to offer advice or mount a serious monitoring mission even if they had wanted to. They opted out, led by the Organization of Security and Cooperation in Europe and the Council of Europe, which diplomatically argued that the security concerns in the republic were too great for them to take the risk; and that the Chechen elections were only regional, not federal, so outside their remit. Instead, it was organizations rather less well known for their own democratic traditions – the Arab League, the Organization of the Islamic Conference, and the Commonwealth of Independent States – that acted as observers, and pronounced the process fair.

On paper, the Chechen election looked like the culmination of initiatives designed to move towards a peaceful solution. There had been a new constitution approved by a referendum in spring 2003, an amnesty for former fighters who laid down their weapons, and the withdrawal of federal troops and military checkpoints. There were delegation of greater powers to the local authorities, funding for economic and social reconstruction, and the prospect of parliamentary elections in the near future. The reality looked very different. There were certainly some signs of physical improvement since my first trip to Chechnya in 2001. By 2003, Grozny was still heavily battle-scarred, but some other villages and towns appeared in better shape. Agriculture was being revived, there were cars in the streets, people on the pavements, goods for sale on ramshackle stalls. Economic activity was under way, and local residents did their best to get by in the appalling conditions.

But with a partisan war still ongoing, with daily clashes and widespread disappearances poisoning Chechens' lives, the very idea of elections seemed inappropriate. The selection of Kadyrov was particularly provocative. None of the candidates were ideal, and Kadyrov at least had muscle as well as newly acquired administrative experience. But to attempt to legitimize him in questionable elections was premature and artificial. While he denied it, many accused Kadyrov of being a warlord himself, with substantial commercial interests. His son Ramzan had frequent run-ins with the police, and headed a military unit fighting 'rebels' in clashes that looked to many like the settling of scores with rival gangs. Money earmarked for reconstruction went missing. Those amnestied included many of Kadyrov's own people, and federal troops who were accused of abuses. There were allegations that Kadyrov's teams were involved in kidnappings and harassment of the local population. A few months before, human rights groups had been calling for the withdrawal of Russian troops. By autumn 2003, faced with the prospect of even more brutal violations by Kadyrov's people, they began to call for federal soldiers to remain. Not because they had improved, but simply because the alternative seemed even worse.

Kadyrov's assassination in May 2004 came as little surprise. He had done little to broaden power-sharing beyond his own group, or to draw different Chechen groups into the decision-making process. He failed to change tack after his election and become more inclusive. Instead, he maintained and even intensified his existing clannish, authoritarian line. It looked as though the Kremlin had attempted to delegate greater responsibility to him while shirking its own role in the process. That risked undermining Kadyrov by limiting his support from the federal authorities, while giving him a dangerously free rein with less scrutiny from Moscow. It created the prospect for a fresh civil war, with further instability. The question was whether Kadyrov – and his successor Alkhanov – resembled more closely Dudayev or Maskhadov. Neither option seemed positive, for Russians and above all for ordinary Chechens.

Despite his normally calm, collected manner, Chechnya was Putin's one clear weak spot. It was a subject almost guaranteed to bring out the rougher side of his personality. His usually civilized language would slip into slang, and his temper snap in response to persistent questions. In late 1999, after repeated quizzing by a Russian journalist on his policy towards Chechen 'bandits', he threw out the phrase 'We'll wipe them out in the shit-house'. In November 2002, when a French journalist in Brussels launched a barbed question about human rights abuses, he began a long response, becoming visibly irritated. He stressed that Russia was a multi-faith country, equipped with experts in circumcision. If his questioner wanted to come to Moscow, he said, he could arrange for them to 'cut it off in a way that it will never grow back'. Asked in June 2003 for his response to a senior US State Department official's comment about the dangers of Russia's policy in

Chechnya, he replied: 'We have a saying in Russia: in every family, there is somebody who is ugly or retarded.'

Whenever Putin travelled to the west, he always seemed to be caught out on Chechnya. Often he was didactic, launching into lengthy explanations of the history of the conflict and how his approach was the best way to resolve it. There may have been an element of histrionics in his explosive reaction, designed for Russian domestic consumption or to frighten off foreign critics. There may have been frustration at what he perceived as western ignorance, misunderstanding and prejudice, without constructive, realistic alternative suggestions. But there also seemed to be hints of Putin's own irritation at the absence of any clear resolution in Chechnya long after he had first embarked on his own policy.

His initial decisive approach undoubtedly did much to improve his image at home, propelling both his Unity party into parliament in December 1999 and him into the presidency the following March. His continued hardline style helped sustain his high popularity ratings by tapping into popular anti-Chechen sentiment. Even as the conflict dragged on, and the polls indicated that the Russian public had ever more mixed views about the desirability of the war, there was little indication that they had any clear alternative solution in mind, or that they blamed Putin for the continuation of the conflict. Above all, the polls suggested that Chechnya was not a top concern for the country, and did not pose him a significant political challenge.

The 'political containment' of Chechnya was as important as the war itself. As the conflict dragged on, efforts to control the domestic media stepped up. Increasingly denied outlets for critical views, much of the political class was in any case itself mute on Chechnya, either sharing Putin's analysis or not daring to defy it. Internationally, the Russian president was able to capitalize on shifts in world opinion in the fight against terrorism, notably after 9/11, twisting it to his advantage. But he was only partially successful in winning the intellectual argument abroad when he drew parallels with Chechnya. While there were undoubtedly foreign fighters and funding in the republic, it was clear that the conflict was largely fought by Chechens within Chechnya and for a Chechen cause. Many foreign leaders were initially reluctant to be too closely associated with Putin as prime minister because of his approach. But as the prospect of his presidential victory approached, the search for non Middle Eastern oil intensified and the fight against international terrorism rose up the agenda, reservations were not allowed to get in the way of realpolitik. Chechnya became the 'forgotten' war.

At home, the idea that Russia was a pioneering victim of and fighter against international terrorism went down well. One extraordinary example was the film *Voina* (*War*), released and even implausibly entered into a Russian festival of human rights films in 2003. Directed by the populist Alexei Balabanov, its script could have been written directly by the state-controlled propaganda machine, Rosinformcentre. The plot involved two naïve British actors supposedly turning up in Grozny to play Shakespeare in the middle of the conflict, before being kidnapped by Chechen warlords for ransom. Screenwriters around the world could have come up with plenty of colourful names that they might have used for their captors, but few would have spontaneously thought of the word that was in fact employed by the characters throughout: 'terrorists'.

How consistent was Putin in meeting his own stated objectives in Chechnya? By summer 2003, he was warning that the return of peace could take decades. His approach had sharply evolved. As Emile Pain, a Russian social scientist and former government adviser, argues, during the second half of 1999 alone, Putin first talked about repelling cross-border aggression by Chechens; shifted to the need for the creation of a cordon sanitaire around the republic; and concluded with the need for the total destruction of terrorists. By January 2000, he was placing particular emphasis on the need to preserve Russia from collapse, warning of the risk of a radical Islamic 'khalifate' spreading up the Volga and raising the prospect of another Yugoslav-style split-up across Russia.

Many Russian analysts were sceptical of such a spill-over threat. Chechnya was a special case, a republic that had been devastated for a decade through political and military adventurism. There were few indications in 1999 that the more stable surrounding republics, such as Dagestan or Ingushetia, would follow the same path, particularly after seeing where it had led during the 1990s. Further north, the Muslim ethnic republics of Bashkortostan and Tatarstan sometimes played the 'Chechen card' in an effort to win concessions from Moscow. But they had no desire to follow suit, were far more tightly controlled, and had little momentum pushing them in a similar direction. A striking aspect of Russia after the break-up of the Soviet Union in 1991 was that despite the painful legacy of the past, the huge distances and varied ethnic patterns and histories of the regions, there had been few such pressures. Russification had provided a powerful glue which held the country together in a remarkably coherent way over the decades. The nationalistic forces in Chechnya were very much the exception.

In early 2000, in a long pre-electoral interview, Putin laid out his approach at the time. When initially appointed by Yeltsin as prime minister in the previous August, he said he had thought that he would have three or four months to 'bash the hell out of those bandits' before being fired. As acting president, and with the Kremlin already within his reach half a year later, he told his interviewers that he would soon push for a by-election in the federal parliament. He predicted the introduction of direct presidential rule in Chechnya for 'a couple of years', followed by regional parliamentary and presidential elections. He also stressed the need for rehabilitation, reconstruction and reconciliation.

The actions that followed were largely true to this plan. Tactically, the Russian army had learned many lessons from the previous war, and used them to reduce its own casualties. But the generals and the country's political leadership failed to draw some of the most important lessons from 1994–6, let alone other conflicts. Intense bombardment and human rights abuses helped create a partisan war. Instead of denouncing NATO's intervention in Kosovo as an attack on their 'Slavic brothers' the Serbs, the generals might have done better to study the modest loss of life and rapid withdrawal afterwards in that conflict. Declarations every few months that the 'military phase' was over looked increasingly ridiculous as dozens of soldiers continued to die each month. In August 2002–August 2003 alone some 4,749 troops perished in Chechnya, according to the International Institute for Strategic Studies – or more than in any previous twelve-month period since fighting began. If Putin had concluded in 1999 that military action was the only remedy possible, he was still faced with the unpleasant fact that the armed forces with which he had to work were weak: ill-equipped, poorly motivated and under-trained.

By any objective standards, it is hard to credit the resulting policy in Chechnya as a long-term success. Even by official figures, more than 5,000 Russian soldiers have died in the conflict since autumn 1999. According to estimates made by human rights groups, the combined total number of casualties among rebel fighters, federal troops and civilians alike may in fact be at least ten times as high, and probably already surpasses the levels of the previous war. An estimated one million servicemen have passed through Chechnya in a decade of war, coming away psychologically disturbed and often drawn into criminal activities on demobilisation. Russia nominally controls most of the territory of Chechnya, but the number of terrorist incidents has increased since the war began, and there are near-daily skirmishes and casualties.

Heavy bombardment has devastated the territory, worsening economic conditions that were already among the toughest in the country. A new generation has grown up knowing nothing but violence and hatred, with little formal schooling and few job prospects. Kidnappings and banditry continued throughout the period. Human rights abuses, including the torture and 'disappearance' of thousands of people, have taken place against a background of impunity. Growing hatred of Chechens has sparked fresh racist attacks across Russia, tensions with the Muslim community and frequent incidents of harassment by the police and the authorities against the Chechen diaspora. There are more than 100,000 internally displaced persons who fled the conflict and prefer not to return to the republic. Thousands travelled abroad, becoming one of the largest groups seeking political asylum or refugee status around the world. Some even returned to Kazakhstan, despite the painful memories of their families' deportation to the country sixty years earlier.

Putin cannot be blamed for the situation that he inherited in Chechnya, from either the Soviet period or the subsequent chaos and first war of the Yeltsin era. But he shares some of the responsibility for the Russian failures during the uneasy peace that followed. In his role as director of the FSB from 1998, and then as head of the State Security Council, he should certainly have been aware of how the situation was deteriorating in the republic. He is far more responsible for opting for a second all-out war, even if he had no role in the apartment bombings and the Dagestan invasion. It could have been possible to prevent or limit military action. Greater efforts could have been made to work with Maskhadov, if only through intermediaries such as the Ingush president Aushev. Maskhadov's was the last generation of Soviet-trained soldiers with whom it might have been possible to reach a compromise, while he still had authority. Even if military intervention was necessary, it could have been accompanied by greater responsibility and moderation. But on Chechnya, Putin seems to have been listening most attentively to his generals. Other strategists in the Kremlin and advisers on Chechnya with experience of the region from the previous period – including Rybkin and Khasbulatov – were ignored. 'There is a Russian political class which is experienced, and interested in negotiations,' Aushev told me. 'But they have been side-lined.'

The hardline approach, and Putin's personal rhetoric on the issue, have helped contribute to a growing sense of nationalism, inter-ethnic hatred and extremism across Russia. The authorities' rapid clearance of the rubble of the 1999 apartment bombings has stoked conspiracy theories. Their refusal to hold public inquiries into the Ryazan 'exercise' or the Dubrovka theatre storming, and to hold trials behind closed doors of those accused of involvement, have helped divide and disillusion the Russian elite. Whatever the truth, a surprisingly large number believe that the apartment bombings were provocations, and not carried out by Chechens. Chechnya has reinforced the role of the armed forces, and set back the cause of democracy in Russia.

In cynical, narrow terms, Putin contained the international and domestic fallout of the war, and has up till now largely succeeded in limiting the fighting to within the republic's own borders. Yet he has poisoned relations between Chechens and Russians still further, creating problems that will at best take years to resolve. The biggest victims are the Chechens themselves. But the nationalistic rhetoric, and the tens of thousands of casualties on all sides create broader generational dangers across Russia. The political and economic instability in the region risks triggering the spread of radicalism and conflict beyond Chechnya into the neighbouring ethnic republics, and creating the conditions for enhanced links with international terrorists. Hundreds of thousands of soldiers and police have been left with untreated post-conflict trauma, spreading pain, violence and hatred throughout Russian society. Putin's approach may result in precisely the internal, regional and even international instability that his policy was supposed to prevent.

SHOOTING THE MESSENGER

AT 3.45 A.M. ON EASTER SATURDAY 2001, the armed men made their way swiftly to the meeting point. They gathered outside the monolithic concrete building at Ostankino, in the shadow of the giant television mast that dominates the city skyline. They were anticipating trouble.

Eight years earlier, in 1993, an irregular militia armed with machine guns and bazookas had assembled at the same place. Sixty people died as crack federal troops fought off their amateurish attempts to seize control of state television on behalf of the old parliament, which was defying Boris Yeltsin with a mixture of ageing rifles and nationalist-Communist slogans. In 2001, under his successor, the chosen weapons were lawsuits, and the rhetoric was capitalist dogma. But the new president stood behind the latest action just as his predecessor had. And his wishes were being implemented equally ruthlessly in an effort to enforce his emerging regime.

This time, private security guards brandishing legal documents were in the front line. Their target was the eighth floor of Russia's crumbling television centre. The building held the operational heart of NTV, the country's leading privately owned network, established and controlled by the powerful businessman Vladimir Gusinsky. His journalists had been in a sleepless state of resistance for ten days. They had refused any compromise, rejecting offers of talks with

Gazprom, the state-backed gas company which had ousted Gusinsky's representatives at a shareholders' meeting earlier in the same month and – on paper, at least – taken charge of the station.

NTV staff had done their best to whip up public support over the weeks since then. Friendly journalists from other media had been brought in to report on the fray. Supporters from the liberal Yabloko party had arranged rallies and round-the-clock vigils with public figures. In the previous few days, the station had abandoned its regular schedule in favour of simply broadcasting an 'open camera' in its own reception area, showing crowds milling around in anticipation of trouble. The tactics made Gazprom hesitant to create a scandal by aggressively imposing its will.

The timing so early on that Easter Saturday holiday was cynically perfect. The atmosphere in NTV's shabby corridors, enlivened and exhausted by frenetic debate and the constant to and fro of outside journalists, politicians and officials, had calmed. Boris Jordan, the US-born financier named general director of NTV by Gazprom, had attempted to reassure the staff. He repeatedly pledged in public and private that he would not take control by force. It seemed that a final decision on the fate of the station would be several weeks away, pending a legal appeal on the validity of the shareholders' meeting.

Most of the NTV staff had left for the long weekend. Yevgeny Kiselyov, the gravel-voiced key anchor and general director who had rallied his colleagues to fight off the new Gazprom team, was following his regular practice in travelling abroad. He was meeting Gusinsky, who, under pressure from the authorities, had fled from Russia to his luxurious villa in southern Spain. He was being held under house arrest pending an extradition request by Moscow as it stepped up the pressure to seize control of his assets.

The men from Invest Security, Jordan's guard service, were the first to arrive. With the simple flourish of a court order to Gusinsky's surprised night duty staff, they took control of the modest desk that served as a control post before dawn had broken. They diverted the lift so that it would no longer stop at the eighth floor, restricting entry. Oleg Dobrodeyev, one of the founders of NTV, who had quit a year before, appeared on the scene. So did Vladimir Kulistikov, who had also resigned but had been hired back by Jordan as his news editor. By 7 a.m., Jordan himself was on his way to Ostankino. Alfred Kokh, the head of Gazprom's media arm, was soon lurking in the corridors, unable to resist witnessing the culmination of the long takeover campaign he had helped mastermind. A struggle that had been simmering for many months had come to a head. A decisive stage of the fight – and a striking symbol of the effectiveness and ruthlessness of Vladimir Putin's one-year-old administration – was over without violence or great drama.

By the time the morning shift of journalists arrived, NTV was already a different company, firmly under new ownership more closely aligned to the Russian state. The atmosphere changed from creative collective to corporate cabal. Security men in dark suits stood in the corridors. The telephones in Kiselyov's former executive office were diverted to ring at the slick offices of Sputnik, the investment fund Jordan ran, which sat several miles away in the centre of Moscow, nestled behind the city hall.

The action triggered widespread indignation and walk-outs by staff. Pasha Labkov, one of the network's stars, lifted his own framed portrait from the wall of NTV's executive corridor and carried it with him from the building. He had mixed views about the power struggle between Gazprom and Gusinsky, but he was disgusted by the way it had been resolved. 'Maybe television is not a place where decent people can work,' he said shortly afterwards. 'I was appalled by the way the takeover happened. I don't want to work for either Trotsky or Stalin.' Vladimir Pozner, one of Russia's best-known journalists and no great fan of the station's ousted management, said: 'I have a painful impression that NTV has been murdered. It was undoubtedly a hostile takeover that had been approved by the authorities.'

The change in management was the final step in an eighteen-month struggle for control of NTV which was clearly sanctioned by Putin himself. The tactics said much about the way the new president wanted the country to operate, and it sent a clear warning to other media owners and editors to bring them into line. The relatively muted reaction of the rest of Russian society was revealing about its willingness to accept tighter controls. But the absence of a greater outcry was also a sign of the ambiguous role that NTV – and the Russian media more generally – had been playing during the 1990s. The state of journalism highlighted the missed opportunities just a decade after being granted freedom to speak out without Communist censorship. NTV was only the beginning.

Blaming the victim?

In October 1999, Vladimir Gusinsky made his way to a decisive meal in the White House, the headquarters of the Russian government. The brash media tycoon – not far from the height of his powers – was due to eat with the country's obscure new prime minister. Vladimir Putin was still a low-key, low-profile civil servant who had been put forward for the job by Yeltsin. Few expected him to last long in office before being fired like his predecessors by the erratic president.

The venue for their meeting, the former home of the Congress of People's Deputies – the anti-Yeltsin parliament that had been dissolved in 1993 – sat on the banks of the Moscow river, overshadowed by Gusinsky's own office. The tycoon had rented rooms on the twenty-first floor of the neighbouring tower block, the ex-headquarters of Comecon, the Soviet empire's economic cooperation bloc. But, as with the collapse of both Congress and Comecon in such recent memory, the fates of the two men coming together to talk were also soon to change radically.

Just a few months before, Gusinsky had wielded extraordinary influence. A flamboyant theatre director turned successful business-man, he had drifted almost by accident into the media in the early 1990s as a sideline from banking and other more traditional money-making ventures. He financed the creation of the national television network NTV, launched the daily newspaper *Sevodnya*, and acquired a stake in the fledgling radio station *Echo Moskvy*. He created Russia's most powerful and professional media empire, a machine that had helped to dictate public policy decisions and private commercial disputes, to splinter governments and even help make presidents. 'He thought he had God by the beard,' says one friend and former partner, using a common Russian expression. Media Most had been intimately linked to the Russian state, taking advantage of political contacts and pressure to gain finance and support. After nurturing the group in the chaotic post-Soviet business environment over several years, Gusinsky was preparing something altogether more ambitious. He had his eye on a global reach. He launched a gargantuan investment to develop his own television satellite service, complete with the purchase of his own satellite. And he was planning a New York stock exchange listing which he hoped would value NTV alone at upwards of $1.2bn.

Russia's financial crisis in August 1998 knocked a huge hole in his plans. The country's fledgling advertising market collapsed, depriving his business of valuable revenues. The economy was plummeting, dealing a blow to other sources of income. The stock market was continuing a downward slide that had begun several months earlier, having reached record highs in mid-1997. The simultaneous rouble devaluation, default on government bonds and refusal by local companies to pay off their creditors created a huge wave of negative investor sentiment towards Russia. One western banker memorably said that he would rather 'eat nuclear waste' than make investments in the country. Gusinsky was left hugely over-exposed and indebted. By summer 1999, he was already flailing as he tried to persuade the government to help him out once more. But the mood was changing, and his political influence was about to be destroyed.

Accounts of the precise content and mood of the conversation between Putin and Gusinsky that October day vary, but there is little disagreement about the topics the two men broached. Gusinsky by his own admission raised concerns about the undue influence of the clan or 'Family' around Yeltsin which had helped pick Putin, and from which he felt isolated. He discussed Putin's hardline approach to the war in Chechnya, with which he strongly disagreed. He talked about politics and the economy. And he also broached the absence of fresh state financing for NTV, while its government-owned rival ORT had recently received $100m to help bolster its falling revenues during the advertising slump. Some suggest that his comments to Putin deteriorated into near-threats. 'Gusinsky said, "I understand that you have very little chance of becoming president, but if we work with you and you do what we say, we'll try to make you win. And we need $100m in credit,"' says one former Gusinsky associate, in a version endorsed by a senior Kremlin insider.

Gusinsky himself denies that he raised the subject of the forthcoming elections at the meeting, or proposed support for Putin in exchange for money. 'Before then, I talked with Voloshin over the summer, and with Stepashin in his office,' he told me in an interview a few months later. 'At that time, Voloshin offered me money and said, "Take it and go, and we'll reach agreement with your journalists. I don't want you to interfere in the elections." I said, "I don't need any $100m. We won't interfere in the elections. We won't be on anyone's side."' But Gusinsky also admitted that he raised the issue of funding with Putin, notably in a second meeting later in the year. He argued that there should be a level playing field between competitors in the television market. If ORT had received government support, in other words, he believed that NTV should receive the same amount, even though it was privately owned.

Different people who know Gusinsky say that the conversation with Putin may well have become emotional. One acquaintance describes a meeting he had with the media magnate a few months later. 'I went to see Gusinsky and came out sweating, I was so afraid "they" were listening to our conversation. He used phrases referring to Putin like "I'll destroy him." Gusinsky sincerely thought he was a puppeteer who pulled all the strings.' Another long-standing colleague says: 'Gusinsky would get very excited about even very minor things, like summoning the waiter if coffee had not arrived and telling him that he was fired. He had an enormous temper. But it was all theatre. He would soon calm down and forget everything. He had no evil, lingering memory.'

Putin was not so forgiving. He had little love for the oligarchs who had become rich in questionable circumstances in the mid-1990s, and he certainly did not like to be threatened. It was only the intervention of Dmitry Kozak, a close adviser and friend, that persuaded the then prime minister even to agree to a second meeting with Gusinsky. But that was no more successful, and it would be the last the two men ever had. A ferocious campaign was already under way that would lead to NTV and Media Most's other assets being wrested from the tycoon's control, and to his fleeing abroad to escape prison as the authorities stepped up their pressure.

Putin's position was still vulnerable in autumn 1999, with little certainty that he would be elected president. The Chechen war was only just getting under way, his own image was ill-defined, and it looked as though the parliamentary elections in December would be won by the Fatherland-All Russia movement. That risked propelling Yevgeny Primakov, the former prime minister, into power, leading to the ousting of Putin and the 'Family' that had backed him. Putin was taking a gamble by defying Gusinsky. But he already had the support of Boris Berezovsky, Yeltsin's *éminence grise*. While nominally in state ownership, the country's most influential television channel, ORT, was in practice under Berezovsky's control. And Berezovsky, at that stage no ally of Gusinsky, was keen to assure Putin that his support would be sufficient for victory.

One year after his successful election as president, Putin would have his revenge. NTV's takeover in April 2001 was portrayed in much of the international media as the most striking and disconcerting example of the authoritarian tendencies of the new regime. 'President Vladimir Putin has flouted the appeals of the United States and other Western governments that he preserve Russia's free media,' wrote the *Washington Post* three days later, calling for Russia's suspension from the G8 group of leading nations. Many other journalists, commentators and politicians all too casually described NTV as an 'independent' station which had exploited post-Soviet Russia's short-lived system of free speech to be critical of the government, and which was now being crushed in retaliation by the freshly reawakened forces of the old KGB. It made an easy story of good versus evil. It also pandered to the residual Cold War mentality towards Russia that lingered as much in the west as in the former Soviet empire. Making such judgements was to gloss over the details in a struggle that involved not only media control but personal revenge and greed; and not just directives from the top of the Kremlin, but initiative from civil servants and commercial rivals below.

Some of the foreign journalists denouncing the takeover spoke little Russian, or had been in the country for too short a period to monitor the network's coverage and that of its rivals. Given the average three- to four-year tenure of most correspondents, diplomats and other expatriate observers, many had above all witnessed NTV's critical reporting on Russia over the previous two years. There was its relatively balanced analysis of the war in Kosovo in 1999, for example, in contrast to the state-backed channels' almost exclusive focus on the bomb damage and the refugee crisis sparked by NATO attacks, while ignoring the Serb atrocities which helped trigger the war. NTV later that year extensively covered the possibility of FSB involvement in the Moscow apartment bombings, the corruption scandals around the 'Family' of Boris Yeltsin, and the setbacks and casualties of the conflict in Chechnya. It would also give far greater air-time to Putin's rivals in the parliamentary and presidential elections than the state-controlled networks ORT and RTR.

Fewer foreign observers based in Moscow had observed NTV's partisan approach a little earlier in its youthful history, when it had other axes to grind. There was little independence in its clear support – alongside the media outlets of other tycoons – for the ailing Boris

Yeltsin during his presidential re-election campaign in 1996 against the Communist leader Gennady Zyuganov. NTV was tardy in reporting on Yeltsin's frequent heart attacks and other health problems. It propagated a false version of the events when two of his aides were caught carrying large sums of cash ear-marked for illegal campaign financing out of the White House, the government headquarters. It claimed that the money had been planted on them by officers from the special services, while aware that this version was untrue. It maintained all-night broadcasts to keep on the pressure for their release. After Yeltsin's victory, NTV served his interests in joining the chorus of criticism against Alexander Lebed, the architect of peace in Chechnya and a rival presidential contender, to undermine him.

If 'objectivity' or 'balance' is difficult enough to achieve in the western media, the wild extremes of Russia's political evolution in the 1990s made such lofty concepts even more remote. For a start, there is little tradition of an independent press in Russia. In the nineteenth century, the tsars imposed limits on the commercial advertising that newspapers could receive, precisely in an effort to prevent them from being self-sufficient. An extensive system of state funding was in place at the start of the twentieth century to help reward loyalty to the authorities. The Communists picked up on and embellished that tradition, imposing tight control over the media. Criticism and exposés of corruption were published, but only when it served the political interests of those in power. The newspaper *Literaturnaya Gazeta* was – within certain limits – allowed to be critical of the state, as part of a policy dubbed 'Hyde Park under Socialism' – a reference to Speaker's Corner in London, where anyone can speak their mind. It was a practice which allowed the intelligentsia to let off steam, and Soviet officials to claim that they had a free press.

It was only in the late 1980s that a brief 'golden period' for journalism existed, according to Alexei Simonov, a writer and director who heads the Glasnost Defence Foundation, a journalists' rights organization. Mikhail Gorbachev's policy of *glasnost* (openness) removed censorship, allowing the free dissemination of ideas. At the same time, the state continued to fund media outlets, pay salaries and subsidise rental, printing and other costs, maintaining comfortable financial conditions. But as Manana Aslamazyan, director of the media training organization Internews, points out, the period until the early 1990s was also one of 'romanticism'. Most journalists shifted from being sometimes reluctant propagandists for Communism to enthusiastic defenders of the new reformist values of Gorbachev's administration. Criticism of the state itself was still not widespread, because the writers shared the same values as the new wave of policy-makers. When Boris Yeltsin first came to power, he helped perpetuate the changes introduced by Gorbachev, formalizing them by severing media outlets from accountability to their former institutions and 'privatizing' them to the journalists. He approved a new media law which theoretically shielded editors from interference by their owners. Most important, he also avoided clamping down on the media, ignoring or resisting any retaliation against even highly per-sonal criticism. That was Yeltsin's contribution to democracy. But it was far from sufficient to create a truly free press.

Journalists' disillusion with the authorities soon set in. Yeltsin's shelling of the government headquarters in 1993 drove a wedge through public opinion. So did his decision to launch the first Chechen war in 1994. Just as divisive – and with even more impact for the nature of journalism – were his market reforms. Many journalists were still surviving on very modest state salaries, while prices rose sharply. Falling living standards ate into the circulation figures of newspapers, and advertising was modest, offering only scant support to media outlets. At the same time, businessmen began to see the importance of influencing public opinion through the media. Soon they were using individual journalists and entire media outlets in their own commercial and political battles.

In some cases, the writers were willing tools. The most notable case was the widespread support for Yeltsin in 1996 out of fear of a Communist revival. That reflected a deep-seated belief by many jour-nalists that their new life was under threat, often lubricated by financial support from business backers who shared their views. It also reflected a tradition in which many journalists considered them-selves writers above all, with stylistic flourish and expression of opinions being seen as more important than gathering or verifying facts. The results were catastrophic for the liberated media. Simonov says: 'The press decided that it could put aside part of its freedom, and get it back with interest. But freedom never grows in the bank.' His foundation, which has played a key role in defending media rights, was founded in 1991 at a time of growing concern over the biased coverage in the state media of the uprisings in the Baltic republics. Significantly, its founder members were film directors, who united in withdrawing their films from circulation as a sign of protest. Only later – belatedly – did journalists join up.

During the 1990s, base pecuniary instincts were given free rein in Russia's media. A widespread system of *zakazuky* or ordered articles sprang up, with journalists individually or collectively paid to write or broadcast positive pieces about their patrons and negative ones about their clients' rivals, or receive 'blocking fees' to desist from producing threatened negative ones at all. Some links were person to person, others institutionalized through editors. There were one-off payments, but also long-term agreements negotiated through commercial departments. There were at times regular contacts between clients and captive journalists. In other cases, the links were more subtle. The system reached its pinnacle with Berezovsky and Gusinsky, who owned entire media outlets, hired like-minded people to run them and paid them extremely well. It was a sophisticated arrangement that did not even require much supervision, and could operate with little direct interference.

On one occasion in 1999, I had a lunch with the oil group Sibneft in the dining rooms of its luxurious central Moscow offices. The company – acquired on the cheap by Berezovsky and his partner Roman Abramovich – boasted in private of its very close Kremlin connections. That helped it win export quotas, buy additional assets and enjoy extremely low tax bills. But Eugene Shvidler, the chief executive, went red when I asked if Berezovsky still held a stake in the company, as the Russian media was widely reporting. 'That's nonsense,' he exploded. 'What the media writes is rubbish. In any case, I dictate half of what you read in the press.'

A few months later, I had a cagey call from a public relations consultant I knew. As usual, fearful that our telephones were being tapped, he went into little detail, but proposed a meeting in the Radisson Slavyankskaya Hotel. It was a favourite hang-out for thick-necked, shaven-haired, leather-jacketed New Russians and their pencil-thin girlfriends. They would play with the food on their plates in the hugely over-priced atrium sushi bar complete with a mini river and bridge, while their even bulkier bodyguards hovered nearby. As we sipped cappuccino in the adjacent bar, my contact explained that he had just received a very lucrative contract from a big Russian metals company, and would be happy to give me a cut in exchange for my 'cooperation'. When he saw my surprise, he quickly added: 'Just joking, of course.' Attempting to bribe foreign journalists was a delicate affair, although Russians frequently believed that even the western media were in the pay of corporate rivals – or were the agents of enemy governments.

Such was the cynical, mercantile atmosphere of the period that any critical article or broadcast was perceived as having been paid for. The reality was not always so simple. There was so much 'dirt' in circulation that it was perfectly possible for a good journalist to unearth true but scandalous materials in all honesty and objectivity. Sometimes one-sided reporting was more the result of a lack of experience by young journalists than payment or pressure. The cult of secrecy and suspicion among companies and government officials encouraged sloppy journalism and conspiracy theories even for those who tried to verify their facts. And public relations consultants often took advantage of the blurred reality for their own benefit. One foreign financier described to me with amazement how the press officer in a Russian stock brokerage firm he had recently joined presented him with a budget showing the substantial amounts to be allocated each year to a range of different newspapers. My suspicion was alerted when he mentioned one publication on the list that I believed did not indulge in such practices. It may well have been that his press officer was simply seeking the release of cash which he then pocketed for himself.

In January 2001, the national newspaper *Vremya MN* ran a curious article describing the imminent opening of an electronics shop in Moscow to be called Traffic Lights. Apart from having minimal news value and reading like a badly phrased press release, there was one other problem with the story: it was pure fiction. The newspaper had been caught running 'hidden advertising'. A media agency had sent the same fake article to twenty publications, asking them to publish it for a fee as though it was genuine editorial material. Thirteen papers agreed. That same year, Boris Fyodorov, a banker and former government minister, circulated a booklet analysing negative articles about him which he believed were retaliation for his campaign criticizing the poor management of Gazprom. He launched thirteen libel suits against nine papers in the space of a few months, and hired linguistic experts who concluded that many pieces had the same style and content, suggesting a single source. 'It turns out that in Russia you can only rely on the western press . . . while at the same time our deputies are adopting laws intended to prevent foreigners from acquiring our mass media,' he wrote.

Oleg Dobrodeyev was in a position to know such games of media influence and manipulation well. As the joint founder of NTV with Kiselyov in 1993, he had played a key role in building up the station and hiring and training its staff. But he quit in 2000, and broke his silence in an extraordinary way just a few days before the Gazprom takeover in the following year. In an open letter published on the front page of the newspaper *Izvestiya*, he bluntly accused Kiselyov and Gusinsky of twisting coverage over the years for their own political objectives. He used the graphic Russian word *zatochka* to describe NTV, prison slang for a blunt instrument that has been carved and sharpened to be used as a weapon. He highlighted how Igor Malashenko, the then general director of NTV, had been seconded as a campaign adviser to Yeltsin in 1996, and how the station's staff continued to write speeches for the president long after he was re-elected.

Kiselyov argues that the media's role in Yeltsin's re-election campaign is overstated, claiming that the former president himself was a natural campaigner with a mastery of sound bites and images. He says Malashenko showed Yeltsin pictures of his dynamic performance during the elections in 1989 – in contrast to his more stilted, restrained appearance in 1996 – and Yeltsin 'instantly understood' and changed his style. 'The other oligarchs always looked on Gusinsky and NTV as friendly aliens,' says Kiselyov. 'We were with them but not part of them. We were supportive of Yeltsin, and critical of Zyuganov. But we covered Zyuganov's campaign, and he was a regular guest, which was very rare on other channels. We thought the best way to destroy him was to show him. It was a mistake to get involved in the pro-Yeltsin campaign. But we were not ignoring the other candidates, we were trying to keep a certain balance.'

In an interview I had with him in early 2001, Gusinsky admitted that he had sided with Yeltsin during his presidential re-election campaign in 1996. But he claimed that it was an error which had not been repeated since. 'In eight years of NTV, how long did we have good relations with the state? For one year, in 1996. Since then, it's been a permanent war. The state is holding us as a hostage,' he said. 'We made a mistake. Not because we supported Yeltsin . . . but because we didn't have the right to decide who would be president. It is the right of the people to chose the president. But we were learning. That period has passed. And today we are paying for 1996.'

In fact, there were plenty of subsequent examples of NTV's partisanship. Its broadcasts did not always favour the authorities, but they certainly did reflect Gusinsky's shifting interests and alliances. The benefits he offered to senior employees were so large even by western standards that they raised questions about the journalists' dependence on the tycoon. On taking over the company, Boris Jordan, the new director, discovered that the salaries to the top dozen staff exceeded $300,000 a year each, and there were 'soft' home loans of up to $250,000 apiece. One acquaintance recalls being at a dinner at Gusinsky's house while Kiselyov's hard-hitting flagship *Itogi* current affairs programme was on air on a Sunday evening. In a sign of his influence, Gusinsky would explain to his guests what the following item would be, then burst into peals of laughter as Kiselyov discussed precisely that. 'We always argued,' said Kiselyov. 'Gusinsky is an ex-theatre director, he wants to be involved. He never puts any pressure on, he's very sensitive. He might say: "If I were you, I'd do it this way." I usually listen to him. He's a source of very bright ideas.'

NTV's output often appeared to reflect its owner's priorities. 'Gusinsky probably created his business using certain privileges and advantages,' says Kiselyov. 'But it was government policy to create a new class of private owners. We needed a class of owners.' Other oligarchs bartered their influence and political support during the 1990s to buy cash-rich Soviet-era raw materials producers in the oils and metals sectors on the cheap. Gusinsky did not acquire any such companies. Yet he extensively used government loans, concessions and regulatory loopholes to create his own business empire. NTV received its original broadcasting licence for a nominal sum. It was granted tax breaks and customs exemptions on imported equipment. In a deal seen as a reward for supporting Yeltsin's re-election in 1996, it received twenty-four-hour broadcasting rights across the country at the low rates usually reserved for state companies.

Over the years, Gusinsky received $42m in loans from the state-controlled Vneshekonombank. Subsidiaries of the Russian Central Bank also came to his aid: Vneshtorgbank lent $40m, Sberbank a further $150m. The Moscow city government lent $223m. As his ambitions became extraterrestrial, he even persuaded the Russian ministry of finance to provide a guarantee of $143m to cover a loan from the US government-backed Eximbank to purchase a satellite. The money raised from such sources helped fund the growth of his companies and the purchase of capital equipment. But it also went to other businesses, and supported an extravagant lifestyle for Gusinsky and his top managers. They built an expensive *dacha* complex in the Moscow suburbs, acquired apartments in the city centre and constructed a luxury new office headquarters. Gusinsky and his lieutenants had the use of spacious houses near Malaga in southern Spain, and ran up costs of $11m a year chartering private jets. 'Gusinsky never considered NTV as a business. It was a cost centre, with the flows all one-way, to the parent. His concept was right, but the execution was totally wrong,' says Jordan.

Gusinsky insists that all the funding from the Russian state was on competitive terms, and adds that few alternative sources of finance existed during the period. 'If you ask any Russian businessman how they created a multi-billion-dollar company, they will all start to tell strange stories. We took credits absolutely openly . . . Did we have any big non-state banks [in Russia] that could lend us money? . . . We took loans here, we took loans there. How else could we have done it? Of course we could have traded drugs or weapons secretly. But we didn't do that.' Whether or not there were alternatives, Gusinsky built his empire on the back of state funding. It gave him the capital to grow. And it become the tool for his downfall when the political leadership of the country changed.

In 1998, NTV did criticize the government. But that came at a time when the tax authorities were vigorously pursuing claims against Gusinsky's then ally and financier Gazprom. A wasteful and corrupt monopoly nominally controlled by the state, Gazprom was a 'state within the state', whose managers were effectively accountable only to themselves. They had built up an alternative power base to the Kremlin, and had no desire to pay the extra taxes the new government was seeking. Gusinsky with his media empire was a useful ally. Gazprom bought shares in NTV in 1996, and went on to make loans and guarantees to Media Most totalling more than $1bn, although there was little economic logic to the deals, no synergy with its own business, and scant prospect of getting repaid. When Gazprom became more hostile to Gusinsky under pressure from the authorities in early 2000, however, NTV was just as quick to switch its orientation.

The broadcaster attacked the gas company, portraying the battle for NTV purely as a fight for freedom of speech and providing endless details to its viewers of how NTV was coming under threat. It said little by way of balance about the state of Media Most's own loss-making finances, the questionable deals it had entered into and the huge debts that it had amassed.

Gusinsky generated hatred, anger and even fear from fellow members of the Russian business elite. He was a pioneer in 'privatizing' the state security services for his own purposes. His own security staff numbered hundreds, and he admitted that he had employed twenty former KGB agents, including Filipp Bobkov, the former head of the Fifth Directorate, which persecuted dissidents. When I asked Gusinsky to comment on reports that he ran his own sophisticated phone-tapping operation to gather material on rivals, he said: 'The FSB itself sells phone conversations. Why would we need to create a special service?' NTV was his principal tool in his commercial battles. Some businessmen claim to have been threatened with negative press if they did not pay Gusinsky money. One leading Russian banker says: 'I met Gusinsky at Davos and he asked me for $25m. We didn't provide the money, and he began a campaign about how we would default on our creditors.' Others made loans just in case, partly as a guarantee against attacks. The oil group Yukos lent $170m in 1999, for example, with no prospect of returns and no obvious business logic. Jordan claims that, after his arrival at NTV, he received many calls from senior Russian executives attempting to negotiate continued favourable publicity in exchange for payment, as they had done in the past. Malashenko and other members of Gusinsky's management team vigorously deny that any such operations took place.

In the most notorious example of partisanship after the 1996 elections, Gusinsky was at the centre of the 'information wars'. Alongside his then partner Berezovsky, he had bid as part of a consortium for a 25 per cent stake in Svyazinvest, a state-controlled telecoms holding company that was being privatized in 1997. As a backer of Yeltsin's successful re-election campaign, he considered the stake his by right – a pay-off like the cut-price deals received by other oligarchs for their political support. But he was too late. The new Yeltsin team, headed by Anatoly Chubais, was becoming more confident, and decided that there would be no more rigged auctions. A rival bid by the businessman Vladimir Potanin won, for twice the $1bn price Gusinsky had offered. Berezovsky and Gusinsky took revenge, through ORT and NTV respectively. Both channels launched aggressive attacks on the new government of 'young reformers' helping force them out of office.

As so often in Russia, no one was pure, but the choice of whom to attack was highly selective. Potanin, who had long balanced political and business interests, had acquired state assets, including the giant metals group Norilsk Nickel, at knock-down prices. NTV highlighted how companies he controlled were behind extravagant 'book advances' paid to Alfred Kokh, head of the privatization department, and to Chubais. Boris Nemtsov, a youthful deputy prime minister, was also singled out by Gusinsky. No surprise that all three were muted in their defence of NTV in the build-up to the 2001 takeover. They remembered how selectively 'freedom of speech' had been applied against them.

Despite such campaigns, NTV's coverage often stood out as the most insightful and balanced among the Russian networks. Kiselyov argues that NTV was often not the first to report *kompromat* or compromising material against people, but rather picked up on it once it was in circulation – albeit giving it additional credibility and power in the process. As Gusinsky put it: 'We had a meeting with Yeltsin at the time of the scandal. He said, "They say you used *kompromat* against the 'young reformers'." I replied, "I don't understand what *kompromat* is. If it's true, then it's true even if it compromises someone. If it's not true, we have very tough laws in Russia. Let them sue us. Why has no one done so?"'

I witnessed Gusinsky's own approach to the media at first hand. While he should have been keen to cultivate western journalists to help in his defence during 2000, he was reluctant to meet representatives of my newspaper. It took months of negotiations and the help of various intermediaries to arrange an interview, by which time he was in exile in Spain. I flew to Malaga, and was driven in a Mercedes to the luxury private development of Sotogrande that had become his base. Behind large, well-guarded gates, his spacious villa was sprawled around an ornamental fountain complete with a sculpted dolphin. I was shown by a maid into a study with multiple telephones, a giant television and expensive art on the walls. Gusinsky appeared dressed in a bright yellow lumberjack shirt, red braces and jeans. As I fumbled to get out my tape recorder, he leaned forward in his chair and whispered: 'Tell me, Andrew, before we start. Why is the *Financial Times* so much against me?' He was convinced that an abortive commercial deal he had once discussed with our parent company – of which I was then not even aware – was somehow prejudicing our editorial coverage of the NTV affair, and that I was getting instructions on what to write. I later heard that a sophisticated (but evidently useless) analytical computer program used by Media Most to scrutinize journalists' articles had concluded that I was in the pay of the Russian oil company Lukoil. In fact, I had never even met representatives from the company at the time, let alone come under any pressure or temptations from it.

As the December 1999 parliamentary elections approached, Gusinsky and Berezovsky split once more. Berezovsky's ORT adopted a blunt but highly effective direct assault on the principal rivals to the pro-Putin Unity party, hiring the 'killer journalist' Sergei Dorenko. It was a classic Berezovsky appointment. Dorenko was handsomely paid then – and still has Berezovsky bodyguards today. As leaked telephone transcripts illustrated, the two men talked regularly about ORT's coverage of the elections. But Dorenko was an extraordinarily effective presenter and had firm convictions of his own. He needed little encouragement to attack Luzhkov and Primakov. He told me he had first fallen out with Primakov in 1996 when he criticized the then foreign minister over the proposed Russia-NATO treaty. When Primakov – never a great fan of the media – became prime minister in 1998, he exacted revenge, insisting that if ORT wanted a $100m rescue package from the state, Dorenko must be fired. The presenter's acerbic reports on cronyism in Luzhkov's administration triggered investigations against him by the Moscow mayor. He believed the Luzhkov– Primakov duo was a threat to both Russia and himself.

As the weeks to the election went by, Dorenko used his Sunday evening 'author's programme' to indulge in ruthless character assassinations of Luzhkov and Primakov. In his deep, convincing voice, he all but accused Luzhkov directly of corruption and murder. He juxtaposed gruesome images of a hip replacement operation with hints at Primakov's failing health, suggesting that he was too weak to lead. The effect was devastating. ORT, the most widely watched network across Russia, was the direct descendant of the Soviet First channel. Its broadcasts were followed religiously; its influence was like a narcotic. 'Luzhkov asked me, "How much do you want for the last two weeks? I'll give you $100m if there is no Dorenko,"' recalls Berezovsky.

While Berezovsky supported Putin, Gusinsky veered towards

Luzhkov and Primakov. He had long enjoyed links with both men, and after his falling out with Putin he had little alternative. The station stepped up its criticism of the war in Chechnya, and its coverage of the corruption and influence of the 'Family' – an idea that it had helped to create and mythologize. It was NTV that Primakov called to complain live on air about the coverage he was receiving on Dorenko's show. And on NTV he was coaxed into announcing that he would stand for president. The station was more even-handed than its rival, but the message was clear. As Igor Kulistikov, the station's then director, told researchers at the time: 'We are sympathetic with the Kremlin's opponents and we give them the floor.'

The sober conclusion on election coverage from the European Institute for the Media (EIM), a non-profit group funded by the European Commission, was a heavy understatement. It wrote in its report on the 1999 parliamentary elections that the Russian media was 'biased' in its reporting. The state channels ORT and RTR gave disproportionate coverage to the pro-Kremlin Unity party, and were negative in their mentions of Luzhkov's Fatherland-All Russia. In the process, they 'failed to live up to the standards set either in Russian law or in international agreements and conventions signed by the leaders of the Russian Federation'. TV Tsentr, a channel controlled directly by Luzhkov, gave him and Fatherland-All Russia extensive positive air-time. NTV allocated just 5 per cent of its news coverage to Unity – much of which was negative – compared with twenty per cent to Fatherland-All Russia and 32 per cent to the Union of Right Forces. EIM's follow-up study of the presidential campaign in spring 2000 showed that, of its total coverage, 45 per cent of the negative mentions of Putin across all the four principle channels were on NTV, along with 65 per cent of the negative coverage in news broadcasts.

'We behaved as the media should,' Gusinsky told me. 'The impression that we were for Luzhkov and Primakov was created because we talked about them. Against the background of the first and second channels, our neutral coverage looked like support.' That did not stop him frequently citing instances when he had personally called up political leaders – including Luzhkov and Zyuganov, the Communist boss – to persuade them to appear on NTV. Gusinsky had created Russia's most professional television network, but he was far from a hands-off manager running a truly independent station.

NTV stood out – and partially redressed the balance – if only because the other channels were so biased in their coverage. It fought to defend itself as a station, and to provide support for candidates other than those chosen by the Kremlin. At the very least, the channel contributed to a diverse range of media opinion at the time. How it might have behaved had Luzhkov and Primakov won the 1999 elections is more open to question. But for a short period, the fierce battle between ORT and NTV was extremely lively. It was personified in the struggle between Dorenko and Kiselyov, and their Saturday and Sunday night broadcasts became compulsive viewing. But it was Dorenko, with the might of the Yeltsin Kremlin behind him, who won out. With the extraordinary landslide for Unity in parliament, and the destruction of all potential presidential rivals, the scene was set for Putin's election the following spring. And for the subsequent dismembering of Gusinsky's empire and his eviction from the country.

Dictatorship of the law

It began as a short news item and quickly escalated into a national tragedy. Just three months after Putin's inauguration as president, he was facing his first real crisis. The *Kursk* submarine, the pride of the Russian navy, had disappeared during a training exercise in the Barents Sea on 12 August 2000. Having located it on the seabed without radio contact but with some of its 118-strong crew supposedly still alive, the armed forces geared up for a desperate attempt to reach the vessel and free those trapped inside. The nation – and a news-hungry world during a quiet August – watched with growing concern. The *Kursk* tragedy offered something for everyone. For those wanting to see the events as the continued legacy of the Soviet state, there was no shortage of evidence. The navy was so underfunded that it had no submersible craft capable of reaching the wreck. It concealed information that might have helped its new-found NATO allies who volunteered to join in the rescue. Its attitude to the whole affair followed a familiar Communist-era pattern: disregard human life, deny the problem and shift the blame onto foreigners. Senior officials implausibly claimed for weeks afterwards that the *Kursk* collided with another country's submarine, which must be hidden in a harbour somewhere nearby being repaired. But as independent sonar soundings and the pictures from the wreck soon proved, the cause was the explosion of an experimental on-board missile.

For those in the west accustomed to following disasters, the most striking image was that of Putin continuing his holiday in the Black Sea resort of Sochi, surrounded by *apparatchiks* in open-necked shirts doing the same. He did not fly back to Moscow, let alone to the naval base of Severomorsk, and for five days he did not even make a statement. 'From the point of view of PR, [it] could have looked better [to travel there],' he told CNN's Larry King in early September. It seemed a fatal misjudgement for a politician. But in Russia, there was a certain logic. Putin would later argue that he was perfectly well informed of the operation where he was, and that to fly up to the scene would simply have impeded the work of the rescuers. The *Kursk* made only a small dent in his popularity rating. There were also some modest signs of post-Soviet progress amid the continuing gaffes and insensitivities. For me, the most striking element was the reporting of the incident in the national media. Despite all the suggestions of a clampdown in the Russian press, coverage was extensive and hugely critical. The tabloid *Komsomolskaya Pravda* led the charge. 'Why has the president been silent?' it trumpeted on its front page. *Kommersant*, Berezovsky's newspaper, launched an appeal for the families.

I was not the only one who noticed the criticism. In the aftermath of the crisis, when it was clear that all the sailors were dead, Putin made an address on RTR, the national television station most firmly under his control. The government press agency Tass flashed up blocks of his text as he was reading them. But a discrepancy very quickly appeared between the prepared words and what the president was actually saying. With anger in his eyes, Putin diverged almost immediately from the comments of his speech-writers. He expressed 'a great feeling of guilt and responsibility' for the tragedy. But he then launched a scarcely veiled attack on Berezovsky and Gusinsky. He suggested that unnamed people who had been the first to defend the *Kursk* sailors and their families had 'long promoted the destruction of the army, the fleet and the state'. Rather than donating money to the victims, 'they would have done better to sell their villas on the Mediterranean coast of France and Spain'. He appeared convinced that the coverage had been deliberately manipulated by his enemies.

Coming so shortly after a campaign of heightening pressure on the oligarchs, it was certainly possible that the *Kursk* reporting represented their revenge. But there were other possible explanations too. When I called a number of Russian media organizations, I found it was impossible to get through to the top editors. Most of the hierarchy of Russian newspapers and television stations – those who had their hands on the 'ideological' control of coverage – were away on holiday. It was their deputies – more focused on news and less under direct political influence from above – who had been left in charge.

Oleg Dobrodeyev, who had taken charge of RTR after quitting NTV the previous year, was an exception. He was on duty, and quick to show his loyalty to the new regime. One of his correspondents, Arkady Mamontov, won the exclusive rights to stand on the deck of the *Peter the Great*, from where the navy was coordinating the rescue. The views of the stormy Barents Sea were hardly inspiring or informative, but they were a reward for RTR's loyalty. When Putin travelled belatedly to meet relatives at the naval base where the sailors' families lived, he was subjected to a torrent of emotion – and retaliated in kind. Dobrodeyev himself sat in the control room, masterminding the choice of images to be sent out by his team to the nation. But ORT, still under Berezovsky's command, had a very different approach. Dorenko himself filmed an item on the widows and sisters of the victims, who were unusually outspoken in their criticism of the authorities during the rescue operation. After RTR had refused to show their complaints, the women called ORT instead. According to Berezovsky and Dorenko, Konstantin Ernst, the incumbent general director of ORT under Berezovsky who was fighting to maintain his job, told Putin that the women were 'prostitutes' who had been hired specially to criticize. As Alexei Simonov of the Glasnost Defence Foundation summed up the recomposition of the media under Putin: 'The other television heads begged for money. Ernst begged for mercy.'

Ernst would survive, adapting to his new masters. But it would not take long for others to pay the price for that extraordinary *Kursk*-related outburst of media freedom. ORT would soon follow the direction of RTR, coming back firmly under state control. The first step was the firing of Dorenko. After a meeting with Putin, when he says he resisted efforts to be 'recruited', he was dismissed by Ernst, after threatening to discuss on air the taboo subject of the state's attempts to claim back Berezovsky's stake in the channel. Dorenko was soon facing curious charges of assault brought by a drunken police officer who stumbled into his motorbike in a Moscow park one evening. Berezovsky says that, after the *Kursk*, he too had his last meeting with Putin, who accused him of 'organizing a campaign to put him in a bad light'. Nikolai Glushkov, Berezovsky's ally who had been running Aeroflot, was arrested in December 2000 and held in detention on charges of fraud. As the warnings against him stepped up, Berezovsky decided to quit Russia. By the start of 2001, he had been persuaded to sell his stake in ORT to the more Kremlin-friendly oligarch Roman Abramovich. He said that in exchange he was assured that Glushkov would be freed. But the Kremlin did not keep its side of the bargain and Glushkov remained in detention for another two years. That left NTV as the next target to be pursued ruthlessly in the coming months. If Putin had needed any further prompting after his previous experiences with Gusinsky, the *Kursk* had provided it.

The cynical brilliance of the Kremlin's strategy was that its attack against Media Most could be dressed up – at least for foreign consumption – as a defence of property rights and the free market, and an attack on fraud. Officials consistently parroted the line that Gusinsky had borrowed heavily from the state, and that now they were simply calling in debts that were overdue. The basis of independent media, as Putin frequently reminded delegations from abroad who raised the issue, was self-sufficiency through profit. And he was right. Gusinsky had heavily overburdened himself with government money and, with his revenues falling, he was in no position to fight back financially. He had received nearly $1.5bn in state support over the years, with little prospect of paying it back. That made him extremely vulnerable. In any other country, he would have been in deep trouble – as politically connected media tycoons like Robert Maxwell in the UK and Leo Kirch in Germany discovered when their empires started to struggle to survive. If Gusinsky had long been able to twist the Russian state to his advantage, the government support that he had once exploited would now be turned against him. On paper, the methods used were legal, in line with Putin's pledge to introduce a 'dictatorship of the law' to Russia. In practice, his policy was more about dictatorship than law.

The campaign against Media Most was unprecedented. The first warning shots came as early as 1999. Vneshekonombank began legal action to seek repayment of its debts. Video International, a powerful advertising group that dominated the market, withdrew its contract with NTV, threatening its revenues. Dobrodeyev's departure signalled the start of an exodus of some of the group's key employees who were hired by other channels as the political winds changed. Rem Vyakhirev, the head of Gazprom, had long kept silent on the media empire in which his company had so heavily 'invested'. But rumours began to circulate of *kompromat* on his son, who ran Gazprom's lucrative export division. After a meeting with Putin in February 2000, Vyakhirev suddenly began to criticize NTV's coverage of Chechnya. The channel's approach offers 'a serious reason for Gazprom executives to start meditating on the question – where do we invest funds?' he said. With the new president inaugurated in May, Gazprom suddenly woke up to the importance of the money it was owed by Gusinsky and began aggressive action to call in its debts. The aim was nothing short of a full takeover of Media Most's assets, to wrest them from their former owner.

Gazprom began aggressive negotiations, and a series of actions in the commercial courts. But Gusinsky had good lawyers and such methods were not enough. The company soon began to draw in Russia's law enforcement agencies, which were only too pleased to help. Over the space of a few months, some thirty raids were carried out on Media Most offices by prosecutors, tax police and the security services. Many took the form of what the Russian media dubbed 'mask shows', involving heavily armed men in camouflage jackets and black balaclavas forcing their way into company offices, accompanied by state television cameras. The inspections were hugely disruptive, with investigators driving off afterwards with computers and bundles of documents, paralysing the group's systems and sharply diminishing its ability to operate.

Gusinsky refused to take the hint. On 13 June 2000, he was summoned to the prosecutors' office for questioning in relation to an inquiry into alleged embezzlement in the transfer of a broadcasting licence. He did not take the matter too seriously, but at the end of his interrogation, without warning, he was turned from witness into suspect, charged and taken straight to Moscow's crumbling Butyrka prison. For three days he sat in jail, one of the country's richest and most influential men reduced to sharing a cell with two petty criminals and a modest refrigerator. His own concern was matched by that of Russia's other oligarchs, unsure who might be the next victim of Putin's new regime. Seventeen of them rushed to sign a petition condemning the arrest. One name on the letter was a particular surprise: Alfred

Kokh, the former state official, newly appointed as head of Gazprom Media. In the next few months, Kokh would exact his personal revenge for Gusinsky-inspired attacks that had hounded him out of government just three years earlier.

With Gusinsky in prison, his colleagues stepped up negotiations with the Kremlin. They agreed to sell Media Most to Gazprom, but insisted on drafting a document with a special annexe – 'Protocol 6'. It said that in exchange for the sale, all charges against Gusinsky would be dropped and he could leave the country. With the document approved and signed by the press minister Mikhail Lesin, the magnate was released from jail. He immediately went to the Moscow office of Akin Gump, his US lawyers, and secretly videotaped a statement that he had agreed to the sale under duress and he would not respect it. Then he headed to the airport and quit Russia for the last time. He would continue his combat from abroad.

As word leaked out of the agreement – and of Gusinsky's refusal to complete the deal – Gazprom stepped up the pressure. A new case was launched by the prosecutors' office in September alleging that Media Most had obtained loans fraudulently. By November, Gusinsky agreed to hand Gazprom 25 per cent stakes in his media companies in exchange for the quashing of all outstanding debts. But Gazprom wanted more, and Gusinsky was still a reluctant seller. As the talks dragged on, prosecutors launched a fresh summons and then an international arrest warrant against him, triggering his detention in Spain pending an extradition hearing. The Moscow district tax inspectorate separately filed a petition to liquidate Media Most, NTV and other subsidiaries, in order to wrest them from Gusinsky's control. It used an obscure piece of legislation never before applied that permitted the winding up of companies judged insolvent – or unable to pay their debts. The law permitted a calculation by which the debts could be re-valued to much higher current levels but the assets could not. By such criteria, almost every company in Russia could have been assessed as bust and closed down the following day. But selective justice was the name of the game. Then in January 2001, the prosecutors' office took a new hostage. Anton Titov, Media Most's finance director, was summoned for questioning as a witness and then, just like Gusinsky and Glushkov before him, arrested, charged with fraud and taken to Butyrka. He would remain in detention for nearly two years before trial. Meanwhile, raids continued on the group's office, and investigations accelerated against other key employees, some of whom fled abroad and have still not dared return home.

By virtue of its existing 21 per cent shareholding and the extra 25 per cent stake negotiated with Gusinsky, Gazprom was close to obtaining majority control of the key asset it sought: NTV. The balance hung with Capital Group, a secretive US-based fund that had bought 4.5 per cent from Gusinsky. Boris Jordan met the head of Capital in New York to discuss other business, and was asked for his views. He soon found himself in Switzerland, interpreting between the fund manager and Kokh, who asked Jordan to run NTV. A deal was brokered, and with Capital switching sides, Gazprom just scraped past the 50 per cent mark, giving it overall control. It called an extraordinary general meeting of shareholders to change the directors. Gazprom had been consistently using the local court close to its Moscow headquarters in its battle, which always delivered sympathetic verdicts. Media Most decided to fight back, seeking an injunction to challenge the legality of the meeting. It found a friendly court in the city of Saratov. 'We thought at least it would not be under the direct control of Gazprom or the government,' said Kiselyov. He travelled there the day before the shareholders' meeting, received the injunction and then tried to return by plane to Moscow, only to find the airport closed because of a 'bomb threat'. He drove the 550 miles back to Moscow instead. But the following day, the Saratov court reversed its decision. When Sasha Berezin, a lawyer representing Gusinsky, arrived at Gazprom's head-quarters, he was met with a classic Russian corporate sleight of hand. His *propusk*, the all-important piece of paper required to gain access to any building, had not been prepared. Security guards refused to allow him even to attend. Inside the luxury glass and marble building, the meeting went ahead without him. Voting was held, and Gazprom became the *de facto* proprietor of NTV, appointing its own directors. That would lay the groundwork for the physical takeover of the assets orchestrated by Jordan two weeks later.

Gusinsky's cynical brilliance throughout the campaign against him was to cloak his commercial interests and political ambitions in the language of freedom of speech. He used it to portray himself as the innocent victim, stoking up concern and condemnation of the Russian authorities. NTV's critical coverage of the Kremlin could earn strong ratings at home, help Gusinsky's own anti-Putin agenda and boost his reputation abroad. Whether reporting on Chechnya, government corruption or the failures of the state in salvaging the *Kursk*, NTV was helping fulfil all three goals. Its broadcasts supported his case whenever the fight spread outside national borders, notably when the Spanish courts ruled in April 2001 against his extradition and Interpol refused to register Russia's request for an international arrest warrant, stating that 'the case has a predominantly political character'.

Gusinsky's tactics were subtle and sophisticated, though ultimately they had little effect at home. The reality of the combat was not always so clear-cut. Protocol 6 was one example. It made little sense to me that Lesin, a government minister, would voluntarily sign a document waiving prosecution. Even in Russia, there was a nominal separation of powers which would embarrass a court trying to accept such a document. In fact, Igor Malashenko, who had close links to Lesin, persuaded him to sign it. It was a tool that would then be used against him, when Media Most made the document public.

Gusinsky did not help his own case. He frustrated potential 'white knights' interested in acquiring and saving his media assets from the Russian state, including the financier George Soros and Ted Turner, the US media magnate who founded CNN. He dragged out conditions on terms and price with them, much as he had with Gazprom. Many of his businesses operated at a loss, creating a pretext for their closure. Gusinsky had – as prosecutors claimed – shifted assets into offshore companies, if only to make their seizure by his pursuers more difficult. He alienated former employees and business partners, who complained that he had left them out of pocket over the years. Dmitry Biryukov, the joint owner of the Seven Days publishing group with Gusinsky, switched sides. He created a coalition with Gazprom, and within a few days of NTV's closure, he shut the newspaper *Sevodnya* under pretext that it was unprofitable (as it had always been). Overnight, he replaced the old team at the news magazine *Itogi* with a new group of more compliant journalists. As Kirill Rogov, a Russian political commentator, put it: 'The problem is that it isn't the good NTV versus the bad guys. It's the bad NTV versus the even worse guys.'

For those who tried to probe deeper into the issues raised by the attack on Gusinsky, the 'other side' did not help its own case. Gazprom was inaccessible, a clannish corporate giant obsessed with secrecy at the best of times. NTV had become so sensitive an issue that it refused almost all commentary. It argued simply that it was fighting a commercial struggle to recover its debts against an intransigent Gusinsky. It did not explain what business logic there was in a gas company lending to Media Most in the first place – let alone to the tune of $1bn. And it did not want to respond in any detail to the widespread accusations of mismanagement and corruption that plagued its own operations and executives. The Kremlin, too, kept quiet throughout the period, except for a few banal and barely credible statements on the importance of free speech, the oft-repeated mantra that the NTV–Gazprom battle was a purely commercial dispute, and the need for the courts alone to decide the issue. Such arguments sat uneasily with the drama unravelling on viewers' television screens. They also looked odd, given that Putin himself had conceded how far from independent the country's judicial system was and how desperately it needed reform.

Those who were most willing to speak out against the attacks included an impressive collection of pundits. NTV allies, they were linked by shared values but also by the fact that they had long been cultivated by the channel. They were part of a *tusovka*, a tight-knit group of friends. They had frequently been invited to appear on its programmes in the past, and felt a very personal connection to the station and its staff. Lilia Shevtsova, for example, a shrewd political analyst from the Moscow Carnegie Centre, who had been a strong critic of Putin from the start, talked to her contacts about how sad the events were for 'Zhenya' Kiselyov, and encouraged them to do whatever they could to protest and help out. It had become an emotional issue as much as one to be rationally analysed. 'Our country is building a Potemkin village, an imitation regime,' she told the TNT channel the day after the takeover. 'The external wrappings of democracy are all the same: in elections, parliament, parties and even an imitation NTV. But the essence is absolutely different.'

Above all, those willing to offer comment and 'spin' on the situation were the NTV journalists and executives themselves. That reflected the education and leanings of many of the key employees at Gusinsky's Media Most group. It helped them speak 'the right language' – literally as well as metaphorically – to those whom they sought to influence abroad. They were *zapadniki*, people who were fundamentally western-oriented. They spoke foreign languages, were educated, had travelled and worked abroad, and sometimes owned property or moved their families there to live. They had foreign friends and acquaintances, and knew how to put a message across to them. By appointing such people in top jobs across his media empire,

Gusinsky had already made his choice of general editorial line without any direct intervention on his part.

Kiselyov himself was the prime example, happy to talk to foreign journalists and keen to cultivate diplomats. He had fluent and near-accentless English, his second foreign language after Farsi. He regularly watched the BBC, and modelled his own broadcasts partly on its style. He had an apartment in London and spent much of his time abroad. His own son had been educated in the UK and now lived there. And he would often draw unfavourable comparisons between Russia and foreign places. 'I want to travel freely from my country and return with dignity,' he said. 'I look with envy when I arrive at most European airports, and the locals just make their way through, waving their passports. Here in Moscow you are subjected to humiliatingly long queues.'

Igor Malashenko, the former Dante scholar turned Kremlin political adviser who became NTV's first general director in the mid-1990s, was a fluent English speaker who spent much of his time lobbying in the USA. His family was partly based in the UK, and his daughter studied at the elite English girls' school Roedean. Mikhail Berger, editor of Gusinsky's *Sevodnya* newspaper, spoke good English, as did Masha Lipman, the deputy editor of the news magazine *Itogi*. Alexei Venediktov, the chief editor of Echo Moskvy, an influential radio station, had impeccable French and was cultivated by the French embassy and the francophone media in Moscow as a result. So was Sergei Parkhomenko, the editor of *Itogi* and a former consultant for the French news agency AFP.

The heavy presence of western-oriented *zapadniki* from Media Most stood in contrast to the *gosudarstvenniki* or statists lined up against them, those with a natural affiliation for the Russian state and its Slavic traditions. They reflected a widespread Russian belief in absolute respect for power, with little sympathy for or even concept of the idea of a developed counterbalance within the media, political groups or civil society. Their number including Dobrodeyev, who had considerable influence behind the scenes, and who struggled in English. There were also others who were more opportunistic and commercially oriented, starting with Kokh.

To the bemusement of many western observers, the domestic outcry following the takeover of NTV was relatively limited. Some pointed to Russian apathy, co-optation or fear. But the explanation was in many ways simpler. Many had little interest in or sympathy for the idea of a media group in opposition to the state. It was not part of their history or culture. Opinion polls suggested distrust of the media in general, and of privately controlled channels in particular. Despite seventy years of Soviet propaganda, most still put their faith in the state networks. Many more, who had been following the saga more closely than foreign pundits, were also deeply sceptical about NTV's claims to have been independent. They had become cynical about any claims of freedom of speech after a decade of media excess. 'The fight over NTV is about one crook stealing the cudgel of another,' said Sergei Gorelikov, a teacher who followed the domestic media closely, using a Russian expression. His virulent anti-Communist beliefs and adherence to the democratic ideals of the late 1980s did nothing to turn Gusinsky into a hero for him.

Given the sensitivities of free speech and journalists' obsession with their own profession, the NTV battle generated considerable media attention. But the issues at stake – and the methods employed – were commonplace in Russia. New and old management teams in a wide variety of different businesses, supported by contradictory court decisions obtained in dubious circumstances, fought for control with the help of muscled interventions by court bailiffs and private militias. Law enforcement and the judicial system had been privatized, and the state itself was often weak. In autumn 1999, I witnessed the forceful eviction of Dmitry Savelev, the manager of Transneft, the state-controlled oil pipeline operator, who refused to leave when the government fired him. Ahead of the NTV takeover, two well-known vodka factories in Moscow, Kristall and Smirnoff, had been the scenes of similar feuds. Dozens of other, low-profile instances were taking place across the country.

The NTV takeover divided opinion-makers. Yuri Luzhkov, the once powerful and outspoken mayor of Moscow who had benefited from Gusinsky's past support and backing, swiftly changed sides. As a political opponent of Putin, he had already felt pressure to become more accommodating. Investigations resurfaced into the business activities of his wife. His control over the city budget was sharply curtailed in favour of the federal finance ministry. He was politically sidelined and his powers cut. In an effort to reconcile himself to Putin, Luzhkov adopted a far lower profile. A few days before the NTV takeover, he had concluded an agreement to unite his Fatherland movement with the pro-Kremlin Unity party as a single voting bloc in parliament. He was not in the mood to jump to the defence of Gusinsky and his 'anti-Putin' channel. He turned his back on the station which had offered him support and credibility a few months earlier, in order to pre-serve his own future.

Grigory Yavlinsky, head of the liberal Yabloko party, was the most outspoken among the handful of politicians criticizing what was taking place at NTV. A former dissident who trained as an economist and was a fluent English speaker, he never ceased to highlight the contrast between Russia and much of the rest of Eastern Europe. In the other countries, he argued, the transition from Communism over the previous decade had been considerably accelerated by the removal of the old *nomenklatura*. In Russia, the old Soviet elite had remained in charge, and the rise of former KGB agents to power – starting with Putin himself – threatened the creation of a police state. Many of Yabloko's supporters – concentrated in the traditional intel-lectual centres of Moscow and St Petersburg – were themselves dissidents who placed a high priority on human rights and demo-cratic freedoms. Yavlinsky also had a personal loyalty to NTV. He had received considerable support from Gusinsky – both financially and in air-time. He was granted extensive exposure during the spring 2000 presidential race, when he stood against Putin. The station had become a natural home for him, the forum for many of his policy pro-nouncements. So it was no surprise that, as the tension grew, he led a night-time vigil in the headquarters to fend off any potential Gazprom attack. His militants also helped organize a rally outside Ostankino that attracted several thousand people, officially in defence of free speech, even if 'Yabloko' and 'Yavlinsky for President' banners were as much in evidence as anything to do with NTV.

But Yabloko's position contrasted sharply with that of SPS, the Union of Right Forces, a conglomeration of different parties on the liberal right. Its members always had an uneasy relationship with Yabloko, and NTV drew a clear dividing line between them. SPS had proved more willing to court power, establishing tight links with the Putin administration. When Yavlinsky stood out by criticizing the second war in Chechnya in autumn 1999 and called for the govern-ment to negotiate a political settlement with rebel forces, Anatoly Chubais, one of the leaders of the SPS, accused him of being a traitor. Yavlinsky retorted that Chubais was the architect of a 'semi-criminal oligarchic state', one of those top officials behind the cut-price insider privatizations that had created a handful of powerful business leaders. As parliamentary elections approached in December 1999, SPS made great play of presenting its economic programme to Putin, hinting at its cooperation with the likely new leader of the Kremlin. Putin reciprocated the noises of courtship, and SPS was rewarded with a record 11 per cent of the votes. Yabloko suffered by contrast, paying the price of Yavlinsky's uncompromising candour. It barely scraped by the 5 per cent minimum threshold to enter parliament.

Philosophically SPS, which represented Russia's new middle class and entrepreneurs, had strong sympathies with democratic values. But it also stressed the importance of property rights, debt reimbursement, and the use of the bankruptcy courts to enforce claims against non-payers. These were essential – and frequently unfulfilled – conditions by which Russia's newly established market economy could function. Yet Gusinsky – like other oligarchs – was far from meeting such standards, bending competitive practices and amassing large debts which he was unable to repay. As Boris Nemtsov, one of the SPS leaders, put it ambiguously on a late-night NTV show shortly after the shareholders' meeting: 'We believe in both freedom of speech and property rights. If we have to choose . . . we want to have both.' As with Yabloko, there was also a personal aspect to the relations with NTV for top SPS politicians. But it was a negative one. Both Chubais and Nemtsov had been attacked in the government by Gusinsky during the 'information wars'. They exhibited a certain ruthless pragmatism, never better illustrated than when they appointed Kokh as their campaign manager for the parliamentary elections in 2003.

NTV's takeover would not be enough for Gazprom and its backers in the Kremlin, who maintained a dogged pursuit of Gusinsky's former journalists and executives. In the hours following the takeover in April 2001, Kiselyov and his team made their way to other televisions studios just across the street. They fled to TNT, a minor television station that Gusinsky still controlled, best known for its dusty repertoire of old films. For a few hours, the rebel journalists even managed to continue broadcasting on NTV's frequency, until Jordan's technicians cut them off. But when they switched to TNT, it too came under threat. Within two days, the Russian tax police launched a series of legal actions. Months earlier, they had conducted raids and accused the chain of underpaying taxes – to a total of just $7,000. The management disputed the bill, which as so often in Russia owed much to the huge contradictions in legislation. Nevertheless, it ultimately agreed to pay. But in a bizarre form of 'double jeopardy', the tax police now began a criminal claim, based on the argument that the top executives of TNT were personally liable for tax evasion – even though payment had been made.

In early April, Gusinsky had hosted an extraordinary secret gathering at his Spanish villa. The shareholders' meeting to oust his directors had already taken place, and although the takeover was yet to happen, he was preparing for the inevitable outcome. The guest of honour was Boris Berezovsky. Between their feuds, he and Gusinsky had forged pragmatic alliances before, including over Svyazinvest. Now the two exiles were brought together again by common interests. 'We have difficult relations,' Gusinsky had said in February 2001, when Berezovsky first publicly offered help by proposing a $50m credit line to Media Most after the Russian authorities froze its bank accounts. 'But at the moment, any help without political conditions is good.'

Berezovsky offered the former NTV team a precarious new chance. He had relinquished his control of ORT, but he still had a controlling stake in a minor channel, TV6. Its ratings were low, but it had a strong regional network and was the nearest thing to a fourth national channel. The Kiselyov team took it over, spicing up a bland mix of cheap foreign soap operas with acerbic news and current affairs. For Gusinsky, the offer gave him a continued outlet for his views within Russia, and support for his loyal staff. For Berezovsky, it provided a fresh weapon in his armoury, a way to build his new-found image as an opposition figure, and a defender of free speech and civil society. He used TV6 as a mouthpiece, appearing on the channel to allege FSB involvement in the apartment bombings and mounting criticism of Putin's administration. But Berezovsky had a reputation for withdrawing rather than investing money in the businesses he controlled. The chances of getting paid, or of receiving future large financing on the scale Gusinsky had offered, were remote. The prospect of outside investors coming in to save the NTV radicals was equally slim. 'I understand perfectly well that Berezovsky is a very contradictory person,' said Kiselyov at the time. 'But we have no other options.'

TV6 was soon under threat too. Lukoil-Garant, the pension fund of Lukoil, one of Russia's largest and most powerful oil groups, which owned a minority (15 per cent) share of the station, started legal action. It was angry at the new format, and believed Berezovsky was trying to dilute its own share down to zero and take full control. It complained that the management changes triggered by the arrival of the NTV team had been made without its approval, and it used the obscure insolvency law only ever previously applied against Media Most, calling for TV6's liquidation. The move made little sense from a business perspective. It risked destroying whatever value could have been generated from the company. Lukoil may have been acting on orders from the Kremlin, or simply trying to please at a time when it too was coming under pressure for its support of Putin's rivals. In any case, the courts had no doubt which way they should rule. As Berezovsky began a process of appeals, the pressure mounted. Mirroring the Skuratov affair in 1999, a Russian Internet site released a video of a man 'resembling Kiselyov' cavorting with prostitutes. Then, even as the prospect of liquidation loomed for TV6, the press minister Lesin took a decisive, pre-emptive step: in January 2002, he ordered the station's broadcast licence to be withdrawn.

The chase of the NTV luminaries by the authorities was exhaustive. One by one, demoralized and tempted by lucrative offers elsewhere, some of the best journalists from the old team were picked off. Svetlana Sorokina, a key anchor, was headhunted by ORT to host her own show, *Basic Instinct*. She had been reluctant to join Berezovsky's camp, but says she opted to work for TV6 after receiving calls from people warning her that it would be inadvisable not to do so. She finally quit only when it collapsed. But Kiselyov had fewer options. He held talks with Russian business figures, including Chubais and Oleg Deripaska, who were sympathetic to the idea of financing a non-state channel. Some officials sought to curry favour with the Kremlin by proposing that the TV6 frequency should be allotted to a sports channel, but Kiselyov and his team won approval to take back the licence on behalf of a newly created company called TVS. He agreed a complicated structure designed to safeguard journalistic independence while ultimately owned by his business backers. The idea was all but stillborn. It was difficult enough to get two of the country's competing business bosses to agree for long, let alone an entire consortium. To obtain the Kremlin's blessing, the company agreed to an advisory board run by Arkady Volsky, the head of the Russian Union of Industrialists and Entrepreneurs, and Yevgeny Primakov. Primakov set the tone, warning in one radio interview that he expected journalists to exercise 'internal censorship . . . let's call it self-censorship' in their broadcasts.

In reality, Kiselyov says that Primakov rarely interfered. A heavy outside hand was hardly needed to scupper the project. It was destroyed from within, weighed down by heavy budgets and by fights between the oligarchs for control. As it struggled from crisis to crisis, there were quarrels over senior management changes, injections of new cash and efforts by its creditors to call in their debts. Reporters grew tired of the endless variations on the theme of business versus freedom of speech. When a final compromise between the owners fell apart, TVS was set to close of its own accord in June 2003. But Lesin again dealt it a pre-emptive swipe, withdrawing its licence just a few days before it would have folded. In its place, the state finally launched its sports channel.

A constant question in Moscow was who was behind the relentless pursuit of NTV. It seemed hard to imagine that Putin himself was coordinating every step. But it was just as inconceivable that such a high profile campaign could have been run without his consent. The persistent, wide-ranging actions suggested a Soviet practice that had re-emerged in many areas of Russian life under Putin. Local bureaucrats – in the prosecutor's office, the tax inspectorate, the security services or the courts – and even private companies would demonstrate 'initiative from below'. Some reacted to pressure. Others to commercial greed. Still more tried to please, doing what they thought would earn them credit from the Kremlin. Once the president had set the tone, officials long used to reading between the lines would react. All it required was the lack of any reprimand, and a modest occasional sign of encouragement. Often, Soviet style, important developments in the Gusinsky saga happened when Putin was out of Moscow and could claim to be removed from the decision. He feigned surprise when he was 'informed' by journalists on arrival for a state visit to Spain in June 2000 that Gusinsky had been arrested. But his subtle smile in front of the cameras was signal enough to proceed. The details such as the amount owed by Media Most to Gazprom that he cited at his press conference showed that he was following the case very closely indeed.

But if initiatives from below were easy to start, they were more difficult to stop. While Putin's motivation may have been political, principally designed to destabilize a potential opponent and bring a powerful media tool under control, others had different motives. The fate of NTV after Gazprom's takeover was a case in point. Although initially decried as an agent of the Russian state, Jordan did a good job in managing the station. The channel maintained criticism of the authorities within certain limits, and remained far more outspoken than many had feared. Jordan's mission was different from Gusinsky's, the economic climate was improving sharply, and the persecutions had stopped. But the peace would not last long. He tried to bypass Lesin and sidestep those in Gazprom Media, cultivating his own contacts directly in the Kremlin. He had his eye on engineering a management buyout that would give him a big stake in the company once he had turned it around. With foreign investors scared away, it was ultimately a curious cabal of Russian state-backed banks led by Evrofinance, a former subsidiary of the Russian Central Bank, which led a partial buyout from Gazprom.

Although Jordan spoke Russian fluently, he was a foreigner, making him difficult to control. The Dubrovka theatre siege in October 2002 provided the perfect pretext for his ouster. Leonid Parfyonov, one of NTV's top journalists, infuriated the Kremlin by employing a lip reader to work out what was going on in a cabinet meeting, images of which had been distributed to the media by officials without the sound. It showed that Putin and Mikhail Kasyanov, his prime minister, were disagreeing about launching a raid. Savik Shuster's evening talk show featured angry relatives of those in the siege who, imbued with the Stockholm syndrome, called for negotiations with Chechen rebel leaders. That same night, Russian special forces attacked. Putin would accuse NTV afterwards of broadcasting the operation live, jeopardizing its success. It was simply not true. Rival channels were broadcasting the test card, or old Soviet films. NTV easily outstripped its rivals in its coverage, but it was not live. After a very brief comment by a reporter standing some way away from the theatre that 'I think something may be happening,' there was no further news while it waited for approval from the authorities. By the time a local crew had filmed troop movements and made it back to their outside broadcast van for transmission by satellite, and editors had studied the material and released it, the raid was over. But the accusation had been made, stirred up by Jordan's rivals, and the ground was prepared to oust him and his management team.

The new general director was Nikolai Sinkevich, the son of a famous Soviet television presenter, who had no experience in either the media or management. He was a doctor specializing in the treatment of piles. Shuster's live talk show, called *Freedom of Speech*, soon underwent a change. It became pre-recorded for a while, allowing the option of editing out embarrassing bits. Parfyonov's Sunday evening *Namedny* show was subject to periodic censorship, notably when Sinkevich ordered him to drop an item in November 2003 on a 'kiss and tell' book by the journalist Elena Tregubova about her experiences as a Kremlin reporter. Whatever the true reasons behind NTV's shifting ownership, the result was that the state reasserted its control – just in time for the build-up to the 2003 parliamentary elections, the first real test of Putin's political regime.

The ultimate extremes

As Alexei Sidorov reached for the entrance door to his apartment block in the Russian city of Togliatti one evening in October 2003, two men rushed up to him and stabbed him repeatedly in the chest. He managed to call his wife on the entryphone, but as she rushed to help him he was already dying. Sidorov had taken over as editor of the *Togliatti Observer* just eighteen months earlier, after an assassin shot Valery Ivanov, the founder of a paper known for its tough articles on corruption, inequality and crime. The latest murder brought to six the number of journalists killed since 1995 in the city, which was dominated by Avtovaz, the automobile manufacturer traditionally preyed upon by organized criminal groups fighting over control of the sales from the production line. None of the killings have been solved, and the efforts of the local police – who initially attempted to claim that Sidorov had been involved in a drunken brawl – appeared risible. Where criminals could not buy off the authorities in the Samara region, there were always other methods, such as the arson of the regional interior ministry's own headquarters in February 1999, which killed seventeen inspectors.

Since 1993, the International Committee for the Protection of Journalists estimates that forty journalists have been killed in Russia in the course of their work, one of the highest death tolls around the world. Many more have suffered from beatings and threats. Statistics collected by different local organizations have given frighteningly large totals. From his small office in central Moscow, Oleg Panfilov, who runs the Centre for Journalism in Extreme Situations, tries painstakingly to keep track of all the cases. There have been clear-cut ones such as that of Dmitry Kholodov, the *Moskovsky Komsomolets* journalist killed in 1994 by a booby-trap in a murder linked to his work investigating corruption in the military. Some journalists have died in alcohol-related incidents, or for reasons only tangentially linked to their work. Others have been killed in disputes over money rather than directly because of what they wrote. The problem is that commercial conflicts and freedom of expression are often interlinked in post-Soviet Russia. Few media organizations are profitable, and their economic dependency makes them tools in broader corporate and political struggles, as Gusinsky's NTV highlighted.

For the vast majority of media outlets, the state remains the dominant influence. Just ahead of the parliamentary elections in 1999, I travelled to Ufa, the capital of the ethnic republic of Bashkortostan, to investigate one such situation. Murtaza Rakhimov, a former 'red director' of the local oil company, had become president in 1993 and created his own dynasty, putting his son in charge of the oil sector and grooming him as his successor. He tightly controlled the local election machine, delivering very strong support for the successive parties that he chose to endorse. He had put his weight behind Our Home is Russia, the 'party of power' of then prime minister Viktor Chernomyrdin in the 1995 parliamentary race, the Communist Party under Gennady Zyuganov in the 1996 presidential campaign, and Yuri Luzhkov's Fatherland-All Russia in the 1999 Duma campaign.

One of his techniques was tight control of the media, earning his republic the dubious prize among national journalists' organizations of the worst place for press freedom in the country. Yavlinsky, the head of Yabloko, cancelled a trip to Bashkortostan in 1999 after his campaign organizers had permission for their rallies withdrawn, and were told that his official plane would be turned back at the airport. The manager of a local television station who had offered air-time to Yavlinsky was fired. With Dorenko bashing Luzhkov and Primakov regularly on ORT, Rakhimov took the station's local affiliate off the air until Moscow intervened to restore it. Boris Shmakov, editor of the anti-Rakhimov newspaper *Vmeste*, had twice been beaten up in recent months. He told me how none of the regional printing presses would take his business, so he had to have his paper produced in Zlatoust, a town outside the republic's borders, and then brought in by truck. That was only the start of the problem. Many newsvendors were reluctant to sell copies, knowing that if these were on view in their kiosks they risked trouble with the police.

Rakhimov exploited the situation. But the majority of journalists across Russia remain closely bound to federal, regional or local governments. Many are in fact civil servants, their salaries paid for by city or regional administrations, their publications receiving rent support and access to state-controlled distribution networks. Local authorities control some 80 per cent of the country's printing presses. They offer cheap loans, bulk subscriptions and payment for the publication of official documents. The resulting heavily subsidised, high-circulation operations suck in advertising and undercut the subscription charges that commercial publications must levy to break even. In the process, they undermine any attempts to create a self-supporting, free press. At the national level, the state is also deeply involved. The very existence of a federal press ministry seems like a Soviet anachronism. In fact, it has a very post-Soviet incumbent, since Mikhail Lesin, the minister, is himself a mini-oligarch, the power behind Video International, which long had a near-monopoly on the Russian advertising market. His department helped create its own captive professional organization Media Soyuz in 2000, to compete with the existing Union of Journalists. The new project was widely seen as a well-financed but bureaucratic body designed to divide and confuse, undertaking such projects as a 'Golden Pen' award offering prizes for the best positive articles and broadcasts about Russia.

Under Putin, the state reasserted its role. When I arrived in Russia in 1998, most important press conferences in Moscow were held in a hall of the private press agency Interfax, decorated with signed photographs of ministers, politicians and top officials who had appeared there. Ria-Novosti, a state-run agency, occasionally managed to lure an obscure bureaucrat to its tatty Soviet-era panelled room. By 2002, it had taken over the market, hosting the best speakers in state-of-the-art surroundings, complete with a giant flat-screen television. For a while, Interfax even had difficulties accrediting its journalists to the official 'pool' in the Kremlin. This was symptomatic of a new recentralization of power, matched by a cult of secrecy, with administration officials more difficult to see than they had been under Yeltsin. Meetings would often begin and end with the desire for any article to be 'objective' – or sympathetic. Many public figures demanded prior approval of any direct quotes they gave.

There was an underlying contempt for journalists. As Echo Moskvy's Alexei Venediktov put it, Putin 'sees the media as someone's instrument. He looks at them as an industry, not a societal institution.' No better confirmation could have come from Putin's own mouth, when he reacted angrily to a *Le Monde* journalist during the EU–Russia summit in Rome in November 2003 who asked him about judicial abuses in the high-profile investigation into the oil group Yukos taking place at the time. 'This bears no relation to cooperation between Russia and the EU, but if this problem interests you, I understand you were put up to it, you must earn your fee. Having earned billions, they [Yukos's shareholders] will of course spend millions, tens of millions, hundreds of millions in order to save their billions. We know how this money is spent – on what lawyers, on what companies and firms, on what politicians, including so these types of questions get asked.'

But despite all its efforts to control information, the authorities were far less effective in resolving the more important structural issues faced by the media. One Sunday evening in October 2003, Panfilov called me with a tip. A conflict was brewing at the offices of *Novoe Vremiya*, a critical weekly magazine. I rushed to the scene, to find the editor standing in the window on the second floor talking to his staff in the street below, a hostage in his own building. A Moscow businessman had appealed to the property registrar and claimed title to the offices that the publication had occupied – and believed it owned – for forty years. Late the previous Thursday evening, nine armed men from a private security company had arrived to enforce his 'rights'. They took the two students who were acting as lookouts by surprise, and kicked them out. On Sunday afternoon, they stepped up their action, refusing entry to the journalists and threatening to break down the inner door to the magazine. When the police finally arrived, they did nothing to intervene. 'How can this happen? We live in a peaceful country,' said one women journalist stranded outside. 'Don't be so naïve, sweetie. Peace was in Soviet times. Now we live in democracy,' replied the policeman. 'This happens all the time – normally over the weekend, when the courts are closed. You should have an "arrangement" with the police.'

The press ministry's own offices were right next door. But more symbolic were the other nearby tenants: a garish casino complete with flashing neon signs, a nightclub and an up-market restaurant. Located on prime real estate near Pushkin Square, *Novoe Vremiya*'s office was one that powerful commercial interests had their eye on turning into a more lucrative venture in the vicinity. The publication was not alone. Just opposite sat *Moscow News*, a liberal weekly which was forced to move to the Moscow suburbs later the same year after problems with its lease. On the other side of the square was the prestigious national newspaper *Izvestiya*. Mikhail Kozhokin, the then editor, told me that Kremlin officials would call up periodically and suggest it was time to reopen the question of ownership of its headquarters. It was never clear whether the threats were politically inspired by their masters, as they hinted, or the civil servants were playing their own games.

In any case, the situation created a permanent climate of tension, a reminder of the post-Soviet ambiguities that hovered over the media and much of the rest of the country. *Izvestiya* had already been split in two during the uncertain privatization of the early 1990s, with part of the editorial team heading off to create a rival paper, *Noviye Izvestiya*. *Izvestiya* itself was caught in a stalemate between two corporate owners which had fought for control: the oil group Lukoil and Interros, the holding company of Vladimir Potanin, the politically influential businessman. Potanin had the majority share, but Lukoil had a significant stake and its own agenda, refusing to approve injections of new money to help the newspaper develop. As Yassen Zassoursky, the veteran dean of the Moscow State University school of journalism, argues: 'The Yeltsin privatizations freed journalists from their former control, but gave no initial mention of ownership, resulting in continued economic confusion.'

If disputes over assets created one form of leverage by mixing the commercial with the professional, Panfilov considers that the most important threat to journalism under Putin has come from another source: the rise in legal actions. He calculated that in the first two years of Putin's term, more lawsuits had been filed against the media than during the previous decade under Yeltsin. Alexei Venediktov of *Echo Moskvy* estimated that 150 laws were passed in 2000–2003 affecting the media in some form. Many threatened severe penalties for trivial offences, providing yet more pressure points. 'Even the new law on the use of the Russian language means in theory that if a broadcaster mispronounces a word, the station could be taken off the air,' said Venediktov.

Libel cases have been among the most worrisome form of pressure. The feisty *Novaya Gazeta*, a weekly paper with an investigative slant, was almost forced to close in 2002 after it received a claim for damages of $500,000. Mezhprombank claimed it had lost business when a corporate client had read a negative article about it and decided to take its money elsewhere. One of the paper's own journalists dug around, and found out that the 'client' was in fact linked to Mezhprombank, and the entire case was a set-up. In a separate case, a judge in the south of Russia had launched and won a $1m libel suit after the paper's articles raised questions about his luxurious lifestyle which hardly tallied with his modest official salary. Even foreign publications were not immune from litigation. Keen to defend their new, improved reputation, some of the country's largest oligarch groups started launching actions abroad: Oleg Deripaska's Russian Aluminium or Mikhail Khodorkovsky's Yukos threatened litigation in Frankfurt and London against the financial news agency Bloomberg, the *Sunday Times*, *Le Monde* and *Frankfurter Allgemeine Zeitung*. But the situation is far worse for Russian publications, dragged into the Russian courts.

The result of such pressure is that perhaps the biggest danger to journalism in contemporary Russia is the return of self-censorship. If Gusinsky and his colleagues faced threats and even the confiscation of assets, they also had enormous political clout and financial support. For the majority of Russian journalists, their working conditions are far more miserable and the risks even greater. The attacks on NTV sent a clear warning to regional television and print organizations across the country about clashing with the authorities. They also indicated to regional and local governments that they had carte blanche to interfere. 'The threat of closure has made editors more careful,' said Vladimir Gurevich, editor of the daily newspaper *Vremiya Novostei*. Alexei Simonov from the Glasnost Defence Foundation said: 'The idea of self-censorship is a long-running one in Russia. We thought that the guard inside each journalist's head had left his post and gone away. Now we have found out that he was just asleep and is waking up.'

For some journalists, threats were not even necessary. Wrested from the hands of Berezovsky, ORT demonstrated a complete transformation. Its prime-time evening news became a case study in sycophancy, a reminder of its Soviet nick-name 'All about Him . . . and the weather,' in a reference to Brezhnev. As Gennady Seleznyov, the then speaker of the parliament, complained once, there were four items each night: 'A disaster, Putin meeting a minister, a glorious act by United Russia and the weather.' He was right, except that the first item was usually Putin, covered at obsequious length whatever the news value of the event, whether it was a technical discussion in his office on health care, or a skiing trip to Magnetogorsk. Such extensive coverage would no doubt have brought joy to Sovietologists starved of information only fifteen years before, but it was hardly news.

When I met Konstantin Ernst, ORT's general director in late 2002, he acknowledged how extensive was the coverage of Putin, but came up with a ruthlessly market-oriented explanation: 'We have to show our viewers want they want.' That included a desire to see their healthy, young president representing their country at every occasion. He had reoriented the station to the state's wishes, even hiring Alexander Zdanovich, the spokesman of the FSB, as a senior executive. Marat Gelman, a political consultant who was also appointed as the station's deputy director in that same year, went further. He said that until his nomination the news agenda had been largely determined by reports on Interfax. Gelman brought in tighter coordination, helped by the 'Friday meeting' in the Kremlin chaired by the presidential chief of staff and attended by the heads of the television channels.

Russia still had considerable freedom of speech. The Internet carried all sorts of inflammatory and unverified information, and there were hard-hitting factual and fictionalized books, as well as newspapers and magazine in Moscow and even in the regions that offered a diet of scandal. In television, the most important influence on public opinion, the appearance of professionalism improved sharply, in large part thanks to the style Gusinsky set and the top-quality journalists he trained. But the content deteriorated sharply. Diversity of opinion diminished. It seemed like a far more positive sign when RTR, the second state channel, acquired a significant shareholding in Euronews, and began broadcasting bulletins drawn from television news services around Europe. But if its headquarters in Lyons in

France chose the running order and pictures to be shown, the translation into Russian was a watered-down version which edited out any Kremlin-critical remarks. When I asked Gelman why ORT had given so little coverage to the enormous scandal around the clearly politically motivated investigations into the oil group Yukos, he replied: 'Yes, it was really curious. That was the first time they didn't tell us about something in advance.' It seems that he had not been given his orders on how to report. Or, in a Kremlin and government that seemed increasingly divided in its approach between competing clans, suddenly they were not sure which clique they should be listening to. That could have resulted in a new form of media diversity. Instead it led to silence on one of the most important topics of the 2003 pre-election period.

AUTUMN OF THE OLIGARCHS

LEANING FORWARD EARNESTLY AS he spoke, Boris Berezovsky lamented the state of Russia under Vladimir Putin: freedom of speech had been crushed, political opposition all but eliminated, the country was returning to totalitarianism. An excitable man with a trophy wife half his age in tow, he made an unlikely dissident. It was July 2001 and we were sitting in Berezovsky's own Challenger jet, in deep white leather armchairs, en route to Paris before he headed on to Tokyo for a weekend trip. His chauffeur had driven us to Nice airport in a Mercedes from his luxurious estate which dominated the tip of the Cap d'Antibes in southern France. His three portable telephones lay on the table in front of us. For once cut off from a ground signal, they were not all ringing simultaneously. He hinted that his wealth came to several billion dollars – not bad for someone who little more than a decade earlier had been an obscure, impoverished academic sharing a rusting Zhiguli car with a colleague.

During the 1990s, Berezovsky had proved lucky, skilful and ruthless in equal measure, putting his university research on decision-making theory to very practical use, building contacts and extracting cash from the crumbling Soviet system. He created the company AVVA, an investment fund which left tens of thousands of ordinary Russians out of pocket when it collapsed in 1993. Most of his future riches would come from links to state enterprises. He established LogoVAZ, a powerful partnership with VAZ, the manufacturer of the Zhiguli, using it to distribute the vehicles on preferential terms and build up a franchise in Moscow. He won control over Sibneft, one of the most attractive state oil companies privatized cheaply to insiders. He fought back aggressively when he lost out in another, the sale of the telecoms holding company Svyazinvest. In retaliation he launched a media campaign that destabilized the government. He exerted strong influence over Aeroflot, the state-controlled national airline, less through owning shares than by appointing his own people to top jobs. As he once memorably put it: 'I don't privatize companies, I privatize people.' Much of the airline's substantial revenue was channelled through his service companies in Switzerland, earning him significant commissions in the process. He claimed a large stake in Siberian Aluminium, a metals giant that dominated the market.

In July 1996, just after the re-election of Boris Yeltsin, Berezovsky boasted that he was one of 'seven bankers' who between them controlled half of Russia's GDP and had masterminded Yeltsin's election. But as he himself put it, 'I use business for political objectives.' Once he had concentrated on securing revenue streams from whatever source, he was far more concerned with how to spend them than with the precise nature of his investments. And his expenditure often bore little relation to the businesses themselves. What excited him was power. In 1996, newly back in office, Yeltsin appointed Berezovsky deputy secretary of the state security council. A year later, he became executive secretary of the Commonwealth of Independent States, the loose confederation of former Soviet countries. More than any of his fellow politically influential business oligarchs who emerged over the period, he was obsessed with the political ends for which business was primarily the means. 'In 1997–8 all ministerial appointments passed through the office of Sibneft,' said one Russian politician. That made him the first among equals as the mood towards oligarchs changed under Putin. As Berezovsky sensed the dangers in 1999, he stood for election to the federal parliament from the North Caucasus region of Karachayevo-Cherkessia, providing him with some immunity from prosecution. But it would not be enough.

To some, Berezovsky's influence was overplayed, not least by the man himself. Critics argue that he used his extensive information network to learn of government decisions before they were made public, and then announce them as though they were his own idea. In the rankings of the country's most influential people published by the newspaper *Nezavisimaya Gazeta*, he consistently ranked near the top. But Berezovsky owned the paper, and its polling techniques left room for doubt about the accuracy of the information. In any case, Berezovsky's word was taken seriously in Moscow's hothouse political atmosphere, and his press conferences were always packed with journalists hungry for his views. He had considerable access to those at the centre of power, and did his best to influence decision-making. Though Yeltsin's own autobiography makes few references to Berezovsky, he was closely associated with the 'Family' around the then president. His partner at AVVA had been Alexander Voloshin, who would go on to head the presidential administration. His commercial alter ego during the second half of the 1990s was the tycoon Roman Abramovich. And as thoughts turned to Yeltsin's succession during 1999, he stepped up contact with Vladimir Putin.

Yevgeny Primakov, the prime minister after the August 1998 crisis, certainly rated Berezovsky's influence as excessive. 'His ambition was to claim no more or less than the management of the country,' Primakov wrote in his memoirs. Under Primakov's leadership, prosecutors began probing the oligarchs' business empires, starting with those under Berezovsky's control. Criminal inquiries were opened at Sibneft and Aeroflot. There were raids on a private security company called Atoll that he controlled. But Berezovsky had powerful allies. As he came under widespread attack, he received an unexpected visitor to his *dacha* on his birthday: Vladimir Putin himself. Putin also visited Berezovsky in the south of France as they hatched his presidential campaign strategy in summer 1999.

If Berezovsky was not the only 'kingmaker' for Putin, he was certainly among the inner circle of counsellors around Yeltsin, and one of the most important in turning the dauphin into the ruler. Berezovsky harboured a strong dislike for Primakov and Yuri Luzhkov, the mayor of Moscow, both of whom enjoyed high ratings and were emerging as strong presidential contenders. He was instrumental in creating Edinstvo, the Unity party, in summer 1999. He put to good use ORT, the state television channel which he controlled, and *Kommersant*, the newspaper which he bought in the same year, initially through the front of an implausibly young Iranian 'businessman'. True to his academic roots, Berezovsky had helped gain his first access to the Yeltsin circle through literature. He arranged the publication of a glossy version of Yeltsin's presidential memoirs in Russian. In 1999, the German academic Alexander Rahr came to him to ask for assistance in a book he was writing on Putin, but says Berezovsky instead helped organize the production of a rival work. Three Russian journalists interviewed the secretive Putin. *First Person*, the result, was designed to help his election campaign.

At first, Berezovksy seemed to reap the benefits of his work. He emerged as a beneficiary of Russian Aluminium, the giant cash-rich metals conglomerate formed by bringing together a disparate series of smelters long suffering from bitter ownership disputes. It sailed through approvals from the state anti-monopoly commission, although it controlled more than 70 per cent of the market. But within months of Putin's victory, Berezovsky was on the run. Berezovsky himself says that he had failed to anticipate the new president's authoritarian twist, and they fell out on policy grounds: the reckless pursuit of the war in Chechnya, the attacks on the regions and the attempt to rein in dissent. One leading Russian journalist says that Berezovsky had told Putin: 'Just because I have supported you up till now does not mean I will continue to do so.' For Putin, so used to absolute loyalty, that may have proved the decisive factor. In any case, as one Russian politician claims, Berezovsky's requests for meetings with Putin were suddenly refused. He no longer had the access of which he had once boasted.

Whatever the truth, Berezovsky's instincts and contacts indicated that the mood had changed. He knew well how to read the signs, fleeing the country in autumn 2000 while he still had the chance, ahead of the jailing of Nikolai Glushkov, his lieutenant appointed to run Aeroflot. Berezovsky says he was tricked into selling off ORT with a broken promise of Glushkov's release. His people were ousted from Aeroflot. His rights to the TV6 broadcasting licence were stripped away. He was forced to sell his stake in Sibneft. As so often in the modern Russian code of honour, he was not left out of pocket. He received $170m for ORT, and $1.3.bn for Sibneft. Nor was he persecuted as ruthlessly as the media magnate Gusinsky. Perhaps he knew too much; perhaps he was more subtle; perhaps Putin felt he owed him something. When I asked him, his own explanation, after a long pause, was that he had not irritated so much with direct lobbying for his commercial interests, which he had left behind when he began to focus on politics. 'Putin remembers the time when we were in the same boat,' he added.

Driven into opposition, and then swiftly into exile, Berezovsky maintained a close eye on Russia. His power-broking role, and his particular knowledge of Chechnya forged through a decade of tight contacts with the diaspora, made him of considerable use to his host governments. He settled first in France, and then took advantage of the more favourable fiscal regime in the UK. In his offices in the West End in London, his employees scanned the Internet, providing him with thick dossiers of information each day on what was going on back in Russia. He was eager to meet with fellow countrymen whenever they were passing through London, sometimes paying their fares so they would come. With a bright, lively intelligence, and his past influence so recent in his memory, Berezovsky was clearly dissatisfied with his self-imposed exile. His analysis was usually shrewd, though always carefully crafted to portray himself as hero and victim.

He used part of his fortune to fund human rights groups and Chechen causes. He supported Akhmed Zakayev, the former Chechen rebel leader, who came to London and fought extradition proceedings launched by the Russian authorities. He did the same for Alexander Litvinenko, his former bodyguard, who had worked for the FSB security services before fleeing abroad. Berezovsky's growing public criticism of Putin's regime helped position him as an opposition figure in a way that dovetailed well with his bid for political asylum in Britain in autumn 2003. But he was no longer a player. Extricated from Russia, he could live well, yet he was frustrated and bored. There was probably nothing more painful for him than to hear Putin's dismissive answer at a Kremlin press conference in July 2001, when a journalist asked him about Berezovsky. 'Who's he?' the Russian president replied. Berezovsky was a prime example of how the relationship between business and power would alter under Putin. The oligarchs had helped create the conditions and the mechanisms for Putin's ascension to power. But he began to appropriate their system, slip from their control and adapt the rules.

The battle for control

The stylish Samotlar hotel would have been strangely out of place almost anywhere in Russia in the mid-1990s. In the drab western Siberian oil town of Nizhnevartovsk, it looked as though it had been airlifted in from Scandinavia by mistake. Like so many provincial centres that had sprung up during the Soviet Union's drive to industrialize, Nizhnevartovsk was an uninspiring collection of weather-beaten concrete five-storey buildings along gridiron streets, built to house those working in the surrounding industrial sprawl. But value judgements operate on a different scale in Russia. Aesthetics were of less importance than pragmatism to the planners and even most local residents. They were proud of their speed and effectiveness in forging an entire community out of a hostile environment. Nizhnevartovsk had been designed to service the extraction of new sources of oil in the 1970s, and to keep the state-planned system alive. More than twenty years – and a capitalist somersault – later, a bust of Lenin still stood guard in the town centre. Roads with names like 60th Anniversary of the Revolution provided a vivid reminder of the vision of the Communist officials who had overseen its construction. They would have been shocked to view the decadent Samotlar, a luxury contemporary half-moon-shaped hotel clad in wood and marble, surrounded by a small forest and a tall fence to protect guests from prying eyes and the ugliness of the environment outside.

In summer 1999, Nizhnevartovsk was the focal point of a bitter business dispute between local interests and powerful rivals located in Moscow, the repercussions of which were felt as far away as Washington, London and Frankfurt. There was a sinister air around town. Mercedes jeeps with dark-tinted glass ferried guests to and fro, and thickset bodyguards hovered in the Samotlar's entrance hall, explaining that they were there 'for your protection' when asked. Over the previous several years, the fight for control of the local oil business had left a messy trail of murders. The town's mayor had only just come out of hospital after several weeks of treatment, the result of being savagely beaten up by unknown assailants. Afraid of ubiquitous informers and bugging devices if we talked inside the hotel, one local man would only agree to discuss the possible perpetrators when we strolled in the gardens outside. It seemed like a throwback to Soviet times – but these days, the 'privatized' security services had adapted

KGB-style tactics and directly hired their staff for commercial purposes, and often with more violent consequences. Despite the uninspiring surroundings, the Samotlar itself – named after the nearby oilfield – was a striking reminder of the rich spoils at stake beneath the nearby Siberian tundra. Cash was being generated, but little of it was reinvested locally. The exception was the hotel, which became the backdrop for a classic piece of post-Soviet, post-privatization asset-grabbing, under the cover of only superficially western-style bankruptcy proceedings.

At stake was the future of Chernogorneft, the most lucrative of the two oil companies that dominated the town. At the beginning of the 1990s, as Communism crumbled, the local managers took over their 'production association', spinning themselves off from the parent company, Nizhenevartovskneftegaz (NVN), which had debts as cumbersome as its name. It operated the older, more mature and less profitable oilfields. It also paid heavy 'social charges' for the upkeep of the former factory-town, financing housing and hospitals, schools and transport. The plum asset of Chernogorneft – with the best oil and modest overheads – had fallen into the control of Sidanco, an oil holding company which regrouped production, refining and sales operations across Siberia. Sidanco, in turn, had been acquired by Vladimir Potanin, one of Russia's new generation of influential business barons.

His close-cropped hair and rough-hewn face made him look like a boxer drawn off the streets, but Potanin was the son of a senior official in the USSR's foreign trade ministry who understood the Soviet establishment perfectly. He had benefited from the lifestyle of the *nomenklatura* and spoke immaculate English. And his newly acquired wealth allowed him to develop a penchant for wild parties well endowed with young women. He got his start in the bureaucracy, and would play on his contacts to win lucrative state contracts for his financial group Uneximbank, which processed wages, pensions and trade contracts for the state. But his masterstroke came in the fashioning of something much bigger for him and for Russia as a whole. The result was to hand away many of Russia's most valuable and strategic state-owned natural resource groups in cut-price insider deals which created a class of super-rich, super-powerful oligarchs overnight, rapidly worth not just millions but billions of dollars. In the process, he laid the foundations for many of the country's future problems.

In 1995, the government was desperately short of revenue, and – with time ticking away towards the presidential elections the following year – Yeltsin was in urgent need of support. Potanin crafted a solution dubbed 'loans for shares'. On paper, the arrangement could have operated fairly: private banks like his Uneximbank would make loans to the government, and take shares in state-owned companies as security. If the money had not been repaid a year later, the shares would be sold off in auctions, with 70 per cent of any increase in their value theoretically going to the government, and the rest to the lender bank. The idea was that the state would receive close to the market value of the companies as a result. In practice, the rules were cynically constructed and implemented to minimize competition – and to maximize revenue to the banks at the expense of the government. No foreigners were allowed to take part and a series of opaque 'investment' conditions left the selection of the winner to the discretion of the self-interested institutions which administered the procedure. Loans for shares bought the loyalty of a small group of big businessmen who agreed to pool resources in order to support the re-election of Yeltsin in 1996. It was a messy compromise, at a time when Yeltsin's rating had fallen to single digits and Gennady Zyuganov, the Communist leader, looked set to win the vote, raising the prospect of re-nationalization and destruction of their newfound wealth. But it also propelled a tiny elite of politically connected businessmen, each with significant wealth built around a captive bank, into an entirely different league. They became – on highly advantageous terms – owners of some of the country's most attractive assets, and big political actors in their own right. The oligarchs were born.

In late 1995, Potanin's own Uneximbank both operated and – through an obscure affiliate called MFK – won the auction to manage 51 per cent of Sidanco's shares, in exchange for a $130m loan to the government. With Yeltsin re-elected a few months later, Potanin was appointed first deputy prime minister. In September 1996, Uneximbank bought a further 34 per cent of Sidanco cheaply, consolidating its control. Four months later, it ran the auction for the sell-off of the shares it held in collateral. The restrictive investment conditions in the tender were ones that it alone could meet: notably the requirement for the winner to transfer to Sidanco a stake in the Angarsk oil refinery, which Potanin already held. His company Interros-Oil was successful, paying just $129.8m in an auction which had a minimum offer price set at $129m. The result was that the government received not one additional kopeck beyond the value of the original loan for the sale of control in one of its more valuable oil companies. And since much of that sum was earned by Uneximbank on government money it was handling in the first place, the total cost to Potanin was symbolic. In real terms, after allowing for the effect of inflation and the previous income the bank earned from the state, the government was all but paying him to take over its businesses.

The deal was not unique. Similar tricks ensured that 'loans for shares' turned a handful of intended beneficiaries of oil company privatizations into multimillionaires. Mikhail Khodorkovsky, once a *Komsomol* (Communist Youth League) leader, became the controlling owner of Yukos through his bank Menatep. Boris Berezovsky took over Sibneft, as always one step removed, via the Stolichny Savings Bank operated by his partner Alexander Smolensky, a former construction manager made good. Mikhail Fridman of Alfa, whose bulky appearance hid a soft-spoken, shrewd interior, acquired the oil group TNK with his partners. Not all the winners were 'outsiders', and nor did their styles or fates resemble one another. Vagit Alekperov, a grey-haired top oil executive who had grown up in Azerbaijan and had been a Soviet first deputy oil minister, carved some of the country's best oil assets out of the state system to create Lukoil, a vertically integrated group with production, refining and sales operations. 'Loans for shares' allowed him to legitimize his ownership. Vladimir Bogdanov, the austere 'red director' already running Surgutneftegaz, got his own privatization in the same way. He shunned the luxury life of Moscow, cultivating an image as the best form of Soviet paternalist manager. He lived and worked in the Siberian company town of Surgut, and insisted that his top managers did the same. Potanin himself received a double prize. With his business partner, Mikhail Prokhorov, he purchased outright a second asset that would prove even more lucrative than Sidanco: Norilsk Nickel, the gigantic Arctic-based producer of rare metals.

Today, the oligarchs insist that they respected the laws that existed at the time – while glossing over the fact that they helped both draft and implement them. 'The laws were perhaps written irresponsibly after the collapse of the totalitarian state,' says Leonid Nevzlin, one of Khodorkovsky's partners. 'But everything we did was legal.' Berezovsky claims that the money paid during the privatizations was considerable, given the financial difficulties of the state and the bidders alike. He said that, faced with the threat of a presidential victory in 1996 by Gennady Zyuganov, many Russians and most foreign investors were scared away, pushing prices down. Others argue that there was competition, and the outcome was not so clear-cut at the time as it now appears. Vladimir Vinogradov, for example, a smooth banker who controlled Inkombank, made an aggressive attempt to win control of Yukos but failed.

Anatoly Chubais has a more pragmatic justification for 'loans for shares'. A tall ruddy-faced economist who mobilized the future oligarchs to support Yeltsin's campaign, he oversaw the second stage of the pact after the victory in 1996, which led to his nomination as head of the presidential administration. Even Putin dubbed him a 'Bolshevik' for his ruthless methods. But Chubais suggested that 'loans for shares' was a Faustian bargain forged between the state and big capital necessary to ensure Yeltsin's re-election and the definitive elimination of the Communists as a significant political force. He believed that it was of little importance who won the auctions or how much they paid. The aim was to prevent a red revanche, and to push big state companies into private hands. That would eliminate their continued mismanagement and theft under public ownership, and create a new class of owners who would build the foundations of a capitalist economy, invest and become ardent defenders of private property.

But as Sergei Vasiliev, an economist and politician, puts it: '"Loans for shares" was a big mistake. You could have designed the auctions differently. What is permitted to lobbyists is not permitted to reformers, if you are building a democratic society.' 'Loans for shares' may arguably have been the inevitable outcome of a late-Soviet system that had been perverted and corrupted beyond redemption. It may have been an inequitable but necessary step to push the country and its economy towards private ownership at a wild period in the 1990s when there were no clear-cut rules and little certainty about the future. It may ultimately even have helped to build the conditions for Russia's investment and economic growth in the following years. But it sent a hugely demoralizing signal to the vast majority of Russian society, who perceived 'their' wealth to have been swindled from them by a ruling cabal. It gave enormous power to a small group of oligarchs whose primary concern became the preservation and expansion of their own commercial interests. And it did little to establish firm foundations for the rule of law, or for the creation and fair operation of the institutions of a modern society, as the subsequent battle for Chernogorneft and countless other corporate struggles in the next few years would show. For Grigory Yavlinsky, leader of the Yabloko party, it created a 'semi-criminal oligarchic system' that corrupted the media, the parliament, the judicial system and government alike.

All would not be easy for the oligarchs in the aftermath of the auctions. Most lacked the financial resources necessary to fully buy up companies even at knock-down prices, and they were forced to forge alliances, not all of which were solid. Some could fall back on long-standing partners. Behind the public face of Mikhail Khodorkovsky, for example, was a tight group of friends who preferred to stay in the shadows. Bemused employees at Yukos observed that after its 'loans for shares' purchase, some executives 'parachuted' into the company appeared to wield power far beyond their official position or competence. That was because they were also shareholders alongside Khodorkovsky, observing and safeguarding their investment from the vantage point of key inside positions. His 'clan' even lived together, in a specially constructed and well-guarded 'colony' of Moscow houses in the chic north-western suburb of Zhukovka.

Other partnerships were more shaky. Vladimir Potanin developed a long-term commercial tie-up with Mikhail Prokhorov. But he also forged a temporary alliance with the Alfa group of Mikhail Fridman and his partners in order to finance and jointly own Sidanco. 'Unfortunately we were not legally strong and we didn't have enough money, but Potanin had political support and promised to protect our rights,' says Fridman. Alfa put up a third of the money, and Potanin pledged them a third of Sidanco's shares in exchange. But after the purchase, the two groups – operating in a difficult environment and still relatively inexperienced – fell out. Potanin decided to reimburse Alfa's money plus interest but to hold on to all the shares, sparking fury from his new partners. Determined to enter the oil sector regardless, Fridman bid for TNK, one of the less impressive remaining oil companies in state hands. He hooked up with Access/Renova, a joint venture controlled by the businessmen Viktor Vekselberg and Len Blavatnik, to raise funding. But by the time of the TNK auction in July

1997, there had been widespread criticism of insider deals. There was more genuine competition in the bidding, and Viktor Paly, the manager of TNK's principal production subsidiary, NVN, fought to maintain his own influence. The result was that Alfa and its partners were forced to pay a much higher price, closer to true market value, for less attractive assets: $820m for 40 per cent of the company.

As the economic climate worsened, the stakes were becoming higher and the tactics more desperate. World oil prices were low, and partly controlled domestic ones were still lower, making it difficult for the new owners to make money. After the August 1998 financial crisis, the oligarchs – most of whom had empires centred around their captive banks – were substantially weakened. Some used the crisis as an excuse to exaggerate the extent of their losses and refuse to pay creditors even though they had the money to do so. There were suggestions of favouritism in the way the Central Bank of Russia propped up a few of the banks in an attempt to maintain liquidity. But many were also left significantly out of pocket, their investments severely impaired when the rouble plummeted and the government defaulted on its high-interest bonds.

Olga Kryshtanovskaya, a sociologist who has meticulously tracked the evolution of Russia's business elite over the past decade, suggested that the oligarchs' political power was always exaggerated, more the result of slick public relations than reality. Whatever control they wielded over state financial flows and political decisions began to wane sharply after the August 1998 crisis, she says. Sergei Kirienko, the prime minister close to the oligarchs, was fired immediately afterwards by Yeltsin. Primakov's criminal investigations destabilized them still further. Iosef Pappe, an academic who has studied their evolution, agrees. 'There is no oligarchy in Russia – there are just some oligarchs,' he says.

There was another practical problem with the chaotic privatizations of the 1990s. The government had held back on the sale of the plum oil holding companies until 1995–7. But as part of the mass 'voucher privatizations' of the early 1990s, it had already sold off stakes in their subsidiaries – the individual oil production and refinery operations around the country in which they held shares. That would create inevitable structural problems once 'loans for shares' progressed. The original idea was to turn managers, employees and the general public into shareholders as quickly as possible. Alan Bigman, an American who worked on the sell-offs in Nizhny Novgorod in 1992, defends the approach of Chubais to wrest control from the state sector at any cost. 'The real priority was to break the back of the economics ministries, and get them into private ownership of any sort,' he said. At the same time, he argued that the process was too complex, reflecting a mixture of Russian's love of technical things, and foreign consultants' desires to transfer concepts from elsewhere. 'I remember how proud the advisers were to show huge diagrams with all sorts of boxes and arrows explaining how it would work.'

In Russia, the rule of the strong dominated. All that counted was the majority shareholder. There was no respect for minority investors, who were seen as a nuisance. Through a mixture of pressure and manipulation, desperation and ignorance, most shares soon ended up in the hands of the incumbent managers. The shift from abstract state control of companies to meaningless individual ownership meant little to most employees. In the harsh economic climate of the period, what mattered to them was cash. Many were glad to give up their apparently worthless privatization 'vouchers' in favour of even modest payments of badly needed roubles. For the managers who took over the companies, ownership was more important. They may not have had the majority of the shares, or considered them of much significance, but they were insiders who knew the business, and they had the ability to divert cash flows for their own gain. When the state started privatizing the oil holding companies – which normally had majority stakes in these local operating businesses – it triggered a clash that was impossible to reconcile easily. The local managers suddenly saw a threat from the far more aggressive new owners. The result was an inevitable conflict. The oligarchs found themselves struggling to consolidate their full influence over not only the holding companies they had bought, but also the subsidiaries theoretically under their control.

Not all privatized companies were entirely mercenary. Some Soviet-era managers, like Bogdanov at Surgutneftegaz, had a clear set of values, and a belief in the long-term value of their businesses. His conservative patriotism, which led him to place surplus cash in Russian banks and bonds rather than shielding it offshore, cost him dearly during the financial crisis of August 1998. But at a time of little certainty over how long any group of managers would retain control, let alone what the political future of Russia would hold, the general mood was 'grab it while you can'. Executives at different levels in the corporate hierarchies siphoned off oil revenues for themselves, and moved the money to safe havens offshore with low or no tax. Reinvesting in their businesses was not a priority, any more than respecting the rights of minority shareholders including foreigners. Without access to the cash flows or even reliable financial accounts, outside investors could do little to police the situation, and were excluded from any share of the profits. As the holding companies attempted to exert full control, the minorities' influence was still further eroded. The oligarchs appointed their own executives, held shareholder meetings to nominate directors for the boardroom and resorted to a series of tricks to exert their full control.

BP was among the western oil groups drawn into the post-privatization mess. Potanin might have seemed a curious partner for the establishment British oil group, but his exposure to foreign cultures, and his mastery of the reassuring vocabulary of responsible corporate governance, worked its charm. BP executives knew the risks of operating in Russia from earlier unsuccessful ventures, but Potanin's status as a minister and a power-broker seemed to offer a political *krysha* or 'insurance' in an uncertain environment. And with its rival Shell simultaneously finalizing a $1bn investment agreement with Gazprom, BP was keen not to be left behind. Russia was becoming the new gold rush destination for the international energy companies. After a brief period of 'due diligence' to study Sidanco, John Browne, BP's chief executive, went against the advice of some of his own consultants and signed an agreement with Potanin at Number Ten Downing Street, in the presence of Tony Blair, in November 1997. BP paid $571m for a 10 per cent stake in Sidanco, allowing Potanin swiftly to recoup his investment four times over. The deal implied that the company was already worth twenty times more than when he had acquired it just nine months earlier.

In a western quoted company, a 10 per cent stake would have been enough to exert enormous management influence. In Russia's winner-takes-all corporate culture, it was close to worthless. BP appointed three executives, but key positions including those related to control of the cash flows remained under Potanin's people. The financial information available was poor, with the company – like its peers – running multiple accounting systems: one for a handful of insiders, another for its commercial partners, and a third even less flattering for the tax inspectors. The chances were that no one knew the full picture, with different executives in the holding company and its subsidiaries serving a multitude of interests, including their own. BP soon discovered that Sidanco had accumulated huge debts. Its efforts to propose improvements were rebuffed. Tensions quickly grew with Potanin. Whether BP was aware of it or not, Sidanco was behaving just like other Russian holding companies in the ruthless struggle to exert full authority over its rebellious subsidiaries. The company even attempted to issue new bonds in December 1997 to two of Potanin's Uneximbank affiliate companies which were designed to be swapped for debt in the subsidiaries, 'diluting' into oblivion the stakes of the remaining minority shareholders.

Under the shroud of secrecy around its internal financial affairs, Sidanco was able to apply one of the most widespread practices of the industry at the time: 'transfer pricing'. It purchased all the oil from its own production units including Chernogorneft. It sold on the oil at a profit, but paid back in exchange only a nominal sum far below world market prices, drawing its own subsidiaries heavily into debt, leaving them with no money to reinvest or even pay wages. It was a mechanism for removing cash from the companies, a rational enough approach at a time when no one knew how long their control over the subsidiary companies would last. But it left the local operations very weak, creating the perfect conditions for a Russian-style takeover.

In December 1998, an obscure company called Beta Echo unexpectedly filed a bankruptcy petition against Chernogorneft in the local courts. Someone obviously had a sense of humour since the name immediately cast suspicion on Fridman's own Alfa group, which had a trading arm called Alfa Echo. Fridman had been determined to take revenge for Potanin's betrayal, and Simon Kukes, the chief executive he appointed to run TNK, was charged with implementation. He dreamed of reuniting Chernogorneft with NVN, ideally drawing on the technical skills and international prestige of BP. But John Browne rebuffed repeated approaches by Kukes, even as relations with Potanin soured. TNK denied that it was behind the bankruptcy. In fact, the local managers of Chernogorneft itself had launched the process. The Russian bankruptcy code, designed to protect creditors and owners, was instead making the situation worse. Other petitions against Sidanco's debt-laden subsidiaries followed, leaving Sidanco an empty shell, deprived of its revenues. Two months later, Potanin pre-emptively filed a petition against his own holding company Sidanco. BP wrote off $200m of its investment, and looked set to lose everything. It had backed the wrong oligarch, in the wrong country, at the wrong time.

By early 1999, global oil prices were rising again. Properly managed, Chernogorneft could have quickly paid off its creditors. In the circumstances, a reputable western-style insolvency practitioner could easily have settled the outstanding debts and handed the company back to its original shareholders. That, in turn, would have salvaged the struggling Sidanco. Yet the bankruptcy seemed to be getting nowhere. I travelled to Nizhnevartovsk to try to understand what was happening, but it was not easy. I arranged an interview with one of NVN's top managers. It was the sort of conversation that was typical of many with Russian businessmen of his generation: he gave short, uninformative answers, and after a discussion that seemed painfully long, I was more confused than ever. He insisted on prolonging the agony at a private dinner in the Samotlar afterwards with his PR manager, during which he hinted at 'coming to an agreement' – presumably designed to see whether I was willing to join the ranks of local journalists whose independence had been bought off by one side or the other.

I got to know the dining rooms of the Samotlar hotel well. As in so many Russian restaurants, the meal was accompanied by deafening pop music. I thought it was perhaps a hangover from the Soviet-style practice of distracting attention from the food and providing a complete 'entertainment experience' for those lucky few who had gained access to a jealously rationed table. But I soon saw another reason: to avoid eavesdropping. As I was attempting to have a conversation at one table, I noticed a familiar face at the next, his voice drowned out by a synthesizer. It was Vasily Bikin, Chernogorneft's court-appointed insolvency manager, whom I had met earlier in the day. Hovering in the corridors later on, I saw that both he and Alexander Gorshkov, his successor, were staying at the Samotlar. But the hotel had been constructed by Viktor Paly using NVN's funds. With its own authority asserted over the company, TNK's blue and white flag now flew prominently outside the building. Chernogorneft operated a rival – albeit less luxurious – hotel across town which was optimistically called the Venezia. In the clannish world of Russian business, all Sidanco and Chernogorneft employees from out of town stayed there instead. It would seem normal that those running Chernogorneft's insolvency would also be at the Venezia – particularly given that the Samotlar charged premium rates hardly affordable on the official daily allowance and salary of insolvency managers. Unless someone else was supporting them.

TNK always stressed that it did nothing illegal, and was acting within the framework of Russia's bankruptcy laws. But it made no secret of its interest in acquiring Chernogorneft, and Potanin's initiative presented it with the chance it needed. 'Potanin was busy having parties in Paris, and BP was not paying attention. It was an opportunity for us,' says one very senior TNK insider. With control established over NVN, it had been anxious to promote a positive local image for itself and co-opt decision-makers. Kukes brought the local mayor and the regional governor onto TNK's board as non-executive directors. He made donations to the construction of a children's hospital. And things were soon going his way in the bankruptcy procedure. Locals said they often saw TNK executives in cahoots with the court insolvency officials. Chernogorneft continued to operate outside the control of its shareholders. It oil sales were diverted from Sidanco to Crown Trading and Finance, a Gibraltar-based operation linked to Alfa.

Without their prior agreement, two of Chernogorneft's largest creditors – the US Eximbank and the European Bank for Reconstruction and Development – had some of their debts paid off, though they should have received no preference over other creditors under Russian law. Other businesses which were owed money had their debts bought out by TNK, until it acquired majority voting rights on the creditors' committee overseeing the insolvency. Instead of paying off the debts with the rising revenues from oil sales and swiftly returning Chernogorneft to Sidanco, the bankruptcy was prolonged until November 1999. BP had launched a bitter lobbying campaign, criticizing TNK on Capitol Hill, and pressing Tony Blair to talk to Vladimir Putin. Asked why he didn't open peace talks with TNK, a top BP executive told me: 'You don't talk to someone who's stolen your wallet.' In December, the company was put up for sale regardless and he would soon be forced into an about-turn. Few of Chernogorneft's disillusioned shareholders and remaining creditors had any doubts who would win the bidding. They were not disappointed. Fridman had his revenge.

The new deal

By the time the invitation came from the Kremlin in late July 2000, the ground had already been prepared. It took only days after Putin's inauguration in May for the first signs of a new era to show. Police and prosecutors began launching inquiries one after another. There were allegations of tax evasion at the oil group Lukoil, privatization irregularities at the metals group Norilsk Nickel, the illegal sale of shares to foreigners at the electricity group UES. A leaked memo from the finance ministry suggested that Sibneft was paying substantially less tax than its rivals. Most striking of all, the media tycoon Vladimir Gusinsky – already subject to an intensive series of swoops by police and prosecutors at his offices – was lured to the general prosecutor's office for an interview. He was arrested unexpectedly, and held for three days in Moscow's crumbling Butyrka prison.

The oligarchs were suddenly under concerted attack. It seemed that they were no longer kicking open the doors of power to demand privileges, gather inside information and dictate their wishes. Through the intermediary of Boris Nemtsov, the leader of the liberal SPS movement which some of them helped finance, they were reduced to pleading merely for the right to a meeting with the president. At issue was the whole scandal-ridden privatization process that had made them rich in the first place.

Putin was fully aware of his debt to certain oligarchs. While legitimized by democratic elections, his political ascension was primarily the work of Yeltsin. He had been rapidly promoted through a series of posts with the president's support, anointed as prime minister in summer 1999, and then thrust into the role of acting president by Yeltsin's decision to resign prematurely in December. The move gave Putin extra credibility and authority, additional access to the instruments of state power, and cut down the time for any rival candidate to prepare a serious challenge. Yeltsin's support meant that of the 'Family' too, which included not only Tatiana Dyachenko, his daughter, and Valentin Yumashev, his former chief of staff who would later marry her, but also Voloshin, Berezovsky and his protégé Abramovich. They were linked in a clan of mutual support, with allies in powerful positions. Their influence suggested continued economic liberalization, accompanied by special privileges for them; and the preservation of their existing spoils.

Some of Putin's first decisions in office suggested that he was indeed the 'Family's' pawn. His first move on becoming acting president was to sign an order granting immunity from prosecution for Yeltsin. Berezovsky maintains that there was no such broader pact for the oligarchs, including himself. 'And I should know,' he says. But Putin regularly paid visits to Yeltsin. He maintained Voloshin in his job, and allowed Yumashev and others to keep their offices – and hence access – within the Kremlin. Khodorkovsky's circle has been credited with devising the idea of the 'Family', and Gusinsky's television channel NTV was responsible for popularizing it to use as a political weapon against them. There was more than a little truth to the group's influence, although in the opaque world of Kremlin politics, the label disguised a rather more complex and shifting set of relations.

Putin was not entirely a creature of the 'Family', nor of the oligarchs more generally. One reason was that the oligarchs themselves were divided, with conflicting commercial and political interests and loyalties. Personal rivalries and jealousies rarely allowed them to agree a common line for long. Some, like Gusinsky, had indicated support for alternative candidates such as Yuri Luzhkov, the mayor of Moscow, alienating themselves from the new centre of power. Others had already faded away, the result of losing out in the 'loans for shares' fight, misjudgement or simple ill-health. Vladimir Vinogradov's Inkombank was dealt a death blow by the 1998 financial crisis, and he disappeared from the scene with kidney problems. The influence of Vitaly Malkin's Rossisky Kredit Bank also dropped sharply.

Putin had his own separate non-family network in the corridors of power. The so-called 'St Petersburg circle' included many with whom he had worked under Anatoly Sobchak in the early 1990s and who had since joined the government in Moscow even before him. There were also his former colleagues from the security services.

While the 'Family' might have provided support to Putin, it was probably the campaign he waged in Chechnya that established him in most ordinary Russians' minds as the decisive leader they yearned for. The conflict had the practical effect of strengthening existing hardliners such as Anatoly Kvashnin, the chief of staff of the army, and Nikolai Patrushev, Putin's friend who ran the FSB. In his attempt to create a new power base, separate himself from those who had propelled him to the top and establish a counterbalance, he drew on others with whom he had worked over many years. This group exerted its influence as the strikes against the oligarchs began in early 2000. The result was an inevitable internecine conflict which would help define his following years.

Putin was pragmatic enough to recognize the destabilizing effect of a wholesale redistribution of property. When he finally met the representatives of big business on 29 July 2000, the discussion lasted two and a half hours. There was technical talk about investment, and plans for entry into the World Trade Organization. But the coverage by Russian state television of Putin's opening address, and an official Kremlin statement issued shortly afterwards, left little doubt about the main message. The press release read: 'The President said that the authorities would not review the outcome of privatizations. At the same time, it was unacceptable for competing companies to use state structures and law enforcement agencies to achieve their goals.' Some participants came away with different nuances, but the overall idea was clear. 'Putin is a well-educated man with certain rules of behaviour. He hinted, but it was absolutely clear what he meant,' said one businessman who was present. 'The situation in the country is difficult, power practically doesn't exist, and you claim that your business is under threat. Do your business and you will get support if your money is working for the country. The president is restoring order and don't make this difficult task more difficult or I will not forgive you, because you are partly responsible.'

The timing was in many ways fortunate for the oligarchs. If Putin was laying down new ground rules, the conditions in which they were operating were also beginning to change for the better. The cut-price insider deals for the purchase of the state's main cash-generating businesses had come to an end. Most of the plum assets had already been sold. The bitter infighting that followed was subsiding, as the different groups extricated themselves from each other's grip and established clear control over their holding companies and subsidiaries. In the accelerated pace of just half a decade, the oligarchs had overseen asset-grabbing and consolidation, and were ready to move to a third stage. Their priority before had been to secure cash flows on companies that generated revenues at a time when they had no idea how long their ownership would be secure and there was uncertainty over future profit. Now the domestic economic upturn and a sharp rise in international commodity prices meant that they could start shifting towards a longer-term perspective. 'The improving security of ownership was something that began with the privatizations and is still continuing today,' according to one businessman. But most of the oligarchs had begun to take a more strategic view and started to invest, putting something back into their businesses – and even contributing to society at large.

If there was the 'stick' of legal threats on one hand for those who broke the pact, on the other there was the softer psychological 'carrot' of a change in approach by the country's leadership as it attempted to restore order and establish new rules. 'Be subservient and you can keep your money' was the message. They recognized in Putin a different personality, and one with whom they could work. 'When I met Putin, I had a much greater sense of stability,' says one top Russian businessman who saw him a few months later. 'He is the same age as me, shares the same view of the development of the country and the economy, and clearly understands what the tasks ahead are. I had a very positive feeling.' The process of change had already started in 1999, but it took off sharply in the following year. Chubais's belief at the time of 'loans for shares' was that the priority was to transfer assets at any price into private ownership and good management would follow. With the new owners investing, it was starting to happen.

Reactions varied widely within business to the arrival of the Putin regime, but few stood still. Boris Berezovsky had already gone south, winning the parliamentary seat for Karachayevo-Cherkessia, an ethnic republic close to Chechnya. There was a logic to the move, given his long-standing interests and contacts in the Caucasus. As one of the most vocal of the oligarchs already sensing the uncertainty of regime change, it gave him a new outlet – direct from the tribune of the Duma. There was even the prospect of parliamentary immunity, shielding him in theory from politically motivated prosecution – although immunity could always be lifted. But by autumn 2000, Berezovsky sensed the dangers, and he fled abroad.

Berezovsky was conspicuously absent from the Kremlin business meeting in July. So was the media tycoon Gusinsky, who had been released from jail and quit Russia just ahead of the gathering. The lack of invitations for two of the most vocal and political oligarchs seemed designed to send a message about a new approach to corporate dialogue that came with the change in regime. Relations should be more balanced, more business-oriented, with everyone 'equidistant from power', as Putin had promised in his election campaign. For those who were willing to keep their head down and obey the new rules, the situation was calmer. 'This much talked about idea of keeping the various representatives of business at equal distance from the political authorities has become reality. As for those who do not agree with this position, it's like they used to say, 'Some are gone and the others are far away,' as he would tell journalists at a press conference in June 2003.

Roman Abramovich, the most low-profile of the oligarchs, was also absent from the meeting, as he moved sharply to the east. Abramovich had been built up into a mysterious, powerful figure during 1999, so elusive that the newspaper *Versiya* offered a prize to anyone who could find a photograph of him. The widely circulated black-and-white image that finally appeared – and was republished for months afterwards in the absence of any alternatives – was hardly flattering, giving him an intimidating dark four-day stubble. Abramovich hated publicity, and would be shown on Russian television fleeing reporters. Yet paradoxically, taking a leaf out of the book of Berezovsky, his mentor and partner in Sibneft, he pushed himself into the public arena. He stood for parliament in December 1999 as the representative of Russia's most remote, far north-eastern region of Chukotka. The following winter, he won election as its governor.

I was among the first journalists to meet him, when Sibneft arranged a trip to Noyabrsk, in Siberia. It was my first visit to the company's principal operation centres, and despite Abramovich's official role as one of the company's top executives, it seemed unfamiliar to him too. His taste for extravagance, chartering Boeings and constructing luxury yachts, would later become more widely known. But for such public outings within Russia, he chose a more modest mode of transport: a Yak-40, a small Soviet passenger plane. I was ushered into a zone at the front with marginally greater comfort, where he agreed to talk for a few minutes. He was no great raconteur, offering short, uninformative replies in a soft voice, but confirming his friendship with Yeltsin's daughter Dyachenko. In person, out of the shadows, his blond hair and demi-beard looked far less frightening. The man himself seemed ill-fitted to his role as a power behind the throne of the 'Family': gentle, shy and an implausible politician. But he clearly had the human touch, asking interesting, intelligent questions and listening at length to local oil workers on arrival. He chose others to play the tough guy in his business, but he obviously did the 'relational' work behind the scenes.

For an orphan turned wheeler-dealer trader with a small fortune and an extravagant lifestyle to his credit, Abramovich would have found Chukotka a form of internal 'exile'. He was like a latter-day inmate on day release in a zone with a horrendous heritage of Stalinist forced labour. He registered to pay his tax there, claiming to contribute $30m a year to the regional budget from his personal income. Separately, he donated another $200m for the construction of buildings, and other activities such as his Pole of Hope fund to send poor children south to the sun for their summer holidays. He also summoned a number of his reluctant Sibneft colleagues to Anadyr, the regional capital, to help him govern. His philanthropy provided him with a way to put a positive spin on his activities, impressing the handful of western journalists he took there on trips. He may have had the desire for a new challenge after having made so much money so easily; and a genuine disgust at the poverty and mismanagement of the place, heightened by his insights during his short period as parliamentary representative for the region, but there was a substantial element of corporate self-interest involved too, however. Sibneft started oil exploration in the region, and exploited local tax loopholes to the full. It channelled its profits through locally registered, short-lived trading companies, gathering still further tax breaks by hiring disabled traders. The result was that Sibneft paid the lowest profit taxes in the industry, at less than half the official nominal rate of 24 per cent – generating savings well beyond the volume of his philanthropy. Whatever the ultimate reason for his decision to seek political office, Abramovich was not using Chukotka as a base for opposition to Putin. Rather, he was pledging allegiance to the new regime, as a loyal cog in the 'power vertical' being constructed by the Kremlin in an attempt to impose its policies across the country. It was that attitude – mixed with the continued influence of the 'Family' in the Kremlin – that ensured his survival.

Vladimir Potanin went north. He would continue to pursue aggressive policies in business, but he seemed to have lost the taste for oil and decided to concentrate on consolidating his hold over the cash cow of Norilsk Nickel instead. In late 1999, I had paid him a visit in his central Moscow office. It sat in the middle of a row of three semicircular buildings on Academic Sakharov street – the former home of the Soviet foreign trade ministry, for whom he had previously worked. The corridors and reception area were bland. His own spacious office looked vaguely like something from a Wild West saloon, with dark wood surround. He had never seemed a man afraid of ostentation. In 1997, he had hired the entire eighteenth-century Kuskovo park and stately home in south-eastern Moscow, and flown in the Australian jet-ski team. He was well known for his extravagant parties on the Côte d'Azure in summer and in the Alps in winter, without attracting any questions from the authorities about the source of his income. But when I asked him about tax bills, he started to look pained and defensive. 'You declare your income and what do they do? They start probing and looking for more,' he complained. A new era was being ushered in.

Potanin would soon begin not only to pay more taxes on the profits earned at Norilsk Nickel, but also to reinvest the money that was being generated. He impressed visitors to the polluted, harsh Arctic headquarters of Norilsk not only by the industrial equipment his team was installing, but also by such human touches as heated bus stops. It was a gesture in a far broader series of efforts begun by the oligarchs to give something – albeit modest – back to society. He would also try to bridge damaged relations with foreigners. His Uneximbank, like other oligarch banks, had defaulted on its creditors in August 1998, including a number of banks that had lent it money. Like his peers, Potanin created a new 'bridge bank' called Rosbank, into which the cash went, leaving the obligations behind. But Potanin did make efforts to restructure his existing debt, a rare example of someone who held talks with his creditors resulting in a settlement that offered them partial repayment. Immediately after Putin's July meeting, companies donated to soldiers' welfare organizations. In fact, many of the country's big businesses had already been funding social programmes and other 'good works'. Berezovsky had been among the first, launching his Triumph Fund to support artists and academics in the early 1990s. But the emphasis and the volume of money started to grow considerably. Potanin had long supported orphans. He became a trustee of the Hermitage in St Petersburg, offering the museum support in its renovations, and donating $1m so it could buy *Black Square* by the Russian artist Malevich when it came up for sale. As his artistic activities brought him to international attention, he would even be elected a trustee of the Guggenheim Museum in New York in 2002. 'The 1990s was difficult for the country, the rules were not established, society was in a pitiful condition and we made a lot of mistakes', he told me. 'We lost the confidence of the people. Our target is to re-establish confidence. I'm not asking for excuses, but I'm ready to help, to work on changing people's attitudes.'

Not all the oligarchs evolved so far or fast. Some of those who had failed to diversify out of the banking sector and find new sources of revenue were crippled by the 1998 crisis and failed to recover. But if they played by the new rules, they were left alone. I was amazed one day in 2001 to be able to track down Alexander Smolensky quite easily. His continued existence in Russia symbolized that loyalty and discretion were more important than ensuring that justice was done. Smolensky had built SBS Agro into one of the most extensive banking networks in the country. Its innovative technology and management could have made it a Russian success story. Its close connections to power were illustrated by the location of some of its branches, including the White House (government headquarters) and the parliament. But the bank was designed so that all deposits collected were quickly transferred offshore. After the 1998 crisis, it shut its doors, leaving a hole of more than $1bn and millions of angry depositors out of pocket – although certain well-connected clients were rapidly reimbursed. A 'bridge bank' soon appeared, called Pervy OVK, which was run by Smolensky's son for a while. It took over the SBS branches, while naturally claiming no link with the previous occupiers or their debts.

I assumed that Smolensky had permanently fled the country to Austria, where he had citizenship and his family had been relocated. In fact, he was sitting in a luxurious top-floor Moscow office with a view across the Kremlin, decorated with ornamental elephants. This was not just any building. Alexander House was owned by one of

Smolensky's companies. During late 1999, it became the headquarters for German Gref's Centre for Strategic Development, as he drafted Putin's economic programme. By early 2000, it was the headquarters of Putin's campaign team, where the newly-elected president himself turned up unexpectedly in front of journalists on the night of his March victory. Since then, the building has continued to hold part of Gref's team, as well as the offices of assorted pro-Kremlin organizations, including the political consultant Gleb Pavlovsky's Effective Politics Foundation. Smolensky told me that the Russian interior police had initially launched an investigation against him in relation to the collapse of his bank, but then sent him a letter saying that all charges had been dropped and he was free to return to the country. He reimbursed the right people, kept a low profile and stayed out of politics. In exchange, he was left in peace.

Plus ça change?

When the hammer went down on the last significant privatization of Putin's first term in December 2002, there was only one surprise. Relieved auction staff presented the winner with an extravagant bunch of orchids. Eugene Shvidler, Sibneft's chief executive, had just paid $1.86bn for the Russian oil company Slavneft. The flowers that went with it were a symbol of what had taken place: beautiful at first glance, but with the initial positive impression soon replaced by a lingering odour. The floral tribute seemed to mark the relief on all sides that the sale had been completed according to plan. And that was the point. Superficially, the ceremony looked diametrically opposed to the 'loans for shares' deals seven years earlier: modern, western, transparent, fair. But it was a ceremony: a ritual performance complete with auctioneer in black jacket and bow tie, designed to give an impression that belied the reality. It was a metaphor for modern Russia.

Slavneft was a showpiece auction that was closely watched by the business community. The sale of the last state-controlled oil company was an ideal chance to demonstrate how relations between the state and business had evolved under Putin. On paper, the process seemed the antithesis of previous deals. The State Property Committee had hired Salomon Brothers, the prestigious international investment bank, as financial advisers, and Coudert Brothers as lawyers. It organized site visits, and three separate 'data rooms' in different locations around Moscow so that potential buyers could carry out detailed 'due diligence' on its assets and finances without rivals even learning of their interest. Foreigners were actively encouraged to bid, and there were 'roadshows' abroad, including one in China. On Salomon's advice, the decision was made to sell off all of the state's 75 per cent stake, rather than an initial piecemeal 33 per cent which would have proved less attractive to potential buyers. A substantial minimum 'reserve' price was also set, the highest ever at $1.7bn. And there were no obscure investment commitments, opaque sealed bids or strange conditions. The sale would take place through an open auction, with the process filmed on closed-circuit television.

It was hardly prime-time viewing for ordinary Russians, but for Moscow-based journalists the Slavneft sale was a hugely important event. Dozens of media organizations were accredited, and warned in a stiff memo by the Property Committee to come to its headquarters by 9 a.m., ahead of the start at 11 a.m. sharp. I almost didn't bother to turn up, assuming a foregone conclusion, but the show we witnessed made it all worthwhile. We were squeezed into a small room high up in the black glass tower, while bodyguards kept us away from the auction hall itself at the far end of the same floor, presumably in case any journalists were tempted to bid spontaneously. It soon became clear that there was a problem. The large-screen television in our room was turned on, complete with a ticking electronic clock showing 10.50 a.m. But only half an hour later did people start filing into the hall, sitting behind desks arranged as if in a school classroom. The names of the bidding companies were obscure, and I was worried that I would not be able to work out who the true owners were. In fact, there was no problem: the bosses would not take any risks by delegating something as important as this to their subordinates. Shvidler himself entered, and sat down behind the sign not for Sibneft but for a company called Invest-Oil. Alexander Korzik, one of his deputies, was at a different desk, supposedly representing the previously unknown Fininvest. German Khan, a top executive and shareholder at TNK, sat behind the name of another recently created front company.

After a nominal opening bid at 11.52 a.m., just two groups took part. Two attractive young women with knee-length boots and short skirts raised the opening $1.7bn offer by $20m, on behalf of Optifor.

Shvidler upped them by the same amount. The process went back and forth just eight times, giving the nominal impression of a competition. The auctioneer hesitated, as if conscious of estimates by financial analysts that the sale could raise more than \$2bn. Then, less than ten minutes after the process began, his hammer banged down. Shvidler had 'won' Slavneft for a mere \$160m above the reserve price. Any pretence that there had been even a little competition for the company was soon shattered. One of the women admitted as she rushed to the lift that Optifor was controlled by Sibneft. Sibneft had fought only against itself. Or so it seemed. Within an hour, TNK put out a press release saying that the winning bid was a joint one from TNK and Sibneft. It was effectively admitting to the existence of a 'dealer's ring' – a pre-auction pact between the two leading contenders for Slavneft, designed to avoid any real bidding war between them that might have increased the price – and the revenue to the state. Instead of a competition, the entire process had been stitched up in advance, leaving the two oligarch-controlled companies to shore up the assets between them in private.

Pre-selection of 'acceptable' candidates for the auction had begun much earlier. The Chinese National Petroleum Corporation had initially been encouraged to bid, and called the Russians' bluff. It resolved to take part and hired J.P. Morgan, the investment bank. Officials at the State Property Committee suddenly started getting nervous. There were hints that it would not be prudent for the Chinese to participate. Meetings were refused. No one would sign to confirm receipt of the application documents they filed. Just ahead of the deadline, they got the message and decided not to proceed. The state-owned company Rosneft was also excluded from bidding – much to its own irritation, but with some justification since this was supposed to be a privatization. Others were debarred by curious last-minute court orders filed against applicants. Even as I waited for the auction to begin, I received a call on my mobile telephone. Alexander Lipsky, a Russian businessman who had planned to take part, was downstairs. Officials had refused to notify him even late the previous evening whether they would accept his bid. That was in violation of their own procedures. When he arrived in the morning, they simply refused him entry. 'I can only laugh,' he said bitterly afterwards. 'We would have been ready to pay a lot more than \$2bn.' The quality of his own bid might have been questionable, but did he have a weaker case than the obscure Russian front companies used by Sibneft and TNK? The property committee was certainly going to take no chances.

In practice, Slavneft had long since been carved up. As part of the same 1990s process of messy multi-stage, multi-level privatization that affected the entire oil sector, the company owned only minority stakes in a number of its oil-producing subsidiaries. A large proportion of the shares in its operating businesses had been bought up over the previous two years by TNK. Legally, it no longer controlled many of its principal assets. Meanwhile, Sibneft made little secret of the fact that it had gradually been 'taking over' the management of Slavneft, starting with the appointment of Yuri Sukhanov, a top executive promoted by Mikhail Kasyanov, the prime minister, as chief executive the previous May. Even if the Chinese, or another outsider, had managed to buy the state's 75 per cent stake in Slavneft at auction, they would have found themselves with little more than an empty corporate shell, while the assets 'walked' elsewhere.

The Slavneft auction did mark some progress over the past. With the exception of the $2bn paid for the telecoms group Svyazinvest in 1997 in an auction that was unexpectedly competitive, $1.86bn was the largest sum ever received by the state for a privatization, and not far below a fair price. Furthermore, TNK and Sibneft were not entirely in collusion. Each had its own competing interests in the deal, and the fact that the state's reserve price was pushed up ahead of the formal auction from $1.3bn to $1.7bn suggested some government pressure to achieve a reasonable deal. 'If there had been a higher bidder, they would have won,' claimed one TNK insider afterwards. 'In some ways, Russia is very transparent. It's money that counts.' If the rule of money was becoming more important, the ability of the state's own institutions or laws to regulate it fairly was not. That was a serious blow to the efforts of the economic reformers, a decade after the privatization process began.

When TNK announced that it was creating a $14bn joint venture with BP just two months later, the Slavneft price was put in perspective. In September 2003, BP calculated that it would pay $1.4bn for its share of Slavneft, suggesting a fair market price at the auction should really have been more than $4bn or twice the price paid. The fact that BP – with all its experience in the Russian market – had not been willing to bid for Slavneft on its own suggested that it understood that the rules of the corporate game were still far from fair. Another indication came from the fact that TNK-BP, the company created, was a joint venture only 50 per cent owned by BP rather than an outright purchase. As Mikhail Fridman, the head of Alfa, which was joint owner of TNK, put it: 'We are in a stage in this country where it is logical for western companies to work in partnership. They can be very successful, but it is premature to go it alone. Our expertise is necessary for the relationship with local authorities, the tax authorities, the government.' BP's own lobbying for Sidanco via Tony Blair, who could in turn speak directly to Putin, indicated the substantial clout that was necessary in Russia to resolve corporate struggles. That did not bode well for other less influential companies trying to survive in such a hostile environment. As Lord Browne, BP's chief executive, himself memorably put it: 'Russia is a country ruled by men, not laws.' His decision to join forces with TNK was striking, just three years after the two companies were in open war over Sidanco. BP later began to argue that it had played a shrewd game all along. Yet Bob Shepperd, whom it appointed chief executive of Sidanco in 1999, admitted that without the upswing in oil prices the situation could have been radically different.

Alfa was the archetype of the Yeltsin-era oligarchic groups that had survived and thrived under Putin. If lobbying under Yeltsin involved frequent visits to government officials, Alfa adopted a different tactic in late 1999: direct and permanent implants. Its former employees Vladislav Surkov and Alexander Abramov were installed in the Kremlin. Alfa even hired Oleg Sysuev, a former top member of the presidential administration. Shortly after, it managed to win a $40m loan from Arco, the Russian agency charged with rebuilding the banking sector after the August crisis. As Olga Kryshtanovskaya, the sociologist, put it: 'After the 1998 crisis, the oligarchs began to appoint their own people, rather than influence decisions directly.'

In spring 2003, I went to see Peter Aven, a partner in the Alfa group and head of its subsidiary Alfa Bank, in his cavernous office in the next building to Potanin's. A former trade minister, Aven made no secret of his continued links to power, and the fact that he had regular meetings with Putin. Earlier that year, he had seen him to seek approval of the joint venture created between TNK and BP. But when I asked him directly how much influence Alfa had in the Kremlin, he vigorously played it down. Then he received a call. 'Shuvalov has resigned,' he told me as he hung up. He was referring to the head of the government administration, whose departure was only made public three days later.

Alfa's success, like that of several of its peers, was partly the result of rising oil prices. But the company also had a commitment to the long term, and was a pioneer in appointing professional external managers. It had survived the 1998 crisis better than most, with its bank remaining in existence and honouring its debts. It had preferred to keep itself a private company, without public scrutiny of its accounts. But – partly out of the necessity of paying a higher price for such privatized assets as TNK than its rivals – it was already more prepared for competitive market conditions. It was forced to raise substantial debt ahead of the crisis as a result, prompting it to develop systems that helped it respect its obligations afterwards. It hired Americans keen for adventure and 'repatriates' born or trained abroad but who now saw more interesting challenges back in their homeland.

Alfa was a manifestation of Chubais's hope that privatized companies – no matter into whose hands they passed or at what price – would lay the foundation for overturning Communism for ever. He had argued that the newly created propertied class would in turn fight to defend and increase its wealth, pushing for the development of property rights and a fair judicial system for all. He was at least partly right. Alfa became an influential lobbyist, among those financial groups that braked rapid banking reform which risked creating competition for its own expanding network. And it also diversified heavily, expanding from oil into telecoms, supermarket retailing and a growing range of financial services. Potanin's Interros group expanded into engineering, agriculture, the media and food processing. 'The major result of the last ten years is that managers are appearing and Russia's wealth is now in the hands of more or less efficient managers,' he told me. He stressed that he planned to spin off the businesses he acquired via strategic partnerships or introductions to the stock market. In early 2004, he even took an important step towards shared ownership when he announced a merger of his heavy machinery division with the rival OMZ group controlled by Kakha Bendukidze. A study in 2001 by the financial analyst Peter Boone suggested that Russia's top twelve privatized groups had revenues equivalent to the entire federal budget. Among the largest sixty-four companies, just eight oligarch groups controlled

85 per cent of the revenues. A more comprehensive 2004 study by the World Bank showed that the key oligarchs held several percentage points of GDP each. It suggested that they were no more efficient managers than their smaller rivals, although their disproportionately cash-generating businesses allowed them to re-invest significantly and made them effective lobbyists. Even as their political influence was waning, the oligarchs' economic weight was growing. Berezovsky's boast about controlling half of the economy may have been exaggerated, but Russia's oligarchs looked as though they were starting to become *chaebols*, the vast, politically connected conglomerates that dominated South Korea in the post-war years. They were reinvesting in the Russian economy and helping it to restructure. They even began divesting themselves of some 'non-core' assets that they had acquired. But their own weight and range of activities in the economy grew ever larger after 2000. There was far less evidence that the regulators could curb their influence, imposing anti-monopoly rulings to prevent them stifling competition.

There were changes to the economic environment under Putin. The mere fact of the meeting that he held with the oligarchs in summer 2000 said something about a new approach. The president committed to regular meetings with the RSPP, the big business lobby, and the oligarchs played the game, engineering a 'takeover' of the organization to use as a vehicle for formal dialogue. The rusting RSPP headed by Arkady Volsky was transformed, and oligarchs suddenly dominated its board. It was partly a sham, of course. They continued to meet one-on-one with Putin and other officials, and even boasted about it in private. But they did not have the open access of the past. And the nature of their lobbying changed, with greater emphasis on the parliament now that it was becoming a place that mattered in getting new laws passed. The attitude of government also began to shift. As Yegor Gaidar, the former deputy prime minister, put it: 'At the peak, seven to ten people were the real Russian government. They could easily change the prime minister, and were able to promote any economic policy they wanted. Now there is nothing like this.'

New oligarchs also emerged. While Abramovich and Fridman continued to wield great power, a still younger and more brash generation appeared. Andrei Melnichenko's MDM bank started building its own empire, expanding from corporate lending into the purchase of industrial assets, including coal mines and fertilizers.

Oleg Deripaska emerged as the power behind Russian Aluminium and diversified into car production. But neither of them appeared from nowhere. They had long-standing links with Abramovich. And Deripaska even cemented his connection to the 'Family' by marriage, taking as his wife the daughter of Valentin Yumashev, the former head of the presidential administration who in turn was married to Tatiana Dyachenko, Yeltsin's daughter.

Just as important was the arrival of new 'statist oligarchs' under Putin. Gazprom, the gas monopoly, proved an early target. The company, which controlled a quarter of the world's gas reserves, was nominally in the hands of the state. But Yeltsin had characteristically given it enormous slack, delegating the votes on the state's formal 38 per cent shareholding to the management. Rem Vyakhirev, the life-long chief *gazovik* – the Russian slang for a gas worker – ran a sprawling empire that operated farms, hotels and yacht clubs as well as gas production facilities and pipelines. In 2000, Gazprom's share-holders and outside directors began to raise questions about its cosy commercial relationship with Itera, a Florida-based company that in a decade had risen from obscurity to become a major gas operator in its own right, largely on the back of work with Gazprom or in its zone of influence in the former Soviet region. The following spring, Putin drew a line under the past. He placed Alexei Miller, a long-time colleague from St Petersburg, in Vyakhirev's place, heralding the start of a purge of former management and the end of the company's autonomy from the Kremlin.

Other groups with powerful links to the Kremlin, notably Rosneft, the last state-controlled oil group, and Mezhprombank, controlled by Sergei Pugachev, began to emerge as strong forces. The Kremlin was proving important in making and breaking the business class. But rather than focus on equality of competition and tough regulation, it seemed to be using politics to boost its favourites and punish those that took an independent line.

End of an era

The operation was executed in military fashion. In the chill Siberian morning, the plane landed to refuel at Novosibirsk air-port. As it hovered on the runway, heavily armed agents of the FSB stormed on board, surprising the occupants. By the time that Moscow, three time zones to the west, woke up to the news of the arrest, the officers were already flying back to the capital with their extraordinary catch: Mikhail Khodorkovsky, Russia's richest man. By that same evening, Saturday 25 October 2003, the mighty oligarch had already been hauled before a Moscow court, charged with $1bn in fraud and tax evasion, and taken into custody. The news made headlines around the world, and when the Russian stock market opened on the following Monday morning, it nose-dived. Foreign investors, excited by more positive recent trends, tried to make light of the news, to argue that it was an exception that could be ignored. But many Russians sensed something deeper and were the first to sell.

The arrest was the dramatic culmination of a series of investigations over the previous few months into Khodorkovsky, his partners and their business activities. Few had anticipated that it would reach such a climax so quickly. And – as in previous such high-profile cases – most believed that the actions were politically motivated, a response to the refusal to play by the rules laid down by Putin three years before. The affair raised questions which went well beyond Khodorkovsky's own dealings, into politics, civil society and the nature of Russian business and its relationship with power.

Khodorkovsky was not someone who inspired immediate sympathy. He had an underlying coolness and arrogance. He was less extrovert than many of his fellow oligarchs, more unassuming and soft-spoken. Employees noticed how he could sit unremarked during meetings, listening and thinking rather than dominating the discussion. They also found him deeply enigmatic. One expatriate who worked for him told me: 'I was once tempted to say, "Look, you can have back all the money you have paid me. Just tell me who you are and what your aim really is."' Khodorkovsky was not extravagant in his tastes, admitting only to a penchant for collecting briefcases. He spurned image-makers, shaving off his moustache and getting rid of his 'tank-top' pullovers and thick spectacles at a late date.

He had played by the same extreme rules as the other oligarchs. In some ways, he had been the first among equals, the most extreme of all. Through his core Menatep holding company, he won a series of questionable privatization tenders, culminating in the cheap purchase of Yukos during the 'loans for shares' saga. After the August 1998 financial crisis, Menatep closed its doors, refusing to pay its creditors. Another bank, Menatep St Petersburg, mysteriously emerged, supposedly with no connection to the original, but claiming its assets. West LB, a German bank, had approved a $165m loan to Menatep with supremely unfortunate timing just weeks earlier. It seemed unlikely that Menatep had even had a chance to spend much of the money, but it defaulted and said it could not repay. The Germans thought they had been clever, securing their money against 15 per cent of Yukos's shares. But when they arranged a meeting with Yukos's management to cash in their collateral, they met a stone wall. First, their interlocuters claimed they had never heard of Menatep and that the share pledge could not be legal. In subsequent meetings, Yukos became more aggressive, threatening to simply issue new shares to dilute the 15 per cent stake to next to zero. They even warned the Germans that they had had their offices bugged and were aware of everything they discussed with their bosses. Many sensitive documents related to Menatep mysteriously disappeared soon after when a truck carrying them 'accidentally' fell into a lake.

Yukos's direct partners fared no better. Consultants went unpaid, local staff suffered wage delays and the financial conditions imposed on the company's businesses were harsh. With oil prices low, Khodorkovsky's management team did everything to squeeze the maximum benefits and tighten control over their sometimes rebellious subsidiaries. Kenneth Dart, an American-born inheritor of a styrofoam cup fortune who had developed a reputation as an aggressive investor in emerging markets, was caught in the middle. He had bought shares in some Yukos subsidiaries in the mid-1990s, and noticed that Yukos was employing 'transfer pricing' to buy the oil from them at low cost, leaving them with little or no profit. As he and minority shareholders fought back in the media and the courts, Khodorkovsky launched dilutions to establish full control over the businesses. At one extraordinary general meeting held in June 1999 designed to seek shareholders' 'approval' for the move, Dart's representative arrived at the venue – Menatep's headquarters in Moscow – only to discover a note on the door. It said the meeting had been moved to another venue in a different town. By the time he arrived, the gathering had supposedly already taken place and the dilution been decided to Dart's detriment.

Khodorkovsky had seemed among the most far-sighted of the oligarchs, the one best able to sense the way the winds were blowing and

to adapt accordingly. By the time he participated in Putin's meeting
with business leaders in mid-2000, he was already responding. He
expressed no interest in politics, but demonstrated a very clear
change in his approach to business. While his rivals were still
indulging in extensive transfer pricing, extracting profits from Russia
for maximum short-term gain, he was already starting to reinvest in
Yukos for at least the medium term. He appointed foreign experts to
senior management positions in the company right up to the level of
finance director. They brought outside experience and acted as independent 'eyes and ears' for him from within. He subcontracted
engineering work to global consultants such as Schlumberger, helping boost oil production levels back towards their late Soviet peak. He
began to bring his income back 'onshore', disclosing a far greater
proportion of Yukos's true profits – and paying tax on them.

Luck played in Khodorkovsky's favour. World oil prices began to
rise sharply in mid-1999, giving him unexpected additional revenues.
Instead of keeping all the proceeds for himself and his partners, he
decided to sue for peace. By the end of the year, he was able to reach
a financial settlement to compensate Dart. Menatep St Petersburg
began to pay off Menatep's creditors, making good on its defaulted
loans. West LB received half of its original loan in settlement. Yukos's
other creditors were paid off. What was never clear was how far the
transformation represented a real shift in mentality, and how far it was
simply a pragmatic response to the rise in oil prices, making
Khodorkovsky a 'fair-weather financier' who might yet again prove
ruthless if conditions became tough once more in the future. At the
very least, his next strategic moves were ground-setting.

With Yukos's cash flows rising fast and its subsidiaries firmly under
control, he had the opportunity to simply buy out all the remaining
minority shareholders and make his company private, removing it from
the stock market with all its obligations for transparency and profit-
sharing. He decided to do the opposite. 'Private companies have a
limited scale of operations,' he told me. 'We had ambitions to build
something huge.' He would turn Yukos into a western-style quoted
company. Instead of increasing his fortune through a large salary or
cash generated by the business, he opted to boost the value of the
company's shares. He adopted international accounting standards,
and released financial statements every three months. He hired investor
relations staff, produced glossy annual reports, launched a slick website

and participated in roadshows abroad. He created a supervisory board, including several foreign directors. He launched a corporate governance code. He also began to pay out cash dividends to shareholders, something almost unheard of in Russia.

Outside observers initially reacted doubtfully, even ironically. Perhaps because of the high-profile combat waged against him by Dart, Khodorkovsky had received substantial – even disproportionately – negative publicity for practices that were widespread among the oligarchs. Over time, the stock market became more impressed. From a brief $6 high in August 1997, shares slumped to just 50 cents at the end of 1998. But then they soared, peaking at $16 in October 2003. Profits rose from $300m in 1998 to $3bn in 2002. Stephen O'Sullivan, the head of research at United Financial Group, a Moscow brokerage, long remained sceptical, but over time even he became more bullish about the company's rising share price. 'We took the view then that it was a fair-weather conversion because of high oil prices,' he said. 'We were wrong.' Three years after he had been seen as the pariah of the Russian stock market, Khodorkovsky became its poster-boy, a paragon of positive change. His envious peers began to plan 'Yukosization' of their own companies. Even one individual close to Dart with whom I talked seemed convinced by the transformation. 'He should have kept the shares,' he said, rather than agreeing to a cash settlement.

Looking back, there was strong financial self-interest in Khodorkovsky's approach. He was no dreamer half-heartedly indulging in commerce, but a hard-nosed businessman at work. He attempted to extract the maximum gain in the minimum time. He maintained an aggressive commercial policy with acquisitions such as Eastern Oil company in Siberia. He lobbied hard to protect his company against legislation which he considered threatening – whether limiting the effect of new oil taxes or sabotaging proposals for a special 'production sharing agreements' regime that would have eased the entry of foreign oil companies into Russia. He extensively used tax avoidance schemes, minimizing profits tax through the use of 'offshore' zones within and outside Russia. The amounts he reinvested in the business remained relatively modest and were focused on boosting short-term production at existing wells rather than exploring new sites. That helped swell Yukos's output and revenues as quickly as possible while oil prices were high. It also improved the value of the company ahead of its future sale. In the final analysis, his moves benefited others, but above all himself.

Khodorkovsky could have simply pocketed the proceeds. Instead, he started cultivating different, much broader interests. Through Yukos, he financed Internet centres at schools in areas where the company was present. There was funding for employee mortgages, and resettlement support to help those who wanted to move out of the most harsh environments where the company worked. He engineered a takeover of the respected Moscow State Humanities University, pledging $100m in support over a decade once his people were in charge. He supported New Civilization, a scouting-style organization complete with summer camps that was loosely based on the Communist-era Young Pioneers, except with the ideology of free markets and democracy, and neckscarves that were not red but in the corporate colours of yellow and green. There was the Young Leaders' Programme, which drew together promising future decision-makers from Russia, the UK and the USA. Yukos funded US Library of Congress programmes, winning photos of himself alongside George W. and Laura Bush. Somerset House in London even opened 'the Khodorkovsky room', containing a new permanent exhibition drawn from the collection of the Hermitage Museum in St Petersburg that he funded.

Separately, he created a charitable endowment called Open Russia. He established links with George Soros, the financier who had donated millions of dollars to Russia through his Open Society Institute. The similar-sounding name of the organization was not a coincidence. Soros was starting to wind down his activities in Russia, and was reassured by Khodorkorvsky's willingness to take up the slack – a rare example of a Russian businessman willing to donate to such causes. Most of his peers gave high-profile support to conventional charitable activities that would do little to change the social structure of Russia: to orphanages, the renovation of Orthodox churches, the upkeep of museums. Khodorkovsky was far more innovative. He supported work with AIDS, foreign policy institutes and the training of politicians and lawyers. He helped regional journalists, and bought the critical weekly paper *Moskovskiy Novosti* although not long before he had been taking legal action against journalists who wrote negative stories about him and his past. Khodorkovsky the businessman was becoming a philanthropist too – and one with a liberal democratic agenda. He said he planned to spend $100m a year on such activities. In spring 2003, I attended an academic seminar on energy in the headquarters of the Moscow Carnegie Centre, a think tank. Its star turn was Khodorkovsky, as if he was directly assuming the mantle of the former US robber baron Andrew Carnegie. Khodorkovsky even began to compare himself openly to Carnegie. But he was a man in a hurry who was trying to roll three generations into just three years – despite the very recent imperfections in his past.

He said openly that he planned to quit business when he reached forty-five to pursue other activities. In public, he talked about his interests in the social sector, but also began to criticize government decisions, and argued for Russia to become a 'parliamentary republic' with greater counterbalances to the Kremlin. In private, he hinted more directly at political ambitions. Some gained the impression that he planned to form a group of deputies, and even had his eyes on being named prime minister. Others understood that he wanted to become president – or at least the person who would name the future president in 2008, as Yeltsin had in 1999. 'He said he wanted to be prime minister, block voting with a third of the parliament, and change the constitution to bargain with the president,' says one Russian businessman who knows him well. When I asked him his ambitions directly, Khodorkovsky refused to comment, stressing instead his growing interest in education and his other philanthropic projects to which he said he planned to devote himself full time. He launched into a vigorous defence of civil society and private property, attacking those who wanted to re-examine the privatizations. 'They want the development of a society in which private property co-exists with authoritarian power,' he said. 'That was possible in the middle of the last century but it's not possible at the start of the twenty-first.'

His most trusted partner and the second largest shareholder in Yukos was Leonid Nevzlin, who had been in charge of 'government relations' and became a member of the Federation Council. His key lobbyist was Vasily Shakhnovsky, a former deputy to Yuri Luzhkov, the Moscow mayor and presidential contender. Like Vladimir Dubov, a member of the pro-Kremlin United Russia and vice-chairman of the parliamentary tax committee, he was a Yukos shareholder. Khodorkovsky provided funding to Yabloko and the Union of Right Forces, and put four allies onto Yabloko's list of candidates for the 2003 elections. Sergei Muravlenko, Yukos's former president, provided support to the Communist Party and stood as one of its candidates. Yukos became

one of the most powerful lobbyists in the parliament. It also had strong
links in the government and the parliament. When it celebrated its
tenth anniversary in the Rossiya Hotel, opposite the Kremlin, in April
2003, Voloshin was among the star guests, and he read out a greeting
from Putin.

Whatever Khodorkovsky's political aims, he began to pose an ever
greater challenge to the Kremlin. He argued hard for the construction of a pipeline from Angarsk in eastern Siberia to China, as
government officials pressed for an alternative route to Nakhodka on
the far eastern coast. It was longer and more costly than his proposal,
but offered multiple outlets for oil, rather than a single captive buyer.
He lobbied for other privately managed pipelines, including one to
Murmansk in the north-west, an ideal location for a deep-sea port for
oil tankers. He criticized Putin's policy on Iraq as war approached in
early 2003, indicating that he believed Russia's paramount loyalty
should be to the USA. He engineered a merger with the rival oil
group Sibneft, creating Russia's most powerful company with a
market value of $35bn, or more than half of the federal budget. And
he launched competing discussions about a strategic partnership –
even a merger – with the US multinational giants ChevronTexaco
and ExxonMobil. Khodorkovsky dared to raise publicly the issue of
corruption in the sale of Severnaya Neft, an oil company that he had
wanted to buy, in the February 2003 meeting of the RSPP lobby in
the Kremlin, despite the advice of his colleagues. 'And a few companies like Yukos, for example, have good reserves. The question is how
did they get them?' Putin retorted sharply, reminding Khodorkovsky
of past problems over tax evasion. 'So I'm returning your puck'. The
ultimate trigger for launching the campaign against him may have
been in June 2003, when the Duma met to discuss the introduction of
a new unified petroleum tax. Alexei Kudrin, the finance minister,
had argued hard for it to be tough, but it was substantially watered
down as a result of intense lobbying, led by Yukos.

Khodorkovsky had made enemies everywhere: among rival oil companies and the state-controlled Transneft pipeline operator keen to
see his wings clipped or to grab a share of his assets; government officials and business rivals envious of his success and seeking spoils for
themselves; old-style statists who hated his Jewish background and
informal style of dressing without neckties, and his unrepentant arrogance. He may ultimately have been trapped by his own success. In

preparing for a full quotation of Yukos on the New York stock exchange in June 2002, he published details of the shareholdings that he and his key partners held in the company. It showed that he personally controlled more than a third of the company, making him worth $8bn. The US business magazine *Forbes* listed him as Russia's richest man. 'He liked being rich and known,' says one of his friends. 'From a statistical fact, it became a social position.' Khodorkovsky became a cover story in glossy magazines, his face increasingly familiar in western as well as Russian publications. That may have led him to believe his own PR, giving him an excessive sense of his importance and influence abroad. He began hobnobbing with top politicians, businessmen and even royalty, some of whom – like Henry Kissinger, Jacob Rothschild and Prince Michael of Kent – he recruited as advisers, trustees or consultants.

Something had to go wrong, and in July 2003 it did. Platon Lebedev, another key Khodorkovsky partner, was warned that the prosecutor general wanted to see him. In time-honoured fashion, to protect himself, he checked into a Moscow hospital, ostensibly for a heart examination. Arrest, by tradition, was taboo in such circumstances. But the prosecutors, accompanied by the FSB, came anyway. Lebedev was interrogated and moved straight into the FSB's own detention centre in Lefortovo. Alexei Pichugin, a Yukos employee in the security department, had been arrested shortly before, on suspicion of murder. When I paid a visit to Khodorkovsky in August, he looked nervous. He kept standing up to pace around the room, fidgeting with a letter opener on his desk and giggling nervously as he related the ironies and abuses in the spiralling investigations. But he also showed a determination to pursue the matter to the very end as he accused his persecutors of falsifying evidence and shrugged off suggestions that he was willing to flee abroad. 'The stakes are very high. This saga unfortunately shows that at least some people are willing to act without even looking at the imperfect body of law in our country. They want either one of their own people or Putin to stand for a third term in 2008. If the next president but one is not theirs, they are signing long sentences for themselves in jail.'

In September, Khodorkovsky met several other oligarchs who were trying to understand whether they could help him, and they urged him to choose between business and politics. 'We said, "You are a businessman but you have started to act like a politician. We agree with your ideas and, if you form a party, maybe we will support you. But only in this capacity,"' said one rival oligarch who was present. 'He replied, "You are all wrong. Civil society is in difficulty and I am going to fight for it."' After this reply, the rival oligarch resolved that he would not even raise the subject in future meetings with Putin. There was no collective letter of support for Yukos as there had been for Gusinsky when he was arrested. Partly the other oligarchs may have resented Khodorkovsky's success. But they also believed that he had broken the terms of the Putin pact, and risked putting them all in danger with his behaviour. A few weeks later, Khodorkovsky himself said: 'I recall our discussions with the president and absolutely agree that businesses should not participate in politics. But at the same time, according to our constitution, I have the same civil rights as other citizens. As long as I have the strength, I am ready to fight the view that I must renounce my civil rights to guarantee my private property. I don't think such a policy of political appeasement is correct. Everyone knows how it ends. In 1929 and 1917, people thought "let's compromise". It ended with five million killed and tens of millions in prison.' Shortly afterwards, he headed off on a week's tour of Russia's provinces, holding what looked suspiciously like political rallies with students, employees and local residents. His trip was cut short after a few days by the FSB, and the same night he too was in prison.

In the words of Stanislav Belkovsky, a political commentator who helped stir anti-oligarch sentiment with a study on their activities published in spring 2003: 'Khodorkovsky wanted to become the majority shareholder, the first among equals.' That – alongside his high public profile – was not a message which sat easily with his peers. 'It was a big mistake to expect business to fight the authorities,' said the rival oligarch. 'Struggling against power is politics. If you are a politician you fight. If you are a businessman you leave.' Then he added: 'The only safe business these days is to be out of business.' The corporate bosses were getting the message. They could keep their money – probably. But they had to toe the party line. Fear and uncertainty were returning. 'Managed business' was joining the new Russian lexicon, alongside 'managed democracy'.

THE PRICE OF REFORM

AS THE MOSCOW WINTER HEADED towards its frosty depths in late December 2002, Vladimir Putin summoned a group of key officials to his *dacha* for a crisis meeting. The harsh climate was a powerful warning of the need for urgent reform of Russia's crumbling energy infrastructure. In the weeks ahead, hundreds of people would die and thousands more would be left shivering as power blackouts triggered heating failures in several regions. Pipes and radiators burst, making the problems still worse. But an ambitious restructuring plan for the electricity sector proposed two years earlier – designed to attract new investment into power stations some of which predated the Bolshevik Revolution – was still awaiting parliamentary approval.

Just a few days before, Vyacheslav Volodin, head of the pro-Kremlin United Russia bloc in the Duma, had warned that draft laws being prepared for the key second reading were too controversial. The reform plan had already been held up for a year, and now he suggested that it was unlikely to be discussed for several months more – which risked deferring it entirely until after the December 2003 elections. Members of his party had raised widespread objections. His comments mirrored very similar statements from Alexander Voloshin, who as head of the presidential administration also chaired UES, the state-controlled electricity monopoly. Greater consensus was still required, they claimed. There were legitimate concerns over the proposals, which risked creating a series of regional monopolies under the control of powerful business groups. That could result in manipulations in pricing and supplies, and would reduce regional governors' influence over the system. But neither the Duma nor the Federation Council, the upper chamber, was the place where the differences would be thrashed out. Instead, a compromise was quickly reached at the meeting between Putin, Voloshin and Anatoly Chubais, the chief executive of UES who had been the architect of the reforms. The command was passed and six weeks later the bills – with only modest modifications – had been passed without incident.

In the imposing grey Stalinist building on Okhotny Ryad opposite Red Square, one instrument of state control was being replaced by another. Gosplan, the state planning agency which had occupied the premises in Soviet times, had drafted ambitious production targets that were impossible to implement. Now the new tenant, the Duma, voted laws *en masse* in a process that bore scant resemblance to western-style democracy, approving government and Kremlin initiatives while having little ability to act as an independent counterweight. The electricity saga showed how far the Russian parliament had received nominally greater powers under Putin; and how little independent influence law-makers had in reality. 'The Duma is weak. It votes without discussion and amendments,' said Vladimir Ryzhkov, an independent deputy from the Altai region. 'The power reform plans were not delayed because of discussion in the Duma but by the opponents to reform within the executive.'

The Duma was not a pure rubber-stamp, though. Party politics played a role in dictating outcomes. So did the growing sophistication and weight of outside lobbyists, led by large business groups. There were differences in views between the Kremlin and the government, and within each of the two bodies. Some laws that were passed were later vetoed. However much the strings were pulled from outside, the basic composition of the chamber had been decided in essentially democratic elections. Compromise was sometimes necessary, and coalition-building became an important part of the process. But despite the caveats, it was hardly a serious debating chamber able to hold decisions in check, or to represent opposing forces in Russian society. The end result was far removed from the parliaments of Europe or North America. The well-equipped main hall, the televised proceedings and the Internet site all gave the impression of an important centre of debate. The reality was less impressive. On key issues, the Kremlin called the shots. With each crisis in Putin's period in top office – the apartment bombings in 1999, the *Kursk* submarine disaster in 2000, the Dubrovka theatre siege in 2002 – attempts to establish independent parliamentary inquiries were quickly quashed. Sergei Stepashin, the former prime minister, even proposed making the parliamentary Audit Chamber a direct agency of the Kremlin, although this was rejected by Putin.

For a group of 'reformers' in government, as much as for more conservative forces in senior positions, the system had considerable advantages. After the feuding and deadlock of the 1990s between parliament and Kremlin, it allowed them to push through economic change and to create a stable political system that helped foster investment and growth. The results were visible in the neighbourhood all around the Duma's own building. When I arrived in Moscow in 1998, the district was gloomy and run-down, with a few grandiose government-run hotels, tatty shops and fading façades. In 2003, it was booming, with the noise of construction and renovation everywhere. There were sushi bars opposite, expensive new private hotels nearby, fancy boutiques and cafés for the middle-class in all directions.

Perhaps most strikingly, the change was visible hundreds of miles beyond Russia's borders, on the Mediterranean island of Cyprus. In the sleepy town of Limassol, an imposing Russian consulate stands on the shorefront. Russian can be heard in the streets, and even in August shops display signs written in Cyrillic offering furs for sale. While rich New Russians have long flocked to the Côte d'Azure for summer holidays and to the Alps for skiing in winter, the bulk of their money has traditionally been concentrated in Cyprus. Ever since the Orthodox monks Cyril and Methodius travelled to Russia and codified the Cyrillic alphabet in the ninth century, there has been a link between the two countries. The Soviet Union was swift to recognize the Greek part of Cyprus as it veered towards civil war in the 1960s against the US-backed Turkish population in the north. Within a decade, it had approved an attractive bilateral tax treaty that would make the island's financial regime as tempting as its weather. As Communism crumbled, Russian money poured in, seeking safety from the regime at home, and notably from the tax inspectors. But by the turn of the millennium, local bankers started to notice a different trend. Cyprus was beginning to rank among the top destinations for capital being invested back into Russia. That meant for the first time in a decade Russians themselves were showing renewed faith in their country. They, who sensed better than any foreigner the nature of the new system and its consequences, began to look back home.

Much of the positive economic change that took place in Russia under Putin was due to high oil prices. Other aspects were the result of a long-term underlying post-Soviet adaptation that owed little to his influence. But his administration could also take considerable credit. It had made indisputable advances, pushing a series of reforms through parliament that helped build the base for longer-term growth and investment. An integral part of that process, the Duma and the upper Federation Council became tools for what its critics labelled 'managed democracy'. They gave the impression of being separate pillars of authority, while resting on modest and ever weaker foundations. It was a process that Russians appeared to endorse, voting democratically in 1999 and again in 2003 in favour of a system that embodied creeping anti-democratic tendencies. It was the price of reform.

Consolidating conformism

Boris Berezovsky watched NTV's Sunday evening news programme *Itogi* with growing excitement. It was November 1999, and Yevgeny Kiselyov, the anchor, was in full flow when the unexpected happened. A phone call came from Yevgeny Primakov, the former prime minister whose electoral movement, Fatherland-All Russia, looked poised to win the largest number of seats in the Duma, threatening Putin's chances for the presidency. Primakov, no lover of the media, was patched live on air, and began to rant about the latest critical report about him on the rival ORT chain's Saturday evening *Sergei Dorenko show*. 'It was then that I understood we had won,' Berezovsky recalls. The now exiled tycoon sometimes exaggerates his role and takes credit for decisions made by others. But he was using substantial money and influence at the time to help ensure Primakov's defeat and Putin's victory. 'I really thought that if Primakov took power, Russia would change course,' he says. 'It was very important that he lost out. It was not possible to think about the presidential elections without thinking about parliament. It was clear that the parliamentary winner would become president.'

Over the summer, Yeltsin had been desperately struggling to find his preferred choice of successor, as the threat from rivals grew ever greater. All Russia teamed up with the Fatherland party of Yuri Luzhkov, the autocratic mayor of Moscow, recruited Primakov and brought in other powerful regional bosses, including Vladimir Yakovlev, governor of St Petersburg, and Mintimer Shaimiev, the president of Tatarstan. Different ideas were being bounced around among Yeltsin's advisers, including a new 'party of power' called Rossiya (Russia). Berezovsky dabbled with a rival party of regional governors. 'I tried to plan a political strategy for the new time,' he says. 'I understood because I spent more than twenty years in decision-making science. A dynamic system is better than a static system. Democracy is dynamic. We need to have balance and competition in politics. We need opposition. It is better if it is constructive, but any competition is better than none. In August 1999, the Kremlin had lost the initiative, Yeltsin had a lot of problems fighting impeachment, and we didn't have enough power to be constructive. We just tried to destroy the opposition.'

Berezovsky says he met Valentin Yumashev and Alexander Voloshin, the past and then incumbent heads of the presidential administration, to argue for the creation of an alternative party. Without a positive channel, he feared that negative campaigning against Fatherland-All Russia risked driving voters directly into the hands of the Communists. The result was Unity, an anodyne political movement with a patriotic Russian bear as its logo, and no electoral platform other than loyalty to Vladimir Putin, Yeltsin's choice as the future president. The party was formally headed by Sergei Shoigu, the technocratic head of a government department that only vast and crumbling Russia could have possessed: the ministry for emergency situations. He came across as inarticulate and incoherent in his rare public statements. But he was widely known and liked for his frequent appearances on television as the saviour who was always on hand to coordinate rescue operations and dispense relief aid after the latest in a series of floods, earthquakes, landslides, industrial accidents and other disasters that regularly befell the country. Alongside him as party figureheads were Alexander Karelin, an Olympic wrestler, and Alexander Gurov, a respected former boss of the interior ministry's organized crime division. 'Unity had no ideology,' says Berezovsky. 'From the very beginning, I said that people don't listen to ideology, they will watch who will be president. They are oriented to power.'

Berezovsky claims the idea of Unity was his, while others say it was above all Voloshin's creation. In any case, he lent the media outlets he controlled – including the television network ORT and the *Kommersant* newspaper – to the cause. Well-known Russian artists, singers and academics were recruited in carefully orchestrated 'photo ops' to lend respectability. In late November, Putin, whose rating as prime minister was already rising remarkably fast, formally endorsed Unity, saying that he would personally vote for his friend Shoigu. The party that had been created from scratch less than four months before was suddenly shooting up in the polls. As I travelled across country in the weeks ahead of the race, I kept coming across the same sentiment from ordinary Russians: 'We need a strong leader.' The parliamentary campaign had, as Berezovsky predicted, become a proxy for the presidential campaign to come. The tactics – with bitter 'media wars', the incumbent's advantage, the backing of substantial state resources, and all manner of other dirty tricks – may have been unbalanced. But Primakov and Luzhkov also had considerable force and money behind them and were employing many of the same methods. The scene was set for a real contest between different political forces.

When voting came on 19 December, the result would surpass all Unity's expectations. Its strikingly high result, with 23 per cent of the votes and almost twice as many seats as Fatherland-All Russia, was a surprise to many, not least its own militants. It helped hand Putin a stronger mandate than he could have imagined. There is little doubt that there was manipulation in the final score. The Kremlin had imposed centralized control over voting via FAPSI, part of the federal intelligence agency. Some regional voting machines – notably in the more autocratic ethnic republics – delivered implausibly high support. Through the media, there was character assassination of Luzhkov and Primakov, juxtaposed with flattering images of Putin, emphasizing his youth, energy and courage, and building up his reputation as a tough, decisive leader. But in a country with little taste for ideology, after seven decades of Communism followed by one of chaos under the banner of 'reform', there was little interest in radical revolutions. The message of stability and unification of the nation under Putin helped consolidate the electorate. The growing inevitability of Putin's victory, shown by his sharply rising ratings in the opinion polls, pushed many Russians to support the party that was set to win. Whatever the weaknesses of Russia's fledgling democracy, Unity and Putin were almost certainly the people's choice.

Dmitry Furman, a historian, argues that even in contrast to its neighbours, there is little culture of political opposition in Russia. Ukraine has natural rift lines, because of its two languages – Russian and Ukrainian – and heterogeneous communities formed by the shifting borders over the past century. In the countries of Central Asia, or of the South Caucasus, such as Azerbaijan or Georgia, there are different clans – some in and others out of power. In Russia, by contrast, with a multi-ethnic population stripped of its identity and faith, widely dispersed and in Soviet times frequently redistributed across the country to meet the central planners' whims, there are loyalties to friends and family but few broader alliances. Even the 'opposition' parties in parliament often played a double game, associating with the Kremlin for influence and support. Anatoly Chubais, a leading member of the Union of Right Forces (SPS), had opposed Putin's candidature as prime minister; and the party was marginalized in its representation in committees in the new Duma. But it presented Putin with an economic plan during the 1999 election campaign which provided core elements of his programme; and Putin's positive comments about SPS helped significantly boost its electoral results. Yabloko was critical of the Kremlin's initiatives on Chechnya, but on other matters Grigory Yavlinsky seemed increasingly close to Putin as his first term continued, notably on foreign policy, and he even hinted at ministerial ambitions for himself and his colleagues. Many politicians peddled the line that the government and Kremlin officials made bad decisions, but that Putin was the 'good tsar' who should always be supported.

The Duma elected in 1999 was far more compliant than any of the parliaments Boris Yeltsin had ever known. Throughout the 1990s, most of the then president's efforts to legislate reform had failed. Draft laws sat undebated or were rejected, and those initiatives that did get under way – such as privatizations – were achieved by presidential decrees, completely bypassing the Duma. There was certainly pluralism. But there was also sclerosis, with resolutions passed but ignored, and many reform projects simply not discussed at all. At times, the Duma's relations with the Kremlin resembled open warfare. Yeltsin's authority was periodically challenged, culminating in mid-1999 in a close-run impeachment vote as the Communists attacked him for the dissolution of the Soviet Union, the shelling of parliament and the first war in Chechnya. 'Not one reformist law was passed via the Duma under Yeltsin,' said Vyacheslav Nikonov, a political analyst close to Primakov.

The new Duma elected in 1999 was not simply a steamroller for imposing the Kremlin's – or the government's – will. The reality was that politicians served a variety of interests, including their own pockets. The Kremlin, as Russian analysts like to put it, has seventeen towers and many conflicting internal views. The government, with its fifty ministries and departments, was not always united within itself or with the Kremlin. And once the Duma deputies – many of whom were neophytes – began to understand how the system worked, they too were open to persuasion from a variety of different forces, political and commercial alike. Business groups, which began to see a shift in power towards the parliament, stepped up their own lobbying with politicians during the term of the Duma – and proved highly successful. 'When you see parties voting entirely against laws that they supported in their own party manifestos, you have to raise questions,' one senior government minister told me.

UES was able to advance its initial electricity reform proposals in parliament through intense lobbying, even though Putin's economic adviser, Andrei Illarionov, and many officials and regional governors were expressly opposed. The Alfa group managed to stall Central Bank proposals on a depositor protection law for retail banks which it felt harmed its own attempts to be a market leader. Oleg Deripaska, the metals tycoon who had diversified into the uncompetitive Russian automobile sector, was able to push through protectionist measures to penalize imported cars and successfully led opposition to Russia's rapid membership of the World Trade Organization. Yukos, much to government officials' annoyance, coordinated a group of Russian oil companies that repeatedly delayed the abolition of a series of tax loopholes and watered down legislation to impose a tough new unified petroleum tax. The Communists, the second most powerful group in the Duma, did sometimes constitute a counterbalance to the Kremlin. They were seen as a sufficient nuisance to be reshuffled out of many of their key committee chairmanships halfway through the parliamentary term.

Nevertheless, the Kremlin was able to ensure that it could achieve a parliamentary majority on most issues of importance. It drove through an unprecedented volume of laws over four years. Whether legislation was popular with the conservative left, such as public sector wage increases, or with the reformist right, such as agricultural land sales, Putin's team was normally able to reach its goals. 'I can't think of any example when Putin did not get his way with something he wanted,' says Boris Nemtsov, head of the SPS. Putin was equally effective in blocking initiatives that he did not want to see passed, such as several proposals for parliamentary inquiries, including one sought by Nemtsov into the circumstances surrounding the authorities' role in the Chechen hostage siege in the Dubrovka theatre in Moscow in October 2002.

The Duma often gave the impression of paying lip-service to being an opposition force. It had the form of a western-style parliament while in substance operating in an eastern way. Government and Kremlin officials would argue disingenuously that they supported certain initiatives in principle, but that their hands were tied as they awaited the necessary ratification of the Duma. Early in his term, Putin managed to push through in record time the Start 2 arms reduction agreement with the USA that had long been stalled under Yeltsin. The Duma stalled discussion on the 'Moscow treaty' on bilateral nuclear arms reductions with the USA in early 2003, as the two countries took conflicting views over Iraq. But as Putin and George W. Bush decided to patch up their relations in the spring, it was suddenly able to push through endorsement just in time for a meeting of the two leaders in St Petersburg in May 2003. On the other hand, Putin and Mikhail Kasyanov, his prime minister, both pledged that Russia would ratify the Kyoto protocol on reducing environmental emissions. But months passed without any parliamentary decision, as Putin hardened his line in an attempt to gain other concessions from the European Union. When Putin vetoed a controversial media law in late 2002 that news organizations warned would sharply cut freedom of expression, it looked suspiciously as though the whole process had been engineered so that he could intervene like the 'good tsar' at the last minute to fight for the liberty of the press.

While many critics talked about 'managed democracy' in the Duma, the primary reason for parliament's compliance was democratic and arithmetic. Unity had won a mandate from the Russian electorate, and Putin's conciliatory style built on it. He regularly met the heads of the different parties in order to reach compromises. The composition of the Duma was predominantly left-wing, although many of Putin's planned reforms were economically liberal. But he could usually find a sufficient number to approve his desired laws through coalition-building. He brought the explicitly pro-Kremlin forces together with the right-wing parties on issues such as land reform, and with the Communists on more socially oriented laws such as pensions and state employees' wage increases. By spring 2001, the Kremlin was able to engineer the merger of Unity and its former rival Fatherland-All Russia, creating United Russia. The old *apparatchiks* who had made up its backbone saw no problems in switching allegiance to associate with the new centre of power. The deal was equally attractive to politicians from the Russia's Regions and Peoples' Deputies groups, drawn from the single-mandate constituencies that made up half of the Duma's 450 seats. All four parties were able to create a 'centrist' bloc that commanded a simple majority.

Voloshin perfected a system to help bring about compliance. His principal channel was his deputy, Vladislav Surkov, the skilled operator who had worked in Menatep and Alfa, two of Russia's biggest oligarch business groups, before joining the Kremlin in 1999. Individual politicians had long benefited from perks provided indirectly by the Kremlin which helped make them dependent on the authorities: salaries, cars, even apartments. Party leaders sought financial support, which was channelled via the Kremlin. Some had top-up salaries, or promises of support in future election campaigns. It was not always a simple question of direct pressure or crude corruption. Payment-per-vote was arguably less significant than it had been during the 1990s. Psychological factors were also at work. 'There is a political culture of conformism more than corruption,' said Vladimir Ryzhkov, the independent law-maker. 'A major part of the Duma doesn't understand what being a politician means. For example, one deputy argued against our calls to invite a government minister for questioning, saying, "Why waste the time of such a busy man?"' Another Russian party leader agreed. 'The Unity people have no principles. They are people who are ready to do what the boss wants, they are *sovok*,' he told me, a derogatory word meaning 'Soviet man' in the worst sense. But he added: 'Surkov is a brilliant manager. The system works in many different ways. He calls, pays money, develops informal relations. A lot of people want some position in government. There are a lot of options,

225

many understandings that are possible. The system is very efficient, but it is not particularly corrupt by Russian standards.'

Such mechanisms gave support to the idea of 'managed democracy'. There were some troubling changes to the rules of the political system, including tough restrictions on media analysis and reporting of elections passed in 2002. But there were few radical amendments to the regulations governing elections during Putin's first term. There was a new law on political parties, applicable from 2007, which imposed tougher conditions for registration and raised the minimum threshold for entry into the Duma from 5 per cent to 7 per cent of the total vote. The initiatives were portrayed by critics as backward steps for democracy, cutting down the number of smaller and regionally based parties. But with twenty-nine movements that stood for election in 1999 elections, and twenty-three in 2003, the Kremlin was trying to tweak a party system that many argued was far too fragmented and ineffective.

If the rise of authoritarianism in the parliament under Putin should not be underplayed, the degree of democratization that took place under Yeltsin can also be exaggerated. For Grigory Yavlinsky, leader of the Yabloko party, the roots of Russia's 'democratic deficit' began with the 'loans for shares' scandal of cut-price privatizations in 1996. As he saw it, the oligarch system that resulted overhung Yeltsin's entire second term and beyond, polluting the political parties, the judicial system, the media and business, locking them into a mutually reinforcing spiral of dependence and 'de-modernization'. There was an element of personal politics to his analysis. Yavlinsky's own '500-day plan' to end economic central planning, drawn up at the end of the 1980s, was swept aside by Yeltsin in favour of still far more rapid reform in January 1992: the overnight liberalization of prices, designed to break the back of the system. In the process, it caused hyper-inflation, wiping out the savings of millions of ordinary Russians. Yavlinsky was marginalized in favour of 'market Bolsheviks' led by Anatoly Chubais, who would go on to devise and implement 'loans for shares', and create Yabloko's main right-wing political rival, SPS. Such personal rivalries helped explain why the two most liberal, democratic movements in the Duma – the nearest it had to western-style parties – were eternally at loggerheads, weakening their support and leaving the way open to the managed democracy they condemned.

I asked Georgy Satarov, Yeltsin's official in charge of relations with the

Duma in the mid-1990s, how pivotal 'loans for shares' had proved to the destabilization of Russia's fragile democracy. 'Why 1996? It began in 1993,' he replied, citing the date when Yeltsin sent tanks to shell the White House, home of the Congress of People's Deputies, the parliament of the time, and imposed a new supra-presidential system that sidelined its replacement the Duma from the start. 'There was the idea that democracy is good – if we are the winners. If we lose, it's a loss of democracy, and we must do everything to stop it.' He pointed to two short periods during the 1990s when Russia had a government formed on the basis of support from parliament. The first was after 1991, when Yeltsin first came to power and was forced to negotiate with the Congress of People's Deputies. The second was after the crisis in 1998, when the Duma rejected Yeltsin's proposed prime ministers, Viktor Chernomyrdin and Nikolai Aksyonenko, in favour of Yevgeny Primakov.

Writing in 1995, Thomas Graham, a US diplomat who was among the first to highlight the idea of oligarchic clans competing for power, put it thus: 'In domestic politics, there are few committed democrats and no clans committed to democracy despite rhetoric to the contrary. Democratic procedures, including elections, are seen largely as weapons in the power struggle. Moreover, all the clans now support law and order and stability, which in the Russian context will inevitably lead to restrictions on democratic freedoms.' He drew attention to a number of private business leaders, but also to commercial groups centred around powerful politicians who were competing for power, such as Yuri Luzhkov, the mayor of Moscow.

Satarov highlighted a range of techniques employed ever since which did little to support and enhance democracy. There was no separation of powers, as members of the Kremlin administration meddled in the election campaigns of national politicians and regional governors. The mass media was exploited to mould public opinion. And there was widespread use of 'incentives' to win the support of the Duma, notably as part of the annual struggle to approve the budget, which did have to go through parliament. 'People did not only use money for votes,' said Satarov. 'They could be secured by different means, including threats. The government traded, winning consensus by offering oil export licences, for example, or if you needed the support of four people from a region, say, agreeing to change the status of some property from federal to regional ownership.' Deputies received apartments in Moscow, which they kept regardless of whether they were re-elected. There were cash payments to supplement their official salaries, and also a range of perks including chauffeured cars and access to elite hospitals, government rest homes and leisure facilities.

If the roots of Putin's managed democracy dated from the Yeltsin era, the new president did little to improve the system. After 1999 he and his advisers created a malleable parliament centred around a political movement that had no life of its own. Sergei Shoigu and other leaders of Unity did not even bother to take up their seats in parliament. That was not illegal, but was hardly a sign of their serious commitment to democratic accountability. In place of Unity figure-heads like Gurov, the anti-corruption fighter, the party filled its ranks with political unknowns, including twenty politicians who had criminal records. Unity's merger with Fatherland-All Russia to become United Russia was so smooth precisely because there was no coherent identity to either movement, except the pull of power itself.

Boris Gryzlov rose to the podium and conducted the business in a firm voice, with all the ease that his well-oiled years as a committee-man had given him. 'Votes for, against, abstentions, passed,' he said with barely a pause between each word. There was no debate from the hall, just a unanimous show of hands as 500 party members mechanically approved the rules, nominations for top posts and manifesto, in quick succession. The colour scheme was yellow and purple, not red; the logo was a map of Russia and a bear, not the hammer and sickle; the books on sale outside offered insights into *How to create strong political texts*, not the collected works of Marx and Lenin. But in other respects, the second gathering of the United Russia party in March 2003 looked suspiciously like a Congress of the Communist Party of the Soviet Union. Ruddy-faced, pot-bellied men in late middle age and polyester suits arrived from Moscow and across the regions. Inside the main conference hall, disagreements were absent, the key decisions had been made in advance. The biggest debate took place in the corridors outside, where analysts and journalists argued over whether it reminded them more of the sixteenth or the twenty-fifth party congress, under Stalin or Brezhnev. 'There was more discussion under Stalin,' said Sergei Markov, a political scientist himself close to the Kremlin. 'Under Brezhnev, like here, everything was decided in advance.'

United Russia's 2003 manifesto was a collection of banal platitudes and empty, populist slogans. 'Democracy or authoritarianism? The market or regulation? Openness or closure of the country? West or east? These are not topical questions,' read the document that had been endorsed. 'Decisive political language and aims should be focused on real problems . . . We plan to become the party of Russian national success . . . We believe in ourselves and in Russia!' United Russia had few active grassroots militants, a weak regional organization and no ideology. But it had a very important patron, Putin, who sent his endorsement in the form of the text of a welcoming address. Gryzlov's own speech praised the policies adopted by the Kremlin in the past three years, concluding that United Russia should be 'the party of the presidential majority'. The only other substance was criticism of the current government, which seemed rather curious given that it had been chosen by and presided over by Putin, and its senior cabinet members included Shoigu, as well as Gryzlov himself, who was interior minister.

United Russia was short on leadership, ideas and charisma. What it clearly did have was money, reflecting its firm backing by the Kremlin. It was a party of bureaucrats, conformists and opportunists. Even those advising it seemed deeply cynical about the whole exercise. In August 2003, I paid a visit to Vyacheslav Nikonov, the political scientist and grandson of the one-time Soviet foreign minister Vyacheslav Molotov, in his comfortably renovated office in central Moscow, in the former headquarters of the *Komsomol* (Communist youth league). He was open about his role as an adviser to United Russia, defending its support for Putin – whom he characterized as a latter-day de Gaulle – for modernizing the country. But he was equally candid in his scepticism in the build-up to the parliamentary elections in December. He lamented the absence of any strong leaders, platform or ideas by United Russia. 'It's going to be boring,' he said. 'This will be a campaign about who loves Putin more. There is no ideology. But no matter, because Russian state television will only show the positive images.'

Taming the regions

The architecture looked European, but the decoration would have been more appropriate in one of the authoritarian ex-Soviet republics of Central Asia. In the streets of Kazan, the historic capital of the Russian republic of Tatarstan, there were smiling pictures of President Mintimer Shaimiev in the shops, and banners bearing his slogans suspended in the streets. It was just ahead of elections in spring 2001, but there was no sign of any challenger. In the national museum, opposite the local Kremlin which contains Shaimiev's palace, there was even a special exhibition on voting. Photographs of only one candidate – the incumbent – were on display.

Sergei Kirienko, Vladimir Putin's special representative for the region, had just arrived in town. He held a joint press conference with Shaimiev, full of complimentary words for the republic's activities, in what looked suspiciously like an official Kremlin endorsement of his re-election campaign. A number of Russia's leading political parties had not even bothered to take part. In particular, there was no alternative Kremlin-backed candidate. There were several politicians running against Shaimiev, but you had to go looking for them. I found Robert Sadykov tucked away in a tiny office a few minutes' walk from the museum. The Communist candidate, he complained that he had had election materials confiscated and that his supporters had been harassed by the police. A few days later, Shaimiev was back in office for another four years, ringingly endorsed by 79 per cent of voters, in an election with an exceptional 79 per cent turnout. Sadykov won just 2 per cent.

Over the previous decade, the hawk-eyed Shaimiev had proved a master at political adaptation and survival. The former Communist Party boss of the republic, he was elected president of Tatarstan after the fall of the Soviet Union, even though he had supported the putschists who acted against Mikhail Gorbachev in 1991. He became the third figurehead name on the list of candidates in the anti-Putin Fatherland party in the 1999 parliamentary races, endorsing Yevgeny Primakov, the former prime minister with whom he had recently signed a new, wide-ranging 'bilateral' treaty. Yet after Fatherland's poor performance, he switched allegiance in time to support Putin in 2000 – and deliver him 69 per cent support in the presidential race.

He ran Tatarstan like a benevolent dictatorship, with family members in key administrative and business posts. He appointed the local mayors, who in turn sat in the regional parliament. He adopted policies which often bore little resemblance to those in the rest of Russia. When most of the country was privatizing its assets in the early 1990s, he defied federal policy. He maintained the regional government's control of strategic state industries, and its rights to mineral resources. Shaimiev pioneered what he called 'the soft entry into the market', which meant continued price regulation and few privatizations. The policy looked wise at first, but has left Tatarstan with an extremely inefficient, opaque corporate sector.

There was no radical overthrow of the past in his republic. The Communist Party might be a spent force, but a statue of a youthful Lenin still stood outside Kazan's well-respected university, from which the Soviet leader had been evicted as a student. Tatarstan had its own flag and language, but also a 'sovereign' treaty governing relations with Moscow, and a constitution which contradicted many federal laws. Shaimiev had the right to grant amnesty to prisoners, for example. He opened Tatar representative offices abroad, issued Tatar passports, and during the Chechen war refused to send young conscripts to the Russian army for military service there. He even resisted efforts by the federal centre to establish local representative offices of the Treasury and the Audit Chamber in Kazan.

Tatarstan had taken to the limits Boris Yeltsin's approach of allowing regions to take as much autonomy as they could handle. With its proud history of conquering Russia and remaining a dominant force until the sixteenth century, the republic had at least two contemporary strengths which helped maintain its position in the post-Soviet world. First, with its oil reserves and manufacturing base, it was a rich region and one of a handful that were net contributors to the Russian budget, giving it substantial bargaining power. Second, with half of the population ethnically Tatar and at least nominally Muslim, Shaimiev had long been able to toy with the panic button in Moscow, warning that the republic could disintegrate into a new Chechnya if his skilful political fingers did not caress its delicate relations. 'The situation was very complex here in 1991–2,' he told me in an interview in 1999. 'Extremist nationalist forces gained the upper hand and called for full independence. I made a speech to the people, and said yes, we need autonomy, but we must negotiate with Russia. Most of the population didn't like my words, and accused me of cowardice in comparison with Dudayev.'

However dangerous the situation had been a decade earlier, it had calmed since, if only because of the 'demonstration effect' of the catastrophic events that followed in Chechnya. Half of the local population was in any case Russian, and the rest assimilated by decades of Soviet rule. Shaimiev was proud of the vista from his presidential palace. As we sat in a large conference room, he pointed out of the window to an Orthodox church – an indispensable feature of every Kremlin across Russia. But then he indicated to his right, where in its shadow he was constructing a mosque inside the same ancient walls. It was the only example of such religious coexistence in Russia, and his officials frequently cited it as a symbol of how Tatarstan refuted the US political scientist Samuel Huntington's theory of the 'clash of civilizations' between Islam and Christianity.

Rafael Khakimov, an academic and former Communist party ideologist turned presidential adviser, argued that nationalism had declined sharply, and that Tatar-style 'Euro-Islam' was progressive and democratic. There were some radical groups in the republic who received funding from the Middle East and had contacts with the Taliban. But local Islam was largely secular, the legacy of generations of Soviet control. There had been only a handful of mosques tolerated in the republic under Communism; and widespread intermarriage that diluted separatist ethnic sentiment. Shaimiev's mosque in the Kremlin was progressing suspiciously slowly, as if he preferred the idea to the reality that it might one day be filled with active worshippers. As we knocked back vodka in a local restaurant, a local Tatar businessman put it colourfully: 'There was an official Tatar delegation that travelled to Malaysia recently. When they attended a banquet and the toasts began, they were appalled to see that there was only orange juice to drink.'

With his own frustrations with the regions still fresh, Putin resolved to tame the governors as one of his first reforms, whatever the risks. During a visit in 1999, when Primakov was still prime minister, Shaimiev expressed his confidence to me about Tatarstan's continued quasi-independence from Moscow. In remarks which revealed much about both his attitude towards the federal authorities and the separation of powers locally, he said: 'If Russia did not prolong our bilateral treaty, the parliament would have decided not to contribute to the central budget.' Khakimov added in a separate discussion: 'We are not going to give a single extra kopeck to Moscow.'

Two years later, the situation was very different. Khakimov estimated that where Tatarstan had previously retained 70 per cent of the tax it levied, now all but 30 per cent went straight to Moscow. Some was then redistributed to the region, but the federal government had reasserted its influence as the paymaster. That not only weakened Tatarstan's financial autonomy; it also played an important psychological role, shifting the loyalties of officials based in the region. Many had nominally been federal civil servants, but in practice felt tied to the republic, which influenced their promotions, supplementing their pay cheques and providing apartments and other perks. In one sign of the change in mood under Putin, the Tatar Constitutional Court in 2001 overturned a local Shaimiev law requiring its presidential candidates to speak Tatar as a clear violation of the Russian constitution. Many other legal contradictions were eliminated. Federal government offices were opened in Kazan for the first time. Shaimiev might have retained his throne, but he would henceforce have to negotiate on rather different terms with Moscow.

The shifts in Tatarstan symbolized a far broader attack on regional autonomy under Putin. Russia was split into eighty-nine regions, each with its own governor and legislature. Even in such a vast country – the biggest in the world with its eleven time zones – that seemed too many to manage. There were wide differences in the implementation of national policy at the local level, and flagrant abuses of the federal constitution. Regions imposed trade barriers to seal off their economies. Ruling alliances of local politicians and captive business groups limited competition and impeded economic growth. The Federation Council in Moscow, the upper parliamentary chamber in which all the governors sat, had become a lobby for regional interests, often acting as a brake on federal legislative reform. The Council was itself hardly democratic. During 1993–5, Yeltsin directly named many of its representatives. In the period since, there had been no direct, popular elections: the governors were automatically given seats. Their presence created a direct conflict of interest, since they represented both the executive and legislative branches of power.

Nor was the Federation Council very efficient, with short sessions for a few days each month when the governors came on brief visits to Moscow. Nevertheless, it certainly acted as a check on the Kremlin's power – albeit for selfish regional reasons rather than because of any broader responsibility to society. Over the period 1996–2000, it blocked on average a quarter of all the laws that it examined. In 1997, it closed ranks around Yevgeny Nazdratenko, the governor of the Primorsky region in the Far East, despite Yeltsin's efforts to oust him after a corruption scandal. Putin, who had worked on regional affairs when he came to the Kremlin from St Petersburg in the mid-1990s, developed an understanding of the existing system and its limitations. He could recall some particularly striking examples of the autonomy of the Federation Council, above all in its repeated refusals of Kremlin demands to dismiss Yuri Skuratov, the prosecutor general who was pursuing corruption investigations touching embarrassingly close to Yeltsin and his immediate entourage.

Once Putin was inaugurated in May 2000, he moved swiftly to curb the powers of Russia's regions, changing the framework in an effort both to push through his own reforms federally and to implement them locally. He announced the creation of seven federal *okrugs* or 'super-districts' across Russia, regrouping the existing eighty-nine republics. Each was run by a *pol pred* or plenipotentiary representative whom he named personally. Their role was to take charge of the federal offices in the regions, supervise government activities, improve coordination, and bring local laws into compliance with federal ones. There was more than a little symbolism to the fact that these districts or *okrugs* corresponded to ones that already existed for the deployment of interior ministry troops. The style of supervision and discipline imposed from the top was also set by the profile of the *pol preds* he appointed: of the seven, just one was a diplomat and one a politician; the remaining five were drawn from the army, the police and the FSB. New laws were passed that gave the president the right to fire regional governors who came under investigation by the prosecutor general; and to dissolve entire regional assemblies if they passed laws judged illegal.

Putin also altered the composition of the Federation Council itself. Governors would in future no longer be allowed to sit in the assembly, but must instead nominate a representative. The second member for each region would in future be selected by the local legislature. The governors protested fiercely, but received only the most mild modifications to the proposals in compensation: they were offered membership of a newly created advisory body called the State Council. Yegor Stroev, the head of the Federation Council and a critic of the reforms, was himself replaced in December 2001 with Sergei Mironov, a close ally of Putin from St Petersburg. The new leaders of subcommittees were pro-Kremlin loyalists. By the start of 2002, all the members had been changed, with about half of the senators drawn from Moscow, and most linked to or approved by the Kremlin. The change in voting patterns was stunning. During its sessions in 2000–2003, an average of just 3–6 per cent of laws that the Council considered were thrown out.

The new rules of the game also led to the persecution of a number of governors, serving as an example to others. Alexander Rutskoi, the governor of Kursk, was an early target. Plagued by allegations of nepotism and mismanagement in his region, he was an easy target. Just one day before voting during his re-election campaign in October 2000, the regional court barred him from standing. It upheld a complaint from two of his rivals, one of whom was Viktor Surzhikov, a former KGB agent who had been appointed as Putin's federal inspector for the region, a deputy to the *pol pred*. They alleged that Rutskoi had abused his official position during his campaign, and that he under-declared his property, including failure to mention a six-year-old Volga car that he claimed he had sold but failed to de-register.

Two months later, in the remote northern region of Chukotka, the oligarch Roman Abramovich, who had been closely linked to the Kremlin, was competing to become governor. His main rival, the incumbent, was suddenly and conveniently called in for questioning by the Moscow tax authorities, putting on pressure until he withdrew his candidature in favour of Abramovich. Putin also tackled Nazdratenko from Primorsky Krai. He was far more successful than Yeltsin, persuading the regional leader to stand down for 'health reasons' in early 2001 after accusations that he had mishandled the winter heating crisis. Ruslan Aushev, the leader of Ingushetia, who had often criticized the Kremlin's policy towards Chechnya, unexpectedly resigned several months before his term was due to expire. In an interview afterwards, he indicated enigmatically that 'one person in the Kremlin' knew why he had left. A court later dismissed Aushev's chosen successor from the list of candidates standing to replace him, paving the way for the election in April 2002 of a former KGB official, Murat Zyazikov. The result was swift conformity with Moscow's policies, including calls for a rapid return of Chechen refugees who had been sheltering in Ingushetia now that 'peace' had been restored in the neighbouring republic.

Putin's success in taming the regions was mixed. Despite his early aggressive rhetoric against corruption, it soon became clear that compromise was necessary. He used persuasion and incentives, backed up by threats where necessary, rather than simply exerting his theoretical right to dismiss governors seen as too troublesome to stay. After conversations with the Kremlin, Nazdratenko announced that he was 'resigning' due to ill-health. He was soon given a face-saving appointment as head of the powerful state fisheries commission in Moscow. Despite numerous corruption allegations, and a strong personal hatred, it took Putin until summer 2003 to remove Vladimir Yakovlev from St Petersburg. The governor also 'resigned' voluntarily, and was named a deputy minister in the federal government in charge of utilities reform. With others, such as Yuri Luzhkov and Shaimiev, former political enemies who had engineered their Fatherland-All Russia's merger with Unity, he was more magnanimous still. He 'grandfathered' them, exempting them from the different conditions that applied under the new laws designed to set a two-term limit for regional leaders, granting them and many other local bosses the chance to stand for a third and last term. Putin rejected Shaimiev's recommendations to the State Council on regional–federal relations, but he compromised on other matters. In exchange for tightening fiscal control, he pledged a five-year investment programme of federal funds to compensate. While the (federal) authorities imposed 357 modifications to the Tatar constitution that contradicted federal law, each had to be negotiated individually. Tatarstan lost some of its autonomy, but Putin allowed the republic to maintain references to its sovereignty, and to retain the 1994 power-sharing treaty. Shaimiev even went ahead with plans to adopt the Latin alphabet for the Tatar script, abandoning Cyrillic. Local observers pointed out that, in the vitally important Russian game of protocol, Shaimiev would not – unlike some of his gubernatorial counterparts – come to meet and greet Kirienko, Putin's *pol pred* for the region, on the tarmac at Kazan's airport.

Such moves suggested that Putin was weaker – or more open to argument and compromise – than his critics suggested. But he set the tone, and he also nominated the key people – the *pol preds* – who would implement his policies, however clumsily. As a result of their periodic interventions in elections, the pro-Kremlin candidate did not always win. But, as Nikolai Petrov, a geographer specializing in Russian regional policy, argues, their role did have the effect of weakening the governor's power and strengthening that of central government at the expense of local democracy. The *pol preds* had a strong nuisance value, adding a new level of bureaucracy and wielding the power to order debilitating inspections. During Putin's first term, most of the country's federal inspectors and their senior officials were changed. The proportion drawn from the military, the police or the security services rose sharply to three-quarters of the total, bringing a more authoritarian and Soviet perspective with them. On paper, the Duma, the Federation Council and the regional governors had been tamed, creating a mechanism to push through votes and impose the Kremlin's new policies. That left questions over how effective the policy would be, and the cost to democracy in the process.

Legislating reform

Stepping into Yegor Gaidar's vast office feels at first like passing through a time warp back into the Communist era. At the end of a long, gloomy corridor, there are dark wooden panels, lumpy furniture and scant decoration apart from official reports stuffed into old-fashioned bookcases. But the rhetoric from the fast-talking economist could not contrast more with the Soviet decor. Officially head of the Institute for Economies in Transition, an academic research centre, Gaidar remains a hate figure among many Russians. He was the architect of price liberalization during his brief tenure as deputy prime minister in 1991–2 at the very start of Boris Yeltsin's first term. People still bitterly remember the huge price hikes that followed, destroying their savings and triggering Gaidar's dismissal in favour of the far less radical Viktor Chernomyrdin as prime minister. Aslambek Aslakhanov, Chechnya's Duma member in 2000–2003, who used to work in the security services and keeps a statue of Felix Dzerzhinsky, the founder of the KGB, in his office, once told me bluntly: 'He should be shot as a criminal.'

While now nominally an independent researcher, Gaidar remains intimately linked to Russian economic policy-making. He is a senior figure in the Union of Right Forces, a coalition of liberal political parties which incorporates his Democratic Russia party. He is also directly connected to power, as the white plastic *vertushki* – the telephones that link top state officials – sitting on his desk demonstrate. 'His' people are in parliament, the Kremlin and the government alike, occupying important jobs and consulting him regularly on policy. If Anatoly

Chubais became the principal implementor of Yeltsin's reforms – most notably the privatization of state assets – Gaidar was the intellectual force. He and his network drafted many of the ideas introduced in Russia over the 1990s, implemented them in government, and were responsible for evaluating the results. While Gaidar's democratic credentials might make him uncomfortable with Putin's authoritarian thrust – and pushed him to sever his links with Yeltsin during the first Chechen war – his connections to the current Kremlin and government remain strong. Probably more than any other interest group around Vladimir Putin, it is Gaidar's economic liberals who represent the strongest continuity over the past decade. And, despite any concerns they might have had about his authoritarianism, under Putin they finally had the chance to push through many structural reforms of which they had long dreamed. It was no surprise that Peter Aven, the former minister who heads Alfa Bank, called for Putin to be a new Pinochet.

When Putin as prime minister created the Centre for Strategic Research in 1999 to draw up policies for his presidency, he initially drew on a broad range of experts to take part in the discussions, from radical neo-liberals to old-style 'conservative' Communists. There was an element of Soviet central planning to the Centre, with its final strategy document of several hundred pages proposing a 'ten-year plan' up to 2010. But German Gref, the close Putin associate who ran the Centre, was soon showing liberal credentials, and its advisers were gradually whittled down until they were dominated by the economic 'reformers'. With its talk about the break-up of monopolies, the reduction of bureaucracy and the targeting of social benefits to those most in need, the text could have been lifted directly from multiple policy documents issued by the World Bank and the IMF over the previous decade. The difference was that this time the new president's team was claiming 'ownership' of the ideas for themselves.

In fact, previous Russian governments had already attempted to undertake such reforms, most recently during the brief rule of the 'young reformers' of Boris Nemtsov and Sergei Kirienko in 1997–8. But factional fighting limited their influence, the system was heading towards collapse, and the entire government was brought to its knees by the August 1998 financial crisis. The subsequent crisis period, with the firing and hiring of three prime ministers in the space of a few months, did little to renew long-term thinking. As Putin said in an interview in *Izvestiya* in July 2000: '. . . take economic policy: for years, it has been clear what needs to be done, all that has been lacking is the will to do it'. The same applied to other reforms. A series of important changes to the legal system had been prepared in the early 1990s but never implemented. Health care and 'administrative' reform of the civil service were repeatedly discussed but never tackled.

Putin's first statement as he prepared to run for office – 'Russia at the turn of the millennium' – was vague. But over time, his pronouncements became more detailed, and on economic matters, his actions more market-oriented. That demanded a degree of political courage in a country where the reformers had been stigmatized in public opinion and the parliament alike. While wrapped in the conciliatory language of social democracy, there was little doubt in his programme of the course he was charting. At times, Putin seemed almost to adopt the tone of a weary economics professor, gently chiding ordinary Russians during a televised national question and answer session in 2002, pointing out the need for efficiency in public services and to cut down waste.

Putin's subsequent nominations in the economic sphere indicated that his ideas were not simply words. He inherited top officials such as Yuri Maslyukov, the powerful deputy prime minister under Primakov, who was a former senior Communist Party *apparatchik* and advocate for greater state involvement in the economy. The new president's own nominations would be fundamentally different. He named as prime minister Mikhail Kasyanov, the deep-voiced English-speaking finance ministry official specializing in foreign debt negotiations. The move would signal the creation of parallel governments, with Kasyanov's cabinet largely focused on technical economic and social policy, while Putin himself was more directly involved in coordinating the law enforcement, military and security aspects of the administration. He named Gref as head of the ministry of economic development and trade, offering clear endorsement of the 'Gref plan'. He hired as his chief economic adviser and 'sherpa' to the G8 nations Andrei Illarionov, an outspoken liberal economist who peppered Putin's speeches with technical concepts like 'rent-seeking'. In March 2002, five months before his mandate came to an end, he fired Viktor Gerashchenko, the head of the Central Bank, who had blocked banking reform. He replaced him with the cautious Sergei

Ignatiev and a team of widely respected deputies with a very strong reputation for integrity, including Oleg Vyugin, a former top finance official. Such appointments meant Putin was putting economic and financial matters into the hands of reliable, professional, market-oriented experts.

With the governors tamed, the parliament more compliant and a new sense of nervousness in the civil service, Putin's administration set about putting the Gref economic reform pledges into practice. The approach was cautious, bureaucratic and unglamorous: the creation of working groups, drafting of laws, rounds of consultation, commissions established to reach compromise in the case of disagreement. The reforms were stop-and-start. But over the first two years of his presidency, the results began to come together. Fierce budget debates in the Duma had previously extended well into the year in which the money was supposed to be being spent. The government moved instead to seek approval well in advance, even introducing a 'zero reading' to agree the main lines in advance with the parliament, sharply reducing dissent and speeding up the process. The list of legislation adopted was long and often seemed boring, but after years of political drama, it was precisely what Russia needed if it was to start becoming a more normal nation.

In the economic domain, the most fundamental initiative was less new policy than a new philosophy of fiscal responsibility. After consistent deficits year after year, the Russian government was able to prepare – and the parliament to endorse – a budget that in 2001 was in surplus for the first time in its history. The administration was helped by three factors. First and foremost, the macro-economic position of the country was sharply improving. In the wake of the August 1998 financial crisis, economic growth rose sharply. Russian companies and the state alike wiped out their debts and cut their interest costs in a single swoop. The fourfold drop in the value of the rouble meant that domestic manufacturers benefited from 'import substitution', with a large jump in demand for their ever cheaper goods in preference to those bought in rising foreign currency from abroad. Above all, there was a leap in commodity prices which benefited Russia's large natural resource exporters in the oil, gas and metals sectors. That led to a growth in profits, but also in tax revenues and export duties, swelling the government's revenues. The state suddenly had money to spend, and could raise wages and invest in public services without triggering new deficits. The Central Bank's reserves grew sharply on the back of export earnings. Foreign debt was paid off. Inflation was brought under control, and the rouble – which had been losing value ever since the 1998 crisis – stabilized.

Second, Russia was starting to benefit from the introduction of systems that had never previously existed, and would finally allow it to manage its public finances more effectively. It was only in 1997, for example, under the then finance minister Mikhail Zadornov, that the government began to establish a Treasury. Until then, the state's finances had been handled largely by private banks, with few controls and considerable scope for them to make money by delaying pensions and wages before – and if – they eventually paid them to the intended recipients. 'Expenditure control was the black box of government fiscal policy,' says a senior IMF official. 'They didn't know what they were spending. It was their Achilles' heel.' Ironically, it was the left-wing, populist government of Yevgeny Primakov, appointed immediately after the August 1998 crisis, which introduced Russia's toughest budget. The government had previously been funding its expenditure through the issue of high-interest bonds, which seemed attractive to investors but bore an unsustainable cost. In the aftermath of the inevitable default, with sharply falling revenues and no prospect of international support, it had to slash spending. The result was a particularly harsh decline in real income for pensioners and government employees. The moves seemed in contradiction with Primakov's image, instincts and political beliefs, but the crisis had left the Russian elite with little choice. The legacy of 1998 was a determination to reform.

Third, the government was helped by Putin's political landslide victory. He had a strong mandate, there was a willingness to accept a new agenda, and there were no electoral pressures to act as a brake. Business was one of the few forces that might have been strong enough to resist. But it had been weakened by the 1998 crisis, and in any case shared the thrust of Putin's policy reform. The government went about the overhaul of the nation's financial affairs with particular dedication. Despite a few early ambiguous signals, Russia's debt to foreign countries via the 'Paris Club' and to institutions such as the IMF was not simply paid off on time. It was reimbursed in advance, more quickly than the schedules required. Putin sent the signal to his ministers that he no longer wanted the terms of his own policies to be dependent upon – and therefore in any way dictated by – foreign organizations or governments. But nor did he want to risk any international opprobrium as he sought the debt upgrades by rating agencies that would attract future commercial lending.

Balancing the budget year by year at a time of fortuitously rising government revenues was one thing. It was quite another to tackle structural reforms designed to sustain growth in a more uncertain future. While the economic climate is favourable, many political leaders around the world have been tempted to spend. There is a temptation to defer difficult reforms when there is no apparent crisis or corresponding pressure for change. In Russia, given the absolute levels of poverty, the sharp decline in GDP that had taken place since the end of the Soviet period, and recent memories of much more difficult times, such complacency might have been more difficult. In any case, Putin demonstrated from the start that he had a long-term strategy, famously raising the prospect of attaining Portugal's per capita GDP, and then setting the task of doubling the size of the economy by 2010. He did not appear complacent, frequently stressing that Russia remained too reliant on the fickle nature of oil prices.

The most eye-catching and swiftest of the reforms introduced by the new government was to the tax system. Ignoring the advice of international institutions like the IMF – but in line with the recommendations of Gaidar – the government introduced a low, flat-rate personal income tax rate of just 13 per cent, in place of a sliding band of up to 30 per cent. Russians had little tradition of paying tax and scant inclination to start. State officials were frequently seen as parasites, hindering rather than providing support to citizens. The results of government policy often seemed designed to make a few rich while the services provided for the average Russian continued to crumble. A simple, low tax, fixed for a number of years, was arguably the most likely way to draw new taxpayers into the net. In 2000 I went to a pilot tax centre in Volgograd that was being funded by foreign aid agencies. What was striking was that the innovations went in entirely the opposite direction to those I had seen in the UK and elsewhere. If there was a growing orientation in the west to 'customer friendly' approaches which encouraged taxpayers to talk directly to tax officials, who identified themselves by name and gave out their direct phone numbers, in Russia the logic was the reverse: simplify procedures and minimize personal contact to cut down on the scope for corruption or arbitrary interpretation of the rules.

During Putin's first term, a series of other important tax reforms designed to improve the business climate were introduced. Corporation tax was reduced, with the basic rate levied on profits coming down from 35 per cent to 24 per cent. The 'road tax' of 1 per cent of revenues – a clear barrier to business growth by discouraging companies from boosting their sales – was abolished. VAT was cut and sales tax abolished. New customs duties were introduced, sharply cutting the rates charged on a wide variety of goods. A series of inconsistencies and special exemptions was ironed out. Other pro-business initiatives followed: measures to improve transparency, corporate governance, minority shareholders' rights and bankruptcy procedures. The aim was to enhance property rights and take measures to prevent a repetition of the scandals that had happened even in the very recent past. There were also initiatives particularly geared to small business, which had less power to fight Russia's substantial bureaucracy. One law cut the number of business activities requiring licences from 2,000 to 120. Another introduced restrictions on government agencies' inspections – a frequent pretext for harassment and bribes. A third created a simplified registration procedure to streamline new business creation.

One of the most symbolic – and delicate – areas of reform was that of land. Ever since the Bolshevik revolution in 1917, private ownership had been forbidden. In practice, widespread quasi-privatization had taken place during the 1990s, with the sale of *dacha* plots, the negotiation of long-term leases and other informal arrangements. But Yeltsin always failed to introduce definitive legislation on the issue, and many politicians in Russia's Communist and Agrarian parties had a financial as much as ideological interest in maintaining the uncertainty and ambiguity of the status quo. Putin was able to introduce a new Land Code in two basic steps. The first part dealt with industrial property – the smallest but most valuable part of Russia's land mass. It legitimized existing informal sales, reduced the scope for local authorities to claim the rights to the land under buildings which had already been sold, broadened the activities that could be carried out on land, and created the basis for its free sale and use as collateral for loans. The second, more controversial, step took longer. But in 2002, the government was able to win parliamentary support for changes to the previously taboo laws governing agricultural land. While much farmland had in practice been leased, there was still a ban on its formal sale. Compromises in the new law included forbidding sales to foreigners, preventing the sales of land close to strategic zones such as national borders, and giving local authorities considerable discretion over how much in their region could be sold. But the reform laid unprecedented foundations for the free trade and inheritance of agricultural land never seen under serfdom or socialism alike.

One of the most comprehensive and fundamental reforms dealt with the legal system. Putin, himself trained as a lawyer and with fellow lawyers among his key advisers, repeatedly stressed his commitment to the 'dictatorship of law'or the imposition of a law-based society. He appointed Dmitry Kozak, who had worked with him in St Petersburg, to coordinate the task in the Kremlin, and by the end of 2001 a series of legal changes was under way. These included a very substantial increase in funding over several years to the judiciary, with pledges to raise salaries sharply, hire additional judges and provide the courts with extra resources. That would help cut their financial dependence on – and hence potential bias in favour of – local authorities. It would help reduce the temptation of bribes. Judges' powers over investigations were enhanced, and decision-making responsibilities on whether to hold suspects in pre-trial detention shifted to them from prosecutors. There were changes to the system of discipline of judges, adding state representatives to the previously entirely self-regulatory panels which had made members of the judiciary a law unto themselves. New civil, criminal and commercial arbitrage codes were introduced. The criminal code introduced trial by jury, attenuating a judge-based system which had an acquittal rate lower even than that under Stalin at less than 1 per cent.

There were hundreds of other laws approved by the Duma during 2000–2003. They may have been significantly altered during the process of consensus-building, but many represented moves towards the 'normalization' of Russia. From the beginning of 2004, for example, a new law finally came into effect introducing mandatory car insurance. There was criticism about the level of premiums that people had to pay, who could participate and the loopholes designed to ensure that insurers did not pay out. But the very principle of such a system – particularly given Russia's fast-rising car ownership and the widespread incidence of accidents – justified its introduction. More extraordinary was that no such legislation had previously been in force.

There were new rules on currency liberalization, allowing citizens to legally take substantial sums of money out of the country for the first time and to invest it abroad. They might have made little difference to the rich, who always found a way round the rules, but they had an important popular effect. Other laws were low-profile, abstract and technical, but also significant for the longer term, including a package of regulations designed to prepare Russia for membership of the World Trade Organization. A new Labour Code was passed thirty years after the previous one, easing the right of employers to fire their staff while imposing new burdens, including fines, in the event that wages were paid late. And pension reforms were launched, to address the growing costs of a pay-as-you-go retirement system that threatened the benefits of future generations. It also offered the prospect of additional money for investment in the stock market, helping boost investment and growth. None of these initiatives might have caught the headlines, but they were signs of a shift towards a more normal, modern, developed society.

Tracking progress

Financial documents do not normally make for gripping bedtime reading, but the densely worded 200-page prospectus prepared for the New York stock exchange listing of the Russian fruit juice and milk company Wimm-Bill-Dann (WBD) reads at times like a thriller. Issued in January 2002, it is one of the most frank exposés of post-Soviet business yet written, even though it was produced by the company itself. It admits that its largest shareholder spent nine years in a Soviet penal colony after conviction for a violent crime, and that some directors are part of the Trinity Group, a firm running casinos and security guard operations 'subject to possible speculation . . . [about] links with organized crime'. It describes the Russian court system as being unreliable and open to widespread abuse. It explains the intricacies of a series of privatizations of state assets which were supposed to involve competitive bidding, but where the 'rival' companies taking part were controlled by WBD or its affiliates. It lists a series of 'related party transactions', where the top managers benefited from commercial deals on favourable terms in clear conflicts of interest. Such information ought to have been enough to dissuade anyone from buying the shares. But it had the opposite effect. Foreigners rushed to invest, pushing up the stock price sharply until the company worth more than $1bn. Danone, the French agro-food group, took a significant stake and even mulled launching a full takeover.

WBD was one of the success stories of Putin's Russia, a sign of both the growth and the diversification of the economy. Created through the purchase of a series of dairies and fruit juice producers across the former Soviet Union, it was a pioneer in the new trend of corporate governance. The company was far from perfect, but it represented something radically different from the more typical Russian business model of the 1990s. Its owners hired professional Russian managers and the best foreign consultants. They lured outside directors to sit on its board. Instead of simply stripping out the cash to siphon off into their foreign bank accounts, they reinvested in the business to generate long-term profits. They signed contracts with top-class packaging suppliers, bought state-of-the-art equipment, and began to spend large amounts on marketing and the development of their brands through television advertising and sponsorship. And they disclosed it all in their financial statements, publishing their true results, not some 'grey' equivalent that was a fraction of the real figures. As a result, they also had to pay significant corporate taxes. In short, they started thinking about the future, and how they could enhance their wealth by improving the value of the company itself. And, under the new rules of the game, they were able to do it and survive.

It was one thing for Russia's commodities groups – the owners of vast oil and nickel reserves with huge political clout – to make easy money by selling their raw materials on foreign markets for hard cash. It was another for a mundane food-processing business to win market share in the domestic market, competing against imports from established foreign companies and creating one of the country's best-known brands from scratch. WBD was one sign of the economic growth across Russia from the start of the millennium. Its operations – which provided local employment, transactions and tax revenues to boost the local economy – stretched from Ukraine in the west to Kyrgyzstan in the east. And its rising sales were an indication of the pent-up consumer appetite for branded premium products. One top

WBD executive told me that the whole process of seeking a New York quotation was designed to provide an exit, to allow him and his colleagues to cash in. Bringing in foreigners would help protect their investment from the authorities, he explained. Whatever the case, their approach represented a considerable improvement in Russian business practices from what had gone before.

WBD was a high-profile example, but it was not alone. When Auchan, the French retailer, opened its first hypermarket in the northern Moscow suburbs in autumn 2002, its decision was impressive enough. For most of the 1990s, foreign retailers had sniffed at the Russian market and then taken fright following the August 1998 financial crisis. Now Auchan was willing to commit to investing tens of millions of dollars to create a network of shops and warehouses around the Russian capital. Located on the city's outer ring-road, the store was difficult to reach, but demand on the first day was huge, with long queues at each of its sixty-eight checkouts. That showed the scope for competition, and highlighted the pent-up demand that existed when someone cut into the substantial margins that a tight-knit group of Russian retailers – in shops and street markets alike – had made by keeping the market closed and controlled. As I wandered Auchan's aisles with the director, just before the opening, he said Moscow's expatriate French community would be disappointed at the absence of their favourite products. His focus was instead on buying from Russian producers for Russian consumers, and that was now possible. I had become used to local supermarkets selling surreally overpriced imported wines, olive oil and even basic goods that could easily have been produced locally such as pasta, beer or butter. But Auchan was able to tap local producers for a large proportion of the enormous range of items for sale. Four years before, I had picked up packages of locally produced *pelmeni* or frozen dumplings in uninspiring packets, only to have the poor-quality flaps swing open, disgorging the contents onto the floor before I could even make it to the till. The quantity and quality had sharply improved, a sign of genuine enterpreneurship.

Such activity reflected – and helped generate – unprecedented economic growth. Russia's gross domestic product far outstripped most other nations', rising by 8.3 per cent in 2000, 5 per cent in 2001, 4.3 per cent in 2002 and 6.8 per cent in 2003. Its stock market was among the best performing in the world for four years running. Its bonds began to be taken seriously by investors, to the point that the rating agency Moody's even boosted their status to 'investment grade' in October 2003. The rouble, which had been dropping sharply since August 1998, had been holding steady since 2000. Russians for the first time since the collapse of the Soviet Union were less swift to convert their money directly into the dollar as a hedge against further falls. They began to have faith in their own currency. The Chicago stock exchange even started trading rouble exchange rate futures – a sign of both growing stability and interest in the currency. As businesses grew, there were steady rises in employment and wage levels. The Central Bank of Russia's reserves rose to more than $77bn by early 2004, against $60m at the start of the 1990s. As oil exports and company profits increased, so did tax revenues. The IMF, a long-standing preacher of financial austerity and a source of desperately needed funding for Russia for much of the 1990s, was suddenly sidelined. Its advice and its money became all but irrelevant, and it was forced to swallow its own medicine and cut its Moscow office to a skeleton staff.

The Putin administration practised fiscal conservatism in its appointments and its policies. The ministry of finance prepared a 'stabilization fund' to put aside money earned from a tax on oil windfall profits for future crises. Where in 1998 it had sought international food aid to cope with threatened famine, in 2003 it pledged food donations to Angola and North Korea, and contributed to the UN AIDS fund. Russia's new-found prudence won it plaudits, including 'market economy' status from both the EU and the USA, which further eased foreign trade. But how far the new economic boom was attributable to the government's reform programme – and the new confidence justified – was more debatable. Growth was, in the words of one banker, largely 'thanks to God and OPEC' – the result, above all, of the rise in the price of oil and other commodities with which Russia was richly endowed. Much was either directly in the oil sector, or in businesses dependent upon it. The sharp rouble devaluation of August 1998, which boosted the competitiveness of domestic producers, played a significant role. So did the simultaneous default on government and private debt. Other factors also helped. Work by Gaidar's institute suggests that a similar economic recovery has taken place in countries across the former Soviet bloc in the past few years regardless of the extent of policy reform or their natural resource endowments. The researchers see growth as a delayed but inevitable result after the end of Communism, as market mechanisms and institutions finally begin to function.

The flip-side of growth linked to high oil prices was that, regardless of Putin's reforms, the Russian economy remained poorly diversified. Investment and growth are likely to drop sharply if oil prices fall. Outside the oil sector, much expansion has been in the state-funded construction sector. Many new jobs have been created by local governments, paid for through higher tax revenues which may prove difficult to sustain. As the Expert Institute, an economic research centre, argued in early 2003, Russia has experienced largely 'inert growth' based on existing resources, traditional markets and ageing technologies. During the second half of Putin's term, the pace of reform slowed while the pressure to increase government spending rose sharply. Any drop in tax revenues in future risks putting fresh pressure on the country's currently sound fiscal position.

Some of the reforms undertaken by Putin do appear to be yielding positive results. 'If the big companies controlled ministers under Yeltsin, now they can only buy deputy ministers,' one executive told me. Twice-yearly surveys conducted by CEFIR, the Centre for Economic and Financial Research, suggest that harassment of business by local officials is starting to decline. The number of inspections and licences fell during 2001–4. Businesses questioned started to rate competition a tougher challenge than regulation, while corruption was only a minor problem for most. The findings are partially backed up by the Business Environment and Enterprise Performance Survey (BEEPS), sponsored by a range of international financial institutions, which studies changes to countries across the former Soviet bloc. It indicated that between 1999 and 2002, the 'time tax' – the time spent by senior company managers dealing with public officials in connection with the application of laws and regulations – dropped sharply, from nearly 14 per cent to just under 10 per cent. Bribes paid as a proportion of total company revenues also fell, from 1.7 per cent to 1.4 per cent. However, the proportion of firms frequently forced to give bribes rose from 30.6 per cent to 38.7 per cent, suggesting that corrupt officials were not keeping up with inflation in the amounts they demanded. CEFIR's study also showed a drop in the rate of improvement in its more recent surveys. The Kremlin's own Control Department concluded in 2003 that bribes were widespread and regulation threatened the survival of small businesses.

The results of changes to the tax system are also mixed. A handful of large Russian oil companies has been required to pay greater tax and excise duties, following more aggressive rules imposed by the government. The BEEPS analysis suggests that Russian companies are increasingly complying with tax regulations. Asked what proportion of their true sales they reported to the authorities for tax purposes, the average response increased from 78 per cent in 1999 to 80 per cent in 2002. Total tax revenues have also increased. However, many businesses complain that the removal of investment deductions that they could previously write off against taxes means that their net tax bills have not significantly reduced. The same applies to those companies fully complying with the new Unified Social Tax, with the result that most still under-report their total payroll. They use a variety of avoidance schemes – such as paying salaries as dividends – or pure evasion, by paying staff a proportion of their salary directly in cash. Since it suits staff not to declare these additional payments, they have little leverage in using the tougher regulations theoretically available with the new Labour Code. Temporary 'off the shelf' companies have been created to avoid paying value added tax. Many Russians remain suspicious that if they declare their true income levels, the authorities will raise tax rates again in the future, trapping them. A detailed 2003 study conducted by the Economic Expert Group, which works as an adviser to the government, concluded that the cut in corporate and income tax rates alike had done little to boost disclosure and raise revenues. 'The measures were not supported by pressure from the tax inspectors,' said Evsey Gurvich, the Group's research director. He judged that the greatest successes were the elimination of turnover tax, and a hike in oil duties – albeit after intense lobbying that meant oil companies were still paying at only modest tax rates compared with their peers in other oil-exporting countries.

There have been tentative signs of positive change in the legal system. Measuring the 'objectivity' of court decisions is difficult, since the loser always assumes that the winning side exerted commercial or political pressure to get their way. But the tax authorities have lost a large and growing proportion of cases – suggesting that judges are no longer making rulings on the basis of 'the interests of the state'. So too from time to time have the FSB and the armed forces in human rights cases. The launch of jury trials across the country likewise seems a positive move towards rebalancing the interests of defendants and prosecutors, with initial indications that acquittal rates are rising as a result. The new commercial code has created a mechanism for removing corporate disputes from less experienced and unreliable local courts into a more specialized system. Corporate lawyers are increasingly recommending their clients to use the Moscow courts rather than seek arbitration abroad. They are also more and more willing to fight in the courts, suggesting growing confidence in the system. How far these changes can be attributed to Putin's reforms is more debatable. Sergei Marinich, head of litigation with Salans Hertzfeld & Heilbronn, an international law firm, says: 'There is a gap between what the government has promised in legal reform, and what has occurred.' He suggests that the principal factor pushing for progress has simply been the rising volume of commercial cases taken by the courts over the past few years, and the increase in law firms arguing cases. With a change in generation among judges, evolutions are being forced through by their accumulating experience and the growing workload of complex cases.

For most of Putin's initiatives, it is too early to tell what the effects will be. Russian reform is still a work in progress. As Gaidar says: 'We will not know what was responsible for growth for another five years.' Land reform seems to be triggering change, with substantial investment taking place. But the social consequences for those existing farmers who are displaced, and the risks that the purchases are dominated by a few oligarchs, are considerable. The same applies to the restructuring of the electricity sector. Greater liberalization is attractive in theory, if it encourages competition, investment and cheaper electricity for consumers. But the current plans risk creating a series of regional near-monopolies which may do little to improve – or may even worsen – the status quo. Pension reform has given Russians greater freedom to choose how to invest funds for their retirement, but within a system where they risk losing everything to private managers with high costs and little experience.

One success of Putin's period in office is cited by business people above all others. It is not the detailed economic reforms or the minutiae of any particular law, so much as the general climate of political stability. That means the mere absence of regular changes in ministers, a sense of continuity, predictability and assurances that the compromises of the 1990s – however bad – will not be jeopardized. It has allowed companies to plan and invest with greater confidence.

Whereas banks in the late 1990s had been reluctant to lend money for more than a few months to companies, they began extending credit for two, three, even five years. Businesses began to issue bonds and investors to buy them. Russian capital was returning to the country. 'The main achievement of Putin is stability itself,' said Sergei Vasiliev, the St Petersburg economist, now a member of the Federation Council. 'I don't put emphasis on economic reforms. If you compare how often governments changed in the late Yeltsin period, things have been very stable. That is a virtue per se, compared with how Russia was perceived ten years ago.'

The downside is that Putin squandered his high ratings and a period of strong economic growth to undertake the 'easiest' reforms when he had most political capital available. The key changes undertaken were pro-business initiatives that preserved or enhanced company profits. Tax cuts, for example, were universally popular. But in areas of fundamental long-term importance where there was little pressure for change, such as poverty reduction, or where there was active opposition, like entry into the World Trade Organization, progress was less impressive. Just two years into Putin's first term, complacency had already begun to set in and policy reform slowed even as the economy boomed. 'Our elite is like a frog in a kettle of boiling water,' said Grigory Yavlinsky, the leader of Yabloko, referring to the addictive nature of growth – and the risk of 'cold turkey' to follow. Administrative reform of the civil service itself was frequently mentioned but repeatedly delayed. Military reform was given such a long timetable for the abolition of conscription – in 2010 – that it was meaningless. Resistance by Gazprom and the Kremlin led to almost no progress with the promised restructuring and liberalization of the gas sector. Banking reform – a low priority for some of the oligarch-controlled banks – shifted only very slowly.

Long timetables are necessary in any country to implement serious reform. Gaidar argues that Putin has learned the lesson of the 1990s, that it is best to not go too far, too fast, but to get a few things done well. As Putin himself shortly after his inauguration told one senior foreign official who was impatient to see the launch of rapid and wide-ranging economic reforms: 'It is better to tackle one thing at a time, to win battles and not lose the war.' But in Russia, the way the reforms were structured created scope for manipulation and left open to doubt how seriously and effectively they would be implemented.

The optimists suggest that Putin's second term will be a period of 'reform crowding', when less popular policies will be introduced more easily. His own team should be consolidated and in theory he will not stand again. The danger is that so many reforms have been deferred that the second term will instead suffer from 'reform overload' with no time to put so many policies into effect.

Growth was also very unevenly spread, concentrated above all in Moscow, the oil-rich regions of western Siberia and a number of other larger cities. Rural areas, many smaller settlements, declining industrial regions and those heavily subsidized in the past – notably in the far north – have continued to suffer. Despite pledges in the Gref programme to introduce 'social targeting' of assistance to the most needy, little was done beyond a few pilot programmes. The living conditions of most Russians remain miserable, with an average annual wage of $2,160 in 2003. Income inequalities have grown sharply, in a country with seventeen dollar billionaires and thirty-one million people living below the poverty line of $840 a year. The collapse of the Communist system has reduced what equality of access to public resources once existed. The former socialist paradise has become the ultimate symbol of 'trickle-down' free market economics, with all its limitations.

While opinion polls suggest strong support for Putin's reforms, they also show a sharp mismatch between those undertaken by the government and those where ordinary Russians had the greatest hopes. A study by the pollster VTsIOM in 2001 suggested that pensions, education and the military were the reforms where expectations were highest. Debureaucratization, energy supplies and tax and judicial reform – the areas where progress was in fact greater – were all ranked lower.

Putin was able to engineer a much more flexible set of political institutions to force through policy reform than Yeltsin ever had. Through elections and subsequent consolidation in the Duma, and a series of tough measures to weaken governors, he created a far more compliant machine to approve legislation. But the problem was knowing how to use that new mechanism. On many issues, there was no clear consensus as to what constituted effective reform. The government was soon facing issues that many western countries had not satisfactorily resolved, whether in the electricity and gas sectors, railways, health care or pensions. The absence of political debate in favour of technocratic analysis and strong commercial lobbying was not necessarily the best formula for success.

A second issue was that, regardless of the reform legislation, much less progress was made in ensuring effective implementation. Demands from the IMF, the EU, the World Bank, the World Trade Organization and other international organizations often focused on the form rather than the substance. New laws were passed and institutions created, but that did not mean they were more effective. Many of the initiatives given legal foundation since 2000 have been stalled or manipulated by the bureaucracy. Administrative arbitrariness and the importance of personal contacts remain paramount. Mikhail Kasyanov, the prime minister, began holding regular meetings with the Foreign Investment Advisory Council, a group of top foreign businesses operating in Russia. He told its members to call him directly if ever they faced problems. Such an approach – even when it worked – did little to resolve the systematic problems for other businesses or individuals struggling with officialdom across the country. It was a continuation of the principle of administration by exception. The head of one major international freight business told me that in the St Petersburg port, where top officials in the customs service have all been replaced, bribes had been sharply reduced and efficiency increased. In Vladivostok in the far east the system remains hugely corrupt, and local officials were indifferent to the changes in regulations ordered by Moscow.

Putin has not engineered a purely authoritarian regime. He has frequently recoiled in the wake of resistance, whether from regional leaders such as Mintimer Shaimiev, whom he has attempted to co-opt rather than crush; or on rarer occasions from people marching in the streets, such as the protesting pensioners in Voronezh in spring 2002, who helped persuade the government to delay its planned housing utilities reform. But he has often had recourse to administrative, bureaucratic means, which have weakened rather than strengthened democracy or the development of impartial institutions in the process. The negative message of a few high-profile manipulations of the court system – such as in the dismissal of Rutskoi or on the attacks on Yukos – have done little to foster a society based on law.

The outcome of Putin's first presidential term has in economic terms been very positive. His role in that transformation – and its sustainability – are more open to question. And the political price paid to get there has been extremely debatable.

A BRIDGE TOO FAR

AS MILLIONS OF PEOPLE REACHED for their remote controls on 11 September 2001, Vladimir Putin reached for his telephone. Russians, like others around the world, watched in horror and amazement as almost every television channel broadcast pictures of New York's collapsing Twin Towers. They were quick to offer their condolences, and many carried bouquets and messages of support to the US embassy in Moscow in the days that followed. But few understood how quickly and dramatically their president would react.

Putin was the first foreign leader to reach George W. Bush, sheltered in Air Force One, his specially equipped plane, in the hours after the attacks. Relations between the two former Cold War enemies had sharply improved over the previous decade, but one relic of the old power struggle which could now be put to new use was the emergency 'hot line' directly linking the leaders of Russia and the USA. It had been designed to prevent 'mutually assured destruction' between the nuclear superpowers as the result of a communications error. While ordinary phone connections to Washington broke down in the wake of the attacks, the special connection became a tool for Putin in his willingness to reach out actively to the USA, linking him rapidly to Condoleezza Rice, Bush's National Security Advisor.

It was a gesture that would impress the US administration, building on Putin's first meeting with his American counterpart in Slovenia just three months before. Despite their very different backgrounds and careers, Bush and Putin had got on then surprisingly well. 'I looked the man in the eye. I found him to be very straightforward and trustworthy . . . I was able to get a sense of his soul,' remarked Bush afterwards. The power of this statement was equally its danger. The Bush administration, after initially ignoring Russia and criticizing the Clinton White House for building a too personalized bilateral 'Bill and Boris show', was in the process of creating a similar 'George and Vlad' number with all the same weaknesses. Bush had fallen for Putin's carefully cultivated charm.

But the Russian president had much more in mind during his September phone call to Bush than mere personal expressions of sympathy. He had ideas for wide-ranging cooperation that would stretch beyond the public statements of concern of other foreign leaders, and which could help transform the relationship between the nations. There followed two weeks of intense debate in Russia. The USA was calling for the creation of an international coalition against terrorism. The mood in Russia quickly became suspicious. There was concern that US military retaliation against the Taliban in Afghanistan would impinge on Moscow's traditional 'sphere of influence' in the region. In the days after 9/11, Sergei Ivanov, Putin's trusted aide and recently appointed defence minister, firmly ruled out the presence of NATO troops in Central Asia.

Despite the initial outpourings of grief – including those for a number of Russian victims in the Twin Towers – there was still deep popular ambivalence towards America. After the erratic Yeltsin period, there was a new expectation in the military and security hierarchy, brought up during the Cold War, that Putin would adopt a more assertive, even aggressive, approach towards the west. Despite the warmer diplomatic and economic relationship of the 1990s, Moscow's elite Frunze military academy was still teaching from older ideological texts. The vast majority of troops and armaments had been redeployed eastwards within Russia's shrinking borders, but they remained oriented towards a confrontation with western Europe and the USA. And while the military had no tradition of ignoring or overruling its political masters, there were increasing indications that it was willing to exploit the silences of the Kremlin. There was the dispatch of troops to Pristina airport in 1999; the carte blanche in Chechnya; or the periodic incursions into foreign territory, notably in neighbouring Georgia. Several generals were even elected as regional leaders and or selected as representatives in the Federation Council.

Anti-American hostility had declined from a recent peak at the time of the Kosovo crisis in 1999, when NATO began bombardments without even consulting Russia. But it remained strong. Living standards and economic growth had only just begun to pick up again after the August 1998 financial crisis. There was disillusion with western assistance during the 1990s, which had failed to make hoped-for progress in rebuilding the country after the collapse of Communism. There was considerable scepticism about the benefits of the economic and cultural model offered by the west. And there was a lingering post-colonial complex, which had seen the former Soviet superpower reduced by winter 1998 to a weakling begging for foreign aid. The most eye-catching symbol of Putin's diplomacy in his first year and a half in office was the near month-long trip with full diplomatic protocol across Russia of Kim il-Jong, the dictatorial leader of North Korea, in a bullet-proof train donated to his father by Joseph Stalin.

Putin withdrew for several days to Bocharov Ruchei, his favourite country retreat near the balmy Black Sea resort of Sochi, to make his decision. He reflected amid the palm trees, in a venue where the senile Leonid Brezhnev used to take his holidays. Putin himself had first got to know the venue at that time, twenty years earlier, when he and his family had stayed with friends in a hostel for the former leader's bodyguards. He had been in the same residence again just a year earlier, in August 2000, when he faced his first serious political crisis during the failed mission to rescue sailors on the *Kursk* submarine. This time, he was far more directly in command of the process, less dependent on the old establishment and more confident of his power. He listened to generals, politicians and intelligence officials as he weighed the options. He held a meeting of the State Security Council to canvass opinions. But the ultimate choice was his alone.

Returning to Moscow on 24 September, Putin called a meeting of the leaders of the different parliamentary factions. In a tantalizing statement shown on television he said: 'I think I have made my decision, but I want to hear your views first.' It was only afterwards, in an evening address on national television, that he made his proposals known. He pledged to work with the Central Asian states in favour of the US operation, establish humanitarian corridors in Russian airspace, and continue weapons support for opponents of the Taliban.

He also set a gambit, in clear defiance of world opinion on Chechnya. 'Other deeper forms of cooperation are possible,' he said. 'The depth and character of this cooperation will directly depend on the general level and quality of our relations with these countries and on mutual understanding in the sphere of fighting international terrorism.'

Many later described Putin's decision to support the USA as a logical continuation of his previous thinking and activities. 'There was no change, it's just that the USA did not cooperate at first,' said Sergei Karaganov, the head of the influential Council on Foreign and Defence Policy. Most in the Russian hierarchy would certainly click their heels in obedience in public once the choice had been made. General Valery Manilov, a former Cold Warrior, told me in a meeting shortly afterwards that he had long been an advocate for tighter cooperation with the west. Some used the decision self-servingly, arguing that it was a coherent response to Russia's long-standing concern about international terrorism reflected in its policy in Chechnya, to which the west was finally waking up.

In the context of the debate raging in Russia at the time, however, the decision was courageous, and far from inevitable. Putin's own background and training in the KGB, an agency at the core of the Cold War struggle, suggested a degree of ambivalence. His first year in office as he shaped his own foreign policy had offered ambiguous signals. He visited North Korea and Cuba during 2000. He invited the Iranian President Mohammed Khatami on a state visit in March 2001, and in July of the same year signed an important bilateral friendship treaty with China. A tireless traveller abroad, he sometimes seemed unfocused in his priorities and destinations, but far from exclusively concentrated on cultivating the west. He could have paid lip-service to the USA after 9/11, while being noncommittal in his real pledges of support.

When the parliamentarians gathered to meet Putin just ahead of his public address, the eccentric ultra-nationalist Vladimir Zhirinovsky called for support for the Taliban. Just two minority fractions spoke out in support of assistance to the USA: the liberal groups headed by Grigory Yavlinksy and Boris Nemtsov. All the rest argued instead for Soviet- or Chinese-style neutrality: an expression of sympathy, but no tolerance for the US presence in Russia's Central Asian backyard. Yevgeny Primakov, always discreet, had already been co-opted and silenced by Putin. But it is difficult to imagine that Primakov, the architect and popularizer in the post-Soviet world of the idea of 'multi-polarity', of competing 'spheres of influence' to counterbalance the USA, would have been so enthusiastic had he been the elected president instead.

There was a strong element of continuity in Putin's ultimate decision. The very existence of the Taliban and Al Qaeda in Afghanistan was the heritage of prolonged meddling through proxy wars by the two superpowers, for which Moscow shares responsibility. The USSR had destabilized the country's successive regimes through years of manipulations and a bloody decade-long war. The USA provided arms and funding, and stirred Islamic fundamentalism as a counterbalance to Communism. There was a symmetry in the two former opponents finally coming together to tackle the mess that they had helped create and then abandoned. Putin himself had a few months earlier threatened to bomb the Taliban, drawing a link between their regime and the destabilization of Russia's southern frontiers, including the simmering conflict in Chechnya. Russia had also been covertly supporting the Northern Alliance as a bulwark against the Taliban since 1995. It had helped created a buffer zone for the Alliance – and for itself – on the borders of Tajikistan, the most pro-Russian of the former Soviet Central Asian states. It maintained a large contingent of border guards, and turned a blind eye to the regular high-profile frontier traffic. Dushanbe, the dusty Tajik capital, had become the de facto second home of Taliban resistance, where Burhanud Rabbani and other Northern Alliance leaders spent much of their time. If the USA, which had turned its back on the problems of Afghanistan even more than Russia had, was now willing to take the risk, provide the technology, fund the fighting, and do a better job than Russia's own ill-equipped and over-stretched army, why not?

In practice, there was little that Putin could do to stop the USA. In Tajikistan, there was still significant Russian influence, including a permanent contingent of troops. Other countries in the region had been largely neglected by Russia over the previous decade, whereas the USA now offered them the prospect of economic assistance. More broadly, by not backing the USA, Russia would risk alienation abroad at a time of almost universal support in the struggle against terrorism. Putin's decision was forged on the basis of realism, pragmatism and mutual interest. It was a significant rebuff to the 'old thinking' of the residual Soviet military establishment, and in defiance of more conservative forces. It was, most important, a departure from the 'you gain – we lose' zero-sum game that had dominated Cold War politics. It reflected the idea that both the USA and Russia could benefit from the bargain.

There was more to Putin's decision than narrow self-interest linked to Afghanistan, however. In private, he went out of his way in his support of the USA, not only defying much of elite opinion by not opposing a military build-up, but extending an enthusiastic hand of friendship. He offered over-flight rights, assistance with search and rescue operations, and authorized the shepherding of CIA agents into the country via Tajikistan. He pledged active intelligence cooperation, and delivered it: notably providing secret logistical information on the topography and caves in Afghanistan, and data that helped US special services find their way to and around the capital, Kabul. It was a calculated gamble based on mutual interest, in the hope of a then-unarticulated desire for tighter links in the future. Western intelligence officials confirm that Russia would go on to collaborate more closely with them, providing information on purported terrorist attacks planned against foreign government targets abroad. The data was not always reliable, its provenance often frustratingly unclear. The working methods were very different, and the enthusiasm from lower officials was not always as great as the pledges from their masters. But such exchanges did represent a 'step-change' from the past.

As subsequent events would show, Putin's decision was not to embrace America's interests at all costs, or to toe Washington's line in future. But 9/11 did provide him with a chance to fully capitalize on a call for help. If Putin had previously been interested in enhancing the transatlantic relationship, the Bush administration held back for several months in a harsh reassessment of Moscow's real level of value and power. After Slovenia and 9/11, the partnership would improve. But insensitivity to Russia re-emerged with George W. Bush's policies on Iraq. Combined with a tougher attitude by Europe, it helped trigger a new change in Russian foreign policy. As his country's bargaining position strengthened, Putin's approach became more assertive. While building bridges to the west, he rekindled other priorities too.

Dancing with the devil

On top of the tall concrete tower, the giant golden statue of Saparmurat Niyazov, the 'president for life' of Turkmenistan, shifted imperceptibly. It edged around on its scheduled once-daily rotation that ensures it always faces the sun. Huge portraits of five heads of state hung from the marble-clad exterior of the luxurious conference centre nearby. At the appointed hour, lengthy cortèges of black limousines carrying the different leaders, their advisers, bodyguards and doctors, drove through the hot, dusty capital, Ashgabat, arriving at the front steps to a grandiose welcome.

It felt like a latter-day gathering of medieval eastern potentates. It was in fact an attempt by Niyazov, the self-styled 'Turkmenbashi' – father of the Turkmens – to gain international credibility as host of the first summit of the Caspian nations in April 2002. A man with no love of journalists, his desire for publicity and foreign attention meant he had little choice but to invite the international media. Not that he took any chances. Visas were issued only for three days – barely enough time to make the flight connections in and out. Troops sealed off the roads around Ashgabat for journalists' 'own safety'. Even within those constraints, I and a number of colleagues spent several hours waiting for the delayed departure of the Turkmenair plane from Moscow – supposedly held up by 'bad weather' despite the bright sunshine at the departure and arrival points. His media minders did not even want to risk leaving curious journalists with a few hours to wander around the capital.

Niyazov hoped to change his image as a pariah of international human rights groups, presiding over a regime characterized by widespread corruption, harsh authoritarianism and a Stalin-like personality cult. But as the official entourages gathered around the large circular table bedecked with flowers, it was another politician who took the limelight. Seated alongside the leaders of Turkmenistan, Kazakhstan, Azerbaijan and Iran, it was Vladimir Putin who really stood out. He was not only the youngest and healthiest by far, and the most recent to rise to power. In contrast to his counterparts, he had been more or less democratically elected to preside over a country which – despite backsliding – benefited from a relatively critical media, freedom of religion and a fledgling market economy. Mohammed Khatami of Iran might have capped Putin's sobriety and even his reformist image with a certain extra pious moral authority, reinforced by his refusal to attend the vodka-soaked banquet that concluded the first day's session. But the appeal of the radical Islamic regime he represented, and his own effectiveness in moderating it, was more open to question.

The Ashgabat meeting said much about Putin's style of diplomacy. His participation was part of an extensive, even exhaustive, programme of foreign visits that began shortly after his election as president. Not all his contacts and destinations were savoury, but they were in large part logical and necessary, reviving links to neighbours and former allies near and far after a decade of neglect. And they were also on very different terms from those of his predecessors'.

Gorbachev had turned his back on former Soviet allies in Latin America, Asia and Africa as he forged détente with the west. He alienated others as rising ethnic nationalism in the Baltic republics and the Caucasus triggered bloodshed in the struggle for independence. Yeltsin, for his part, signed away the last remnants of Moscow's control over its satellite republics in 1991 as the price for liberating Russia from the ideological yoke of the USSR. It was the way to undermine his enemy Gorbachev. His subsequent priorities, and Russia's lack of resources, led to a decade of abandonment of the 'near abroad'. Even today, formal border treaties have yet to be concluded with most of Russia's neighbours. The relationship was symbolized by the vacuous nature of the 'Commonwealth of Independent States' (CIS), established to represent their mutual interests, but rarely capable of taking any significant decision. The absence of active Moscow involvement in the region was perhaps necessary for a period. 'Benign neglect' at least allowed the emergence of a series of independent countries, however shaky their foundations. It permitted the collapse of the Soviet empire with remarkably little conflict or loss of life over a very short period. And it was accompanied by an extraordinarily smooth removal or neutralization of Cold War nuclear, biological and chemical weapons complexes across the region.

But the end of the USSR also created a dangerous vacuum. A decade of Yeltsin's erratic approach to foreign policy had created the need for a practitioner of statecraft who was more sober in every sense. The ailing former president's appearances had increasingly become a comedy of errors. During a planned stopover in Ireland in 1994, he failed to get off his plane, triggering undignified debates over whether he was simply too drunk, or fought in vain against his bodyguards who thought it wiser that he stay on board. At the start of a summit with Bill Clinton in Moscow in September 1998, he mixed up his briefing notes and began reading remarks prepared for the concluding press conference. On a visit to Uzbekistan in October 1998, he collapsed into the arms of President Islam Karimov on arrival at the airport, in front of the television cameras, and had to be swiftly flown home. Pained officials frequently had to perform tortuous linguistic gymnastics to explain what the president had 'really' meant to say. Yeltsin's broad thrust might have been westernizing and democratic, but his threats, U-turns and unpredictability gave the impression of a leader to be treated cautiously while not taken too seriously.

It would not have taken much to bring about an improvement at the personal level, but Putin certainly fitted the job description well. He was the opposite of Yeltsin in terms of health, energy, sobriety and diplomacy. According to an estimate by the *Komsomolskaya Pravda* newspaper, in the first two and a half years of his term he spent 1,154 hours in aeroplanes, more than half of them abroad. He travelled to former Soviet allies, whether in Cuba, North Korea or China. He revived his links to the surrounding CIS states, placing fresh emphasis both on Russian citizens living abroad and on the former 'colonies' which were still tightly linked to Russian culture, education and language. Through geography and history, Russia was their most logical partner. Putin joined the Organization of the Islamic Conference, and boosted Russia's role in the Shanghai Five, the Asia–Pacific Economic Cooperation forum, and the Association of South-East Asian Nations. He wanted to be friends with everyone. But throughout his presidency, Putin never lost sight of the further horizon, establishing even tighter and ever more frequent links with the leaders of Europe, the USA, Canada and Japan. The 6.6 million square miles expanse of Russia – the largest country in the world – may be wedged between the Caucasus, Central Asia and China to the south and east, but Putin seemed at least as interested in points further west. An analysis by *Kommersant Vlast* magazine suggested he spent more time with European and US leaders than with some of his own ministers.

Many have argued that Russians are 'Eurasians', European-looking on the surface but Asian under the skin. To others, they are more

'Asiopean', dominated by the east in their thinking. But Putin's own orientation was at least to be international, not centred purely on Russia and its supposed exceptionalism. His thinking seemed more European – if not Anglo-Saxon – than Asian. He relished foreign relations – a traditional domain for heads of states who can flee their domestic challenges, and exercise freer reign abroad than at home. He grew in confidence as he impressed other world leaders, outstripping their expectations. And he visibly relished his chance to enter the court of the great, rubbing shoulders with them and gaining the impression of being treated as an equal.

In his visits and his statements, Putin might not have had much political experience but he could use his KGB training to the full. He always had a positive word to say about his hosts to win them over, showing interest, enthusiasm and respect, even humility or contrition. In green-sensitive Canada, he claimed that he had been a lifelong environmentalist. In Japan, he donned a judo suit and allowed himself to be thrown during a match. In China, he declared that one of his daughters was studying the language. In France, he said his favourite painter was Renoir. In April 2000, on the sixtieth anniversary of the Katyn massacre, where Soviet troops murdered 15,000 Polish officers near the city of Smolensk, he called the Polish president to offer cooperation on an investigation. He went to the St Geneviève de Bois cemetery near Paris, resting place of many White Russians who had fled Communist oppression, as a sign of reconciliation to those who had fled the Soviet terror.

It was clear that Putin did not see Russia as simply one ordinary nation among many, in a world dominated by Washington. In his speeches, he frequently made references to his country as the *derzhava* or superpower it had once been, and which he wanted to see rise again. 'Russia was and will remain a great power,' he wrote in 1999. But he also recognized a new reality, and switched his methods accordingly. Russia would never be great again without an economy to match its historical ambitions. That was best achieved by pragmatic choices, aligning itself in the meantime with those countries which were powerhouses, starting with the USA itself.

The summit in Ashgabat was an example of Putin's new approach. The Caspian Sea had always been a key strategic frontier in Central Asia. Its rich minerals, fishing resources and transport links gave it an ever growing economic role. But its full exploitation had long been deadlocked. Iran argued that the Caspian should be developed jointly, with its wealth split equally five ways 'condominium-style' between the littoral states that surrounded it. The authorities in Tehran were attempting to rebalance a geographical disadvantage, since they controlled just 13 per cent of the shoreline – and in the waters of the southern Caspian at that, which are far less abundant in oil reserves. In the past, Russia had taken the same view for different reasons. It still saw itself as the main negotiator with Iran, a legacy of the Soviet period when all the remaining shoreline was directly under Moscow's control. It had attempted to maintain its regional influence after the collapse of the USSR by keeping a veto over future development. But history had moved on. The former Soviet satellite states were no longer under Moscow's control, and they – as well as Russia – wanted a healthy share of future sources of revenue. Kazakhstan and Azerbaijan had already begun developing oil and gas projects regardless of the objections of Russia and Iran – even triggering a skirmish between the Iranian navy and a BP exploration vessel that entered contested waters in 2001. Moscow had begun to cooperate on bilateral deals with both states in the mid-1990s, but had never fully followed through.

Turkmenbashi had hoped to reach an agreement on the division of the Caspian. But the preparations were insufficient, and the feuding parties too far apart. Iran was still a long way from its partners on points of principle. Other bilateral disputes – notably between Azerbaijan and Turkmenistan over the division of their shared seabed – hindered progress. On the second day, the five assembled leaders mumbled a few diplomatic niceties in front of the cameras. Despite the slot allocated in the official programme, they left without even bothering to hold what would have been a very empty concluding press conference.

The inconclusive Caspian summit was a symbolic trigger for Putin, who made the best of an unproductive gathering. He was determined to break the deadlock, regardless of the remaining countries' objections. Within weeks of its conclusion, Russia had swept away its old-style legalistic objections and finalized bilateral agreements with both of its direct Caspian neighbours, Kazakhstan and Azerbaijan. The three states – the best endowed with proven hydrocarbon reserves – formalized a division of their sea borders, the pooling of oil resources, and an agreement to ensure that the Russian state-backed energy companies Rosneft, Lukoil and Gazprom would be significant partners. The initiative reflected a new pragmatism, effectiveness and above all commercial drive in Russian foreign policy. It was far from the only example. On his trips abroad, Putin regularly brought large delegations of businessmen, as well as regional governors keen for investment deals, and government ministers prepared to seal contracts and open detailed discussions with their counterparts. Rare was a foreign trip that did not conclude with the signature of trade contracts, and often with the restructuring of Soviet-era debts.

Waiting in the cavernous halls of the conference centre in Ashgabat while the closed-door discussion of the leaders was under way, I noticed an unexpected figure hovering nearby. It was Alexei Miller, who had worked with Putin in St Petersburg, and had been named by him a year earlier to run Gazprom, the state-backed gas monopoly. Miller, a cautious, shy man, forced a half-smile, raised his mobile phone to his ear as a pretext, and scurried away when I introduced myself. A few months later, the reason for his decision to join the Russian delegation would become clear. Itera, an obscure Florida-based company suspected of close links to Gazprom's former management, had eaten deeply into the company's market during the 1990s, acquiring gas contracts across the former USSR from under its nose. Itera had established particularly strong ties with Turkmenistan, controlling its gas output and becoming one of the few companies allowed to use Gazprom's pipeline to transport it – on opaque financial terms – for sale to Ukraine. After Miller's appointment, Itera's position began to weaken sharply. The biggest blow came when Gazprom took direct control of the lucrative Turkmen gas contract a few months after the Ashgabat summit.

As Russia's key export, energy was a vital source of foreign exchange, particularly as international oil and gas prices rose. But it was also the lifeblood sought by many other countries. It became an important lever in Russia's foreign relations with its neighbours near and far, and Gazprom one of Putin's principal tools. Miller was a guest of honour on many trips. For the EU, the USA and Japan, Russia offered long-term strategic energy supplies from a partner that appeared increasingly friendly and stable at a time of growing political turmoil in the Middle East. For Russia's more traditional, poorer and captive nearer neighbours in the CIS, dependent on subsidized energy inputs or reliant on Russian pipelines to export their energy, there were more aggressive undertones, albeit dressed up in the clothes of market economics.

'Europe's last dictatorship', Belarus, ruled by the erratic Alexander Lukashenko, had long benefited from a romantic courtship with Russia under Yeltsin. The two leaders had talked dreamily of a union of their two countries. Under Putin, the relationship became frostier, and more practical. While Lukashenko paid frequent trips to Moscow, return journeys were rare. He would make short, conciliatory statements at a concluding press conference, sometimes sweating, as Putin spoke out. Later – safely back on home soil at Minsk airport – he would give a harsher, more nationalistic spin to the talks. The tall, balding authoritarian leader, with his clipped moustache, anti-western outbursts and intolerance of domestic opposition, became an increasing embarrassment. The Kremlin made clear that any political union would be on its terms, essentially implying that Belarus should be absorbed by Russia. To drive home its point, Moscow got tough over gas exports. Just as winter 2002 was approaching, it demanded the payment of outstanding debts, and said future supplies would be on new, higher, 'market' terms.

In energy-starved Ukraine, Putin named Viktor Chernomyrdin, the former prime minister who had built his career inside the Soviet energy sector and maintained very close links to Gazprom's old guard, as his high-profile ambassador. One of his prime tasks was to put an end to the theft of gas from Russia's pipelines, and to get Ukraine to pay up on its outstanding debts. In the South Caucasus, poverty-stricken Georgia had long proved an irritant to Russia, with its attempts to take an independent policy line, alleged harbouring of rebels from neighbouring Chechnya, and direct links with the west – including discussion of NATO membership. Moscow started to add new economic pressure points. Itera found its long-standing gas supply arrangements challenged by Gazprom, and in summer 2003, UES, the state electricity monopoly, took over power generation contracts from the American group AES. In other republics such as Armenia, Russian state energy groups also reasserted their control, edging out Itera.

Putin's foreign policy tactics towards his near neighbours would not be purely commercial. Flying back from the Ashgabat summit in 2002, he stopped over in the Russian Caspian port city of Astrakhan. In a carefully orchestrated series of 'photo opportunities', he paid a visit not only to one of Lukoil's oil rigs that was carrying out offshore drilling, but also to the Russian naval fleet. He pledged fresh money and new military exercises. Implicit muscle would become part of the new regional discourse. The pragmatic approach to the Caspian, he seemed to be saying, would be backed up if necessary by force.

As part of his efforts to reassemble the ruins of empire, Putin began to revive the CIS, as well as other regional organizations. He relaunched the idea of a free trade zone; and even of a common currency. The first step came with a union announced in 2003 between Ukraine, Belarus, Russia and Kazakhstan. He delegated leadership of the CIS – which Yeltsin had always claimed for himself by an unwritten rule – to the then Ukrainian president Leonid Kuchma. It was a neat way of deferring responsibility, while giving the impression of magnanimously sharing power. But the mere fact of paying attention to questions of leadership, and handing control to a close ally, also suggested that he wanted the organization to become more active. Spurred on by the US military build-up in Central Asia, Putin finalized his own new security partnership in the region in 2003, the Collective Security Treaty Organization, with half of the budget financed by Russia and the remainder by the other five member states. In October of the same year, he inaugurated the Kant air base in Kyrgyzstan: the first new Russian military outpost abroad since the fall of the Soviet Union. It was no coincidence that it was in Central Asia, just nineteen miles from Manas, location of a base controlled by the USA-led anti-terrorist coalition.

Putin brought to his foreign policy a fresh emphasis on the protection of the interests of ethnic Russians living outside the country, many of whom had lost status, jobs and pension rights since the collapse of the USSR. There was also a Cold War element to Moscow's priorities. The authorities harshly criticized the second-class status of Russians in the Baltic states, which had shifted their allegiance westwards, opting for NATO and EU membership and to some degree turning ethnic Russian residents into scapegoats for the sins of their former imperial masters. But Moscow was quieter about the larger-scale abuses and much poorer living conditions for its citizens within the CIS states. Gazprom may have gained control over Turkmen gas in 2002, but Turkmenbashi succeeded in exchange in ending the dual citizenship status of Russians living in his country – and swiftly clamped down on those who chose to remain Russian passport-holders.

The tensions between Russia's traditional and newer allies, its Soviet versus its modernizing priorities, cut through many aspects of Putin's foreign policy. In some ways, they have accentuated precisely because his administration was more effective in implementing its different and sometimes contradictory aspects than had been Yeltsin's. It highlighted a tactical rather than a strategic approach, a sense that Russia was indulging in foreign relations more than a coherent foreign policy.

One result was the conflict of clashing world views. Putin was no doubt right in attempting to improve relations with his neighbours, as well as more distant states. It made good economic as well as political sense. His approach – notably to some of the more unstable states along its own borders – lent itself to Russia's re-emerging role as a regional broker. It also allowed for some cynically clever ruses. He constructed imitation western-style elections in Chechnya, for example, but used observers from the CIS and the Muslim world to endorse them. But there have been limits to his policy of making friends with everyone. It has raised false hopes, and risked creating future fissures.

Putin re-established ties with North Korea, while maintaining the links with South Korea that had helped isolate Pyongyang. He tried to balance links with Syria and with Israel, once conducting conversations by phone with Tel Aviv on the day the Syrian vice-president, Abdel Halim Khaddam, came to Moscow. He invited President Pervez Musharaf of Pakistan on a state visit, and even attempted to mediate in the Kashmir dispute, while continuing to cultivate long-standing links with India. Above all, he tried to become best friends with the USA, while offering political, commercial and even military support to regimes it viewed with great suspicion, including China, Iraq and Iran. Russia stressed its commitment to regional stability, a reduction in arms and drug trafficking, and a clampdown on a political vacuum that could create conditions to lure terrorist groups. Yet in at least three 'frozen conflicts' – in South Ossetia and Abkhazia in Georgia and in Transdniester in Moldova – it played a double game that helped perpetuate them as zones of non-law. While not officially recognizing these breakaway states, it maintained peacekeepers, provided economic aid and trade, conducted quasi-diplomatic relations and operated open borders.

Another problem with Russia's policy was the friction between commercial and security interests. Putin attempted to rationalize the country's defence industry, centralizing weapons exports into the hands of two state agencies. He gave new impetus to the sale of civil nuclear technology, putting his own people into top jobs in MinAtom, the atomic energy ministry, and its subsidiaries. The two fields – military and nuclear – were rare examples where Russia could capitalize on its Soviet expertise, prove internationally competitive and generate substantial foreign revenues from the sale of sophisticated exports. The trade also helped to placate financially and politically the traditional military-security lobbies at home.

By 2003 Russia was the world's second largest arms exporter after the USA, with $4bn in annual revenue. MinAtom was generating a similar amount from sales of its know-how, equipment and fuel. The brake came as much from Russia's new businesslike insistence on full payment in cash as from any strong philosophical worries over weapons proliferation. The inability to pay appeared to be the main reason that arms sales were not greater to North Korea or Iran. Its policies towards such countries clearly set Russia on a collision course with the USA. Putin played tough, resisting American pressure to cease its $1bn contract to built the Bushehr nuclear power station in Iran. He called for Tehran to accept spot checks by the International Atomic Energy Authority without making them a condition for continued work. His discretion paid off when Iran agreed in late 2003, and immediately launched talks for new civilian nuclear contracts with Russia. Such cooperation raised concerns over the potential threats to Russia's own territory. As the evidence grew of Iran's desires to develop a military nuclear programme, and the indications were that it had already developed medium-range missiles that could reach well into southern Russia, Moscow's sales of sophisticated missile, anti-aircraft and nuclear technology to Tehran sat increasingly uneasily with its own more aggressive policy in the Caspian.

The rise of moral equivalence

When Tony Blair, the British prime minister, decided to pay his first visit to St Petersburg in March 2000, the pretext for his short trip could not have been more symbolic. Seated in the royal box of the Mariinsky Theatre alongside Vladimir Putin, he watched Prokoviev's opera *War and Peace*. The military phase of the bloody conflict in Chechnya was in full march against a backdrop of international criticism, but the bilateral political spirit was of explicit conciliation. The message was clear to the Russian public. An important foreign leader had come to Putin in his home town. The Russian leader-in-waiting could capitalize on his association with a new-found friend, adding one final gloss of credibility as an international statesman to his standing in the build-up to the presidential election the following month. Putin was still only acting president, but Blair was keen to build bridges with the man set to be the new incumbent of the Kremlin. He seemed unconcerned about the signal he was sending of preference to one among several rival candidates, destabilizing further any pretence of a democratic race in the coming weeks.

The choice of St Petersburg allowed Blair to play with protocol, claiming that he was simply visiting Putin informally as a friend, whereas a trip to the capital would have been considered an official visit. That made no difference to the Russians. For Putin, aside from any electoral fillip, the most significant message of the St Petersburg meeting was that western public opinion towards Chechnya was shifting in his favour. As he told Russian journalists, it had proved difficult for him to travel abroad as prime minister because foreign leaders 'didn't really want to meet us because of Chechnya . . . [or only] if we agreed to change our position on the Caucasus'. If criticism of Russia's policy in Chechnya was an irritation for Putin, it became an element, at times an obsession, in his own thinking, and a tool in his tactics.

Blair's St Petersburg trip set a softer tone on Chechnya that would soon be followed by his western peers. The clashes in Yugoslavia had triggered enormous international pressure and intense foreign military and diplomatic interventions over the previous decade. Just a little further east in Chechnya, still on Europe's borders, another conflict had taken more than 100,000 lives and left tens of thousands more abused, displaced or destitute. But the international community drew a curtain around Chechnya: it was an internal affair to be left to Moscow; Russia's forgotten, invisible war.

The early military fighting in 1999–2000 in Chechnya brought inevitable deaths of troops on both sides. Europe and the USA might have had little stomach for new secessionist battles like the ones they had tackled in Yugoslavia, and no sympathy for the Chechens in particular. But the continued disappearances and other human rights abuses that intensified once the large-scale military conflict came to an end ought to have provoked greater international outrage. Instead, the reverse was true. The climate of impunity grew more powerful, the approach of the west weaker than ever.

If the Cold War balance of power had restricted the sphere of action of Russia's critics in Soviet times, its residual nuclear weapons no doubt played a continuing role in limiting subsequent intervention. There was a strategic desire to bring Russia 'on-side' after the memory of the Communist period, and the growing demand for access to its market and resources. But 9/11 would increase Russia's margin for manoeuvre still further. Probably the most significant fresh factor behind the silence of the west over Chechnya was the change wrought by the terrorist attacks against New York and Washington. In his television address two weeks after the Twin Towers attacks, Putin established a clear link for domestic and foreign consumption alike: we are committed to the international coalition against terrorism, and our fight in Chechnya is an integral part of that battle. The Al Qaeda actions in the USA were appropriated by Putin as a logical extension of Russia's own conflict. Russian officials would make the connections with increasing intensity in the future. When in late 2002 the British detained and then released Akhmed Zakayev, the Chechen rebel leader, the Russian foreign minister Igor Ivanov stretched Cold War-style rhetoric to its furthest extremes when he equated Zakayev to Osama bin Laden.

The argument was not very convincing. Some radical Muslims had come from abroad to fight in Chechnya, and Chechens had established financial and personal links in both Afghanistan and the Middle East. But the connection seemed largely opportunistic: part of a bargain between those willing to fund, and Chechens willing to seek foreign support for a struggle tightly focused around Chechnya itself and its regional problems. There was scant evidence of Chechens fighting alongside the Taliban or in Iraq, or of Chechen terrorist activity beyond the territory of the republic itself or the surrounding region. But the connection, however tenuous, provided a convenient smokescreen behind which world leaders could hide.

International terrorism more generally was a new lowest common denominator on which politicians could agree. It handed a trump card to Putin. Russia's weak economy could not truly justify its membership of the G8. Its internal distortions and imperfectly formed market economy posed problems in its candidature for the World Trade Organization. Its lax border controls weakened its case for visa-free travel with the European Union. Its politicized witch-hunts, harsh prisons and corrupt court system meant the credibility of its arrest warrants or judicial decisions were viewed sceptically abroad. But when Putin joined other foreign leaders for bilateral or multilateral talks, they suddenly had a common language. They could discuss cross-border cooperation between their intelligence services, and common initiatives on the fight against terror. At the very least, they had a broad theme on which to agree in public, despite any private tensions or the absence of any other issues to discuss.

Just as important, 9/11 helped create a growing climate of 'moral equivalence' to Russian abuses in Chechnya that Moscow used in its defence. Officials could draw from the old Soviet armoury of 'double standards' to parry their critics. In the USA in particular, Al Qaeda created a mood of fear that helped prepare public opinion for a clampdown on human rights. Freedom of expression suffered as a result. There was formal and informal pressure on media that criticized Washington's position on the war in Afghanistan – and later Iraq. If reports of Saddam's weapons of mass destruction were instinctively treated too sceptically by the Russian media, the US media seemed too quick to believe them despite their dubious provenance. Even the internet was a victim of the new mood. Shortly after the US bombardments against the Taliban began, I tried to track down an analysis of the Soviet conflict in Afghanistan produced by Fort Leavenworth, a US army research centre. Although it had been freely available on-line in the past, it had suddenly been withdrawn from cyberspace and was inaccessible. I eventually did find a copy of the document – on a server in Belarus.

The US approach to judicial procedures created a similar climate of hypocrisy. There was the use of the 'offshore' internment centre of Cuba's Guantanamo Bay away from independent scrutiny, the label 'illegal armed combatant' to justify closed military tribunals carrying the ultimate threat of the death penalty, and indefinite detention without formal charges or trial. There was pressure for extradition without clear evidence, and allegations of sleep deprivation and other techniques to extract information beyond normally accepted US practice, notably with the delegation of interrogation to Egypt, Pakistan and other US partners. Al Qaeda and the US response to it brought new pressures on civil liberties elsewhere, and diminished concern over abuses among the coalition's partners. Uzbekistan with its horrendous record of human rights abuse was suddenly receiving substantial US aid. Pressure tightened for a European-wide arrest warrant, and for extraditions based on scant evidence. In Georgia, a beneficiary of US military trainers, the authorities said they had immediately dispatched 'Arabs' arrested during a wave of anti-terrorist round-ups on their territory to Guantanamo Bay. That raised particular Russian ire, because Moscow's extradition demands for a group of Chechens caught during similar operations were rebuffed pending lengthy appeals to the European Court of Human Rights.

Whatever the absolute level of abuse in the new get-tough, anti-terrorist approach from the west, it provided a moral cover for Russia to relativize its fight in Chechnya – not to mention its clampdown on freedom of speech. Russians loved to argue that the British had their own problems with the IRA – while failing to continue the argument to its end: Belfast was never blanket-bombed; and the British accepted international mediation. Putin became a master at dressing up initiatives in Chechnya in forms palatable to the west. He now created a virtual political solution in Chechnya through a referendum, a new constitution, elections and endless promises on the restoration of normal life. The moves gave cover to the western leaders, even if the reality was very different.

Other factors also played in Putin's favour to mute foreign criticism of his policies. One was the changing nature and beliefs of his interlocutors, whom he skilfully played off against each other. Blair's realpolitik towards Moscow was mixed with a certain understanding of the Russian position forged from his own frustrations with Northern Ireland, and the memory of British victims of Chechen kidnappers. Another sympathetic ear was José Maria Aznar, the Spanish prime minister. A past target of ETA, the Basque nationalist organization, which placed him in the middle of his own bitter terrorist fight in addition to the new struggle against Al Qaeda, he was easily won over to Putin's cause. The arrival to power in Italy of Silvio Berlusconi, plagued at home with just as many accusations of his manipulation of parliament, the judiciary and the media, also played to Putin's favour. So did that of Junichiro Koizumi, the Japanese prime minister keen to build bridges with Russia and kick-start long-stalled economic and energy cooperation.

Likewise, Jacques Chirac's re-election as president of France in May 2002 changed the nature of bilateral relations with Russia. The victory of his centre-right coalition in parliamentary elections freed Chirac from his lengthy 'cohabitation' with a left-wing government, which had periodically criticized Russian policy. One of the unshack-led Chirac's early foreign policy initiatives was to fly to Sochi for a meeting with Putin, at which he made sympathetic noises on Chechnya. A year later, welcoming Putin on a full state visit to Paris as he sought his support in opposing the war in Iraq, he went out of his way to endorse Russia's latest controversial initiatives to impose a political solution to the conflict. The following summer, his own UMP movement would 'twin' with Putin's United Russia party. The back-drop was set above all by the election of George W. Bush. Many Russian analysts welcomed his victory at the time, anticipating that a shift from a Democratic to a Republican administration would reduce criticism and pressure. They would not be disappointed. The State Department, like the EU's leaders, issued periodic, ritualistic criti-cisms over Chechnya and other issues, but there were few signs that they took the matter too seriously, or that they would prove a stum-bling block to improved relations.

There was no shortage of non-governmental organizations criti-cizing abuses in Chechnya, from the Russian groups Memorial and Moscow Helsinki Group, to the relief agency Médecins sans Frontières, Human Rights Watch and even the United Nations. A few politicians took note, such as Anders Fogh Rasmussen, Denmark's prime minister. Public opinion was sensitized in Copenhagen if only because of the considerable practical knowledge of the situation from the Danish Refugee Council, a relief agency that was one of the most active in the North Caucasus. But overall, the critical regard of such bodies translated into only very modest action in the international political arena.

There were no repercussions from the persistent refusal to grant access to the UN's own human rights commission. Nor was there great outcry when the mandate of the Organization for Security and Cooperation in Europe (OSCE) in Chechnya, which had done much to broker a peace at the end of the previous conflict in 1996, was sharply diluted. Indeed, so keen was the OSCE to regain a foothold in the republic that it abandoned its human rights mandate in favour of a much more limited one focused on humanitarian assistance, and agreed to pay for Russian-provided security including rocket launchers for its bodyguards. It even sent a technical mission to observe the referendum on a new constitution organized in spring 2003, adding credibility to the process.

The one official organization that was consistently critical on Russia's role in Chechnya was the Strasbourg-based human rights body, the Council of Europe. The Chechen separatists were sceptical of its role: they argued that it gave credibility to Russian expressions of concern over human rights, while carrying out few investigations and proving unable to end the conflict. But it was the only body to have expatriate observers based in Chechnya from 2000–03. The Council's diverse membership and its obligation to work on the ground with the Russian authorities under protection of security guards limited its freedom. Nonetheless, its staff did provide information on what was taking place in the republic, documenting abuses and establishing an office where Chechens came to file complaints. By the Council's own estimates, it was directly involved in tracking down and releasing up to 500 prisoners.

The Council of Europe probably carried more weight in Russia than in many other member states, in part because so many in Russia confused it with the European Commission. It was an organization, in the scathing description of one observer, for 'has-been politicians from the west, and up-and-coming ones from the east'. But it held firm in stalling Russia's membership – which was being pushed by Yeltsin – until the conclusion of the first Chechen war. It regularly condemned the second conflict, suspended Russia's voting rights for nine months in 2000, and threatened to establish an international criminal court on Chechnya in 2003 in the absence of adequate domestic measures to prosecute human rights abuses. That provoked ugly rhetoric from some of the Russian politicians who sat in the Council, including Dmitry Rogozin, then head of the Russian parliament's foreign affairs committee. In the absence of domestic efforts to punish abuses systematically, the Council's sister organization, the European Court of Human Rights, may yet prove the most important foreign pressure point on Chechnya. It has already agreed to examine eight cases brought against the Russian authorities by the families of Chechens killed or persecuted during the conflict. Dozens more are under consideration.

Russia's own irritation with the Council of Europe was clear during the visits of its official delegations to Chechnya, notably those headed by the British Labour peer Frank Judd. It felt obliged to play host and provide security, but cooperation often stopped there. I attended Judd's final trip to Chechnya in January 2003, when the protocol department 'forgot' to send an official car to pick him up on arrival at the airport in Moscow. The Russians made a point of bringing his delegation twice to Dubrovka, to pay respects to the victims of the theatre siege. Akhmed Kadyrov, head of the pro-Moscow Chechen administration, was away during the time the delegation was in Chechnya, just catching a few words with Judd as their paths crossed at Mineralnye Vody airport en route. Rogozin, not for the first time, delegated one of his brash junior assistants to chaperon the delegation in Chechnya rather than attending himself. And in line with past practice, bad weather, security or technical problems were cited as the reason for substantial delays for helicopter flights from there into the republic. Along with banquets and protracted sterile discussions with government officials, that left little time to talk to ordinary Chechens. Nevertheless, the imminent arrival of the Council's delegations usually did trigger action – even if it was temporary. The creation of the office of the presidential representative on human rights in Chechnya, Order 85 to demand that a prosecutor be present during arrests of terrorist suspects, and statistical reports on how many human rights cases had been tried all came just before or after such trips. So did a decision to reduce military checkpoints and total troop numbers, and the shifts in command from the military to the intelligence agencies and the civilian administration.

The contribution may have been modest, but the Council of Europe was more active than most quasi-government bodies, and it showed what might have been achieved had foreign leaders proved more aggressive individually, let alone acting jointly. Putin clearly loved attending summits abroad, and was visibly irked by criticism on Chechnya. What foreign pressure did exist earlier in the conflict almost certainly had an impact, such as in extending an ultimatum that Russia gave to residents of Grozny to flee ahead of bombardment in late 1999. The high-profile foreign campaign no doubt helped in the swift release in 2000 of kidnapped Andrei Babitsky, the Russian journalist, and in 2001 of Kenny Gluck, a top Médecins sans Frontières official. When the UN and the EU's human rights commissioner publicly criticized efforts by the authorities to force

Chechens displaced by the conflict into Ingushetia in late 2002, the pressures temporarily eased.

A more intense and consistent international campaign could almost certainly have had a greater impact on pushing for the punishment of abuses, introducing mediators and even imposing foreign peacekeepers, encouraged by the carrot of international reconstruction. Instead, the foreign community's half-hearted approach led to the quasi-endorsement of a sham election in autumn 2003 against the continued backdrop of conflict. There were no cancelled summits, no threats of sanctions or withdrawal of financial aid, no hesitation over Russia's membership of the G8. At a time of big strategic choices – energy and terrorism – realpolitik dominated. 'As a human rights expert, I am appalled that energy and the T-word [terrorism] dominate all discussions,' said one senior member of the OSCE.

While charities and advocacy groups have documented abuses in detail, their governments have done little to support serious reflection on alternative approaches to resolving the conflict. There was a failure of initiative from abroad. 'Where were all the peace plans put forward by the international think tanks?' lamented one Moscow-based European ambassador. In bilateral and multilateral discussions, if Chechnya was brought up at all with Putin, it was normally a brief mumbled comment phrased in sympathetic terms over coffee without conviction. Other issues – such as the conflict over the import of frozen chicken legs by the USA – seemed to vex politicians more, and occupy greater time. 'Since the time of the USSR, we thought that we would move towards Europe. But it's you who have started to become like us,' remarked the politician Grigory Yavlinsky wryly.

A Europe divided

At first glance, the two documents looked identical. But as I compared the final declaration of the May 2002 EU–Russia summit with an earlier version slipped to me by a contact, I noticed that two crucial paragraphs were missing. As the meeting drew to a close in the Kremlin, Putin could congratulate himself on a series of important victories over his European counterparts. Most important, all written references to Chechnya had been excised. The EU's draft statement expressed concern over human rights abuses in the republic, and the need to ease the work of humanitarian organizations working on the ground, had been removed. Member states had expressed concerns about continued abuses; and its own officials working with refugees in the region had been frustrated in their long-standing and very practical request to improve security for their local staff by authorizing use of the United Nations' short-wave radio networks. The absence of a public statement might have been acceptable had tangible promises been given in private. Yet apart from a brief mention over lunch, the subject had barely even been raised. No such breakthroughs were made in the closed sessions. The negotiators seemed to judge that positive mood music was the top priority.

Asked during the concluding press conference why the Chechen references had been eradicated from the joint declaration, Romano Prodi, president of the European Commission, said simply: 'There was nothing new . . . so we saw no need to include them.' In fact, it had more to do with the man sitting on the far side of Vladimir Putin from Prodi: José Maria Aznar, the conservative Spanish leader, who was the EU president at the time. Putin had prepared him well, inviting him to stay the night in his country home outside Moscow. Aznar's own experience with domestic terrorism, and his strong support for Bush's anti-terrorist coalition, in any case made him sympathetic to Moscow's handling of the conflict. He gave in easily, while Putin took full advantage and threw the west's language back in its face. He attacked EU plans to introduce visas for transit travellers from its exclave of Kaliningrad as a human rights abuse for Russian citizens. His comment appeared rich given the gross violations perpetrated against Chechens, but it went unchallenged.

A back-down on Chechnya was not the only concession given by the EU to Russia without anything significant in return. Casting a nervous glance over its shoulder at the USA, which was preparing similar initiatives to strengthen its bilateral relations, the EU's leadership extended 'market economy status' to Russia at the same summit as a way to streamline procedures for its exports. In exchange, it received only limited promises on gas market liberalization without any clear timetable on its implementation. It also announced the creation of a vague 'energy dialogue' and an even vaguer 'common European space' linking Russia with the EU. A few weeks later, as had been widely anticipated, the USA also granted Russia market economy status, and unveiled details of a bilateral summit with oil companies in Houston as part of a broader energy partnership.

The summit highlighted a number of characteristics of Russia's relationship with Europe. On one hand, there were signs of tightening links under Putin. The very idea of high-profile bilateral EU–Russia summits represented a step forward, and seemed to indicate a fresh interest by Putin in Europe after Yeltsin's almost exclusive obsession with the USA. On the other, it showed how Russia was able to exploit interstices within the EU, and play off the EU against the USA for its own advantage. If his decision after 9/11 suggested a clear push towards the USA, Putin sent a rebalancing signal by flying immediately to Germany for a visit, during which he spoke in German at the Bundestag and linked Russia's fate firmly to Europe. If Russia was a tough negotiating partner for the Europeans, the EU's approach to Russia was cumbersome, inconsistent and lacked a clear strategy.

Putin's ascension to power should have been good news for Europe. 'Russia is a very diverse country, but we are part of Western European culture. No matter where our people live, in the Far East or in the south, we are Europeans,' he told Russian journalists just ahead of his election. He grew up in an era focused on the relationship with the USA as the primary foreign interlocutor – albeit a hostile one – and inside a fundamentally anti-western institution, the KGB. But he was raised in St Petersburg, the 'window on Europe' often seen as the most European of Russian cities. He had lived in Germany and spoke the language fluently. On his appointment as a deputy city mayor in the early 1990s, he travelled extensively across Europe. All the signs were that, after Yeltsin's focus on transatlanticism, Putin would at least partly redress the balance with more pan-Europeanism.

Logically, the EU should be Russia's closest partner. Russia is culturally, historically and geographically bound to Europe. Economically, the two regions are closely tied together. Russia is already a significant supplier of energy to Europe, and potentially an enormous provider of labour, an important export market and location for growing investment flows. Half its trade goes to the EU. Geo-strategically, the Russian elite often whispered more or less openly about the long-term threat of China, and how Russia and Europe should forge a common bond to counterbalance it. The EU is also the only possible serious potential counterweight to the US hegemony which Moscow and a number of European nations view with concern. In terms of future security, Russia's location as a buffer zone to points east and south make it important. Ideologically, much of Europe's twentieth-century identity had been forged in opposition to the Eastern Bloc, and the collapse of Communism is an ideal opportunity to rethink and exploit that changing relationship.

In practice, many Russian officials continue to look to the USA – if only as the best way to spur a recalcitrant EU into action. Moscow had stepped up its relations with Brussels early in George W. Bush's presidency, in part because the new US administration seemed less interested in engaging than the old had under Bill Clinton. Yet to the EU, Russia often seemed to be just one of many neighbours, a secondary priority after enlargement into Eastern Europe. In a policy paper on 'wider Europe' issued in 2003, for example, there was hardly any specific mention of Russia. It was lumped alongside, and apparently considered in the same way as, Israel, Morocco and other neighbours of varying significance. Other policy initiatives seemed sometimes to have been dreamed up on the spot. As we nibbled our starters during the concluding dinner for the May 2002 EU summit, I obtained a copy of the speech that Prodi was about to make. I nearly choked when I read that he was proposing to create a new economic union between the EU and Russia, on top of the newly launched but very abstract 'common European economic space'. But when he spoke, he made no such reference. Officials had hastily excised the reference from the text.

For all Washington's relative neglect of Russia as Communism collapsed – with its attention focused instead on the Gulf War – the US invested far more than the Europeans during the 1990s. The Nunn–Lugar disarmament initiative alone amounted to $1bn a year, although decommissioning nuclear weapons was an issue that affected Europe at least as much as the USA. The EU's TACIS programme, by comparison, which provided technical assistance largely spent on hiring foreign consultants, amounted to less than a quarter of that. With a few notable exceptions – such as Sweden, Holland and the UK – bilateral European assistance to Russia was far more modest still. When the EU occasionally decided to criticize Russia – such as over Chechnya or a clampdown on media freedom – it did so incoherently, with statements so squeezed through the multinational diplomatic sieve that they ended up saying little and being issued far too late to have any impact. But the EU also had a greater challenge in its relations with Russia: it had to deal with the daily realities, rather than the grand visions. Its member states had far greater trading links with Russia than the USA did; and much more practical knowledge of the quality of its borders, handling the transit of goods, or dealing with foreign investors. Skilfully, Washington let Brussels take the flak for aggressive negotiations around membership of the World Trade Organization, though it fully shared the position adopted.

Russia needed tough, consistent interlocutors. It loved to focus on high-level political solutions, while failing to meet the norms and technical criteria essential to the implementation of agreements. In 2003 it set visa-free travel within the EU as an objective, for example, but then wanted all discussions to be among ministers while shrugging off calls for meetings with experts who were needed to set concrete conditions. It was delighted to join a combined NATO–Russia Council, but it still wanted to be granted a veto, rather than be treated as just one equal member among others. As Juho Paasikivi, a former Finnish ambassador in Moscow and later president of his country, said of the Russians in 1941: 'It has been their irrevocable policy to get what is to be obtained for as little as possible, and then ask for more. They never sacrifice their instant gains for future objectives.' Or as former US arms negotiator with the USSR, Raymond Smith, put it: 'A [Russian] negotiator will not view the signing of an agreement as the end of the negotiation, but as a stage in the process.'

It was not that the EU was always ineffective in its negotiations with Russia, so much as incoherent. With some officials and on some issues, there was a real tussle. In discussions over the World Trade Organization, the EU took a tough stance under Pascal Lamy, its austere trade commissioner. Deadlock on many matters of substance forced frequent announcements of a 'dead-end' by Russian officials, and numerous extensions in their timetable for accession. But more generally, the six-month rotating European presidency was catastrophic for developing any consistent, effective policy. The contrast between the Spanish and the Danes, the successive EU presidents during 2002, illustrated how alternative styles could bring very different results.

The Danish premier, Rasmussen, inherited a difficult set of Russia-related issues at a particularly awkward time. The key debate by autumn 2002 concerned the fate of Kaliningrad, formerly

Königsberg. As the Soviet Union crumbled, Moscow was determined to maintain this strategic seaport and naval base, even at the price of its growing isolation from 'mainland' Russia's shrinking borders. In the early 1990s, the belt of neighbours separating it from the mother country seemed unthreatening: Poland, Lithuania and Belarus. The awkward arrangement was a small price for Europe to pay for the USSR's withdrawal from the rest of the Eastern Bloc. But EU accession changed the rules. Lithuania and Poland opted to reorient westwards, and their decision meant the need to impose tough 'Schengen' travel rules for those from Kaliningrad crossing their territory to and from the rest of Russia. That meant issuing visas for everyone travelling by road or rail – and the humiliating risk of their applications being rejected.

Neither side helped the situation. The EU dogmatically insisted on the strict interpretation of Schengen rules, even though the imposition of visas would demand additional cost, time and inconvenience for local residents while arguably doing little to cut down on illegal flows of people and goods. Moscow denounced it as a new Berlin Wall being put up by the west. Russia had long ignored the problem, spurning efforts by the Germans to open a consulate in Kaliningrad, failing to help improve its corruption-ridden, inefficient border controls, and overseeing an economic and social decline in the region that turned it into a pariah compared with the surrounding countries. Instead of making the region a pilot project for enhanced cooperation with the EU, Moscow seemed determined that Kaliningrad should not have any preferential benefits – condemning it still further in the process.

It fell to the Danish presidency to try to resolve the problem, as the timetable for EU accession drew close. The Danes found themselves handed one of the most sensitive external issues for Russia just as they were dragged into an explosive internal concern. Denmark, traditionally sympathetic to concerns over Chechnya, was the venue for a conference on peace in the North Caucasus in October 2002. It was scheduled to take place just as the Dubrovka theatre siege occurred in Moscow. One of the keynote speakers was Akhmed Zakayev, as the representative of the rebel leader Aslan Maskhadov. In a move that Danish diplomats saw partly as a provocation while they negotiated over Kaliningrad, Moscow demanded Zakayev's extradition. A year earlier, Zakayev had been judged an acceptable interlocutor by the

Kremlin for exploratory peace talks with rebel leaders. Now he was branded a terrorist. As Denmark held out, demanding extra information and launching formal extradition hearings, its imports to Russia – notably bacon and building materials – were held up by customs for unusually long periods at the border. The country was criticized publicly by officials. Shortly after, Russia introduced new meat quotas, which hit Denmark particularly hard.

As the spat intensified into a full-scale diplomatic war of words, Russia threatened to boycott the EU–Russia summit which was scheduled for Copenhagen in November 2002. Rasmussen seemed to be giving in when he quickly shifted the venue to the more neutral territory of Brussels. But on other matters he held his ground. 'It's a case of what's mine is mine, and what's yours is negotiable,' lamented one Danish diplomat, describing the Russian negotiating tactics. The prime minister did not interfere before or after the Danish courts dismissed Russia's request for Zakayev's extradition. He brushed aside attempts by Russia to control questions at the concluding press conference to avoid any quizzing over Chechnya. He insisted on maintaining a phrase on Chechnya in the draft joint declaration, triggering a dispute that meant no statement was ultimately issued.

Above all, Rasmussen held firm on Kaliningrad. Putin's negotiators agreed to a final compromise on the Friday before the summit on the following Monday, but then hoped to push still further when the leaders met. When Putin began listing a dozen points on which he still wanted to talk, Rasmussen cut him off. He agreed simply to allow a handful of technical advisers from each side to sort out the first few points Russia had raised, sending Putin's advisers scurrying back and forth in confusion. Unprepared, Putin agreed, winning modest concessions on the first few – and the least important – items. The Russians would be given assistance in preparing for the new regime, the costs would be low, the processing rapid. It would be called a 'facilitated travel document'. But, to all intents, they had lost out. Russian citizens would require a transit visa. Rasmussen's was a high-risk strategy which could have led to Russia simply refusing to reach agreement, but for once it worked in the EU's favour. The long-term justification was more open to question, however, as it soured relations.

Without a coherent counter-party, Moscow often proved effective in pushing through tactical victories, while neither side gained strategically. The EU's bureaucracy, the changing priorities of each presidency and the serious divisions between member countries often resulted in weakness towards Russia. The respective Danish and Spanish summit negotiations highlighted just how inconsistent the EU could be. Aside from differences in their technical capacities as negotiators, each of the European countries holding the six-monthly rotating presidency had wildly fluctuating priorities. The Finns and other Scandinavians stressed the northern dimension, a vague concept that concerned cooperation across their borders with Russia. The Greeks emphasized the southern zone, touching the Balkans. For other European countries, Russia featured much less significantly in any coherent foreign policy.

It often appeared that different European leaders wanted to compete with each other in being Putin's best friend for their own bilateral advantage, rather than coordinating any coherent joint approach. The Italians, the French, the Germans and the British all arranged state visits in the space of a few months, each geared to their own national interests and not necessarily coinciding with a broader European agenda. The Scandinavians, more directly exposed to Russia through their common borders, were more cautious. The EU accession states in the east risked sparking greater internal division within Europe and making it more inward-looking as it concentrated on integration. They were likely to generate additional suspicion and hostility into relations with Russia. While the legacy of their Soviet-era education system meant that they remained for at least one more generation russophone, their suspicion of their former political masters in Moscow meant they were often for the same reason russophobe.

Russia may have partly been trying to indulge in 'divide and rule' politics as it had in the Cold War. But it was also responding to the cumbersome reality of how the EU operated. It was much easier for Moscow to negotiate with Washington if only because it was dealing with a single group of interlocutors, and a more consistent message. Talking with the Brussels bureaucracy, by contrast, was like 'like fighting through cotton wool', in the words of Vladimir Chizhov, the Russian deputy foreign minister in charge of European relations. Kaliningrad was a bitter lesson for the Russians. St Petersburg may have been Russia's 'window on Europe', but it was a window that was often closed – from the outside as much as from within.

The battle over Iraq

US–Russian relations may have thawed rapidly after summer 2001, but inside the American embassy in Moscow, diplomats were revising Cold War techniques of Sovietology. With the leaks of the Yeltsin era replaced by the discretion of Putin's tight-knit staff, analysts sought how best to divine the Kremlin's thinking from the most subtle nuances. 'We spend a lot of time trying to understand who is influencing Putin,' said one official. Their predecessors had pored over Communist newspapers to read between the lines, and mulled over the significance of who stood next to whom at the May Day parades in Red Square. Now they studied Putin's every word, and quizzed endless Russian specialists from the think tanks who delivered voluminous policy papers to officials in the uncertain hope that they might have some influence on decision-making.

The USA stepped up the pressure on Saddam Hussein in the second half of 2002 with rhetoric that seemed to be leading inexorably to war. Moscow's ministry of foreign affairs responded with a more dove-ish line: non-military means have not been exhausted, weapons inspectors are making progress and should be allowed to carry out their work, and any decisions should be taken within the framework of international law and through the UN Security Council. It seemed that Iraq risked becoming a 'relationship-breaker' between the USA with Russia only a year after the bilateral partnership had started to bloom.

But as Putin's decision after 9/11 had shown, the Russian president alone called the shots on important matters of foreign policy, let alone on one as fundamental as this. The foreign ministry might have a more pro-Arab, anti-western line by instinct, but it was ultimately subordinated to the Kremlin. In the wake of Putin's support for the international coalition against terrorism, many pro-USA foreign policy analysts in Russia were gaining confidence, predicting that the Kremlin had made a historic choice in favour of the USA, and would stick to it. Ironically, a dissenting view came early on from Grigory Yavlinsky, leader of the Yabloko party and normally pro-USA in his orientation. He argued vigorously that Moscow should support Washington because of their common interests in fighting terrorism, without seeking any quid pro quo. But he also warned that if Washington wanted to rely on Moscow's future support, it must make sure to consult its partners regularly and not to act unilaterally.

Other more traditional commercial, political and military interests in Russia were resistant to further support for the USA. Russia's
stake in Iraq was far greater than it had been in Afghanistan, or even
across much of Central Asia. In Soviet times, Moscow could trace a
long period of diplomatic contact with Baghdad. Yevgeny Primakov,
the former foreign minister and prime minister who influenced a
generation of diplomats, had known Saddam Hussein personally
since 1969. Soviet military experts had been providing their expertise
over four decades, and continued to do so unofficially until weeks
before war broke out in March 2003. Two retired generals confirmed
to the *gazeta.ru* website that they had travelled to Baghdad just before
and received medals from the Iraqi army. Most of the Soviet-era debt
Iraq owed to Russia was for arms sales. Russia had long betted that
international sanctions would be lifted while Saddam Hussein
remained in place, and committed itself to maintaining links with
the regime. Lukoil, the energy group, signed contracts to develop
the \$3.7 bn West Qurna field in 1997. And Russian companies have
been the largest beneficiary of the UN-sanctioned oil-for-food programme, winning \$4.3bn in contracts since 1996.

Russian involvement in any campaign against Iraq risked repercussions among its own – albeit largely secular – twenty million-strong
Muslim population. Iraq had an important role to play in the Middle
East, as one of the few areas where Russia still retained some significant – if largely symbolic – diplomatic input. Most important, the
campaign around Iraq was a first test of the USA's willingness to consult, exploiting the international goodwill it had triggered after 9/11
and working with the anti-terrorist coalition that had been created.
Iraq became a sign of Russia's modest but growing new status in world
affairs. And the Bush administration was riding roughshod over it.

Putin's own utterances on Iraq were rare, and his occasional statements delphic. He had avoided meeting Tariq Aziz, the Iraqi foreign
minister, on trips through Moscow in the preceding months, although
no protocol constraints prevented him from holding talks with equivalent government officials from 'friendlier' states. Even Aziz's Russian
opposite number, Igor Ivanov, did not meet him during a stopover in
Moscow in early 2002. Broadly, Putin kept the line of the foreign ministry. Then in Kiev, in late January 2003, he first hinted to a group of
students that if Baghdad refused to cooperate, he would consider

moving closer to the US position. In his next pronouncements, he swung the other way again. On a trip to China in February, Ivanov mentioned the hypothetical use of Russia's veto at the UN Security Council. He also broached the phrase 'multi-polar world', beloved of his mentor Primakov. It was clear code for creating a counterbalance to the USA – and language that appealed to France, just as Jacques Chirac was stressing the idea of different 'poles of influence' in a world veering towards US hegemony.

Putin even dispatched Primakov to Baghdad to meet Saddam Hussein in late February. It was a mission that Primakov's friends say he was reluctant to undertake. Many recalled his failed shuttle diplomacy ahead of the Gulf War in 1991, and his attempt to broker peace in 1998, splitting the coalition against Iraq and leading to the withdrawal of UN weapons inspectors. It seems that Primakov attempted to persuade Saddam to go into exile, or at least to step down and allow elections to take place. Had it worked, it would have been a diplomatic masterstroke boosting Putin's international prestige. But it failed, leaving Russia's case as an influential intermediary little enhanced.

After weeks of speculation, Putin broke his long-cultivated silence on the first day of a state trip to France, direct from a visit to Germany. He endorsed a joint declaration with both countries opposing military action, which 'the French thrust under his nose', as one foreign diplomat put it. In interviews with the French media the following day, he hinted at the possibility of a veto at the United Nations 'with or without' France.

For a while, US diplomats and others who believed Putin had made a strategic choice in favour of the US after 9/11 played down the significance of the latest comments. But with the deadline for a second UN resolution rapidly approaching, it became clear that he had come to a final and different conclusion, based pragmatically on Russia's interests and the divisions within the west. Early on during the Iraqi talks, there were hints of economic demands by Russia as a condition for its support of the USA. 'We got the impression they were waiting for us to offer them something,' said a senior US diplomat. Putin's foreign policy was certainly not all about principles. As the EU pushed for Russia's ratification of the Kyoto environmental protocol, the Kremlin 'linked' it to easier conditions for entry into the World Trade Organization. Economic imperatives and political bargaining had played a role in the past, and would do so again. The US journalist Bob Woodward writes that when Putin met Bush in Slovenia in summer 2001, he was preoccupied with seeking forgiveness on Russia's Soviet-era debts to foreign governments. As the debate over Iraq heated up, SPS, the western-oriented Union of Right Forces, explicitly called for guarantees over oil prices, assurances on business contracts and write-offs of Soviet-era debt. Vagit Alekperov, the head of Lukoil, even hinted that Putin had assured him his company's contract would be safe.

Russia was at a different and more dangerous stage of the electoral cycle than France and Germany. In Germany, Gerhard Schroeder had capitalized on an anti-war stance in Iraq to cultivate left-wing support to win re-election. France's Jacques Chirac adopted the same stance to bolster his credentials as the successor to his spiritual hero Charles de Gaulle, while strengthening his hand in the – notably francophone – Arab and African Muslim world. With their elections behind them and their credentials established, both of these Western European leaders could begin to tone down their rhetoric. But Putin was only gearing up for parliamentary and presidential elections in the year to come, at a time of disgruntlement about his pro-western foreign policy.

Most of all, there was a wide-ranging belief that Russia had not received anything significant in return for its support of the USA after 9/11. The list of Russian frustrations with the USA was long. In April 2000, almost immediately after his election, Putin used his parliamentary majority to push through ratification of the Start 2 arms reduction treaty and the comprehensive test ban treaty long stalled under Yeltsin. He had played down the fears of NATO's eastern expansion, even hinting early in his term that Russia might eventually join the organization. In the days after 9/11, he closed Russia's Cold War intelligence posts in Cuba and at Camran Bay in Vietnam. In Georgia, which Russia argued was serving as a base for rebels from just across the border in Chechnya, Putin did not flinch when the USA encroached again on his traditional turf by offering military trainers and support for President Eduard Shevardnadze's local troops and border guards.

Yet only weeks after the Twin Towers attacks, Bush announced that the USA was unilaterally withdrawing from the 1972 Anti-Ballistic Missile treaty. That undermined a foundation stone of nuclear strategic stability. It weakened one more element of international consultation and influence that Russia still had, inherited from the Soviet regime. The USA sent U2 spy planes to fly near the Russian border over Georgia, supposedly in order to spot Chechen rebels. The US administration lobbied against the new joint NATO–Russia Council, which the British and Italians had proposed as a gesture to Moscow. On economic matters, US concessions to Russia were also disappointing. An 'energy dialogue' had produced relatively few results. Despite years of lobbying, the Jackson–Vanik trade restrictions introduced against the Soviet Union in the early 1970s as a lever to permit Jewish emigration were still in place. Steel quotas were imposed, which discriminated against Russian producers.

Two months after the fall of Saddam Hussein, an extremely senior Kremlin official could still barely conceal his frustration and irritation at the way in which the relationship with the USA had evolved in the previous eighteen months. 'What sort of allies are we?' he said, in a tellingly lengthy answer to a neutral question I asked him on the subject. 'Russia undertook lots of steps for the USA. We closed our radar stations in Cuba, offered intelligence and communications with the Northern Alliance to help bring victory in Afghanistan. What was the response? The USA tried to push Russia out of Afghanistan and oust members of Karzai's government who supported us. It has fought against Russia's interests in the CIS, encouraging Radio Liberty to broadcast in Ukrainian. It is really aimed at weakening Russia's position. Jackson–Vanik has not been rescinded twelve years after the collapse of the USSR. It's a political signal that we are not good partners. We are glad-handing, and there are no real tangible steps being taken towards us.'

The complaints of one-sidedness were not entirely fair. By supporting the USA, Putin had achieved his own goals of crushing the Taliban, weakening Al Qaeda and reducing pressure from radical groups within and around Russia's own borders. The operations had been conducted more efficiently than his own forces could have managed, and paid for largely by others. While unable to stop the revocation of the ABM treaty, Putin did manage to impose on Bush the Treaty of Moscow on nuclear arms reductions by both countries – admittedly a short and hollow document – despite initial US opposition to any written agreement at all. That allowed him to save face, while benefiting because he understood that Russia could ill afford the costs of maintaining Russian military bases abroad, let alone an ageing nuclear stockpile of Cold War proportions at home. In Georgia, the Russian military had failed to end the war across the border in Chechnya over the previous three years. There was little reason either to place the blame on the adjoining Pankisi Valley in Georgia, or to assume that giving the Russian army carte blanche would have eliminated the rebels based there. In a few months, US military training and pressure had Georgian officials who previously denied any presence of Chechens in the valley, vying with each other over claims on the number of rebels driven out. Russia also earned greater US acquiescence over Chechnya. And its economy benefited hugely from the rising oil prices, which were partly due to the uncertainty over Iraq.

The importance of Russia's public arguments against armed intervention in Iraq should not be downplayed. There was genuine scepticism about the presence of weapons of mass destruction, and about the destabilizing effects on the region that would follow any initial military victory. Subsequent history would prove these doubts to be valid. The weapons inspectors did appear to be making progress, and the connection of Saddam's regime to any proliferation of WMD, let alone international terrorist networks, was flimsy.

Over time, a mixture of the inability to articulate or win any economic concessions may have played a role in Moscow's decision on Iraq, but the reasoning within the Russian establishment also shifted from the mercantile to the intellectual. If there was a hidden economic agenda, it seems in any case that the authorities increasingly came to believe their own public argument. Some Russian foreign policy advisers say Putin was told by his own intelligence services that the war would drag on for a long time – providing him with a chance to intervene as a peacemaker. Putin has denied it, claiming the information he received accurately predicted the outcome.

At root, there may also have been an important question of pride at stake. Putin seemed to recognize that Russia was not negotiating from a position of strength, but he had at least won some respect through his diplomacy in the previous three years. He might have been a junior partner, but he had 'a seat at the table', with a voice and a right to be consulted. That was a big achievement after Yeltsin, who was regarded in the west with suspicion for his ranting and unpredictable decisions. Now on Iraq – as on Kosovo – Moscow was being ignored. While some top-level telephone conversations took place during the Iraq negotiations, senior US officials offered little 'face time' with their Russian counterparts. Rumours of a meeting with Bush came to nothing, and it was only after the war began that Condoleezza Rice, his national security adviser, finally came to Moscow – on the day that a Russian diplomatic convoy was shot up by US forces as it left Baghdad on its way towards the border.

As the top Kremlin aide put it: 'Since the USSR collapsed, the USA has believed that they are the only dominant power and they will prove it.' He expressed particular frustration over the double standards of the USA with its concept of pre-emptive strikes in Iraq to counter future terrorist threats, compared with very real Russian concerns in Georgia. 'When we wanted to strike pre-emptively because of a real threat to our citizens, rather than Iraq where it was hypothetical, they criticized. We are not happy that there is one approach when talking about Russia, and another about the USA.'

Russia was fundamentally aided in its approach by strength and safety in numbers. It seems unlikely that Putin would have been so outspoken had Germany and France not also so strongly criticized US policy towards Iraq. The mere fact that they were so negative gave Putin 'cover', and even created a situation in which it would have seemed curious were Russia to be even more pro-American. The European 'coalition of the unwilling' opposed to war in Iraq gave Putin new options, the chance to trade off alliances. France and Germany might have drawbacks as coherent long-term strategic partners, but they were at least attractive tactical mates. Schroeder had growing personal links with Putin, and Chirac was in office for another five years, an important factor for future bilateral relations. Such continuity was very important.

Having identified itself as an opponent of military action, Russia did not want to have to go through with the threat of a veto on Iraq at the UN, however. One danger was that other US opponents might ultimately renege at the last minute, leaving Russia exposed. More fundamentally, Russia did not want to do anything that further diluted the influence of the UN. In the G8, the NATO–Russia Council and even in the EU, Russia had managed to increase its influence. One of its most significant Soviet legacies remained its disproportionate influence through the UN where it still punched above its weight as one of the five permanent members of the Security Council.

Russia lobbied for there to be no second resolution. It judged that it would be better to feign surprise and anger, criticizing as ill-advised and illegal a US decision to bypass the Security Council, rather than to head into a confrontational vote that would be directly defied by the USA. Preventing a showdown meant both diverting a crisis that could undermine the Security Council itself, and avoiding the ultimate, direct, public rebuke to the USA of a veto. As Mikhail Margelov, head of the Federation Council's foreign affairs committee, argued, 'It was great victory for Russian diplomacy that there was no second resolution vote.'

The cover provided by Germany and especially France allowed Putin to avoid triggering a particularly aggressive reaction against Russia by the USA in the wake of Iraq. The US White House was visibly irritated by aggressive French attempts to block the UN resolution. It actively lobbied the states which had temporary Security Council seats to oppose military action, and briefly blocked NATO's support for Turkey as Ankara hesitated on whether to allow coalition troops into Iraq. Russia, by contrast, kept a low profile. Other factors also played a role. 'We had lower expectations of Russia than [of] France,' says one senior US official. He argues that Moscow did not capitalize on the situation by whipping up anti-Americanism. Washington also had its eye on the situation in Central Asia, and on Russian energy. Moscow could yet prove an important ally. And the personal relationship between Putin and Bush – the very factor for which the new US Republican White House had criticized its Democratic predecessors – still seemed to have a soothing effect. In the weeks that followed the showdown, Putin's periodic comments hardly proved his abilities as a silky-tongued professional diplomat. They hinted instead at an element of dogmatism and emotionalism that ran alongside his better-known quality of pragmatism. While his prepared statements and speeches were usually measured, he proved less restrained during press conferences. At one, he reminded journalists that it was America's ally Saudi Arabia, not Iraq, that had supplied the suicide hijackers for the 9/11 attacks. When Tony Blair came to visit in Moscow in May in 2003, he could not resist embarrassing him with a barbed remark questioning the grounds on which the British leader had justified the war. In response to a question on why he was opposed to lifting sanctions, Putin said: 'Perhaps Saddam is sitting in an underground bunker on a case of weapons of mass destruction, preparing to blow them up.'

But Putin also attempted to reconcile the different parties. I attended one summit in April in St Petersburg, which had long been scheduled as a regular bilateral meeting with the Germans. Gerhard Schroeder was set to receive an honorary law degree from Putin's alma mater, the university law faculty. The event was expanded at the last minute into a 'coalition of the unwilling' with the addition of Jacques Chirac. It was too late to arrange a similar honour for him, so with just one week's notice the professors hastily pulled together a conference on international law, inviting distinguished academic speakers from around the world. The fresh paint was still drying as Chirac arrived to deliver the keynote speech on the importance of the UN – the message for which the entire gathering was the pretext. In fact Putin had tried to bridge the tensions in the international community, inviting Blair and Kofi Annan along too, although they both declined.

As he glanced around the circular table just one month later, Putin could scarcely conceal his satisfaction. In front of him sat the heads of government of fifteen European states, an extremely rare gathering of so many senior politicians outside the EU. It was 31 May 2003, and the EU had come out in force to St Petersburg for an exceptional EU–Russia summit. The previous evening, he had hosted an unprecedented gala for the leaders of more than forty of the world's most important countries. The following morning, he would hold bilateral discussions with George W. Bush. Bush and Chirac, still feuding over their disagreements on Iraq from the spring, claimed 'diary clashes'. The French president flew out just as his US counterpart arrived, so that the two men did not have to meet. But both travelled to St Petersburg, a credit to Putin's ability to steer a middle course in the conflict, and to his lucky timing, just long enough after the war and its diplomatic consequences that the different leaders were starting to seek a rapprochement.

In the previous few months, thousands of workers had been drawn from Russia's north-west region and beyond to St Petersburg to beautify it for the 300th anniversary celebrations at a cost of $1.5bn. Façades on the main roads were repainted, crumbling palaces repaired, long-neglected pot-holes filled, and tatty cottages in the suburbs on the routes to be taken by the foreign dignitaries were concealed behind specially-constructed tall green fences. The local police rounded up the homeless and beggars, 'cleaning' the streets by taking them to shelters far away from the centre for the duration of the festivities. The centrepiece was the Konstantin Palace where Putin hosted his summits. A former royal residence turned into a naval academy and an orphanage, it had been left a burnt-out ruin. But workmen had laboured round the clock to restore it to its former glittering gold and marble grandeur at a cost of more than $300m, supposedly financed by 'donations' from private companies and state-controlled enterprises.

But – like the cracks in the newly-painted buildings – the hollow nature of the summit rapidly began to show. Russia and the EU agreed a bland 'joint declaration', focused around the objective of visa-free travel between their regions, and the creation of a series of 'spaces' to tighten their cooperation. But the two sides grew further apart in the months that followed. A deeper 'economic space' first required Russia's accession to the WTO, but Russia became increasingly insistent that it would not budge on one of its main disagreements with the EU – liberalising its gas market. It became more active in promoting its own alternative CIS free economic zone, uniting with Belarus, Ukraine and Kazakhstan. And, whenever EU officials expressed concern about continued abuses in Chechnya, their Russian counterparts warned that they would in response raise the issue of abuses of Russian citizens in Latvia.

When US energy companies met their Russian partners in the same venue in St Petersburg the following September, they failed to cement any significant deals. Russia had done little to improve the rule of law or security of property rights, and the growing scandal around the oil company Yukos sent out a contrary signal. When Putin travelled to Camp David for a return bilateral summit with Bush a few days later, his trip was overshadowed by criticism of Russian human rights abuses. As Washington continued active intervention around the world, Moscow also began to exert its new-found economic strength and gave voice to political aspirations – especially in the 'near abroad'. By the end of 2003, the USA saw its influence rise in Georgia as the US-educated Mikhail Saakashvili was elected president in place of Eduard Shevardnadze following the collapse of his regime. Russia had little sympathy for Shevardnadze, but was nervous of how the situation might evolve and quickly stepped up its solidarity with

Georgia's breakaway Russian ethnic regions of Adjaria, Abkhazia and South Ossetia. The US began deploying its forces further eastward towards Russia, in line with NATO's expansion.

Russia under Dmitry Kozak, the newly-appointed deputy head of the presidential administration, attempted in November to by-pass the five-way talks with the Ukraine and the Organization for Security and Cooperation in Europe and find its own solution to the breakaway Transdniester region of Moldova. It had already broken its pledge to the OSCE to withdraw 'peace-keeping troops' by 2002 and Soviet-era arms stockpiles by 2003. In November, it tried to impose its own solution for a federal state in consultation with Vladimir Voronin, the Communist-elected president of Moldova. But as word spread of the terms, which included recognition of Russian as an official language and veto rights of Transdniester over political decisions for Moldova, local people took to the streets of the capital, Chisinau, to protest. What was planned as a triumphant victory for Russian diplomacy turned instead into a public relations catastrophe, which came in for sharp criticism at the OSCE shortly afterwards.

The rhetoric – let alone the actions – had not returned to Cold War levels. But there was a new frost in the east–west partnership. And the substance often seemed far less significant than the form. The St Petersburg summit was a reminder of Russia's economic, political and spiritual renaissance. It drew in foreign leaders and enabled it to show off its best side, financed by sharp growth over the previous four years and a resurgent national pride. But it also highlighted how fundamentally different its culture and orientation remained, despite the superficial European appearance of the city. There was under-lying progress and integration of Russia into the world community, and both sides were willing to pay lip service to their common goals. Putin had re-established links with his neighbours near and far, and put Russia's relationships on a more sober, realistic footing. But there was also a new assertiveness, as he demonstrated that he might not be a pariah but neither was he a lackey of the west. It was a relationship of *realpolitik*, a balance of forces and economic interests far more than a true meeting of minds or values.

TOWARDS LIBERAL
AUTHORITARIANISM

IN SEPTEMBER 1973, STIG FREDRIKSON received a curious early morning call in his apartment on Kutuzovsky Prospekt. The Swedish journalist lived in a Moscow block allocated by the Soviet authorities to foreigners, where they could be kept under close observation. The phone rang before his secretary, who doubled as a KGB informant, had arrived for work. To those who were eavesdropping, the brief conversation sounded like a banal wrong number. But the voice was unmistakable to the 27-year-old, who had developed an elaborate system for secret meetings with Alexander Solzhenitsyn, the dissident writer. 'We carried everything in our heads, never wrote anything down, never communicated by phone and never met in apartments,' he recalled thirty years later, sitting in his office at Swedish Television's headquarters in Stockholm. 'Each time we met, we agreed the date and hour of our next meeting, and a fall-back date. We had an alarm system using the telephone. He would ring, and pretend to be asking for the dry cleaner's or the supermarket. I would say, "wrong number", and hang up. That was the sign to meet.'

Over several months, Fredrikson had become Solzhenitsyn's main 'courier', his most trusted source for smuggling messages and texts abroad despite the considerable dangers. They had first met during negotiations to hold a Moscow ceremony for the writer to receive the Nobel Prize he was awarded in 1970. It was scuppered by the interference of the Soviet authorities and the refusal of the Swedish embassy to host the event for fear of damaging bilateral relations. But the discreet contact between the two men remained. With every rendezvous Fredrikson risked expulsion, while Solzhenitsyn juggled with arrest and the discovery and destruction of his precious secret texts. They would meet near the Belarus or Kiev railway stations in Moscow, usually in the evening after Solzhenitsyn had spent the day switching trains and metros, engaging in elaborate manoeuvres to shake off his KGB tails. Through microfilms hidden in packets of aspirins, papers taped to his back and notes concealed in a transistor radio, Fredrikson shipped much sensitive material out of the USSR.

None of their encounters was more important than that September meeting. Solzhenitsyn had just received word that a draft copy of the *Gulag Archipelago*, his explosive condemnation of Soviet repression, had been seized by the authorities. Elizaveta Voronyanskaya, one of his trusted friends from Leningrad who had been typing it, had been arrested a few weeks earlier by the KGB. She was taken to its head-quarters in the 'Big House' for five days of harsh interrogation, just two years before Vladimir Putin entered the same building in a very different capacity. She cracked under pressure, revealing the identity of her friends, and the location of the secret text. Shortly after her release, she hanged herself. The news accelerated Solzhenitsyn's plans. He sent a message via Fredrikson to his lawyer in Switzerland to authorize the swift publication of *Gulag*, which had already been smuggled abroad. A few months later, the book was out, and Solzhenitsyn – whom the authorities had considered imprisoning and even attempted to assassinate – was expelled.

Fredrikson never believed it would be possible to make his secret role public. In the 1970s it seemed that the totalitarian Soviet regime was ruthless and solid enough to continue for many decades, and it would always remain too dangerous to reveal the identities of Solzhenitsyn's clandestine network of helpers. Only twenty years later, with the collapse of Communism and Solzhenitsyn's own return to Russia under Boris Yeltsin, did the writer reveal the names in his book, *Invisible Allies*. It is a striking reminder of how radically the political situation has changed in just three decades. Today, most critics of the Russian authorities will talk openly on the telephone, meet with foreigners in Moscow's plentiful cafés without fear, and usually live without repercussions when their comments are published.

Compared with Central Asia, China or Cuba, and their tight state controls on the media and political expression, Russia – the archetype of ruthless totalitarian control for much of the twentieth century – is relatively free. Indeed, one reason that the country today has such a bad image for corruption and scandal is precisely because the foreign media enjoys widespread access, and the domestic media are able to report openly on issues that go unexplored and unpublished in more repressive regimes. There has been a convergence towards western-style 'tabloidization' of newspapers and trivialization of radio and television, even if the objectives, mechanisms and historical resonances are different. The diversity of media ownership and output has undoubtedly declined under Putin. But Russia also remains a country in which the editor of an extremist newspaper can publish *Mr Hexagon*, a book which clearly alleges the complicity of special services in the 1999 apartment bombings as a prelude to the Chechen campaign. Or where the weekly paper, *Novaya Gazeta*, lambasts the authorities, and the internet site *kompromat.ru* spreads salacious rumours on public figures with impunity.

If Russia's political system has changed significantly since Soviet times, its economy has been even more transformed. The small variety of shoddy goods and the widespread deficits and lengthy queues of the past have gone. At least when shopping, personal contacts and party privileges have been replaced by markets. The new challenges are liberalising and regulating monopolies, and managing the widening gaps of inequality and injustice. Much painful transition remains to take place, notably in remote regions that were heavily subsidised under central planning. But opinion polls suggest that while many Russians still consider that they lived better in Soviet times, most have adjusted to the new realities.

Many of the evolutions that have taken place over the past few years have been eased by the Soviet-era legacy. Over-engineered infrastructure that has survived beyond its theoretical lifespan has helped compensate for the neglect of public works in the past decade. The free apartments given to ordinary Russians, and the residual subsidies of gas, electricity, heating and water, have helped them overcome the most painful period of economic transition by minimising their basic living costs. The kindergartens, schools, higher education institutes, hospitals and cultural centres across the country have provided a social glue to help keep society together. It is a remarkable achievement that the Soviet empire, which was built on so much blood, collapsed with such little loss of life. Whatever its many faults, the political transition from Gorbachev to Yeltsin and then to Putin has been relatively smooth, if far from painless. The challenge today is whether the benefits of market-led economic growth can compensate, as the reserves of the past run out.

Russia in the 1990s created a distorted mirror of the west, with the semblance of western-style democratic institutions in its media, parliament, laws and regulatory bodies welcomed and often demanded by foreign partners. Their existence created expectations which were probably too great, offering signs of 'progress' that were sometimes superficial. Russia had no significant legacy in Soviet or pre-Soviet times of a free press, an independent judiciary, the separation of powers, private property rights, or democracy, any more than it did a market economy. There was no recent memory of any such institutions, as there had been in its former 'colonies' in Eastern Europe. Those who claimed to champion such values, including the oligarchs, had only limited legitimacy in so doing as they played to their own agendas. Russia remained a country that was still only beginning on the path to modernisation, and was not necessarily moving towards westernisation at all. Compared with other parts of Europe, Russia looked disappointing. It came out much better when measured against China, Central Asia or – above all – its own Soviet past. The question is what influence Putin is having on these evolutions, as he risks over-compensating in a country shifting from anarchic liberalism towards liberal authoritarianism.

The roots of economic change

Shortly after arriving in Moscow in late 1998, I went in search of a decadent western item: a lettuce. After failed attempts in three different shops, I stopped at an old-fashioned supermarket on the way home. Its tatty, Soviet-era aura had put me off going inside before, but I was getting desperate. I should have known better. Behind the vegetable counter, there was an open box containing freshly-delivered lettuce. But the green luxuries were still awaiting the complex task of being lifted out onto the empty shelf above. 'Come back in an hour,' snapped the idle shop assistant when I asked if I could have one.

Without authorization from her supervisor, who was inevitably unavailable, nothing was possible.

It was a typical 'shopping experience' in Russia, from which neither pleasure nor convenience could be derived. Long after prices had been liberalised and goods miraculously appeared on the shelves, the culture of customer service still had a long way to go. Vendors had no interest in serving and would stand guarding their own section of counter, always refusing to help a colleague serving a long queue of customers, even if they had nothing else to do. Goods were concealed behind thick glass, and difficult to inspect. To make purchases, you first had to prise the price of every item from a grumbling shop assistant, mentally tally the total, walk to a separate booth, and bend over to explain the sum to a cashier (often still equipped with an abacus) through a tiny window. You had to pay with the exact money in cash (change was hardly ever available and credit cards rare), take the receipt, and hand it back to the original vendor in exchange for the purchases you wanted – assuming someone else had not taken them first. Then you discovered that even a plastic bag to carry your purchases in cost money, and you had to repeat the entire process.

By the turn of the millennium, a transformation in retailing was finally taking place. In the case of my local service-challenged supermarket, it was little short of extraordinary. In 2001, when I next ventured back inside, extensive renovations has taken place. State-of-the-art shelves and cold-storage devices had been installed holding an enlarged stock of goods that you could simply pick out yourself. There were newly-laid floors, bright lights and fish tanks offering the fresh, live catch of the day. But the biggest change was the attitude of the staff. When asked for a particular item, one vendor replied: 'First of all, good afternoon,' before providing all the help necessary. At the multiple cash-desks, staff with name-tags would greet you, pass your goods through bar-code machines, and – as another person packed them deftly into unlimited quantities of free plastic bags – say: 'Thank you for your purchase, please come again.' They offered change without complaint, took credit cards, and even issued a discount loyalty card. And the shop was open twenty-four hours a day.

There were, of course, still some special Moscow touches. A young security guard in a jacket and tie hovered at the entrance, gruffly demanding customers put their bags into a storage rack for fear of theft. His colleagues lingered conspicuously in the aisles, surveying the customers and keeping in contact by walkie-talkie. Certain lines of stock would mysteriously disappear just as you were getting to rely on them being there regularly. And there was a particularly copious collection of alcohol, with a focus on the more expensive varieties of wine and a wide range of vodkas. Prices could mysteriously change at short notice, and sometimes you were billed more than the amount shown on the label at the cash desk. Average prices were certainly not cheap, but nor were they abnormal, any more than the customers, who were predominantly Moscow's burgeoning middle-class rather than thick-necked mafiosi carrying wads of dollar bills.

Our local supermarket was not unique. Soviet shops, with no use for marketing, preferred to hide their existence. In the 1990s, nervous about attracting the unwanted attention of low-level mobsters or other undesirables, many outlets continued to maintain a low profile. Finding Moscow restaurants and clubs like Petrovich or OGI required some very well-tuned radar and a guided tour by an initiated friend to get in. You had to ring an unmarked bell at the bottom of the dark steps of an inner courtyard without a single sign. But window decoration in high street shops started to become more important, signifying the revolutionary idea that eye-catching displays might be a way to attract customers. Despite Moscow's harsh winters, outside terraces with heaters to prolong the alfresco season began to appear all over the city. If finding a cosy place for a quick and cheap snack had proved difficult in the recent past, there was a sudden explosion in cafés, buffets and sushi bars.

While Russians can always be charming if you are part of their group, introduced by someone, drunk, or on an official delegation, 'cold contact' can be a different matter. Yet friendly customer service also began to arrive. In a Japanese-style (but Russian-managed) restaurant, an over-enthusiastic waiter who whisked a beer away before the final mouthful returned a minute later with a full, free glass in compensation. In a Chinese restaurant where I ate, the service was incredibly slow, with dishes arriving heavily staggered. My rice was cold before the chicken it was supposed to be served with arrived, while my friend was still waiting for his soup. But a complaint brought the manager, a plea for forgiveness that they had only been open for a few weeks, and an offer of free beers all round.

Nor was the new culture of customer service confined to Moscow. In the Arctic city of Murmansk, a local journalist took me to a little café which even had a children's playroom at the back. I booked at random into the Northern Lights Hotel, which looked like a stan-dard-issue 1970s Soviet concrete block. I was expecting the usual creaking old corridors, a ferocious female *dezhurnaya* guardian on each floor, 'wake-up' calls from propositioning prostitutes in the middle of the night, a decor untouched for twenty years, and a curious breakfast like the one of meat cutlets and ketchup I had been offered a few days before in Astrakhan. Instead, I could have been walking into a hotel somewhere in Spain or Holland.

There was a tastefully furnished room in contemporary style, a money-back guarantee for dissatisfied customers, payment by credit card, and English-speaking staff. They offered a packed breakfast for early risers, a kettle and tea in the room, even umbrellas to borrow on rainy days from the reception. Such innovations might have seemed trivial to those used to the US, western Europe, or even the neigh-bouring Baltic countries. But for Russia, they were radically new. Andrei Milokhin, a former teacher who became a leading investor and manager in the early 1990s, willingly drove from his home to join me in the restaurant for a drink at 11pm when I asked the duty manager if I could chat to him. In place of the flashy jeep so typically bought by Russian 'businessmen' with their first revenues, he arrived in a rusting second-hand Opel. His team had had to cope over the years with a hand-grenade thrown through a window and an explo-sion in the bar, but he said the hardest task was changing the attitude of staff. Waiters used to expect to steal food and money, and staff at the front desk sat shielded behind a glass screen, afraid of drunks, infection and customer contact. 'We had to change the mentality,' he said. 'We can buy crystal dishes and install gold toilets, but if clients do not feel comfortable, it's worthless.'

The creation of such businesses was an important sign of change. Official statistics showed their numbers remained low by interna-tional standards. But they pointed to a clear trend, a change in culture and environment. Their existence suggested that entrepre-neurs were beginning to overcome the obstacles of property rights, racketeering and regulation that had previously stifled them. It also indicated growing optimism about the future. If so many people were willing to borrow and commit substantial sums of their own money, they believed that Russia had a long-term future which would allow them to make money. They had a stake in the preservation of the newly-emerging capitalist system, and would be a force for further improvement. They created political pressure to ensure that property rights were respected and liberalisation continued.

The retail revolution revealed huge pent-up demand. Ikea, the Swedish home-furnishings group, became a symbol of this new Russia. It took nearly a decade to negotiate, but when its long-awaited first suburban Moscow store opened in spring 2000, the reaction was astounding. There were enormous queues along the road to Sheremyetevo airport, where it was based, as tens of thousands of customers arrived on the first day alone. The managers had anticipated that each client would spend a few dollars. In fact, the typical Russian bought almost as much as their counterparts in western Europe. The planners were flying blind. Ikea's typical customers in Russia were not the same as in other countries. Chauffeur-driven Mercedes of rich Russians, and well-paid expatriate families' Toyotas stood in the car-park alongside more basic Zhigulis and Volgas. An estimate by Renaissance, a Moscow brokerage firm, suggested Muscovites had an average disposable income of 42 per cent of European levels. Ikea reflected the extent of Russia's hidden income, and the scope for greater competition.

Many Russians spent a far higher proportion of their incomes than their counterparts in other countries. That reflected greater incomes than the official statistics showed, low taxes even on the money they declared, and living costs well below European levels. There was also a process of post-Soviet adaptation at work, with many starting to make purchases that they never could before, including one-off renovations to their ancient apartments. And there was a cultural aspect, with Russians often generously and extravagantly spending, rather than saving for the future. In a striking reversal over the past few years, Western expatriates are often conspicuous in Moscow today because they are dressed more shabbily than the locals.

The situation is distorted in Moscow, with its 15 million-strong population and heavy concentration of wealth. But smaller versions of the same retail boom are taking place in many other Russian cities. Ikea already operates three stores in Moscow, and one in St Petersburg, with expansion plans in Nizhny, Novgorod and Kazan. Elsewhere across the country, mail order tapped an important vein. Pascal Clement, a young French businessman, has built a booming sales business in remote parts of the country. Many of his customers had little access to shops and had never received letters before. They hoarded his glossy catalogues for months.

Parts of Moscow are surreally geared to the rich. Marble-clad shopping centres stand alongside luxury goods shops, high-class restaurants and beauty salons. Not surprisingly, most are empty, raising suspicions about their use as outlets for money laundering, or their sustainability as little more than whims for frustrated businessmen, or their mistresses and trophy wives. But there has been a growing shift towards the mass market. Arkady Novikov, Moscow's restaurant king, is a case in point. Fired by a Soviet chef for being too innovative in his cooking, and spurned by McDonald's for being too ambitious when all they sought were hamburger-flippers, he launched his own up-market fish restaurant, Sirena, in 1992. Complete with a giant under-floor aquarium where the daily catch swim beneath the clients' feet, it was not cheap. He went on to establish a range of pricey restaurants, such as Grand Opera, which provided an evening opera performance, and the theme restaurant Byelo Solntse Pustinye, inspired by a cult Soviet film. But since the 1998 crisis, he has increasingly targeted the growing middle-class market, opening the Yolki Polki chain, and then Kish Mesh, offering Central Asian dishes and salad bars at affordable prices.

Intrigued after spotting a distinctly western-style chemist one day, I went to see the owner of the fast-expanding chain 36.6 – the healthy body temperature according to Russian doctors. A typical Russian *apteka* was even more drab and intimidating than most ordinary Soviet-era shops, with white-coated pharmacists hidden behind tiny windows and barricades of obscure-looking medicines. 36.6 was a pioneer in modern branded design, with bright turquoise and blue signs outside, and open shelves and welcoming assistants within. Artem Bektemirov, one of the founders, told me that when one of his staff smiled and offered help to a Russian pensioner, the woman was so shocked that she turned on her heels and fled. Its first store opened with catastrophic timing on the day of the August 1998 financial crisis. But the formula was successful, and the company now operates a chain of several dozen outlets. 36.6 was not just a model of customer service, but also a pioneer in tapping Russia's fledgling equity markets. Just four years after the crisis, it made public its finances and issued shares on the Moscow stock exchange.

The advent of 36.6, and the start of rival chemist chains in response, hinted at the emergence of a more dynamic market. Russian groups filled in the gaps where foreign investors did not want to tread, or imitated and improved on them. In 2003, the Alfa group opened a network of modern Alfa Express retail bank branches, as deposits from Russians rose beyond the volumes at the time of the 1998 crisis. In the oil towns of western Siberia, the local operators had to start sending trains and planes to bring in skilled workers from Ukraine as their expanding demand out-stripped supply. Cities like Surgut began paying honoraria to Moscow musicians and paid higher fees than they would earn travelling to the west.

The bureaucrats hassled, the regulators and courts failed to ensure fair competition and financing was difficult to raise. Personal contacts and trust counted for more than contracts, in what was a rapacious business culture. The state was exerting fresh influence over strategic sectors of the economy, and in many others there were cosy and murky relations between business and the local and federal authorities. Sonic Duo, a mysterious company with powerful connections at the highest level with the ministry of telecommunications, won a licence to be Moscow's third operator – and the only one with a federal licence – without any tender, for just $275. But between 2000 and 2003, more than eighty regional traditional fixed-line telecoms companies across Russia were restructured down to just seven, allowing them to become more efficient and to invest. From a crude, expensive single mobile phone provider in the mid-1990s, Moscow – and much of the rest of Russia – had the choice of three rival operators with state-of-the-art equipment by 2000. Tariffs fell sharply, there was a boom in sales, and by the end of 2003 there were more than 36 million subscribers. The context may have been very specific, but market mechanisms were beginning to work. Foreign investment remained at very low levels. But – because of or despite Putin – for those willing to play by Russian rules, the benefits were there to reap.

The return of hyper-legalism

Anton Drel was preparing for an important court hearing when the call came on his mobile phone. It was 9 October 2003, and he was seeking the release on bail of his client, Platon Lebedev, one of the key shareholders in the oil company Yukos, who had been held in pre-trial custody for nearly four months. An employee rang to warn him that on the other side of Moscow prosecutors were raiding his law office. They were studying his computers and taking away documents related to Lebedev's case, and the affairs of other clients too. Drel rushed to the scene and demanded to see their search warrant. The officers refused, and barred him from even watching what they were doing inside. A few days later, using material gathered from his office, they launched charges of tax evasion against another of his clients, Vasily Shakhnovsky, an important Yukos executive and shareholder.

By the standards of western legal procedure, the raid was a clear violation of the principle of 'lawyer–client privilege'. It constituted a 'fishing expedition' by prosecutors seeking evidence without respect for due process. The action was one in a long series of abuses in the spiralling legal attacks for fraud and tax evasion against the Khodorkovsky clan, which had challenged Putin's regime with intense lobbying, political criticism and international ambitions. It was part of a far broader shift to 'hyper-legalism' as a weapon used by the authorities under the lawyer-president Putin. The Soviet state had always used the pretence of respecting the law in its actions against dissent. Secret service officers took the trouble to employ witnesses during round-ups, and nominally follow written procedures during the purges. Stalin's 1937 constitution was billed as 'one of the most democratic in the world'.

Under Putin, the role of law as a political tool was coming back into fashion. Many of the country's criminal procedures still dated from the totalitarian era, as did the judges and prosecutors implementing them. But more recent changes ought to have helped curb their powers. A new legal code adopted under Putin stipulated court approval for search warrants. Prosecutors appeared so confident that they did not even bother with this formal step. As a member of the Council of Europe since 1996, Russia had agreed that the FSB internal security police should no longer maintain its own detention centres. Yet Lebedev, like Alexei Pichugin from Yukos' security department, who had been arrested a few weeks earlier, and Khodorkovsky himself later in October, were all held in the FSB's Lefortovo prison.

As the Yukos probe gathered pace, there were further extraordinary events. Prosecutors attempted to call in Drel and other company lawyers for formal questioning, in violation of laws on the rights and duties of lawyers. Defence lawyers were periodically blocked from meeting their clients. Private notes made during consultations in prison with Khodorkovsky and Lebedev were confiscated, with officials claiming they were secret instructions designed to hinder the criminal inquiries. Hearings for the detainees were held in closed court sessions despite Yukos' demands that they be open to public scrutiny. The operations of Moscow's Basmanny Court – where the judges had close connections to the Kremlin and the prosecutor's office, and consistently found in their favour – even gave rise to a new derogatory phrase: the *Basmannisatsia* of the legal process.

Allegations of abuse in the case went much further. Yukos executives claimed that the FSB had injected Pichugin with psychotropic drugs, and let hardened criminals into his cell to 'persuade' him to talk. They said the SVR, the foreign intelligence service, had tracked Khodorkovsky on his trips abroad, secretly recording – and doctoring – his conversations with US politicians and business people to present Putin with a warped version of his discussions. Armed FSB officers consistently accompanied prosecutors on their raids, and worked with them to gather and process information. They were also used to intimidate. Two FSB officers even went to the Moscow school where Khodorkovsky's 13-year-old daughter was studying, and demanded that the headteacher hand over a list of the names of all children of her age. They claimed it was part of an 'anti-terrorist' initiative, although there were no reports of any similar moves elsewhere.

The Yukos case is important in Putin's Russia not for the details so much as the broader picture it paints of the continued failings in the country's law enforcement system. It was an exception in the volume of resources it absorbed, and the amount of media attention it received. But it was more typical in reflecting abuses throughout the system and across the country. The two previous feuds by politically ambitious oligarchs under Putin showed suspiciously similar patterns: Vladimir Gusinsky and Boris Berezovsky were subjected to intense investigations, were driven abroad under threat of imprisonment, had 'hostages' from among their key executives imprisoned in order to step up the pressure, and eventually saw their businesses stripped away. In both cases, the law became the state's principal tool. But it was used selectively, and then cast aside once the main objectives – asset seizure and exile – had been achieved.

The techniques did not only apply to those with political ambitions.

In January 2002, the state-backed company Gazprom was struggling to boost its influence and recover assets from Sibur, a petro-chemicals group which was tightly linked to its former management. When it failed to reach an easy agreement, Jakov Goldovsky, Sibur's chairman and major shareholder, and his deputy Yevgeny Koshchits, were arrested and held in detention. Once a settlement was reached, they were released. Such instances of manipulation of the legal system were widespread, as businesses struggled with each other and with the local authorities for the control of assets.

Similar tactics applied outside the corporate sphere, with individuals frequently subject to police torture and unjust prosecution across Russia, while well-connected criminals went unpunished. Shortly after I arrived in Moscow in autumn 1998, Galina Staravoitova, a leading democratic politician, was gunned down in the streets of St Petersburg, creating a national scandal. More than five years later, the case was still open. Her hitmen were belatedly put on trial in early 2004, but the identity of those who had ordered her killing remained unclear. It was one of dozens of such high profile cases of murder – let alone corruption – where the authorities had failed to provide justice. Had they wanted such crimes to be solved, or devoted anything like the resources they did to the Yukos case, the results might have been very different.

A few weeks after Khodorkovsky's arrest in late October, I went to see Alexei Kudrin, the Russian finance minister and a close ally of Putin. He had no love for Khodorkovsky, whom he portrayed as the engineer of the most aggressive tax avoidance schemes employed by any Russian company. He claimed that there was nothing political about the Yukos case, but nor should people concentrate on the procedural abuses involved as anything out of the ordinary. He cited the cases of a former finance minister and another top official who had been held inconclusively in pre-trial detention without bail for many months, while no-one defended them in the media. It was hardly a vote of confidence in improvements to the rule of law under Putin.

It may well have been that Yukos and its key executives and shareholders were involved in all manner of crimes, as the authorities alleged. But they were hardly alone if so, and had done more than many to reform and become transparent. In any case, if the charge against them was so clear-cut, why did the methods used to bring them to justice need to be so crude? If, on the other hand, the action was revenge for political influence-peddling, why not instead pass urgent legislation to ban such methods, and then use the FSB to catch the lobbyists red handed? It seemed to suggest how weak Putin still considered the state. It was inconceivable that the president was not personally involved, and the way the case was conducted suggested that he saw it as a struggle for the very essence of Russian society. Resorting to muscled 'hyper-legalism' seemed to be his principal recourse.

To endorse such techniques suggested how fragile he thought Russia's new legal code, its parliament, media and government really remained in the face of wealthy opponents. His instinct was to distrust such more democratic institutions, preferring to rely instead on the more centrally-controlled ones of law enforcement.

There was little doubt that some oligarchs did still wield much power at the conclusion of Putin's first term. Their influence stretched from favourable journalistic coverage, to compliant Duma deputies, and sympathetic government officials and judges. After initially denying that he bribed, one oligarch told me: 'As long as all issues were determined by government officials, corruption was at crazy levels. Do you think we should just fold our arms and wait, when the security agencies and the mass media belong to the government?' He even showed me in private a copy of a secret prosecutor's report that he had managed to obtain about his company. A senior state official told me that a top Yukos executive had warned him that if he did not get his way on an important new law, 'we will start a war against the government.' As Khodorkovsky himself once told a friend of mine: 'With money, you can ultimately buy anything.'

In Moscow's conspiracy mill, it was soon being argued that Roman Abramovich, who had first proposed the merger of his company Sibneft with Yukos at the start of 2003, was behind the entire legal attack on Khodorkovsky. The idea was to destabilize the company so that he could cheaply gain full control. That was probably pushing things too far. But Sibneft, which preferred to keep a low political profile and concentrate on making money, had long boasted in private of its political connections. It was the most 'aggressive' company in minimising its tax bill, using Yukos-style tactics and paying a lower rate on its profits even if Kudrin insisted that Khodorkovsky's group was worse. Yet shortly after Abramovich held a meeting with Putin in November, the interior ministry and the state Audit Chamber both spontaneously issued statements saying that they had no claims against Sibneft. It was hard to believe in coincidence when on the day in December that Abramovich hinted that the merger with Yukos was definitively cancelled, tax police launched fresh raids on Menatep, Khodorkovsky's holding company, and investigators went to Yukos' headquarters to study alleged violations in licence requirements at its oil producing subsidiary Tomskneft. It suggested that some oligarchs were still capable of exerting extraordinary influence. And that those who remained on Putin's side were above the law.

Pitched against this corporate might were the prosecutors' office and the security services. Putin seemed to believe that only by picking on the biggest, most powerful oligarch group and using the most crude methods could he send a message about his power. When experienced judges and investigators received just a few hundred dollars a month in salary at best, it was no surprise that bright young law graduates went instead into commercial law firms, where they could earn starting salaries of $50,000 a year. The young lawyers employed by the oligarchs exploited Russia's weak and ambiguous legislation to the full, interpreting to the letter laws that had been dictated, blocked or manipulated by their own lobbying in order to preserve tax loopholes and maintain their privileges. They shielded ownership behind offshore trusts, and used the best tax advisers to create special structures that cut their bills. They could spend millions of dollars in their own defence.

The prosecutors and judges, in contrast, still exhibited a Soviet-era mentality. 'Understandings' and orders – commercial or political – were more important than procedures. They seemed to have little concept of the separation of powers or the presumption of innocence. When Vladimir Kolesnikov, the deputy general prosecutor, talked to a group of parliamentarians about the Khodorkovsky case in November 2003, he said it was 'regrettable' that the charges which the tycoon was facing only carried a maximum sentence of ten years in jail. He questioned the legality of a final settlement reached in late 2002 between Khodorkovsky and the federal property fund over a 1994 privatization deal and approved by his own boss, the general prosecutor. He said that although Khodorkovsky did not present a physical danger to society, his pre-trial detention was in effect justified because of the large sums of money at stake, which could have been paid out to pensioners and other needy groups.

The Yukos case was also an indictment of the state of civil society in

Russia. Khodorkovsky, with his robber baron past so recent and his aggressive commercial lobbying still underway, was hardly the best poster boy for democracy. US AID and other private foreign funders, led by George Soros, the US financier and philanthropist, began winding down their substantial charitable support to Russia in 2002, feeling that it was time to shift priorities elsewhere. Khodorkovsky – and Berezovsky through his New York-based Civil Liberties Foundation – were almost the only Russian businessmen willing to take up the slack. A parade of human rights groups came out to defend Khodorkovsky as their new benefactor, weakening their own reputation in the eyes of the authorities. While his motives may have been lofty, and the beneficiaries worthy, it showed how little broader support there was in Russian society for such causes, and how imperfect were the 'heroes' to whom they had to turn as a result.

The irony was that Khodorkovsky's actions may have helped set back democracy, if only by directly compromising the organizations to which he gave money, and dissuading other Russian businesses from supporting them in the future. His purchase of the weekly newspaper *Moskovskiye Novosti* and appointment as editor of Yevgeny Kiselyov, the former NTV anchor under Gusinsky, looked provocative and risked turning the staff into targets. More than eighty Russian charities which received support from his Open Russia foundation were subject to tax audits at the end of 2003, creating a huge strain on their meagre resources. And as the 2003 elections approached, prosecutors found a link to Yukos in order to raid the Agency for Strategic Communications, a political consultancy working for the liberal party Yabloko, which received substantial Khodorkovsky support. They raided the building, leaving with all its records, and disrupting the party's campaign.

Khodorkovsky was a man in too much of a hurry. He tried to call Putin's bluff, directly challenging the Russian president's commitment to the 'rule of law'. Like Berezovsky, he could talk about political rights. Like Gusinsky, he could cloak himself as a defender of the free press. Unlike either of them, he could also use the ultimate tool of capitalist success, portraying himself as a champion of property rights through the 'weapon' of the transparent, profitable company that he had created in Yukos. But as one of the key actors in shaping Russia's fledgling and imperfect new society, his attempts challenge Putin's bargain with the oligarchs so bluntly and so soon risked destabilizing the entire system. He was being consumed by the imperfect society he had helped to create. In trying to promote civil society and democracy, he not only risked charges of hypocrisy. He injured the very cause he was publicly trying to advance.

The relentless measures taken against Khodorkovsky snowballed after his arrest. His shares in Yukos were frozen, the planned merger with Sibneft was called off, and the company came under growing attack as inspectors examined the conformity of oil licences and tax bills. His partners came under investigation one by one, and their businesses were brought to a standstill by the raids. At a meeting on Christmas Eve 2003, Putin sent an unwelcome present to the country's oligarchs. Speaking to the Russian Chamber of Commerce, he warned that a handful of other 'illegal' privatizations might also be re-examined. While repeatedly stressing that there would be no general re-opening of the sell-offs of the 1990s, and the need for the respect of due process in judicial inquiries, his tacit endorsement of actions taken against Yukos sent out a different message. He was calling into question the fragile truce over property rights that had contributed to Russia's economic recovery. If he had a genuine desire to build strong, fair judicial institutions, rule of law and stability, the signals he was sending had the opposite effect. They would be heeded by many state officials only too pleased to respond.

The revenge of the *nomenklatura*

On 20 December 2002, I bumped into an acquaintance from the Kremlin administration during the interval at a concert in the Moscow Conservatory. As an old-style cultural institution that had defiantly refused to adjust to the city's increasingly intense work rhythm, its evening events still started at 7pm, a surprisingly early time for him (and me) to have left work. 'There was no point staying any later in the office today,' he shrugged. 'All my colleagues are out celebrating Chekists' Day.' It was the date when Felix Dzerzhinsky founded the *cheka*, the forerunner of the KGB. And it was an anniversary that was coming back into fashion.

As President, Putin consolidated and enhanced the powers of his former agency, placing back under its authority FAPSI, the government communications agency, as well as the border guards service.

He reasserted his personal control over the 'security ministries' – the law enforcement, defence and military agencies – bringing them firmly under the Kremlin's wing while leaving the more technical functions to the prime minister. The Kremlin's staff ran into several thousands, re-creating a form of Communist Party Central Committee that shadowed, duplicated and supervised the government. Above all, he appointed many of his former colleagues from the security services to a wide variety of posts in the Kremlin and government ministries, and in regional administrations across the country.

Viktor Ivanov, a long-time colleague of Putin from the Leningrad KGB, took on the sensitive responsibility in the Kremlin of the appointment of 'cadres' or managers. Personnel management might seem a secondary, technical function in the west, but the Soviets always thought otherwise. As Stalin once said: 'Cadres decide everything.' Many of Putin's people were not high-profile nominations to the top job, but deputies who held influence behind the scenes. Five of Putin's seven *pol preds* or special plenipotentiaries in the seven super-districts he created were drawn from the FSB or the army. And each of these people, in turn, hired their own teams drawn from similar backgrounds. The 'men in epaulettes' sprang up everywhere, and members of the FSB proudly began to refer to themselves as *chekisti* again.

Olga Kryshtanovskaya, a sociologist, has spent years painstakingly following the evolution of the Russian elite. Under Gorbachev in 1988, she estimates that less than five per cent of the top echelons of federal power were held by so-called *siloviki* – the uniformed members of the security services, the military, and the prosecutors. The figure began to grow under Yeltsin, reaching 47 per cent by 1999. But the greatest increase came with Putin, rising to more than 58 per cent in 2002. Over the same 14-year period across the country's leadership, government, parliament and regional elites, the proportions grew from 4 to 17 and then 25 per cent. More than half of Putin's Security Council today, an unofficial *politburo*, has FSB affiliations. She calculates that 70 per cent of the top jobs in the regional *pol pred* offices are taken by members of the security services or the military. Like previous leaders before him, Putin recreated an elite in his own image. After the disruptions and erratic appointments of the 1990s, the average age began increasing again – reaching 51.5 years old in 2002. The proportion of women, those with elite higher or further education declined. By contrast, those with a military education rose, along with those from St Petersburg.

At the height of the Khodorkovsky scandal, top Yukos officials as well as commentators led by Gleb Pavlovsky, a close political adviser to the Yeltsin Family, argued the investigations were part of a chekist coup. But the 'hyper-legalistic' techniques being employed were identical to those applied in previous struggles, notably against Gusinsky and Berezovsky. At that stage, no-one suggested that the so-called *siloviki* were acting on their own. They were taking orders from Alexander Voloshin, the head of the presidential administration. If such people were really behaving more independently in 2003 than they had in 2000, it was as a result of instruments already perfected by others. As Grigory Yavlinsky from the Yabloko party put it: 'Anyone would have used the same approach in a fight for property. It wouldn't have mattered who was rising to power in the Kremlin. Artists, men of culture, anyone who didn't have assets while others did. These are Soviet and pre-Soviet instincts, not just KGB ones.'

It would be too simple to say that officials in the Lubyanka, the FSB's sinister headquarters in Moscow, somehow engineered the rise to power of their alumni, or that they had any master plan. The agency was heavily demoralised during the 1990s, with funding sharply down, prestige falling, staff leaving to take up jobs in the private sector, and companies exploiting its resources for their own commercial ends. In Soviet times, it had long been subordinate to the Communist party. Its officers remain instruments more than instigators. Nor did all *silovoki* share a tight bond. There were always rivalries between the KGB's domestic and foreign intelligence arms, let alone with the GRU (military intelligence). It was clear soon after Putin appointed Sergei Ivanov, his former KGB colleague as a nominally civilian defence minister, that his man was strongly resented in the military hierarchy as an outsider.

But the domination of any single group in power was unhealthy, regardless of its background. And those from the KGB and the FSB were linked by a common mentality. The resurgence of its cadres, even those who had long since quit, implied the propagation of a certain set of values. 'They consider it patriotism and statism, but it is inseparably linked to fear,' said Kryshtanovskaya. She argued that they tended to guard a greater cameraderie than other Russian groups. Nikolai Patrushev, Putin's long-standing friend who took over from him as head of the FSB, said in a reference to the period when he entered the agency: 'It was generally accepted that you had to serve twenty-five years.' As Putin himself joked: 'There is no such thing as a former *chekist*.' Many of his new nominations to government jobs remained in the FSB's 'active reserve', receiving a second salary, sending back reports, and remaining accountable to the agency rather than their nominal ministerial bosses.

The good side was obedience to the state, and a sense of integrity. The temptations of corruption seemed often less important than loyalty. The bad aspect was conformism and respect for the *vertikal* military-style command structure, with an emphasis on implementing orders rather than questioning them. That had its drawbacks in the Soviet system. It was ever more counter-productive in the evolving state of modern Russia. Such people in key positions were hardly best placed for laying the foundations for democracy, decision sharing, or responding to the complexities of a free market economy. They might have no track with Stalin-style repressions or even Andropov-style threats, but they were above all bureaucrats embittered by the erosion of their status during the 1990s. Their philosophy was above all that of statists, those who believed first of all in the importance of the state itself. Their influence was visible in hard-line policy decisions, whether in boosting military spending, pursuing war in Chechnya, refusing to negotiate with rebels in the Moscow theatre siege, or drafting tough immigration and citizenship laws that did little to meet Russia's needs to find new sources of labour or to integrate its own people and those from the 'near abroad'.

The *siloviki* were appointed under Putin to an ever growing number of spheres of public administration, well outside their traditional areas of expertise. While they were logical choices in the security services, the military and the police, it seemed stranger that four deputy ministers for economic development and trade, and the same number in the telecom ministry were drawn from their ranks. Alexander Zdanovich, the FSB's former press spokesman, was made a director of the state television channel ORT. Yuri Zaostrovtsev, the agency's deputy head, was appointed to the board of Aeroflot, the state airline. What Kryshtanovskaya dubbed Putin's 'neo-authoritarian militocracy' made up a third of all deputy ministers appointed during 2000-03.

Not all Putin's people were drawn from among the *siloviki*. But many others shared a statist philosophy. A classic example was Gazprom. The state had a nominal 38 per cent shareholding, but the gas group had been all but privatized to its own top management, led by the diminutive Rem Vyakhirev. It became a power to itself, an unwieldy 'state within a state' with its own yacht club, luxury hotels and contracts on favourable terms with businesses controlled by its own managers and their families.

When Putin came to power, everything changed. The state firmly re-established its voting rights, and increased its control to 51 per cent. Assets sold off cheaply were recovered. Alexei Miller, a long-time Putin acquaintance from St Petersburg, was made chief executive in 2001, and began a purge of Vyakhirev's team. But the initial optimism of investors that the company would become more efficient and transparent soon dissipated. Despite vast investment spending, it was unable to raise the level of gas production. Cosy new deals were signed with obscure companies. Calls for oil companies to gain access to Gazprom's monopoly control over the pipeline network, and to liberalise the domestic gas market went nowhere. A private near-monopoly had been replaced by a total state one. Miller had proved a loyal bureaucrat and a statist first of all.

Soviet leaders always tended to appoint a 'mafia' of their own acquaintances when they came to power. But they could also rely on a well-developed system for developing cadres from across the country, which fell apart along with the USSR. Yeltsin had neither option, as the system collapsed and his rapid hirings and firings soon exhausted any immediate circle. Putin's choices were not easy, given the questionable backgrounds and character of many of the country's newly-emerged business people and officials. But he was particularly reluctant to give important jobs to people he did not know and trust. Those he selected were not always as effective as he himself was at adapting to the demands of their new responsibilities. His style of *tusovka* management, of drawing on a tight group of his own friends, was not by any means limited to those from the KGB. But his nominations were largely from the narrow circle of his own professional life in St Petersburg.

Jokes began to circulate on the growing role of Russia's second city. 'Are you from the Kremlin? Are you from the KGB? Are you from St Petersburg?' asks one man to another in a tram. 'No? Then get off my foot.' Another tells of the Kremlin becoming so desperate to find any remaining *Petertsi* – St Petersburg residents – to hire that the police are employed to drag reluctant tramps out of the city's main station waiting room and onto the Moscow train. One Russian businessman told me with a wink that he was learning German. 'Eventually the president will run out of people from the KGB and St Petersburg, and then he'll start recruiting German-speakers,' he said.

Putin's approach to management was also deeply conservative. He preferred continuity to change, avoiding any significant departures during his first year in office, and only promoting one: Leonid Reiman, a close ally from St Petersburg, to the newly-created post of telecoms minister. That gave time for his 'power ministers' to adapt, and for the elites of the Yeltsin era time to sort out their affairs. Then he launched the only important reshuffle of his first term, appointing his KGB colleague, Sergei Ivanov, as minister of defence, and Boris Gryzlov, head of Unity, as interior minister. Even by early 2004, his cabinet was largely the one he had inherited from Yeltsin, including Mikhail Kasyanov, the 'Family's' candidate as prime minister.

The Kremlin reinstituted the practice of life-long public sector careers, which had been broken when Gorbachev began ousting those he did not want in the Soviet hierarchy. Anyone who followed the rules of '*nomenklatura* ethics' and bowed to the new authority could find their place in Putin's hierarchy, even former enemies. That enabled him to continue drawing on the past experience of many officials, who instead of losing face were granted a dignified sinecure. Potential enemies were incorporated, as part of an *apparatchik* merry-go-round.

Gorbachev himself was given a degree of access to the Kremlin that he had never had under Yeltsin. The last Soviet leader had in 1999 questioned Putin's appointment as prime minister, but by the end of 2003 had been so charmed that he was calling for a constitutional amendment to allow him a third term in office. Yevgeny Primakov, the former prime minister and one-time prospective presidential candidate, became a foreign policy adviser to him and intermediary in Transdniester and Iraq. Sergei Yastrzhembsky, a diplomat who had jumped ship to Primakov's camp in 1999, was given a second chance as Putin's spokesman on Chechnya. Yevgeny Nazdratenko, the outspoken governor of the Primorsky region in the far east, resigned in early 2001 after a phone call from the Kremlin. He re-emerged as head of the lucrative State Fisheries Commission, and then as a member of the Security Council in change of environmental affairs. Even Putin's arch-rival Vladimir Yakovlev, who stepped down as governor of St Petersburg, was compensated with a job as a deputy prime minister.

There was a logic to the system, which kept potential enemies under control. Nazdratenko, for instance, remained a powerful and popular figure in the far east who might always run again if alienated. Yakovlev – apart from knowing much about Putin's own past – enjoyed strong support which could be channelled towards the Kremlin's preferred replacement to run the city, Valentina Matvienko. Rakhlin, Putin's judo trainer, told me: 'There are people in Putin's circle who are not very suitable, but it is very difficult to make choices and find good people. He knows their limits. It is like the story of two shopkeepers. One says to the other: "Your assistant steals, why don't you sack him?" The other replies: "Because I know his limits. With someone else, how would I know how much they steal?"'

When asked the question as a press conference in summer 2003, Putin himself replied: 'I cannot think of a case when someone who really could not handle their responsibilities was promoted if he had done something that should have led to very different decisions being taken . . . It's very easy to chop off a few heads, fire a few people and look like a tough boss. But I think it is far more important to treat people with care, especially people who, being in very public positions and therefore exposed to a hail of criticisms . . . have nonetheless carried this burden with dignity and have looked after sectors, companies and regions. We need to make use of their skills and experience. It is true that we don't have so many modern management specialists.'

The danger with Putin's overly-cautious approach was that it created sclerosis. Ageing governors and officials were allowed to retain power and create dynasties. Co-opting enemies avoided conflict, but limited the scope for the creation of any alternative centres of power. It also sent out a message of immunity. Few senior civil servants were punished, providing a green flag to further corruption and abuse. It smacked of the old KGB tactics of management-by-*kompromat* or compromising material. Rather than choosing people who were scandal-free, it was better to use any 'dirt' to keep them 'on the hook', or easy to manipulate on pain of prosecution. One Russian politician told me that the FSB had blocked his appointment to a more senior job because it had no dirt on him. Another public figure said that when he went to the office of Vladimir Rushailo, the head of the Security Council, for discreet meetings, the minister would lead him into a corner and make notes on a slip of paper for fear of being overheard.

As Putin's first term came to an end, debate continued about the influence of the competing circles of power around him. The Yeltsin 'Family' was gradually being pushed aside, and those from Putin's own circles promoted in their place. A common denominator among the new people was St Petersburg, but there were rival challengers: the 'liberals' such as Kudrin, and the *siloviki* like Patrushev. When Alexander Voloshin resigned in late October 2003, in what appeared to be an acknowledgement of his failure to prevent the escalation of the Khodorkovsky affair, Putin surprised many by turning to a different group to replace him: the St Petersburg 'lawyers'. He named as the new head of the administration Dmitry Medvedev and as his deputy Dmitry Kozak, both fellow graduates of the Leningrad law faculty. They were classic Putin appointments: low-profile professionals with whom he had already worked for a decade, and who owed their loyalty and success entirely to him.

Both men were relatively young and open. They provided an apparent counter-balance to the competing groups of power. It was unclear in reality whether they had anything like the power of their predecessors, or how far they were free from the pressures of the *siloviki* or other groups within the Kremlin. But their track record provided hints at trends likely to gain momentum in Putin's second term. Kozak had been charged with legal reform, which provided many improvements on paper, the limits of which were highlighted by the Khodorkovsky affair. Medvedev had chaired Gazprom's board of directors, and was responsible for a restructuring which reasserted the state's control but deferred liberalisation. They symbolised a new, modern-looking but more statist style of governance to come.

The death of (virtual) democracy

As the sun rose on 7 November 2003, the formal launch of Russia's parliamentary election campaign, workmen put the finishing touches to a giant stage they had constructed in Red Square, in the shadow of the Kremlin towers. It was the date of the former October Revolution Day holiday, and the Moscow authorities were hosting a free public concert. City officials claimed it was a non-partisan event sponsored by the independent Capital Foundation, created in 1996. But there was no doubt who was the beneficiary. The backdrop of the stage carried a huge banner remarkably like the logo of the pro-Kremlin United Russia party, accompanied by a Soviet-style slogan attributed to Vladimir Putin calling for a 'Strong, United Russia'. Just three people were allowed to speak during the performance: the party's joint leaders, Boris Gryzlov, the interior minister, Sergei Shoigu, the emergencies minister, and Yuri Luzhkov, the mayor of Moscow.

It was typical of what Russians call the use of 'administrative resources', exploiting the institutions of state for their own advantage. By 2003, United Russia was by far the best equipped to do so, drawing into its net of supporters and candidates some of the country's most important federal leaders and heads of regional governments. No support was more important than that of Putin himself. Despite an election law that forbade top officials from endorsing parties or candidates, the president made it quite clear where his support lay when he personally attended United Russia's pre-electoral party congress in the autumn. Giant posters went up bearing his 'Strong, United Russia' slogan in prominent places, including opposite the Duma building. One week before voting on 7 December, Putin stressed on television how important the party had been in assisting the implementation of his policies over the previous four years. United Russia had no programme beyond a single idea summarised in its election catch-phrase: 'Together with the president'.

Gryzlov, the grey, uncharismatic figure who chaired the party, went further in his unconventional approach to electioneering. United Russia refused to participate in what it dubbed the 'populist' television debates arranged with rival candidates – even those which the state-controlled media had pledged to pre-record, allowing censorship of any gaffes ahead of broadcast. 'For parties with no political weight at all, taking part in the debates with United Russia is the same as a substitute goalkeeper of a street hockey team posing for a photograph with Tretyak,' Gryzlov said, in a reference to a legendary Soviet-era player. Why lend credibility to second-rank parties who were hoping that some of the achievements of his party over the previous four years would rub off on them, he argued.

When I asked the exiled tycoon Boris Berezovsky if he thought the media – which he had helped manipulate so extensively in the previous campaign in 1999 – would play an important role in 2003, he grinned and said: 'I think we used up nearly all trust in the last elections.' But in the absence of active campaigning, journalists again made a big difference. Four years before, there had been a real struggle for power between Putin's Unity party and Luzhkov and Primakov's Fatherland-All Russia. The television networks with their varied owners and vested interests were not objective, but they reflected different opinions in their broadcasts. By 2003, all the principal chains were under government control, and that 'resource' was used in a single direction.

ORT, the station with the widest reach across the country which had reverted to its Soviet-era name, the First Channel, was the main vehicle. Its prime-time evening news broadcasts gave a highly distorted view of Russia. For months, it raised Gryzlov's profile through coverage of his meetings and regional trips which were a thinly-disguised form of canvassing. As the elections approached, he was shown taking the credit for anti-corruption operations, pledging improved law and order, or rewarding brave police officers. The state-owned RTR, renamed simply Rossiya (Russia), showed similar slanted, one-party coverage. Opposition politicians like Grigory Yavlinsky, on the other hand, claimed that they were frequently barred from even appearing on television. On the rare occasions the Communists were covered, it was usually to highlight mismanagement by one of their regional governors.

On the surface, Russian television looked increasingly professional. Well-dressed presenters read the news in slick modern studios. They illustrated their reports with sophisticated graphics. But the degree of manipulation was striking. A study by the election monitors of the Organization for Security and Cooperation in Europe concluded that during the month-long campaign there was significant bias. Putin himself dominated the news bulletins, his high ratings lending credibility to his party. United Russia was by far the most frequently covered party, accounting for 18 per cent of coverage on the First Channel, 16 per cent on Rossiya and 22 per cent on TV-Centre, a local chain controlled by Luzhkov. Nearly all of that coverage was rated neutral or positive, whereas other parties, led by the Communists, were shown in a predominantly negative light. While Gryzlov's speeches to war veterans or his appearances helping deal with voter's day-to-day problems were shown uncritically, the Communist leader Zyuganov was pictured being humiliated by a tomato thrower, or struggling to defend himself against (true) allegations of his funding by oligarchs. NTV remained more balanced, although its reports on the Communists were also predominantly negative.

Other 'administrative resources' were widely applied during the elections at the federal level, and across the country. Government buildings were allocated and state civil servants seconded to help United Russia. Vladimir Uspekhov, a student who told me he supported the liberal SPS partly because of its pledge to abolish conscription, was summoned like dozens of his contemporaries to his local military headquarters two days before voting. He was told to surrender his passport temporarily for an obscure administrative reason, without which he and hundreds of his peers were deprived of the right to vote, disenfranchising core SPS supporters.

The Central Election Commission itself, which governed the whole process, was not exempt from such influence-peddling. Charged with supervising the fair conduct of the vote, it had steered laws through the Duma in 2002 that gagged the media. In the build-up to voting, it forbade journalists to comment on parties or candidates in a way that might be considered partisan. As Alexander Veshnyakov, its chairman, argued, the idea was to compensate for 1999, when hidden funding had created bias that had much less to do with the personal opinions of journalists than with earning cash. There was little doubt that the previous system had been highly corrupt. The danger was that the compensatory mechanisms being put in place were not only ineffective, but had swung too far in the other direction. They handed discretionary judgements on media objectivity to members of the Commission and its regional affiliates, who were predominantly Kremlin supporters. When the rules were applied, it was usually selectively. *Kommersant Vlast* was reprimanded for criticising Luzhkov's effectiveness as mayor of Moscow, for example. Images on state television of Putin's attendance at the United Russia congress or his meetings with officials went unchallenged, however.

Across the country, local authorities mirrored the federal use of administrative resources as thirty of the eighty-nine regional governors aligned with the party of power to serve their own interests. Vladimir Kara-Murza, who decided to run for the Duma in a seat to the south of

Moscow for the liberal SPS party, also had the support of Yabloko. The double endorsement was perfectly legal – though rare – but it was swiftly challenged by his opponent from United Russia. The weight of Luzhkov's administrative apparatus militating against him was overwhelming. He had managed to install a large poster of himself in an eye-catching position on a busy road in his constituency. But in the winter gloom of the election evening, it was barely visible. 'They turn off the lights on billboards carrying my posters every night,' he said. 'They would not distribute a local newspaper in which I had advertised, and cut off the sound when I was speaking in a debate on the local Stolitsa television channel.'

Many governors standing for re-election locally fell in with United Russia to combine forces. Luzhkov himself, who was one example, plastered the city with posters and banners urging voters to support him and the party. He played heavily on his weight as the incumbent, as if by chance choosing 5 December – just two days before the elections – to inaugurate both a new metro station and the city's third ring-road, to widespread media coverage. There was pressure on shopkeepers to display his posters, and on companies that ran outdoor advertising space to only handle 'suitable' clients. Alexander Lebedev, a former spy turned banker who ran against him for Moscow City Hall, was reduced to buying up space in the suburbs outside Luzhkov's control, and despatching vans carrying his posters to drive around central roads. Many of his media appearances were done from afar: he campaigned via the BBC and Radio Liberty, beamed into the city from the outside world.

In many ways, Russia's short-lived democracy had always been virtual. The country had no tradition of power-sharing in tsarist times, let alone any living memory under one-party Communist rule. That makes it fundamentally different from many of the countries of Eastern Europe, which are geographically closer to the west and were politically more diverse until the second world war. During the 1990s, Russia experienced the imposition of a supra-presidential system by military force under Yeltsin in 1993; and the heavy hand of oligarch lobbying thereafter. Under the constitution, the government was formally independent, and in practice the prime minister and cabinet chosen by the president with little accountability to parliament. The media may have been unrestrained, but it was also partisan, notably during the election campaigns of the period. State television coverage was heavily biased in favour of the Kremlin in the 1999 parliamentary vote, and in the presidential elections in 1996 as well as 2000.

The privatizations and other economic liberalisation measures launched by Yeltsin were in clear contradiction to the dominant ideology of the successive nationalist and Communist forces in the parliaments in 1993 and 1995. Russians may have gradually begun to benefit from Yeltsin's economic reforms by the turn of the millennium, but they were objects in a system that was imposed on rather than chosen or controlled by them. Their mixed views on the result were summed up in two joke words that had become popular during the 1990s. Many Russians referred to *privatizatsia* (privatization) as *prikhvatizatsia* (seizure), and *demokrati* (democrats) as *dermokrati* (shitocrats). 'The problem is that we mistook the chaos of the 1990s for democracy,' one long-time Russia observer told me. Presidential rule was not so bad, he argued. Otherwise the ultra-nationalist Vladimir Zhirinovsky might have ended up as foreign minister.

United Russia may have been the dominant force in the 2003 elections, but it did not have a monopoly of influence and nor was it alone in using its resources to the full. As Valery Bogomolov, secretary of its 'central committee' complained on the eve of voting: 'many regions where there are "red governors" are making full use of administrative resources against us.' In Tula and Bryansk, both controlled by Communists, he claimed that his candidates had been barred from the local media and unable to hold public meetings with voters. He cited 'provocations', including campaigning calls to people's homes at 4 am purportedly from United Russia, and slanderous leaflets distributed in its name. In Bashkortostan, supporters of Murtaza Rakhimov, the president, were caught printing false ballot papers three days before the elections, as he fought a Kremlin-backed candidate put up against him.

The 'liberal democrats' were not above playing tricks too. In the weeks ahead of voting, Anatoly Chubais, one of the leaders of SPS, raised his profile as a can-do manager by holding press conferences and sending out letters to millions of Russians supposedly in his other capacity as chief executive of UES, the electricity company. Yabloko's Yavlinsky did his best to have some of Putin's magic dust brush off on him, holding a meeting with him in the Kremlin shortly ahead of the election that was broadcast on state television. The message, as so often in Russia, was the primacy of individuals over laws. There were no well-grounded institutions that ensured a consistent, fair political process. Instead, those in charge at whatever level and in whatever organisation sought to impose their own will without check, using all the mechanisms under their influence.

On voting day on December 7, there seems little doubt that falsification took place during the count. Several politicians confirmed that they had had contacts with the Kremlin or governors over the previous weeks offering to 'help' their campaigns. Yavlinsky, who had looked extremely sanguine in television appearances during the evening, told me that Putin called him at 2 am to congratulate him on Yabloko's re-election to the Duma. But as the count was finalised during the night, total turnout figures swelled mysteriously, and Yabloko dropped sharply in the tally. It ended up alongside its rival SPS below the five per cent minimum entry threshold for parliament. Whether Putin himself was involved in influencing the counting is unclear, but it looked, in the words of Andrew Kuchins, one political observer, as though those compiling the figures for United Russia had mimicked the Soviet era and 'over-fulfilled the plan'.

The following morning, election observers from the OSCE and the Council of Europe concluded that there was a 'regression' in democracy compared with 1999. The result, they said, was 'overwhelmingly distorted', and voting was 'free but not fair'. Yet if manipulations tweaked the final result – as an independent tally by the Communist party also suggested – it was probably only by 2–3 per cent. The media may have been partisan, the campaign lacklustre, and the weight of the state heavily brought to bear in favour of Putin's party. But for many voters, the alternatives were still less attractive. The previous four years coincided with a sharp improvement in the economy, a resurgence in national pride and a political stability not seen during the 1990s. Russians rewarded those trends, which they linked to Putin, allowing United Russia to share his glory. It reaped 37 per cent of the votes, or almost three times more than the next largest party. By the time the new Duma began to operate in January 2004, the 'party of power' had already drawn in so many politicians from the single-mandate constituencies that it commanded more than the 300 seats required to give it a two-thirds majority, and appointed itself in charge of every committee.

The Kremlin set the dominant theme for the elections during 2003 when it began to pick away at the messy compromises of the 1990s by attacking the oligarchs. United Russia was able to capitalise on public support for the imprisonment of Khodorkovsky. But the absence of anti-oligarch rhetoric in its statements, and the modest coverage the clamp-down received on state television, suggested that the Kremlin was reluctant to exploit the mood too far. In that vacuum, others would take advantage. Vladimir Zhirinovsky, the outspoken ultra-nationalist leader of the LDPR, raised the theme early. He was rewarded with 12 per cent, putting him in third place in the Duma. Sergei Glaziev, leader of the Rodina (Motherland) bloc, jointly led by Putin's ally Dmitry Rogozin, went furthest, making his central campaign message a new squeeze on oligarchs' money and influence. Created just a few months before, Rodina proved the biggest surprise of the election, gathering 9 per cent of the total votes and becoming the fourth-largest party.

The flip-side of Rodina's success was the failure of the Communist party, which saw its support halve to 13 per cent. The out-dated rhetoric of Gennady Zyuganov, its leader, did nothing to help rejuvenate the party's support and make it relevant to the new era. His defence of the oligarchs, and funding from Khodorkovsky and Berezovsky, made it difficult to keep a coherent line. The ousted opposition parties, SPS and Yabloko, were caught in the same trap. SPS, in choosing to put Chubais on its slate for election, firmly associated itself with the man who helped create the oligarchs, and who remained a hate figure for many Russians as a result. His vigorous public defence of Khodorkovsky after his arrest alienated the public and the Kremlin alike. The irony was that the economic growth the leaders of SPS had helped create in the previous decade was being turned against them. Putin had usurped its reform agenda, and was best placed to capitalise on the nostalgia for lost Soviet pride and power that came with improved living standards. SPS's cynical choice of Alfred Kokh, the architect of NTV's takeover, and aspirational campaign adverts showing Chubais and his running mates using lap-top computers onboard a luxurious private jet, did the rest.

Yabloko was tarnished by the reputation of its leader Yavlinsky as a figure of permanent opposition, who denounced corruption and the errors of previous administrations, but was unwilling to make the messy compromises of leadership himself. During Putin's time in office, Yavlinsky did try to re-position himself, even hinting at his interest in becoming a minister. But that sat uneasily with his outspoken criticism of key aspects of the Kremlin's policies including the war in Chechnya and electricity reform. His party took a fiercely anti-Chubais stance, defining itself in opposition to the 'loans for shares' scheme that Yavlinsky charged had created a criminal oligarchic class corrupting parliament. The result was that two parties with much in common eroded each other's support. But Yabloko was also weakened by its heavy dependence on Khodorkovsky. While insisting that it often voted against his interests, its significant financing and the fact that six Khodorkovsky allies stood as candidates on its party list, did little to improve its image.

Vladislav Surkov, the deputy head of the Kremlin administration and one of the engineers of 'managed democracy', said the 2003 elections marked the end of the transition period, and the emergence of a new Russia. Those parties that had been eliminated 'should understand that their historical mission is finished.' If he was right, Russia's political future looked bleak. While respecting the façade of democracy, it had no depth. It was artificially constructed, a system which had parties without ideas, debates without the most important participants, media without criticism. There was no institutional framework, no broader political culture to help foster diversity of opinion for the future. Whatever the shortfalls of democracy during the 1990s, Putin had done little to help create a more diverse and competitive political environment during his first term. The result was a parody of a new system, the old Soviet one-party system genuinely endorsed by the people.

Many foreign investors and commentators welcomed the United Russia landslide as a sign that Putin would have stable support and a free hand in his second term, allowing him to implement liberal economic reforms. But it was not clear how desirable or effective those reforms would be, let alone how well they would be prepared in the absence of those experienced, liberal lawmakers who had drafted and eased them through in the past. Even if the previous Duma had been dominated by the Kremlin, there was some public debate and modifications to laws following suggestions from minority parties. That process was now likely to be entirely squashed, with policy-making increasingly opaque, and accountability still further reduced.

In the absence of an enemy from without, there was the growing threat from within. Putin faced fawning but hollow support from politicians. Many were allied for purely pragmatic reasons – linked to fear, money or power – and owed less allegiance to the Kremlin than to the commercial groups or regional governors who had helped them get elected. They could easily change tack again, undermining his support in the future. The president, always sensitive to his opinion ratings, could also not ignore the shifts in the composition of the parliament towards a more nationalistic and populist line, just three months before his own re-election campaign in March 2004. It risked pushing him towards a more traditional, anti-western stance on foreign policy, and a less liberal, more statist and socially-oriented economic policy.

Managed democracy brought another danger: that of apathy. In the weeks before voting, nervous political leaders from Gryzlov to Putin began to plead with the electorate to come out and vote. Shoigu even proposed stripping Russians who did not vote of their citizenship. Not only was his suggestion unconstitutional, it was also hypocritical, from someone who had refused to participate in debates, and who did not even plan to take up his seat in the Duma despite his figurehead role with United Russia. When voting day finally came, turnout was low. It fell from 62 per cent in 1999 to 56 per cent in 2003 – and possibly nearer to 50 per cent without manipulation. Those who voted on the ballot for the special category marked 'against all' rose to nearly 5 per cent, making it the fifth most popular choice. The two factors together suggested an electorate which was increasingly disillusioned and disengaged with the democratic process itself.

As Russia headed for presidential elections in March 2004, there was no surprise about who would win. The Kremlin's concern was to find a respectable 'democratic' rival to create the impression of a meaningful race, and to ensure that turnout reached acceptable levels. But the usual candidates from among the Communists, SPS and Yabloko were too humiliated and angered by their poor showing to stand. Most of the dozen people who put their names forward stressed that they were not running in opposition to the president, but to support his ideas. The compliant Zhirinovsky, whose charisma risked unintentionally eroding at least some support from Putin, took no chances. He put up his own bodyguard to stand instead. It was a sorry sign of the state of Russian democracy, but at least it highlighted the absurdities in all their glory.

The shape of things to come

Boris Yeltsin kept his greatest political surprise until the end. On New Year's Eve 1999, with three months to go before his presidential term expired, the man who had aggressively accumulated power over the previous decade told astonished Russians in a national television address that he was relinquishing it with immediate effect. On the same day, a statement that would prove just as significant was released into Moscow cyberspace. Signed by Vladimir Putin shortly before he became acting president, it was called 'Russia at the turn of the millennium'. It laid out the vision of the country's new leader, now into his second term, and it provides a revealing insight into his views and a blueprint that he has since followed.

Firstly, Putin called for consolidation and stability to overcome 'the still deep ideological and political split in society'. He asserted that 'Russia has reached its limit for political and socio-economic upheavals, cataclysms and radical reforms.' He warned that 'the mechanical copying of other nations' experience will not guarantee success,' and said 'our future depends on combining the universal principles of the market economy and democracy with Russian realities.' His conciliatory words, attempting to build a bridge to the Soviet past while nurturing a new Russian pride, reflect one of Putin's greatest achievements. His varied, ambiguous ideas – sometimes vague and even contradictory – may ultimately trip him up. But during 2000-04, they proved a symbol of his strength. By his gradualist policies, his refusal to create political upheaval, and his varied gestures to different groups, 'morphing' to say what they wanted to hear, he acted as a uniting force for the country. In so doing, he cemented the transition from communism to capitalism, in a way that neither of his predecessors was able to achieve.

Both Gorbachev, who undermined the old system, and Yeltsin, who created the conditions for a new one, still suffer from very low popularity today. Putin, by contrast, has enjoyed 70–80 per cent approval ratings throughout his term, proof of a necessary solidifying role for Russia. Little blood had been spilt to defend and legitimise the shift to democracy, the market economy and private property during the previous decade. Many people still remembered the Soviet period with nostalgia, and resented what had come since. Putin's consolidation was just as necessary as the more radical gestures of those who had gone before. He is unlikely to go down in history as a great, transformational leader. But he may yet be viewed as playing an essential role of cohesion, stability and predictability – in domestic and even in international affairs.

A second theme which Putin repeatedly mentioned in his millennium address was economic growth as a way to restore Russia's competitiveness, well-being and status as a 'great power'. He set ambitious but realistically long-term goals, raising the prospect of attaining the per capita GDP of Portugal by 2015 if the country was able to achieve growth rates of 8 per cent a year. While the pace has been a little slower, Putin has presided over a period of unprecedented economic expansion and investment in modern Russia. It was precisely his first achievement of stability, providing continuity and rebuilding confidence, that helped with that process. And it was the economic renaissance that in turn proved most important in helping rebuild a broken society.

Putin's third theme was that of order, and the recreation of a functioning administration. He called for 'the restoration of the guiding and regulating role of the state', and for coordination between government bodies, the parliament, the regions and society at large. It is likely that his judgement on the 1990s would have been tougher still in the statement had he not been so firmly under the influence of Yeltsin's team at the time. The new president created a process, imposing mechanisms of Russian governance and policy-making on the chaos that he inherited. The institutions of state may have been rubber stamps, but there was an attempt to establish a coherent approach, calling on experts to draw up policies, consulting with ministries, and debating in parliament rather than ruling by decree or whim, or not governing at all.

In meeting his objectives of consolidation, economic growth and order, Putin has proved a more effective leader by outcome and by the objectives he set than either of his predecessors. Gorbachev's actions may have resulted in the collapse of the USSR, but his vision of reformed Communism – never daring to criticise Lenin – seemed warped, and he was unable to control the processes that he unleashed. Yeltsin may have had a clearer, more attractive vision, but his ability to implement it was equally questionable and his legacy in many ways deeply unstable. Putin's rhetoric was clear and logical, and his ability to put it into action has so far proved much greater.

The reasons for his success are a different matter, however. Putin was, above all, extremely lucky. Like other leaders around the world, he may like to claim the credit, but much was taking place despite rather than because of him. Domestically, the trend lines for modern Russian society were already sketched out, and the modernizing pressures of an evolving market economy and a population that had tasted freedom were already in operation. He inherited the slow but steady results of economic transition that had led to the creation of the private sector, and a healthy restructuring that followed the 1998 financial default. He came to power as commodity prices began a sharp rise to high levels that have been maintained ever since. Just as the strengthening rouble risked damaging domestic companies, the weakness of the dollar helped limit the fall-out.

In foreign affairs, the new mood of *realpolitik* also played to Putin's favour, as Russia wrapped its war in Chechnya in the justification of the fight against international terrorism. Its growing potential as an energy supplier at a time of growing instability in the Middle East helped keep the west quiet. He could have antagonised the USA over Iraq, but France's aggressive stance pushed him into a secondary role which allowed him to avoid most of the fall-out. With some justification, he could rebut criticism of human rights abuses by resorting to the armoury of Soviet-style accusations of double standards. The strength of the economy and the sharp reduction in his dependence on foreign assistance meant he was less vulnerable to threats from abroad.

Nevertheless, good leaders make – and use – their luck. Putin could have squandered the increase in government revenues triggered by growth. Instead, he limited state spending, paid off international debts, built up foreign currency reserves and endorsed a 'stabilisation fund' to ring-fence high oil tax revenues for long-term use. He pushed ahead with reforms, and put good managers into key financial positions. He could have offered far less cooperation with the west in Afghanistan, or been a more difficult negotiating partner on Iraq. He could have inflamed greater tensions in Georgia, or acted more defensively on Iran. But he steered a middle course, defending Russian interests among its neighbours in the 'near abroad' and fighting for its commercial interests further afield. He proved a far more reliable partner than Yeltsin, with a more realistic view of his country's capabilities.

Putin generally chose to adopt the 'easiest' reforms where there was minimum conflict or opposition, such as tax cuts. But he also laid some foundations for longer-term institutional change. He embedded and enhanced market reforms with a series of new laws. In the legal sphere, his contribution was the adoption of new civil and criminal codes, paving the way for the launch of jury trials across the country. The uncontested nomination of the highly respected liberal judge Valery Zorkin as head of the constitutional court in 2003 was a positive sign for the future.

While inheriting a society in need of substantial transformation, Putin was also fortunate in facing few serious crises during his first term. He was, in other words, a 'fair-weather leader' yet to prove himself in more difficult circumstances. On the occasions when he did face challenges, the results were less impressive. He left Chechnya no more stable than he found it politically, after the loss of tens of thousands of lives. He came out of the botched Kursk rescue badly, and his approach to handling the challenges posed by the oligarchs – notably Gusinsky and Khodorkovsky – smacked of personal vindictiveness and over-kill.

Another drawback was the flip-side of Putin's trademark stability: an unwillingness to act. That may have helped consolidate Russian society in the short term, but it did little to lay the foundations for the long. His preference was to defer decision-making, and to send out confusing signals. 'He says "yes" to everyone, giving them the impression that he supports them,' argued Boris Nemtsov, the leader of the SPS fraction in the Duma in 1999-03. 'Like a typical KGB officer, he lets others take the initiative, but then jumps on the moving train and takes the credit if it works,' said a Russian journalist who knows him well.

Paradoxically in view of the strong growth that Russia experienced during his first term, Putin can arguably be criticised as much for his economic advances as for his democratic regressions. It is what he has *not* done that is most open to fault. His inherently cautious nature – perhaps combined with his political inexperience and the failures of the apparatus he inherited – meant that much of the considerable scope he had for reform was wasted. Critics even started to compare his rule to the stagnation that accompanied the oil-rich Brezhnev years in the 1970s. He could have done far more at a time of growth and goodwill to implement restructuring, and to address the needs of the victims of the transition of the 1990s. That should have precisely included taking more impartial, less political and more economic action to curb the influence of the oligarchs.

By 2001, the policy pledges made in the Gref reform plan were already being sharply diluted and delayed. The promises of rapid gas liberalisation and restructuring – essential if waste was to be cut and Russian industry to become competitive – had been broken. Efforts to improve competition through tougher anti-monopoly and anti-trust regulatory bodies had very limited success. Social policy reform had gone almost nowhere, leaving a sharply divided society. The reform of the housing utilities and the banking sectors progressed sluggishly. 'Administrative reform' of the civil service – to improve efficiency and cut corruption – did not progress beyond protracted discussions in a series of working committees. It is still too early to assess how successful will be most of the reforms he carried out, to the railways, electricity, pensions, land reform and the legal system itself. Realistically, most will take a decade or more to show results. But they will require smooth implementation relying on precisely the overhaul of the public sector which is waiting to happen.

Putin's blackest mark appears to be democratic back-sliding. The Kremlin has sharply centralized political control, cutting down on the autonomy and independence of the Duma, the Federation Council, and regional governments and governors. Diversity of media ownership has declined, and the rise of litigation has helped stifle free speech among journalists, while state-controlled television has become an increasing parody of filtered, Soviet-style propaganda. The growth in *siloviki* in many senior positions around the country has hindered open discussion, the diversity of views and the emergence of civil society. The law enforcement agencies have been used for political purposes. And abusers of human rights, above all in Chechnya, have operated with impunity.

The Putin that emerges at the end of his first term is a liberal chekist like his Soviet mentor, Andropov. His economic vision is largely pragmatic and liberal, relatively open to the market and to foreign investment – if only as the best tools to rebuild Russia's influence in the world. But his view of how to impose change remains narrow, technocratic and authoritarian. He has shown an impressive command of detail, but that has fuelled an excessive desire to centralize power. He has failed to provide necessary support to strong independent institutions, instead largely exercising his personal authority on those around him to achieve results. Secrecy, manipulation and arbitrary decision-making remain the hallmarks of his administration more than transparency, justice and consistency. These traits risk limiting his enduring legacy.

But Putin should be judged in the context of his own background and the post-Soviet environment he inherited. His personalised management style, often relying on close friends and trusted colleagues, is very Russian. His economic pragmatism was born of the self-evident failures of the Communist planned economy he witnessed in his native Leningrad, and into which he gained a privileged insight in Germany and beyond. His authoritarian side is partly explained by the fifteen formative years he spent as a KGB officer, but also reflects the experiences of his more recent past. His post-Soviet political mentor Anatoly Sobchak combined democratic principles with an autocratic style. Yeltsin took the characteristics to further extremes, and in many ways was a Bolshevik democrat who had no faith in power-sharing. Whatever his style, the chaos he bequeathed to Putin would have led many leaders to stress the need for greater controls.

A share of any blame for Putin's policies and approach should significantly rest on Yeltsin and the 'Family', who helped nominate him in the first place in full knowledge of his character. It was they who prepared the ground for his election and that of his parliament, and who provided many of the key advisers starting with Alexander Voloshin who ran the Kremlin for most of his first term. It was they who presided over the society with all its limitations that he was to run. Any assessment of their decision, in turn, and of Putin's subsequent actions, should also take into account the limited alternatives that existed at the time. By mid-1999, the obvious political rivals for the presidency were probably far worse, notably the still older and more Soviet *apparatchiki*, Primakov and Luzhkov.

One problem in evaluating Putin's first term is what geomorphologists call 'equi-finality of form'. While the Russian political landscape appears less democratic today than it did in 1999, the final result now on offer could have come about in many different ways. It may have been caused by a range of processes, the result of interference by many individuals with varied motivations. Given the secrecy of Russian decision-making, it is difficult to judge the truth. And five years is too little to assess how permanent will be the current outcomes, in a society engaged in the painful process of reconstruction.

The war in Chechnya has proved catastrophic, for example. The policies pursued in Chechnya and decried by Berezovsky have proved bloody and destabilizing. But whether the special services were involved in the events that triggered it completely changes the assessment to be made of Putin. It is undeniable that the seizure of NTV from Gusinsky was part of a process that has left the Russian media more tame than it was. The abuses of the legal process in the attacks against Khodorkovsky and Yukos are flagrant and damaging. It is less clear what sort of Russia would have been built had all three oligarchs been left with their former influence. Or how far Putin alone, even with his attempts at recentralizing control, could have determined the outcomes of processes he helped unleash, in a country with so many vested commercial and political interests, and the actions of officials keen to demonstrate 'initiative from below' in their efforts to win approval from the Kremlin. As the former prime minister, Viktor Chernomyrdin, once put it so memorably: 'We wanted to make things better, but they turned out like they always do.'

The 2004 Duma may look like a return to the one-party state, with its two-thirds majority and all committee chairs held by United Russia. But it is an outcome that largely reflects the will of voters, however little may have been done to foster a culture of greater political competition. Nor can Putin be accused of concealing his views. He made the 'rules of the game' of political non-interference quite clear to the oligarchs, however unproductive or unjust they might have seemed. In his millennium statement in 1999, he criticised totalitarianism and pledged his commitment to democracy, but added: 'Russia will not become a second edition of, say, the US or Britain, where liberal values have deep historic traditions . . . For Russians, a strong state is not an anomaly to be got rid of. Quite the contrary, it is a source of order and main driving force of any change.'

Given his own background, Putin has already evolved considerably. The awkward fledgling bureaucrat thrust into national political prominence in 1999 is very different to the smooth statesman now on public display. His growing confidence in meetings with world leaders, and his slick ability to spontaneously handle lengthy press conferences and public question-and-answer sessions is at least equal to that of many of his counterparts abroad. His capacity to invent policy on the spot, and come up with surprising decisions, has been demonstrated on a number of occasions. His strategy – in as far as he has one – is not set in stone. His stated commitment to modernisation and democracy could still be realised if he begins to place greater confidence in the rudimentary institutions he is creating.

In the remainder of his second term, Putin still has the possibility to show a more progressive side with his new-found experience and reinforced authority. With a strong new electoral mandate, a compliant Duma, and his own people firmly installed in positions of power, he has everything in his favour. He can push through tougher economic reforms, overhaul the government administration, and clamp down on corruption. He has the chance to impose future discipline on business through membership of the WTO. He could ensure leniency in his treatment of Khodorkovsky, and ensure other oligarch companies are not pulled apart like Yukos. A test will be whether he limits incompetence and cronyism by keeping confiscated Yukos assets out of the hands of the state-backed Rosneft and Gazprom, and punishing abuse. If he keeps his word and continues to consult with the liberal groups that are no longer in parliament, he may help broaden policy-making and foster a climate of improved consultation. A key litmus test will be whether he maintains the current constitution and relinquishes power in 2008.

But judging by his words and acts so far, it is difficult to offer the benefit of the doubt. The president, nowhere more than in Russia, sets the tone. Putin must ultimately also take the responsibility. Whether he has personally coordinated some of the darkest moments of his two terms, endorsed them after the event, or simply been unable to control those who were behind them, the results stand against him. For Russia's foreign partners, understanding the challenges he faces should not mean glossing over the drawbacks of his policies. Countries should continue to engage with Russia, if anything being tougher and more consistent in their criticism of its shortfalls. It is through greater openness and an increase in contacts and trade that improvements are likely. Given Putin's desire to cultivate a positive reputation in the west, it is also in their interests to be tough with him. But expectations should also be realistic. Putin is building a Russia that will certainly not resemble a western-style market democracy for many years, but will be infinitely better for most of its own citizens and foreign partners than the USSR. It may not be a very enviable regime in the eyes of the west, but it is one that the country's own people have endorsed. Its partners will have to treat it on its own terms.

For an older generation, the memories of the totalitarian past linger. Shortly after Khodorkovsky's arrest, one Russian business-man described his own fear of broader repercussions, and in the same words explained why he believed the imprisoned tycoon – then aged forty – had not thought he would ultimately end up in jail. 'The difference is that he is nine years younger than me. He had no experience of a strong state. He grew up when the system was already collapsing, when it consisted of weak bureaucrats who could be bribed. I remember the earlier period. I had two grandfathers killed, and my grandmother spent fifteen years in the camps and seven more in exile.' Putin's own generation was the last brought up in the shadow of Stalinism. It was born too late to share any of the Bolsheviks' original ideals or struggles, but too soon to be fully incul-cated with the culture of corruption and chaos that took hold from the 1980s.

'Russia is a country divided between two generations,' Leonid Parfyonov told me in his cramped office in Moscow's television centre just ahead of the 2003 elections. His influential prime-time Sunday evening show, *Namedny*, on NTV can be hard-hitting and critical of the authorities, but it is not dominated by politics. 'Everyone understands that these are not exactly elections. They are not interesting as a polit-ical struggle. We have a president who is more than a president, and a parliament which is less than a parliament. The fate of Russia does not depend on the result. People work, travel abroad, go to cafés, use the internet, and live as they want. That is how freedom grows. Anyone who is honest sees that Russia is freer in 2003 than it was in 2001. Young people are happier and more open to the world. They see democracy as a decoration. If the authorities try to remove their freedom, say by restricting the internet, then they will protest. Then I'll go into Red Square to demonstrate.' But at least judging by the 2003 parliamentary vote, it is not clear that they will prove much of a brake on Putin's power or be the kernel of future opposition. According to exit polls, the greatest support for United Russia came from the 18–24-year-olds, followed by the 25–34-year-olds.

So far, Putin's Russia is one that has exceeded the dreams of its people in the 1980s while failing to match their hopes in the 1990s.

The state of the country today is probably consistent with the realities that the new president faced on arrival at the turn of the millennium. But the contradictions of economic liberalism and political authoritarianism will eventually clash. With a more tightly gagged media, the president becomes the first victim of censorship. With a monolithic public political culture, he risks being the target of behind-the-scenes intrigues. With a less transparent approach to policy making, the outcomes will be increasingly sub-optimal. In the absence of a sharp reduction in bureaucracy, corruption and state interference, economic growth is likely to slow, hindering efforts at reconstruction and reconciliation that Russia has begun over the past few years. He finished his first term with an aura of unpredictability about how the next will evolve. That risks turning the valuable stability he has so far delivered into stagnation. As Yabloko's Yavlinsky puts it: 'The president is a good skier, but you cannot go very far when your skis are pointing in different directions.'

Russia in 2008 is likely to be a country in better shape than some now fear, but not as impressive as it might have been had Putin used his potential to the full. It will probably be significantly richer and more self-confident than it is at present, with further economic growth and additional – though slowed – market reforms. Conscious of his legacy, Putin may well keep his word and not change the constitution, instead trying to name his successor as Yeltsin did – or even taking over as prime minister and head of United Russia. But slowed economic growth could ultimately weaken his broad but shallow support. Corruption and bureaucracy will remain a huge burden, and companies linked to the state will be stronger than they were for much of the 1990s. Chechnya will remain a running sore, while foreign policy will become more assertive. Much of the media will be compliant, and the population indifferent as they focus on improving their own well-being.

It is ironic that Alexander Solzhenitsyn – who was persecuted under Andropov and never got on with Yeltsin – has found common ground with Putin. His criticism is less about the democratic deficit of this decade than insufficient action to curb wild capitalistic excesses of the last. There may be cynicism on both sides in the relationship, but their bond is also a symbol of reunification of a shredded society. Yet Putin might do well to reflect on the downside of his Soviet past, and the limits to Andropov's never-achieved ideals. As Solzhenitsyn wrote in *Gulag Archipelago* a third of a century ago: 'Those same hands which once screwed tight our handcuffs now hold out their palms in reconciliation. "No, don't! Don't dig up the past! Dwell on the past and you'll lose an eye." But the proverb goes on to say: "Forget the past and you'll lose both eyes."'

EPILOGUE

'When two schoolboys fight during the break ... the one who is thrashed is guilty, because you don't judge a winner.'
Vladimir Putin's response to a multiple-choice question on the Kremlin's website for children

On 1 September 2004, Russia's traditional 'black August' became swiftly longer and darker. As the enormity of the brewing crisis emerged through radio reports, I prepared to travel to a sleepy town in Russia's ethnic republic of North Ossetia. Beslan would shortly be known to the world as the scene of the most horrendous act of violence the North Caucasus had yet seen. The events about to unfold were a gloomy symbol of the legacy of Putin's first presidential term, and the still more worrying prospects for his second.

The previous day, a 'black widow' suicide bomber had blown herself up at Moscow's Rizhskaya metro station in the evening rush-hour, killing ten people. That event, which in other circumstances would have shocked the country, seemed almost trivial after the mid-air explosion of two domestic airlines one week earlier, taking 90 lives. As an inquiry would later show, a bribe of just Rbs1,000 to bypass airport security was enough to bring Chechen terror to the Russian skies for the first time.

Yet both attacks would soon fade from memory because of what followed. A group of gunmen burst into Beslan's main school on the first day of term, and held more than 1,300 people hostage in humiliating conditions for more than 50 hours. On the third morning, two explosions inside the building triggered an intense gun battle. The roof collapsed and many of those not crushed inside were caught in the crossfire as they fled in panic. By the time fighting ceased four hours later, at least 330 people – more than half of them children – had been killed.

The handling of the Beslan siege was so bad that it seemed almost a parody, making the Nord-Ost crisis of two years earlier appear almost efficient. Back then, the FSB's crack Alfa squad had acted swiftly to neutralize hostage-takers during the Moscow theatre siege and to prevent any explosions from within; the principal failure came in the inadequate medical treatment that followed, leaving 139 hostages dead. This time, Alfa's best troops had withdrawn from the scene to practise storming a building nearby. Those who remained, including some of the best interior ministry soldiers, were drawn unprepared into battle without their bullet-proof vests, and sustained heavy casualties. Parents dodged bullets as they desperately searched for their children, and access by the emergency services was hampered by the many cars blocking the streets.

There were signs from the start that all would not go well. Despite claims that airport security had been tightened following the August plane crashes – let alone since the start of the Beslan crisis – no one even bothered to check my documents before my flight took off for the regional airport of Mineralnye Vody. The only attention on arrival was from corrupt local police trying to extract a bribe to resolve a spurious documentation error. When I arrived in the town's main square, hundreds of tense people were standing around in vigil, anxious for news of their relatives.

Local hostility towards the authorities – above all the leaders of North Ossetia itself – was extremely high. Information was scant, and none of the locals believed the modest total of 350 hostages that officials claimed were being held inside. There was widespread anger about the corruption and security failures that had allowed so many heavily-armed gunmen to cross into the republic through several police checkpoints. And there was a desperate hope that the authorities would negotiate in order to avoid a bloodbath.

The security cordon separating bystanders from the zone around the school was leaky at best, with local residents, journalists and all variety of uniformed services passing back and forth. There was no meaningful coordination or control on the ground. I saw teenagers with shotguns patrolling the streets nearby, and local militia in semi-military costumes with improvized white rags tied to their arms to distinguish them from their foes. Most likely, these irregulars helped spark the uncoordinated gunfire that led to the final gruesome body count, and participated in the vigilante killings of hostage-takers who had been captured alive.

Yet it was the media that became the first scapegoat of the tragedy. As I checked in for my flight bound for the Caucasus, I noticed Andrei Babitsky, the veteran Russian war broadcaster and critic of government policy in Chechnya, coming up behind me. But he never made it onto the plane, held up first by security and then arrested on trumped-up charges of involvement in a scuffle. At almost the same time, the writer Anna Politkovskaya was taken severely ill on another flight into the region, in what appeared to be a crude attempt at poisoning. Neither journalist was able to reach Beslan ahead of the denouement.

State television kept its coverage of Beslan low-key. NTV was better than its rivals, but still frequently repeated the low official hostage count. The day after the siege came to a bloody end, Putin's own carefully orchestrated trip was given ample air-time. He held talks with local officials and visited hospitalized victims, but avoided any other meetings with members of the public and headed quickly back to Moscow.

The feisty radio station *Echo Moskvy* stood out, broadcasting detailed reports as the events unfolded. But during the fighting, it was forced to rely on CNN reports on the ground rather than on Russian sources. Some of the Russian print media also functioned well, notably *Izvestiya*, which reported the crisis as the culmination of two weeks of incompetence by the security services. Within two days of the siege's end, Raf Shakyrov, its editor, had been sacked. His coverage may have been a little emotional and insensitive, but that hardly merited his dismissal. He was more likely the victim of the oligarch Vladimir Potanin, his proprietor, who did not want to displease the Kremlin at a time when big business was rightly afraid that the persecution of Yukos might spread.

The authorities were swift to deflect blame from themselves. The local head of the FSB said on the evening of the massacre that 'a dozen Arabs and a nigger' were among the hostage-takers. The claim, offered without any proof and subsequently shown to be false, played to Moscow's line that Beslan was the latest victim of 'international terrorism'. Sergei Lavrov, Putin's new foreign minister, wasted no time in proving his credentials when he berated the UK and the US for failing to extradite Chechen rebel leaders, whom he claimed were behind the attack. Other officials focused on the complicity of the authorities in neighbouring Georgia. Speaking the day after the crisis, Putin aimed even higher, pointing to unnamed foreign powers which he claimed sought to destabilize the region to take 'a juicy piece of pie'.

In reality, the greatest 'foreign involvement' was probably that of an armed group on the scene headed by Eduard Kokoiti, the self-styled president of South Ossetia, a separatist region propped up by Russia but formally just across the frontier in Georgia. On a visit to his 'republic' a few weeks later, I got the impression of a zone run principally by the local Russian military and its cronies. More than a decade after the territory had been ceded with the collapse of the Soviet Union, Russian army officers controlled both sides of the border to serve their own interests, with little regard for the sovereignty of Georgia that Moscow formally recognized. Arms, people and contraband passed freely in either direction.

At Beslan, Putin could no longer use the 'Kursk defence' as he had in front of the angry relatives of dead submariners three months after his first presidential inauguration in 2000. Then, he claimed that he had had little time to make a mark on his country, and that much blame should be allocated to his predecessors. Four years later, his own role in failing to resolve the conflict in Chechnya could not be dismissed so easily. Nor could the questionable quality of his tactical decisions in the face of the crisis.

By 2004, his own close aides had long been in key positions of responsibility, including Sergei Ivanov as minister of defence, the logical person to coordinate the military response at Beslan. State television showed Putin personally despatching to the scene Nikolai Patrushev, his longstanding friend who headed the FSB, and Rashid Nurgaliev, his sidekick who had taken over as interior minister. Yet neither was visible on the ground, any more than Murat Zyazikov, the FSB officer whom Putin had installed to run neighbouring

Ingushetia, or Vladimir Yakovlev, whom he had named his special representative for the region. Only Ruslan Aushev, Zyazikov's predecessor who had been pushed out of power by Putin, had the courage or political credibility with all sides to negotiate face-to-face, in the process saving twenty-six hostages.

The most important lesson for Putin after Beslan might have been to question the wisdom of some of his own nominations to top jobs, let alone the broader idea of centralizing power and appointments in his hands. Yet when the Russian president spoke to the nation a few days later to lay out his response, there was no such turnaround. He used the events as a pretext for launching reforms long dreamed of by Kremlin advisers but considered too sensitive to implement. He called for the abolition of elections for the country's regional governors, and the elimination of the 'first past the post' method in local constituencies by which half of the Duma was elected. In future, only proportional representation on national party lists would be used, marking a further tightening of the Kremlin's grip on federal politics. Putin went further shortly afterwards, strengthening his power in the appointment of judges. His only concession to accountability was to create a 'citizens' chamber'. In a nod to his Soviet reflexes, he even called for the re-creation of a network of paid civilian informants to keep an eye on their neighbours and cooperate with the police and security services, which in turn had their funding further increased.

In Putin's defence, Beslan would have been any politician's nightmare. Any world leader would have struggled to negotiate with such a group of ruthless – and nervous – hostage-takers. The corruption and incompetence of local officials reflected continued and widespread problems that Putin had inherited in regional administrations across Russia – a country that seemed at times almost ungovernable. After all, Alexander Dzasokhov, the North Ossetian president, was no recent Kremlin nominee, but a hangover from the Soviet era, like so many other governors and top officials.

The failure of the regional elites to better manage Beslan was the one justification officials could – and privately did – use to justify the fresh centralization of power that they were now undertaking. What western critics saw as further democratic backsliding, many Russians interpreted instead as a necessary response to the state's failure to be sufficiently assertive. The local people with whom I talked vented their anger primarily against Dzasokhov, as well as the security and law enforcement agencies. There was no love lost in North Ossetia for the Chechens or the Ingush. But only very few held Putin himself to blame.

There were a few modest positive signs to emerge from the crisis. Despite initially dismissing calls for a parliamentary inquiry as something that would turn into a manipulated 'political show', Putin did finally agree to a probe – albeit one controlled by trustworthy hand-picked senators. He oversaw the dismissal of some corrupt and incompetent local officials – albeit largely low-level functionaries. And the appointment of his trusted aide Dmitry Kozak as presidential representative for the region suggested he was finally taking the need for social and economic reconstruction in the Caucasus seriously – albeit at the price of removing one of his most talented aides from central government.

More generally, Beslan was a stark reminder of the limitations of Putin's approach to governance. His style of leadership was centred on himself, reinforced by an opaque, Byzantine and bureaucratic 'closed system', with few solid institutions, serious counterbalances to executive power, or independent sources of information. It worked well enough in fair weather, giving the appearance of progress in the initial stages of reform, against the background of strong economic growth. It allowed him to push aside his opponents and help engineer the strong popular support that ensured he won re-election with 71 per cent of the vote in March 2004. But the faults of his approach became clear when things started to go wrong.

One example came on 9 May 2004, just two days after Putin's own inauguration for his second presidential term. As the Chechen leader Akhmed Kadyrov watched a victory day parade in the Dynamo stadium in the heart of Grozny, a bomb went off, killing him and throwing into chaos Kremlin efforts to use a trusted strongman to centralize power in the republic. The balance of power was so delicate, and the mechanisms to allow the emergence of any legitimate successor so limited, that Putin was forced to pander to Ramzan, Kadyrov's thuggish son, while putting his weight behind Alu Alkhanov, a weak political neophyte, as the formal successor.

The most striking aspect of the episode was Putin's remarks after a rare visit to the Chechen capital soon after the assassination. He expressed shocked at the scenes of devastation he had seen from the air. Any visiting journalist or civil servant, let alone local resident, could have vividly described the ruins of the capital to him. Given the vast intelligence, military and civilian resources under his control, Putin's reaction suggested a worrying ignorance, matched by indifference or fear from his underlings who failed to report the situation on the ground to him.

The only alternative explanation was that he was being disingenuous, feigning surprise as a way to mobilize his officials. That was also the best – but equally implausible – interpretation I could come up with for the dull meetings broadcast almost daily on national television between Putin and ministers, governors and other officials. The dialogue was formulaic, long-winded and banal. Perhaps Putin was using coded Soviet-era language that had much greater resonance with bureaucrats. Maybe once the cameras were turned off, he slammed his fist on the table and demanded action more aggressively. But the sterile, stylized exchanges looked more like a game that one Russian described to me, updating a Soviet-era expression, of 'you pretend to lead, and we'll pretend to follow'.

Putin's own access to information may have been limited by the imperfect flows fed to him by his staff, and by a hamstrung media which provided a poor additional 'safety net' of data on what was happening in the country. He also appeared to be increasingly surrounded by a government of 'yes-men'. Georgy Arbatov, the founder and emeritus head of the US–Canada Institute, a think-tank that advised successive leaders from Khrushchev to Yeltsin, put it bluntly to me: 'More than anyone, Putin needs opposition as a source of help and new ideas. But I am not optimistic. I don't see strong people around him.'

There was certainly little sign of political debate in parliament. Boris Gryzlov, the ultra-loyalist speaker of parliament and head of the dominant Kremlin-controlled United Russia party, told me directly that the Duma should be a place 'not for political battles, but for technical debate'. There was frustration among the more liberal ministers in the government – notably German Gref and Alexei Kudrin. But Mikhail Fradkov, the low-key bureaucrat named prime minister by Putin shortly ahead of his election, showed no sign of matching the influence of his predecessor, Mikhail Kasyanov. If the president wanted someone less likely to subvert his policies or present a potential political threat, the result was an individual who seemed incapable of taking decisions on his own, let alone putting them into practice.

Plans to switch pensioners' multiple in-kind benefits for cash were badly conceived and still more poorly explained. The promised restructuring of the electricity and gas sectors was endlessly delayed. Civil service 'administrative reform' dragged so much that the head of one agency told me it was four months after the reshuffle before he received prime ministerial approval even to change the official acronym of his organization. Without that, he could not make the new circular rubber stamp that was necessary, in Russia's cumbersome bureaucracy, to legitimize every written order he gave.

Putin did seek some talent outside the ranks of his unquestioning supporters. He named Pavel Krashenninikov, a former justice minister from the Union of Right Forces movement, as head of the Duma's legal affairs committee. Yabloko's Vladimir Lukin became parliamentary human rights commissioner, and its former St Petersburg deputy Igor Artimiev was appointed head of the anti-monopoly agency. And Putin oversaw the removal of some of those on his watch who had performed less well, such as Vladimir Shamanov, the former army general who had been elected with Kremlin support as the governor of Ulyanovsk.

At best, Putin favoured technocrats such as Igor Shuvalov, a quick-witted official who drew up a series of complex economic and social policy reforms – with scant consultation with the ministries and regional authorities that would need to implement them. Often, he fell back on his St Petersburg networks, reinstating as telecoms minister Leonid Reiman, despite persistent allegations of commercial conflicts of interest. Reiman had overseen a significant restructuring and growing competition among fixed and mobile phone operators. He had also employed Putin's wife Ludmilla as a consultant during the 1990s. Competence was important to the president, but connections and loyalty at least equally so.

In the economic sphere, loyalty and the growing centralization of power were also in evidence. No example was clearer than the attacks on the oil giant Yukos. By the end of 2004, Mikhail Khodorkovsky, the leading shareholder, and his partner Platon Lebedev, were facing the prospect of long jail sentences, and their company was being pulled apart and re-nationalized. Yuganskneftegaz, Yukos' main production subsidiary, was sold in a rigged auction to a company ultimately controlled by Rosneft, a state-run group chaired by Putin's own Kremlin deputy Igor Sechin. At best, that meant a shift away from the free-market and towards 'state capitalism'; at worst, cronyism. The tactics employed were crude, stretching even Russia's legal loopholes to their limits. They served as a further blow to the autonomy of the country's shaky institutions, rule of law and property rights. Vladimir Ustinov, the prosecutor general responsible for the Yukos criminal cases, should have been held responsible for numerous procedural violations. Instead, he was rewarded for his services to the state with an honorary doctorate from Putin's alma mater, the St Petersburg Law School.

Despite the gloomy background, there were continuing signs of economic success. In comments to journalists at the end of 2004 to sum up progress during the year, Putin spent little time on politics and much on growth, rising reserves and incomes, and a fall in debt and unemployment. The US magazine *Forbes* launched a Russian-language edition in the spring with a striking analysis which said much about fast-growing inequality and the absence of fair competition. It estimated that Moscow alone had more dollar billionaires than any other city in the world, at thirty-three compared with thirty-one in New York. The total of thirty-six billionaires across Russia controlled $110bn between them, or 24 per cent of GDP. In the US, by comparison, there are 227 billionaires, representing just 6 per cent of GDP. But most growth was taking place despite rather than because of Putin, whose assault on Yukos undoubtedly helped dampen investment. And the contract killing in summer 2004 of Paul Klebnikov, the managing editor of *Forbes Russia*, was a stark reminder that the risks for foreigners as well as for locals operating in the country were not purely financial.

In foreign policy, a shift in circumstances threw Putin into a less favourable light with the west from the start of his second term. He had withdrawn from some of Russia's far-flung Cold War military commitments, and accepted with little complaint the painful eastward expansion during 2004 of the European Union and NATO into former Soviet satellite states. He became more defensive as his closer neighbours risked upsetting his attempts to reassert Moscow's influence in the 'near abroad', notably when the 'rose revolution' in Georgia was succeeded by the 'orange revolution' of Ukraine.

In Georgia, Putin had initially welcomed the downfall of Eduard Shevardnadze in late 2003, but the reformist zeal of Mikheil Saakashvili, the new president, soon destabilized the situation. When

Saakashvili began reining in Aslan Abashidze, the autocratic 'ruler' of the autonomous region of Adjara, Putin reacted calmly. He stressed Russia would not support the use of force by Abashidze, and brokered safe passage for him across the border. As Saakashvili turned his attention to the more virulently breakaway regions of South Ossetia and Abkhazia, bilateral relations became still more frosty.

The Kremlin's attempts to interfere in Abkhaz politics backfired, however, when local residents voted against the new presidential candidate whom Putin had clumsily endorsed. Instead of heeding this message, the Russian leader was even more heavy-handed in Ukraine in late 2004. He sent officials, political consultants and money to help his preferred presidential candidate, Viktor Yanukovich, whom he openly supported during two pre-election trips. When widespread vote-rigging triggered popular protests and the eventual victory of his rival, Viktor Yushchenko, the result was to leave Russia more isolated than it need have been.

To some degree, Putin could point to 'double standards' in criticism of his foreign policy. Just as he was supporting Yanukovich, western governments and organizations were behind Yushchenko – as was Saakashvili, a long-time friend. US criticism of Russian human rights abuses in Chechnya looked increasingly hypocritical as the revelations of prison abuse at Abu Ghraib emerged. Concern about Kremlin-orchestrated democratic regression expressed by George W. Bush and Colin Powell was undermined by the fact that they only became so vocal in the build-up to presidential elections in their own country after nearly four years' frustration with the modest progress of their Washington–Moscow partnership.

A mixture of encroachment onto his 'reserved territory' and the confidence brought by oil wealth made Putin more bristly. He wanted to be treated as a partner and an equal by western leaders, and sought foreign investment – at least in principle. He continued his push to join the World Trade Organization, locking Russia into a system of competitive economic standards and international laws. But he was not going to let western moral values dominate over *realpolitik*. The lesson for the west was that it needed to be both tough and consistent in its message, but also to remain engaged and sensitive to the risks of increasing isolationism by Russia at a delicate time in its evolution.

Reform had been possible during Putin's first term, without much accompanying democracy. That was partly because his policies had been relatively limited, technical and uncontroversial, during a period of strong economic growth and political stability. Similar modernization using authoritarian methods had taken place in the 'Asian Tigers', in China and in Kazakhstan. Most significantly, it had been the hallmark of the liberalizations of the 1990s in Russia itself, where a small group pushed through privatizations regardless of public opinion and opposition from parliament.

Predicting the future in Russia is always more difficult than rationalizing the past. But continued strong growth during the remainder of Putin's second term seems likely, given the current prospects for oil prices and the continuing rebound of the post-Soviet economy. Further liberal reform is possible using more or less authoritarian measures, though the process is likely to be less swift as the issues become more complex and the will to implement them reduces as elections approach and those making the decisions change. It will be counteracted by a growing domination of the state in the natural resources sector, and of bureaucrats rediscovering their Soviet reflexes.

There are few signs under Putin that there will be much greater democracy, serious taming of the bureaucracy, or the creation of more solid, independent institutions to counteract the power of those on top. The paradox of Putin's Russia – and an explanation for his continued popularity – is that the combination of new-found wealth and post-Soviet freedoms means that many people have never had such personal liberty to spend, travel or communicate. As long as democratic restrictions do not encroach on these aspects, there is unlikely to be a fresh revolution or major turmoil any time soon.

But Putin's current policies are renewing uncertainty and stunting growth, while doing little to lay the foundations for a more stable political succession. He seems likely to bequeath a society of increasing inequality and limited accountability, where property rights remain insecure and arbitrary justice holds sway. The best that might be hoped is that he meets his pledge to stand down in 2008, in the meantime retaining a balance of power, minimizing further state intervention and maintaining some stability to encourage and effectively manage growth. But Putin's second term has become distinctly less liberal and more authoritarian. As Boris Yeltsin is now realizing, his protégé's patriotism may be irreproachable, but his commitment to democracy and market reform is questionable.

351

As I lingered by the staircase to the marble hall of the Kremlin after Putin's state of the nation address in 2004, I bumped into an unexpected figure in a smart suit with a clipped greying moustache. I recognized the elusive Viktor Ivanov, the KGB general brought by Putin with him into the Kremlin, who was starting to raise his profile. He was hovering, almost inviting journalists to interview him, confident in his position and new role. 'Did you have a problem with the speech?' he asked me. 'No,' I replied. 'My doubt is whether it can be implemented.' Ivanov smiled and replied, 'Ah yes. In Russia, the questions have always been *kto vinovat* (who is guilty) and *shto delat* (what to do). Not *kak delat* (how to do it).' It was his colleagues' concentration on the first more than the second, let alone the third, that was likely to prove the greatest challenge in the years ahead.

INDEX

Abashidze, Aslan, 350
Abkhazia, 97, 296, 350
Abramov, Alexander, 203
Abramovich, Roman, vii, 81, 140, 152, 176, 192, 195–7, 205, 206, 235, 310–11
Academy of Sciences, 17
Access/Renova, 184–5
Adjaria, 296
Aeroflot, 152, 175, 176, 177, 316
AES, 267
Afghanistan: and Chechens, 272; Russian policy, 256, 257, 259–60; Russian support for USA, 260, 290
Agency for Strategic Communications, 312
Akademgorodok, 41
Akayev, Adlan, 112–14
Akayeva, Roza, 112–14
Akhmadov brothers, 97
Akin Gump (law firm), 154
Aksyonenko, Nikolai, 227
Al Qaeda, 108, 259, 272, 273
Aldi (Grozny), 115
Alekperov, Vagit, 182, 289
Alexei II (Russian Orthodox patriarch), 75
Alfa, 182, 184–5, 188, 190, 203–4, 225
Alfa Bank, 203, 238
Alfa Echo, 188
Alfa Express bank, 306
Alkhan-Yurt (Chechnya), 114, 115
Alkhanov, Alu, 125, 346
All Russia Public Opinion Research Centre (VTsIOM), 31, 253
Alrosa, 21, 77
Altimirov, Aindi, 114
Andropov, Yuri, 4, 14, 18, 24, 51, 61, 62–3, 339
Angarsk oil refinery, 181
Anikin, A. G., 73
Annan, Kofi, 294
Anti-Ballistic Missile (ABM) treaty, 1–2, 3, 289

Arab League, 124
Arbatov, Georgy, 347
Arco, 203
Armenia, 267
arms industry, 269–70, 287
Arsanov, Vakha, 98
Artimiev, Igor, 348
Ashgabat summit (2002), 261–2, 264–6
Asia–Pacific Economic Cooperation forum, 263
Aslakhanov, Aslambek, 122, 237
Aslamazyan, Manana, 138
Association of South-East Asian Nations (ASEAN), 263
Astana (Kazakhstan), 82
Atgeriyev, Turpal-Ali, 104
Atoll, 176
Auchan, 247
Audit Chamber, 218
Auschwitz, 10
Aushev, Ruslan, vii, 94, 99, 129, 130, 235, 345
Aven, Peter, 203–4, 238
Avtovaz, 166
AVVA (investment fund), 174, 176
Azerbaijan, 222, 265
Aziz, Tariq, 287
Aznar, José Maria, 274, 279

Babitsky, Andrei, 117, 277, 343
Balabanov, Alexei, 127
Baltic states, 268
Barayev, Arbi, 88, 97, 99
Barayev, Movsar, 88
Bargishev, General Shaid, 98
Basayev, Shamil, 97, 98, 99, 102, 103, 104, 104–5, 106, 107, 108, 108–9
Bashkortostan, 100, 127, 167–8
Basic Instinct (TV programme), 163
Basmanny Court, Moscow, 308
Bazhiyev, Nurdi, 98